D0071908

INDIA'S NUCLEAR POLICY

Praeger Security International Advisory Board

Board Cochairs

Loch K. Johnson, Regents Professor of Public and International Affairs, School of Public and International Affairs, University of Georgia (U.S.A.)

Paul Wilkinson, Professor of International Relations and Chairman of the Advisory Board, Centre for the Study of Terrorism and Political Violence, University of St. Andrews (U.K.)

Members

Anthony H. Cordesman, Arleigh A. Burke Chair in Strategy, Center for Strategic and International Studies (U.S.A.)

Thérèse Delpech, Director of Strategic Affairs, Atomic Energy Commission, and Senior Research Fellow, CERI (Fondation Nationale des Sciences Politiques), Paris (France)

Sir Michael Howard, former Chichele Professor of the History of War and Regis Professor of Modern History, Oxford University, and Robert A. Lovett Professor of Military and Naval History, Yale University (U.K.)

Lieutenant General Claudia J. Kennedy, USA (Ret.), former Deputy Chief of Staff for Intelligence, Department of the Army (U.S.A.)

Paul M. Kennedy, J. Richardson Dilworth Professor of History and Director, International Security Studies, Yale University (U.S.A.)

Robert J. O'Neill, former Chichele Professor of the History of War, All Souls College, Oxford University (Australia)

Shibley Telhami, Anwar Sadat Chair for Peace and Development, Department of Government and Politics, University of Maryland (U.S.A.)

Fareed Zakaria, Editor, Newsweek International (U.S.A.)

GRACE LIBRARY CARLOW UNIVERSITY
PITTSBURGH PA 15213

INDIA'S NUCLEAR POLICY

Bharat Karnad

Foreword by Stephen P. Cohen

HD
9698
I52
K37
2008

PRAEGER SECURITY INTERNATIONAL
Westport, Connecticut · London

CATALOGUED

Library of Congress Cataloging-in-Publication Data

Karnad, Bharat
  India's nuclear policy / Bharat Karnad ; foreword by Stephen P. Cohen.
    p. cm.
  Includes bibliographical references and index.
  ISBN: 978–0–275–99945–2 (alk. paper)
1. Nuclear energy—Government policy—India. 2. National security—India. 3. Nuclear weapons
—India. I. Title.
HD9698.I52K37   2008
355.02'17—dc22   2008028217

British Library Cataloguing in Publication Data is available.

Copyright © 2008 by Bharat Karnad

All rights reserved. No portion of this book may be
reproduced, by any process or technique, without the
express written consent of the publisher.

Library of Congress Catalog Card Number: 2008028217
ISBN: 978–0–275–99945–2

First published in 2008

Praeger Security International, 88 Post Road West, Westport, CT 06881
An imprint of Greenwood Publishing Group, Inc.
www.praeger.com

Printed in the United States of America

∞

The paper used in this book complies with the
Permanent Paper Standard issued by the National
Information Standards Organization (Z39.48–1984).

10 9 8 7 6 5 4 3 2 1

For Renu

ABS $49.95 3-4-10 POLS

Contents

Foreword

While the United States will retain its lead along many social, economic, and political indicators of power, the rise of China and the hesitant movement of Europe toward coherency ensure that for much of the twenty-first century the world will be increasingly characterized by multipolarity, not one-power dominance. This will also be a world of significant environmental and climatic change, the further spread of nuclear weapons, and a world increasingly tied together via the revolutions in communications and transportation (of both goods and people) that are collectively called globalization.

In this world India will play a special role. It is close to the epicenter of Islamic turmoil, it is one of the newest nuclear powers, and it will be deeply affected as global warming proceeds. India also has strategic potential, evident in its assertive business community and its world class cultural power (in the shape of films, ideas, and a new generation of global Indians).

These developments, and India's potential role as a balancer of China, were the major reasons the Bush administration decided to encourage India's rise. This encouragement took the form of unprecedented joint military exercises, a renewed arms-sale relationship, and, as its centerpiece, an agreement to support India's civilian nuclear-energy program. The last has turned out to be a deal too far. As Bharat Karnad notes in this book—and he is one of the experts on the agreement—India would have been eligible to receive advanced U.S. nuclear technology, uranium fuel for its reactors, and its weapons program would have been blessed *ex post facto* as legitimate. In exchange New Delhi was to separate its civil and military nuclear programs and agree to restrictions on nuclear expansion. Thus strengthened, India would presumably be better able to stand up to an assertive China.

The goal was both breathtaking and misguided. It was breathtaking, in that one clear—but unstated—objective was to enable India to join with the United States and other Asian states in the long-term containment of China. The new relationship with India was to be reinsurance against a malign China and, if carefully managed, would not precipitate a Chinese counter-reaction. It was misguided in that the structure of opinion in India was such that India could not bring itself to say "yes" to an agreement that was probably (if not overwhelmingly) in its favor.

As Karnad explains, the deal was opposed by quite different elements of the Indian political spectrum and there were few enthusiastic supporters (for India, foreign policy is not a central political concern). The left parties, living in the past, opposed it because of anti-Americanism and the fear that India's "nonalignment" might be compromised. However, the opposition of others, such as Karnad, was quite different: he makes a powerful case against the deal on the grounds that it failed the very test that was its foundation: *realpolitik.*

This is why this book is critical for understanding India's evolution as a great power. Karnad agrees that the U.S. tie is very important to a rising India, but he and others are unwilling to cripple India's military nuclear potential not only because they see nuclear weapons as a mark of a great power, but because these weapons have practical military consequence. Without the ability to escalate up the ladder to nuclear weapons, and to fight a nuclear war, a small nuclear state will be forced to back off in the face of a superior one. India, Karnad argues, already has that capability vis-à-vis a declining Pakistan, but not against a rising China. Thus, he argues, India cannot accept restrictions on a program that is part of its core strategy for emergence as one of the world's major power centers. Very much like the liberal arms control and nonproliferationists in the United States, he argues that the failure of the agreement is no great loss—it can be negotiated by new governments in both countries to the advantage of each.

Only time will tell whether this prediction is correct, but one of the many virtues of *India's Nuclear Policy* is that the author sets out clearly the kind of nuclear capability that is minimally essential. It will probably require more testing, it will involve a seaborne leg and an improved missile capability, but it will not be an open-ended system. Above all, it will require a political leadership that does nor shrink from the exercise of coercive power. Karnad is as scathing of the nuclear minimalists (those such as the nuclear physicist Raja Ramanna who argued that all India needs is a few nuclear weapons) as he is of the nuclear abolitionists (those who would abandon the Indian nuclear program altogether). The former do not understand the logic of nuclear weapons, a logic that has been developed and tested over a 60-year period; the latter do not understand the continuing importance of nuclear weapons, even in today's multipolar world.

Bharat Karnad is widely recognized as one of India's leading strategic thinkers. He is part of an expanding community of military and civilian strategists who challenge fundamental assumptions about nuclear policy. The group includes many alumni of the recently established National Security Advisory Board. While they do not necessarily agree with each other, they carry on a vigorous debate in the press and in books such as this over the relevance of nuclear weapons to India, inter-service cooperation, strategic ties with the United States, and the nature of threats faced by India.

That the views of this group, of which Karnad is an influential member, do not exactly reflect those of the present government makes them all the more interesting and important. India is a vibrant and fluid democracy; ideas and theories held by a few can quickly become state policy. Thus, Nehru's expansionist view of India as a major power, a view that held open the possibility of becoming a nuclear weapons state, was followed by a far more constricted view of India and outright opposition to "going nuclear" or military rearmament by most of the political class. The policy wheel may turn again.

We are thus doubly in Karnad's debt for this book: first for summarizing so concisely many of the arguments he has developed at length elsewhere and, second, for forcing the reader to think through, once again, how the logic of nuclear weapons operates in a globalizing world. These devices are not museum pieces or artifacts of the Cold War: they are today in the arsenals of at least eight states and potentially many others. One accident, one miscalculation, could change the course of history.

Sir Michael Howard, the leading contemporary war theorist, has said that only after our deaths will we find out whether two theologies are right or wrong: one theology is a belief in the afterlife, the other is a belief in the efficacy of nuclear deterrence. In this book Bharat Karnad has taken the lead in exploring the relevance of nuclear deterrence to India, the most important of the new nuclear states. The reader may agree or disagree with his conclusions, but there is no doubt he has asked the right questions.

Stephen P. Cohen
Senior Fellow, Brookings Institution, Washington, DC

Introduction

The center of gravity of the international nuclear security system since the end of the Cold War has moved from Europe to Asia, and the focus from the major players of that era (the United States, the North Atlantic Treaty Organization, Russia, and the Warsaw Pact countries) to the outlier regions with second-tier nuclear-weapon states (China and, prospectively, India), third-tier states (Pakistan and Israel), the threshold countries (North Korea, Iran), and aspirant states (Japan, South Korea, Taiwan, Saudi Arabia, Egypt). Increasingly, peace, order, and stability in Asia and the world will rest on the behavior of these "new nuclear nations,"[1] and managing security will require a better understanding of the nuclear politics and strategic thinking in these countries.

This book seeks to reveal the workings of India's nuclear strategy and posture. It deals not so much with the theory or the evolution of Indian thinking on "minimum deterrence," which has been tackled comprehensively in a previous book by the author,[2] as with the translation of the "credible minimum deterrence" concept into a militarily sustainable stance—in other words, with the nitty-gritty of realizing a credible, effective, and survivable thermonuclear force. Nineteen-ninety-eight, the year India resumed nuclear testing, was a watershed. Other than proving to be something of a dam-burst of desire for the bomb among the nuclear have-not states, in India the deliberately ambiguous notions of "recessed" or "non-weaponized" deterrence prevailing until then were shoved aside by the real-world concerns about how to deter potential adversaries and with what armaments, strategy,and tactics. Weaponization by autopilot—the process of nuclear arms development and acquisition initiated and managed by the senior scientists at the nuclear complex in Trombay (near Bombay or Mumbai) with only vague directions from, and supervision by, the government gave way to more institutionalized decision-making, involving other agencies, including the Defense Research and Development Organization (DRDO) in the Defense Ministry and the Armed Services. The *ad interim* strategizing by the nuclear scientists, who originally propagated "minimum deterrence" featuring a small number of basic weapons, was supplanted by the more sophisticated and elastic concept of "credible minimum deterrence" (CMD). Professional deliberations involving the newly founded National Security Council and its various arms, such as the National Security Advisory Board, the Strategic Policy Group in the Department of Atomic Energy, and the Strategic Forces Command, fleshed out this concept over the years.

The CMD concept is more an organizing theme than specific guidelines, and, in that sense, the Indian nuclear force is still evolving. There is consensus, however, on a staged buildup initially to some 200 warheads and weapons. In consolidating the country's strategic nuclear assets, the upsizing of the force or qualitative improvements in the nuclear weaponry will be dictated by the changing nature of threats, technology trends, and regional and international security developments. The strategic triad, conceived by the nuclear doctrine in 1999, will become fully operational by 2012. The development of the triad—bombers, and medium and intermediate range ballistic missiles deployed on rail and road mobile platforms and embarked on warships and nuclear powered submarines able to fire nuclear tipped ballistic and cruise missiles (SSBNs), and still longer range missiles based in tunnels excavated in the mountains—is detailed. The nuclear-powered submarines are set to assume the principal role in tackling the primary threat, China, which maritime strategy to strategically deter China is explicated in the book.

The credible minimum deterrence idea provides a flexible policy instrument enabling many diverse views about strategies and tactics, force structures, and nuclear-weapons use and targeting schemes to compete and coexist under one conceptual umbrella. Such differences have not turned into institutional barriers to development of the deterrent. While India's nuclear strategy and posture are a work in progress, this study will show that the direction in which they are headed is clearly away from the minimalist notions of nuclear deterrence. Politically, the government has found the credible minimum deterrence concept useful as it reflects the key attributes of moderation, economical use of scarce resources, low key efficacy, and the "responsible" state behavior that it swears by.

The fact that Indian nuclear thinking is couched in language borrowed from the dominant western discourse on nuclear deterrence of Cold War vintage has led many Western and even Indian experts to think of the Indian strategy as a replay of familiar Cold War concepts with predictable outcomes. Alternatively, they have looked at the Indian nuclear program through the nonproliferation glass darkly and/or from the U.S. national interest angle. In either case, what has resulted is a sort of nuclear determinism, by which reckoning nuclear weapons in South Asia constitute a "flash point," destabilize the region, undermine the existing nonproliferation regime, and set a bad precedent for threshold Non-

Proliferation Treaty signatory states, "rogue" and otherwise.[3] But the flash point thesis has rapidly passed into cliché, especially as it is unsupported by evidence. It is argued in the book that nuclear deterrence overlays a conflict system peculiar to the subcontinent marked by extreme restraint and controlled India-Pakistan wars and, hence, if nuclear weapons have had any effect at all, it is to reinforce these positive qualities. Since 1990, several conventional military crises passed off without escalation to the nuclear level. The relatively smaller weaker and nuclear-armed Pakistan now feels secure enough to seek an easing of bilateral relations. A more self-confident India has widened its strategic horizon and is exploring a defense perimeter beyond the subcontinent. It is getting ready to play the part of a "swing state," strategic system balancer, and effective counterweight to China.[4]

Central to the analysis is how CMD is viewed and implemented by the main actors, namely, the Indian political leadership, the nuclear establishment, DRDO, and, most importantly, the military brass whose thinking on a range of issues relating to nuclear deterrence—highlighted in this book—is increasingly shaping the nuclear policy. India's nuclear outlook, this study will show, is influenced as in other countries by considerations of national interest and hard *realpolitik,* and the official agencies and the Armed Forces in the loop are acquiring the requisite strategic mind-set and expertise to match the reach and punch of the nuclear hardware and delivery systems.

Among many important aspects of the Indian nuclear policy that will become evident are, first, that in the context of the international technology-denial regimes the development of nuclear-weapon and missile technologies was propelled by the desire to overcome technological challenges and to show the world that Indian scientists and engineers were as good as any and could cope well without outside assistance. Second, that a system of "differentiated deterrence" has emerged to deal separately with Pakistan and China, and the more difficult China-Pakistan nexus. The analysis will make clear that credible nuclear deterrence is ultimately a matter of like deterring like. In a dyad involving absolutely unequal states, such as India and Pakistan, deterrence will not work for the weaker country because it lacks the capacity to survive the nuclear pain and punishment, and will likely fold after the first Indian retaliatory salvo. And third, as the military sees it, it is the indecisiveness and lack of will of the Indian political leadership to take hard national security decisions that is the weak link in the deterrence chain.

The chapter contents are as follows: Chapter 1 reviews the international security milieu in the first decade of the twenty-first century and the direction in which the U.S., Russian, Chinese, French, and British nuclear policies, strategies, and arsenals are moving and why lesser nuclear powers and non-weapon states will try to emulate them.

Chapter 2 provides a brief historical sketch of the fast-paced development of the nuclear infrastructure and dual-use capabilities in India, which early created the nuclear-weapons option, and of the much slower and more deliberate manner in which the decision to weaponize and the minimum deterrence philosophy evolved from 1947 until the 1998 tests.

Chapter 3 discusses the capability growth as regards nuclear weapons and missiles and the operationalization of the Indian strategic deterrent. The accompanying changes in thinking about nuclear weapons use and the relevant strategies and tactics, are analyzed. For example, under the rubric of "massive retaliation," the policy of graduated retaliation is being honed as the practical thrust of deterrence policy, with the response hinging on the nature of the provocation. Of particular interest are the views of Indian nuclear scientists regarding the development of the designs for fission, boosted-fission, and thermonuclear weapons.

In Chapter 4, the unique nature of the India-Pakistan wars are commented upon, the Indian military's views on "limited war" and strategies are examined, including the army's "Cold Start" doctrine, along with the military's ideas on preemption and preventive war. In addition, the possibility of high-value theatre-level and strategic conflicts with China are discussed. It will become apparent that the Indian military is geared, as in the past, to fight severely curtailed wars with Pakistan and that conflict with China could be triggered by five sets of reasons: the undemarcated border; the damming and diversion of major rivers originating in Tibet, especially the Yarlung-Tsangpo River in southern Tibet that becomes the Brahmaputra River as it enters India; ramped up help and material assistance by China to Pakistan's nuclear-weapons program; the Tibetan independence movement supported by India as a function, among other things, of intolerable levels of military material help to secessionist elements in Indian northeastern provinces; and conflict over energy and natural resources. India's conventional military weaknesses vis-à-vis China in Tibet will be discussed along with the need for the government to sanction offensive mountain warfare capability. The controversial Indian-U.S. civilian nuclear cooperation deal, which has divided the country and the Indian parliament, is subjected to a broad brush analysis, and the conclusion is that Washington, contrary to its own strategic intent, seems more determined to see the Indian nuclear capability curbed than to want India to emerge as a credible countervailing presence to China in Asia.

CHAPTER 1

New Attractions of the Bomb: The Nuclearized Twenty-First–Century World

India finds itself in the most dangerous, unstable, and anarchic part of the world in terms of endemic violence, social turmoil, and political and religious strife in a string of failed or failing states in the neighborhood. It is a region sourcing Islamic extremism and its offshoot—unbridled terrorism with a potential for turning nuclear. Several countries (for example, Iran and Saudi Arabia) in the vicinity are threatening to acquire nuclear weapons, and active nuclear and missile cooperation is ongoing between China and Pakistan as well as between Pakistan and a crypto–nuclear-weapon state, North Korea. India, moreover, faces an economically and militarily assertive China seeking to push it to the margins. Destabilizing U.S. and Western interventions in nearby countries complicate India's relations with these states even as its foreign policy seeks to forge close relations with the West. It is reason enough for India to be on guard, have a strong conventional military, and build up a powerful nuclear deterrent.

Whether or not the Indian nuclear tests in 1998 led other countries to think of nuclear weapons as a way both to shore up security and to blunt great-power attempts at coercion, it strengthened the different motivations of threshold powers seeking nuclear weapons. Predictably, it unhinged the international nuclear order. The root cause of nuclear proliferation, however, can be found in the policies of major nuclear-weapon states' endowing nuclear weapons with enhanced political and military value in the twenty-first century. The nuclear "renaissance" is attributable to the recognition by the nuclear haves and have-nots alike that the atom holds the key to energy security and the protection of the nation-state.[1] While the more ambitious but cautious countries hope to reach the weapon threshold using the civilian nuclear-energy channels open under the Non-Proliferation Treaty (NPT) regime, the risk-taking states are trying to acquire through underhanded means the requisite technologies to cobble together a bomb. The resulting "delicate balance of terror" that once principally involved only the United States and the erstwhile Soviet Union now engages many more countries. It may lead to the subsidence of interstate wars,[2] and to international relations becoming simultaneously stickier and more sensitive to the lesser, nuclear-armed, states. Weak countries, either taken over by terrorist organizations or unable to prevent terrorists from using their territory as base, could face nuclear first strike as preemption or retaliation by powerful states.[3] What is emerging is an international security system resting on nuclear eggshells, at once driven both to conciliate and to hit out.[4]

The value of nuclear weapons has increased manifold in part because major powers have thought nothing of violating the sovereignty of lesser states and using force to advance their interests, disregarding diplomatic understandings, UN resolutions, and international laws.[5] With the Westphalian system virtually in tatters, countries have ultimately to rely on themselves for their own security —Kenneth Waltz calls it the "military logic of self-help"[6]—and there are no better means of self-protection than nuclear weapons.[7] This was, in a sense, inevitable. With the restraints of the Cold War bipolar system removed in the *fin de siècle,* large heterogeneous countries fragmented or were helped to fragment along ethnic and religious lines (the Union of Soviet Socialist Republics [USSR], Yugoslavia), small conflicts (India-Pakistan) spurted as did civil wars (Kosovo, Somalia), the United States and the North Atlantic Treaty Organization (NATO) indulged in armed interventions (Kuwait, Kosovo, Somalia, Iraq, Afghanistan), and all great powers and would-be great powers rushed in for a neocolonial grab at scarce natural resources (oil, gas, minerals, diamonds, wood) in Africa, central Asia, and elsewhere.[8] While inter- and intrastate eruptions have continued into the new millennium, the tendency to mount military campaigns in the garb of "humanitarian" intervention by the United States and its European allies has, post-9/11, become more pronounced, further eroding the concept of sovereignty already unavoidably affected by economic globalization, and otherwise weakened the concept of territorial integrity and inviolability of individual states. The inclination of the United States, the preponderant power of the day, to use violence and, more generally, its "hard power" ostensibly to combat terrorism and prevent the proliferation of weapons of mass destruction and WMD technologies, far from addressing the fundamental concerns of the weak countries fearing assault, has exacerbated them. Military solutions for difficult political problems have seeded endless trouble.[9] With the decimation of the Cold War alliance structures that sheltered regional states,[10] moreover, the pressure to be self-reliant for security has led many countries, which for a host of reasons find themselves in adversarial position to the United States or to neighboring states with nuclear weapons, to consider asymmetric means to counter conventional military superiority. In this age, the asymmetric means of choice are terrorism and the nuclear bomb.[11] With nuclear technology spreading fast and nuclear weapons gaining credence, the sanguine attitude toward nuclear proliferation of the United States and the West of the early Cold War years[12] has given way to paranoia.

Libya, Saddam Hussein's Iraq, Syria, Iran, and North Korea were seen as "potentially irrational and undeterrable" and hence labeled "rogue" states.[13] These countries, with varying degrees of success, sought the protection of the "absolute weapon" in violation of their obligations under the 1968 Non-Proliferation Treaty. North Korea bought immunity for itself from Western threats by securing entry-level nuclear armaments (accessing uranium centrifuge enrichment technology peddled by Pakistan in return for its missiles).[14] On the other hand, Libya's agreeing to shut down its covert nuclear military programs suggests that appropriate incentives combined with intense international pressure sometimes works. The carrot-and-stick policy may have persuaded North Korea too, except it intends to keep the small number of nuclear weapons it has already produced as insurance.[15] Other states, such as Syria, with low-key nuclear programs, have faced forceful preemption.[16] Iran is adamant about noninterference in its nuclear program and will end up, in all probability, having the capability and, in due course of time, nuclear weapons.[17] "Shaking the US nuclear stick at adversaries," writes Harold Brown, U.S. President Jimmy Carter's Secretary of Defense, "probably encourages proliferators."[18]

Most of the states of proliferation concern, other than North Korea, happen to be in the unsettled Islamic belt. Among them, India's immediate neighbor to the west, Pakistan, occasions special worry as it is at once the source and the victim of highly effective international terrorist organizations, such as Al-Qaeda and the Taliban, which have put down roots there and are drawing ferocious jihadi fighters to their ranks from all over the Muslim world, including the Arab states, Chechnya, and central Asia.[19] Until the Pakistani government-sponsored A. Q. Khan-run "nuclear Wal-Mart" was officially shut down, it was also the main source of clandestine nuclear technologies, materials, and skills. There is no guarantee that the store has not been taken over by new management.[20] The perception of the threat emanating from nuclearized Islamic countries and Iran in particular to international peace and regional order is a mix of equal parts dread evoked by terrorism and a "clash of civilizations"-kind of antipathy.[21] One danger is of a self-fulfilling prophecy with such a campaign being perceived as "war on Islam."[22] Overhanging this scene rife with tension and violence is the specter of terrorists wielding nuclear devices. It has led to redoubled efforts at reviving the tottering Non-Proliferation Treaty regime and, on the flip side, to nuclear-weapon states promising nuclear retaliation against countries potentially sourcing nuclear terror. It has prompted the targeted states to try to reach, as quickly as possible, the safety provided by nuclear weapons.[23] It is a witches' brew of poverty, social ferment, religious tumult, terrorism, failed or failing states, military weakness, imperiled security, threatened sovereignty, nuclear weapons proliferation, big power paranoia, counterproliferation strategies, colliding national interests and, above all else, the reaffirmation of the political and military value of nuclear bombs. It has generated violent action and reaction and extreme fear and uncertainty all round. The situation is so bad, the initial speculations about the "second nuclear age" seem relatively tame by comparison with the new reality.[24]

In this milieu fraught with risk, the five NPT-anointed nuclear-weapon states—the United States, Russia (as successor-state to the erstwhile Union of Soviet Socialist Republics), China, France, and the United Kingdom (P-5), who, as role models, have discovered new missions and roles for nuclear weapons and novel rationales for their strategic arsenals. In effect, they have reissued nuclear weapons as currency of power in the new century. The bulk of the nonnuclear-weapon states feel shortchanged by the NPT-based global nonproliferation order that, contrary to its promises, has neither achieved any significant progress beyond arms control and toward genuine disarmament nor made the benefits of civilian nuclear energy widely available to the signatory states.[25] The various nonproliferation and arms control treaty regimes and measures (such as the United Nations Resolution 1540) were never designed other than to perpetuate the P-5 nuclear weapons monopoly.[26] The "new" millennium thinking on nuclear security as has emanated from the P-5 states has stuck faithfully to the contours of the self-serving policy. Consider the "nuclear weapon free world" schemes lately proposed by eminences of the American foreign policy community. Two years running, former U.S. Secretaries of State Charles P. Schultz and Henry Kissinger, ex-U.S. Defense Secretary William J. Perry, and retired U.S. senator Sam Nunn have, as joint New Year offerings, asked for continuing efforts "to reduce substantially the size of nuclear forces in all states that possess them"—to take just one of their points—without differentiating between the huge American and Russian arsenals, smaller Chinese and French strategic forces, and the miniscule weapons holdings of India, Pakistan, and Israel. The benefits of a nuclear weapons-free world are touted by stalwart British leaders as well.[27] Such proposals are, perhaps, well-meaning recipes for culling the nuclear arms inventories of the United States and Russia even as other countries reduce to zero and does not address the issue—unless this is what is intended—of a world freed of nuclear weapons being made safe for conventional war and "coercive diplomacy" using the unmatchable American and P-5 military wherewithal. Or take the Carnegie Report—*Universal Compliance: A Strategy for Nuclear Security.* After noting in passing that the P-5 had not delivered on the Article VI commitment, it suggests without any apparent irony that because the nuclear threat remains, the United States should retain a strong and effective nuclear deterrent.[28] It echoes the comments made by the U.S. Assistant Secretary of Defense for International Security J. D. Crouch at the time of the release of the declassified Nuclear Posture Review in January 2002 that a substantial and responsive U.S. nuclear arsenal was necessary to "deal with a broad range of the potential capabilities that adversaries may array against us."[29] Worse, the Carnegie report recommends more of the same nuclear medicine to the NPT signatory states as has stuck in their craw, namely, strengthening the existing nonproliferation order by expanding the membership of "export control regimes" to include all states with relevant capabilities, providing incentives and inducements to prevent nonweapon states from acquiring nuclear weapons, facilitating the development and transfer of proliferation-resistant reactor technologies and fuel supplies, and legitimizing forceful counter-proliferation actions and strategies.[30] Other than the purported desire to prevent nuclear terrorism, at the heart of the Western thinking about proliferation, is the assumption most Third World-signatories to the NPT find unacceptable, namely, that nuclear weapons possessed by aspirant states are, as Sisir Gupta, an influential Indian policy analyst of the 1960s had written, "like guns in the hands of juvenile delinquents."[31]

In fact, the principal reason for the growing desire in the world for nuclear weapons is the search for security in an anarchic world[32] and, even more fundamentally, to enforce the right to equal security for states that supposedly enjoy equal sovereignty. If nuclear weapons are prized by certain countries as symbols of power and as an all-purpose hedge against uncertainty and threats to security, other countries are bound to hanker for similar instruments. Of course, it is a historical truism that some states are more sovereign than others, that sovereignty and security are a function of the power of the state, and that the stronger the country the more easily it can resist foreign interventions into its affairs, disregard international conventions, deflect international pressures, and obtain the level of conventional military and nuclear security it desires. In the context of the nonproliferation order, moreover, nuclear security is seemingly related to a state's position in the rank-ordering of nations, with the richer more powerful countries exclusively enjoying the political and military benefits of nuclear weapons. It, therefore, follows that the great powers can try to secure absolute security for themselves—however chimerical such a goal might be, unmindful of treaties signed and commitments made by them. These great powers are limited only by the extent of resources they are willing to deploy and the costs they are prepared to absorb in terms of the relative neglect of economic and social sectors at home, the alienation of the international community, and of the weakened systems of regional and international peace and stability.[33] It may also be that North Korea and Iran, in particular, seek nuclear weapons to deter the United States by threatening to strike American assets in the region and its closest regional allies (Japan and Israel and major Arab states such as Saudi Arabia, respectively).[34]

Nuclear weapons regained importance with the U.S. *Nuclear Posture Review* (*NPR*)[35] and America's prosecution of the Iraq War. The *NPR* stressed the continuing centrality of nuclear weapons in America's national security plans and policies and, by blurring the distinction between conventional and nuclear weaponry, indicated the development of a seamless but usable military prowess in total disregard of the Non-Proliferation Treaty strictures.[36] Further, when the United States, on the basis of unverified reports of Saddam Hussein's weapons of mass destruction programs, initiated a war without United Nations sanction and affected "regime change" in Baghdad, it put all states that did not get along with Washington—and not just those labeled "rogue"—on notice of the fate awaiting them in case they crossed America. Iraq's misery juxtaposed against North Korea's nuclear bluff and brinkmanship rewarded by payoffs from the "six party talks" convinced the skeptics that the high cost of acquiring nuclear weapons capability was well worth paying, that a nuclear bomb guarantees, as nothing else can, not just the survival of a regime and national system at odds with Washington, but security and diplomatic leverage and political and military autonomy of action. This was no mean revelation for states compelled to deal with an overbearing America. The tension between states possessing nuclear weapons and those countries and nonstate actors endeavoring to acquire them in the face of forceful attempts by the former to deny it to the latter now defines international conflict. The eventual outcome of this tussle may fundamentally change the distribution of power and hence the structure of the global system.

The flawed Non-Proliferation Treaty regime, designed primarily to prevent more countries from developing nuclear weapons, i.e., proliferating horizontally, is central to this fight.[37] In the main because the maintenance of this regime is a priority for the United States, the lone superpower, which portrays the status quo as beneficial for the world and something that needs to persist. Because of the heavy American nonproliferation hand, however, this spin on the NPT regime is apparently less and less convincing. "I believe that unipolarity is not only unacceptable but also impossible in today's world," said Russian President Vladimir Putin in February 2007 when he warned against the United States' "almost unrestrained hyper use of force in international relations, a force that is plunging the world into an abyss of permanent conflicts" and added that America's "dominance inevitably encourages a number of countries to acquire weapons of mass destruction."[38] This last being precisely what many nuclear have-not states are seeking, it has resulted in a world on the cusp of breaking away from the nuclear security paradigm dominated by the United States and the P-5 that was bolted into place by the NPT.

The twenty-first century is likely to see more states relying on nuclear weapons for security than ever before, pushing the world beyond the "nuclear tipping point."[39] If as Henry Kissinger claims, "A single country's acquisition of an atomic bomb alter[s] the balance [of power] more significantly than any territorial acquisition of the past,"[40] then a bunch of new countries going nuclear, many of them with no great stake in the present international system, will result in a radical diffusion of power globally and, at a minimum, the dilution of the coercive capability of major states. For that very reason "life in a nuclear armed crowd" could be tense but turn out to be less conflict-prone than some have predicted,[41] because the fear of starting a nuclear affray and its consequences will inhibit the risk-taking propensities of small and big powers alike.[42] Then again, the scenario could be more problematic. A recent Weapons of Mass Destruction Commission report concludes: "In 2020 or 2025, we might confront the world that was President Kennedy's nightmare, a world with twenty or so nuclear-weapon states, some of which would be located in the world's most volatile regions. Whoever believes that in this constellation, stable deterrent relationships will blossom and we will keep nuclear weapons and fissile materials out of the terrorists' hands may as well believe that the world is a disk, and the moon is made of cheese."[43] In the interim period, the likelihood is of disturbed relations and heightened strife owing to the unwillingness of the nuclear haves to either disarm completely, reducing their nuclear arsenals to zero, or to accommodate the security and status concerns of the nuclear have-nots. This accommodation should start with the proliferation-problematic countries and the "middle powers."[44]

However a more proliferated world turns out, in the near-term to medium-term future what India does and how it does it will be of special interest to the threshold states in the developing world, which signed the NPT but resent and envy India for going nuclear and for having had the foresight to safeguard its nuclear-weapon option.[45] Of the three NPT non-signatory nuclear-weapon states, India alone has the traditional attributes of great power in terms of size, strategic location, population, growing economic presence, and natural resources, as well as a mature, broad-based, nuclear program that is as adept in exploiting the military atom as in the civilian uses of nuclear energy. More specifically, India's evolving nuclear policy and posture will, in the main, be influenced—as subsequent chapters will show—by its legitimate great-power ambitions and search for strategic independence, the international and regional security imperatives, the technological momentum of its strategic weapons programs, and by the nuclear military policy and actions of the United States and China. Continued U.S. and Chinese *realpolitik* use of the nonproliferation issue and mechanisms could lead to India's observing less restraint than it has done so far. In any case, as a would-be great power India may be beyond imitation by other threshold states. It could well turn out, as Victor Gilinsky, a former member of the U.S. Atomic Energy Commission has stated, that India's and Israel's nuclear status will be "laundered" leaving Pakistan as the lone pariah state.[46] This will only hasten India's gravitation toward the P-5 and *de facto* membership in the club.[47] Given its financial dependence on the United States and its political isolation in the region, Israel will try to keep its nuclear weapons under wraps and its role as the American point-man in west Asia afloat.

Pakistan, a marginal state that was enabled to sneak in under the nuclear wire owing to the intersecting lines of great-power politics and an expedient nonproliferation approach of the United States and China, has given rise to hope for other Islamic nuclear have-not states determined to breach the nuclear weapons barrier, except that Washington and Beijing are unlikely to enact for them the helpful roles they parlayed for Pakistan. On the other hand, its record of brazen proliferation may have finally caught up with Pakistan, making it the nation of prime international proliferation concern. If it benefited from the deliberately lax U.S. and international oversight in the past, it will be under the gun from now on, forced to adhere to far higher standards of probity and more strictly enforced norms of behavior, with any egregious slipups triggering actions to capture, destroy, or disable its nuclear arsenal.[48] Such preemption is likely because of the increasing concern about Islamic extremists gaining access to the Pakistani nuclear arsenal and materials in a country suffering from interminable social and political turmoil, sectarian strife, and growing religious radicalization of the masses. It raises the specter of the Pakistani Army losing or ceding control of the nuclear weapons in its employ and of the nuclear weapons manufacturing facilities to a regime of Islamic zealots. A talibanized Pakistan (following up on the experience of the talibanized Afghanistan in the past) with an "Islamic bomb," is a prospect to be justly feared.[49]

Short of this development, India will try to balance the internal, strategic, political, and military pressures to continually strengthen its nuclear military capabilities and the external pressures emanating from the United States–led P-5 efforts to limit its strategic capability and arsenal, to get it to adhere to restrictive nuclear export norms, and to rope it into the extant nonproliferation arrangements. How India manages this balancing act will impact the global balance of power, the nonproliferation system and the outlook of nuclear threshold states.

RETURN TO THE FUTURE?

The parallels in the way the situation evolved post-1945 leading to the ideological tussle and the Cold War between the United States and the Soviet Union, and the manner in which international events have unfolded in the new century cannot be missed. President George W. Bush in October 2007 alerted the world to "the great ideological struggle of our time—the global war on terror" in which the United States has been engaged since 9/11 and the extreme means the United States has threatened to use. In much the same way, international relations in the Cold War were defined by the "free world" vs. communist bloc rivalry with massive nuclear arsenals on both sides maintaining the peace. "In an age when terrorist networks and terrorist states are seeking weapons of mass destruction, we must," Bush said, "be ready to defend our nation against every possible avenue of attack."[50] Compared to the essentially reactive U.S. policy in the period 1945–1993, described by its principal author—George Kennan, head of policy planning at the State Department in the late 1940s—as one of "vigilant containment of Russian expansive tendencies" and of responding to "Soviet pressure" with the "adroit ... application of counter-force at a series of constantly shifting geographical and political points, corresponding to the shifts and maneuvers of Soviet policy,"[51] the new American strategy is proactive and the U.S. national security agenda more ambitious. In September 2002, Bush articulated the U.S.

national security strategy of "preemption" and "preventive war."[52] As he explained to his audience at the West Point Military Academy: "We must take the battle to the enemy . . . If we wait for the threats to materialize, we will have waited too long."[53] A later elaboration of this strategy conflated the threat from terrorism with a generalized existential threat posed by proliferating nuclear weapons and missiles every where. "In 1972, just nine countries had ballistic missiles. Today," President Bush asserted, in a speech at the National Defense University advocating strong antiterrorism measures and missile defense for Europe, "that number has grown to 27—and it includes hostile regimes with ties to terrorists." It thus brought within the U.S. threat ambit those countries seeking WMD means for defensive reasons—to deter the United States. Because the emphasis is on tackling the threat before it fully materializes, there is the likelihood of the states labeled "rogue"—who, more properly, may be regarded as "nuclear cheats" for reneging on the NPT they signed,[54] being punished for possessing skeletal capabilities if not on mere suspicion of harboring nuclear ambitions.[55] This last is an extreme version of the preemptive war doctrine propounded by the U.S. National Security Advisor, Condoleeza Rice, in 2003.[56] Worse, the long-term solution the United States apparently prefers for "transforming" the targeted countries into well-behaved states is to impose democratic governance on them. The record and experience of an imposed democracy is spotty, as Iraq and Afghanistan show.[57] Its "transformative" nature involves the denaturing of the nuclear/WMD/terrorism threat by militarily reducing a potentially troublesome country before grafting some form of democracy on the ruins of the predecessor system in the hope that it will be accepted. It has been applied to Iraq and Afghanistan and could be extended to Iran and Pakistan or any other country Washington decides is in need of political-structural modification for its own good and the good of the world.

In regional polities that often have no history of rule by elected representatives, this entails major social and cultural engineering and is a recipe for unrest, especially because the usually traditional host societies straddle deep sectarian, regional, and ethnic fault lines. Making over such countries in the West's image, as the United States and its NATO allies have learned, is a nearly impossible task.[58] The Marshall Plan kind of programs, which revived the Second World War-devastated Western Europe and Japan, worked because the subject nations were abjectly defeated in war. In Iraq and Afghanistan, where fears of terrorism and WMD precipitated American involvement, the United States is barely able to handle the guerilla jihadi fighters who came on the scene after the initial easy military successes against technologically obsolete local armies had lulled the U.S. forces into complacency, and the "democratic" experiments in Baghdad or Kabul are floundering. In fact, the military quicksand the United States has stepped into in Iraq and Afghanistan is in contrast to what transpired in the U.S.-USSR military face-off. In the Cold War, the bloc rivalry stabilized very quickly at the level of matching nuclear inventories. In the present day, American prowess, while able to sweep aside quickly any conventional military resistance, finds itself no more capable of coping with the highly trained irregular tribal and Islamic militants and the Taliban active in Iraq and in Afghanistan than it did with the insurgents in Somalia in the 1990s.

The troubles the United States has faced on this account notwithstanding, there is political consensus not just about America's mission to spread democracy and the rule of law but, tied in with these aims, the need forcefully to deal with nuclear proliferation and to wipe out the scourge of terrorism. The differences are over how much force to use and in what manner.[59] With the Democratic Party becoming more hardheaded on defense and national security issues and unwilling anymore to cede this electoral issue to the Republican Party,[60] the "aggressive unilateralism" of recent U.S. government initiatives relating to the increased use of U.S. forces in the Global War on Terror (GWOT) and the counter-proliferation effort, are unlikely to be reversed anytime soon. It has led many American political scientists to rue the "demise of liberal internationalism."[61] The world today is much changed from Kennan's time in other ways as well. True, the United States' political and military preeminence is unquestioned. And, as the sole super power, it establishes the standard for military wherewithal, military efficiency, and policy much as Great Britain did in the late nineteenth century when the Royal Navy set the Dreadnaught standard for countries desirous of projecting power globally and able to afford the gun-laden warship-heavy navies and the sort of thinking that went with it. With the United States showcasing its advanced nuclear armaments, sophisticated cruise and ballistic missiles, missile defense boasting cutting-edge sensor and interdiction technologies, and nuclear-powered submarines, all as symbols of great power and as tools of political and military coercion, other countries are bound to take their cue from Washington where their military technological and strategic priorities are concerned. Thus, the U.S. actions in the nuclear sphere, not the official American nuclear nonproliferation rhetoric, point the direction in which other states may be headed. The international leadership subsumed by the United States is not affected by this development because most countries accept there is no other country with the requisite all-round heft to mobilize international resources and to give direction to global campaigns whether relating to security, trade, environment, or anything else. Such leadership by the United States is fine, said the Russian Foreign Minister Sergei Lavrov, provided Washington "is prepared for this status and can cope with it [and is willing] to listen . . . and be involved in collective work." Clearly, he implied the United States is not ready to do other than act on its own accord in a hegemonic manner.[62] It is another matter that hegemony of any kind, benign or otherwise, is an unrealizable goal because, as Francis Fukuyama has argued, it rests on the belief in American exceptionalism, which is not shared by other countries, and on the presumption of a high level of competence as a hegemonic power, which is belied by the United States' numerous foreign and military policy failures after 9/11. It is also unrealizable because such policy does not factor in the limits of the American people's willingness to support and subsidize the necessary level of activism that is required without their espying clear and direct benefits to the U.S. national interest.[63] Moreover, unlike in 1945 when, among the war-destroyed major powers, America alone stood unscathed and ascendant, it is today, relatively speaking, in decline, its diplomatic and economic resources hemorrhaging in distant political-military ventures,[64] and decisive nuclear and thermonuclear weapons capabilities are possessed by many states. Its European allies are uncomfortable about the United States starting a preventive war even when the pretext of a clandestine nuclear bomb is unavailable,[65] and newfound democratic partners, such as India, and sometime adversaries, such as China and Russia, far from uncritically following Washington, are quietly exploring avenues of cooperation to contain American influence and power. So much so, it has fueled talk of a Russia-China-India triumvirate firming up to balance the U.S. power.[66] Worse, Washington is in no position to prosecute a successful "preventive war," as the chances of locating and destroying underground and hardened facilities or taking out carefully dispersed nuclear weapons are not high. Washington also has to bear in mind the possibility that the threat of preemption can deter but also stimulate nuclear weapon acquisition, and it has to weigh the danger of delaying the preemptive strike against the political damage of such action. And it has to worry about its record of mismanaging regime change.[67] The fact is the United States lacks the local intelligence wherewithal and the military manpower for mounting sustained out-of-area operations, leading apprehensive American armed forces leaders to advise against getting bogged down in new slugging matches.[68] The regimes that possibly face an American military onslaught are quick to capitalize on such anxieties. The commander of Iran's Islamic Revolution Guard Corps, Mohammad-Ali Jafari, for instance, promised a "tsunami" of undefined actions in response to any U.S. preemptive attack.[69] And, as if to back up his words, Iran test-fired a new, possibly nuclear-capable, 2,000 km-range ballistic missile a few days later.[70] States seeking deterrence capabilities aside, several countries are rising fast as centers of genuine all-round international power, especially China.[71] This is again unlike the post-Second World War years when there was only a militarily impressive USSR with which to contend. Besides, the end of the Cold War, far from denuding Russia of military muscle, divested that country of an inefficient communist command economy and burdensome "soviets" that spun off into independent central Asian republics. It left Russia, in many ways, far better placed to offer America serious geopolitical competition. A new U.S.-Russian rivalry, many experts feel, is inevitable and could acquire a hard military edge owing to Washington's "arrogant and misguided policies."[72] Most significantly, however, while the unmatched conventional and nuclear military capabilities of the United States translated into irresistible political power and obtained a pliable international system and the ability to shape the international agenda starting in the 1950s, in the twenty-first century such military superiority has been effectively and hopelessly stymied by the new age adversary states and groups and terrorist organizations engaging in asymmetric warfare.[73] If the U.S. military were driven out of

Vietnam by the resilient Viet Cong guerilla and the poorly equipped but hard fighting North Vietnamese army regulars and out of Somalia by a rag-tag bunch of armed men under the warlord Mohammad Aideed, U.S. forces in Iraqi towns and the Afghan countryside alike, as Brent Scowcroft, U.S. National Security in the early 1990s has written, "are being wrestled to a draw"[74] by suicide bombers, squads of deadly snipers and agile hit-and-run specialists able to fight dispersed and to negotiate their way around the maze of streets in cities and towns or in difficult mountainous terrain, in classical guerilla style. And because the religiously motivated jihadi fighters are supported in the field by loose and shadowy support organizations in the host societies instinctively opposed to Western military presence and values, organized violence directed at U.S. troops and between domestic groups at once saps the American will and undermines the U.S. efforts at democratic "nation-building." In the era of "post-heroic warfare,"[75] mounting casualty rates, the consequent erosion of the political will in Washington to stay the course, the calls for a military pullout, and finally the resort to face-saving cut-and-run strategies, is an all too familiar chain of events. Thus, in order to screen off the withdrawal of American forces, the U.S.-installed governments in Baghdad and in Kabul will be asked to do more of the fighting, even if this means fielding ill-trained indigenous military forces to counter the rampaging Iraqi nationalists, tribal insurgents, and the Al-Qaeda and Taliban cadres.[76]

Difficult-to-manage expeditionary wars, however, only highlight the U.S. propensity to use force. Russia's presidential Security Council, in fact, in a March 2007 statement, called for a revision of the country's 2000 military doctrine keeping in mind this fact, new geopolitical changes, and the improvement in Russia's economic conditions. "An analysis of the international situation shows that military force has become an increasingly important factor in the policy of leading nations [who]," Putin said in February 2007, "are paying increasing attention to the modernization of their military forces and the improvement of their armaments. Means of modern warfare are being actively implemented, modes of using force are being reviewed, the configuration of the military presence is being changed and military alliances, particularly NATO, are being strengthened." The "almost uncontained use of force in international relations," he warned, was prompting countries opposed to the United States to seek nuclear weapons.[77] With Washington brandishing the nuclear threat and going in for active counter-proliferation measures, the highly motivated nuclear aspirant states have cultivated the qualities of stealth, resolve, and asymmetric craft shown by the jihadi fighters. Both North Korea and Iran, for instance, plugged creatively into the nuclear black market established by Pakistan. Sizing up the scene, the Kim Jong-il government in North Korea acted fast, bartering its long-range missiles and missile manufacturing technology for Pakistan's uranium enrichment paraphernalia and ex-Chinese weapon design, and presented the United States with the *fait accompli* of near-finished nuclear bombs. Iran, on the other hand, showing the same kind of flair but working at a more leisurely pace and paying for nuclear technology with cash or oil, finds itself short of the weapons threshold and in the American crosshairs. With the Al-Qaeda and Taliban terrorist organizations apparently facing no dearth of financial resources and, discounting for argument's sake the ability of these outfits to either buy "loose nukes" or to manufacture simple nuclear weapons with gun-assembly type mechanism,[78] the possibility is nevertheless real that Islamic jihadi gangs will get hold of a nuclear device in a situation of confusion and strife within Pakistan [79] or incrementally build up a small stockpile of fissile material for eventual use in a crude radiation diffusion device or an "improvised nuclear device."[80] Either of these contraptions could be exploded in a crowded metropolis anywhere in the world, the effect of which can only be imagined. For the United States, nuclear terrorism neatly telescopes the threat from nonproliferation and terrorism posed by "rogue" states comprising the "axis of evil."

Dealing effectively with this triple threat is complicated by the American nonproliferation policy dictated mostly by *realpolitik* considerations. Pakistan used the uranium enrichment technology pilfered from Europe, the nuclear weapons design and weapon productionizing assistance offered by China, and the missile technology delivered by North Korea to build its nuclear deterrent. Thereafter, it set up the Dr. A. Q. Khan–run convenience store peddling nuclear wares to any group or country with cash to spare, which worked only because of the international protection provided by the United States. Khan has revealed this,[81] and, in any case, it is by now well documented.[82] U.S. Senator Larry Pressler, first sounded the tocsin, revealing America's role starting in the latter part of Jimmy Carter's presidency in helping Pakistan acquire nuclear weapons capability and, more deliberately in the 1980s, when the Reagan Administration chose not to diligently apply the provisions in the 1985 "Pressler Amendment"—amended Section 620E of the Foreign Assistance Act. According to it, any sale of "military equipment or technology" to Pakistan was prohibited without annual presidential certification to the U.S. Congress that "Pakistan does not possess a nuclear explosive device and that the proposed United States assistance program will reduce significantly the risk that Pakistan will possess a nuclear explosive device." He had warned in 1994 that "US export decisions that have steadily provided Pakistan with the wherewithal to modernize its nuclear weapons capabilities have created military and political consequences for all of South Asia . . . Unless the United States acts decisively to stop nuclear proliferation it will not be able to defend its non-proliferation policy."[83] If, as is clear, Washington egged on Pakistan's not-so-secret nuclear weapons program, which was seminally assisted by China, can other states be asked to refrain from doing what China and the United States have done and subordinate their national interest to proliferation concerns? Pressler recognized that America had created a proliferation double standard that would be hard to justify. "Other countries seeking membership in the nuclear club," he asserted, "surely will reach their own conclusions from any failure on the part of America to act with resolve."[84] To deter China from carrying on illegal nuclear commerce with Pakistan and, simultaneously, to seriously pressure Islamabad into giving up its nuclear ambitions was apparently not the politic thing for Washington to do. Instead, deliberately turning a blind eye to China's and Pakistan's transgressions served U.S. short-term national interests better. It also served the larger geopolitical purpose the United States shared with Beijing, of nuclear-arming Pakistan in order to contain India—an informal Soviet ally during the Cold War—to the subcontinent, and limit its influence. In any event, what has eventuated is a curious approach, noted by a former U.S. Assistant Secretary of State for Nonproliferation, Robert J. Einhorn, of the states—China and Pakistan, in the main—supplying sensitive WMD goods, materials, and technologies being let off with a rap on the knuckles but countries (Libya, North Korea, Syria, Iran) shopping for these items being threatened with elimination.[85]

Keen to have Pakistan as a "frontline" state—a role it last played in the war against the Soviet occupation troops in Afghanistan in 1979–1993—in the post-9/11 Global War on Terror, and to shield it from the harsh U.S. nonproliferation laws, President George W. Bush enunciated a policy of differentiated proliferation, positing "responsible" nuclear-weapon states and problematic countries.[86] Separating states, in effect, into "good" and "bad" proliferators has led to the former being periodically chastised and told to behave and the latter being threatened with preemptive strikes and pressured into abjuring the nuclear weapons option. India and Israel are by this reckoning "good" proliferators and, Pakistan and China, despite their horrendous proliferation records, are not "bad" proliferators. Reduced to its essentials, the United States' proactive nonproliferation policy of labeling established, new, and aspiring powers as responsible or irresponsible nuclear-weapon states or as good or bad proliferators in order to act or not to act punitively against them, has depended on the nature of that country's relations with, and its potential political or military utility to, Washington.[87] If these relations are good, the country, such as Pakistan, is deemed useful to the U.S. interest and accorded the soft-glove treatment, or if riling a China engaged in brazen proliferation actions is considered risky, it is forgiven its proliferation excesses. This self-serving nonproliferation policy has shredded the credibility of the NPT order and spurred on the nuclear aspirant states. It has also impacted negatively on India's nuclear policy, sowing distrust about U.S. motives—something reflected in the strong opposition in Parliament to the much ballyhooed Indian-U.S. deal for civilian nuclear cooperation.[88] The U.S. policy turnaround on its earlier stance of studiously ignoring Pakistan's destabilizing nuclear activities has not reassured India as it is akin to closing the barn door after the horse has bolted.

The good proliferator–bad proliferator concept is, in any case, too arbitrary a U.S. policy construct to be accepted as universal nonproliferation criterion, especially as the distinction is not sustainable in reality. The Pakistani army has clandestinely nursed Islamic militants and insurgent organizations as state policy, supported the Taliban, Al-Qaeda, and the jihadi actions in Afghanistan, India, and points farther afield, including, perhaps, 9/11,[89] established the A. Q.

Khan–operated black market for forbidden technologies, and arranged the meetings of Pakistani nuclear scientists with the Al-Qaeda chief Osama bin Laden, reportedly holed up, with Islamabad's help, somewhere in the country's rugged North-West Frontier Province.[90] As the main pillar of the Pakistan state, it could shift allegiance and go over to the Islamic militants along with the nuclear arsenal under its control. The danger the West has been apprehending these many years will then be fully realized. The accelerated talibanization of Pakistan has already consumed Benazir Bhutto—America's last best hope for a democratic facade in that country[91]—and has targeted the Pakistani Army and the military leadership. The coming "nuclear anarchy," Jonathan Schell suggests, can be prevented if the United States takes the lead in nuclear disarming itself and the four other NPT-recognized nuclear-weapon states, not partially but wholly and within a set time frame.[92] Disarmament has been suggested by many to replace the NPT regime,[93] and the schemes resemble the "Action Plan" tabled in the UN General Assembly in June 1988 by the Indian Prime Minister Rajiv Gandhi, who on the verge of making a decision formally to acquire nuclear weapons, offered it as a last, good faith, attempt on India's part to obtain disarmament by 2010.[94] Disarmament, however, a "practical impossibility" according to Harold Brown, a former U.S. Defense Secretary, is not a viable solution considering that U.S. policy is moving in the opposite direction, toward finding new roles for nuclear weapons, stocking its inventory with new more usable armaments, configuring new strategies for their use, and upgrading the existing American nuclear weapons design and production facilities. [95]

A DANGEROUS NEW NUCLEAR DAWN

Soon after being sworn in as president, George W. Bush declared his commitment "to achieving a credible minimum deterrent with the lowest-possible number of nuclear weapons consistent with our national security needs, including our obligations to our allies."[96] The Treaty of Moscow signed by Bush and President Vladimir Putin in May 2002 requiring the reduction by 2012 of the extant U.S. and Russian inventories to 1,700–2,200 "operationally deployed" weapons with each country, put upper and lower limits on the size of the "minimum deterrent." It did not mean, however, lowering the U.S. nuclear profile. The U.S. Assistant Secretary of Defense, Crouch, disclosed that there would be no real arms reduction, that while a ceiling was established, few of the 10,000-odd weapons in the U.S. inventory would actually be retired or destroyed, that weapons considered in excess would merely be transferred to the "inactive stockpile" and could be returned to service whenever required. Releasing the *NPR* in January 2002, he defined the new U.S. nuclear agenda as enhancing capabilities to deal with, what he called, "multiple potential opponents, but we are not sure who they might be" and maintaining "sufficient nuclear forces to put us, in effect, beyond [the] reach [of any country that may want] to develop themselves as a peer competitor to the

United States."[97] The instrument conceived to ensure continued U.S. nuclear and strategic military dominance was the "new triad": incorporating the U.S. edge in computing and information-processing technologies; bunching together the conventional and nuclear strike forces; and ensuring active and passive defenses, including missile defense, and capabilities-based nuclear and conventional military planning based on a "revitalized defense infrastructure." The mission of the U.S. strategic nuclear forces (SNF) was stated to be fourfold: to assure security partners, to dissuade potential competitors and adversaries "from pursuing threatening capabilities," to deter capable would-be enemy states with missile defense coupled to "the certainty of U.S. ability to strike in response," and to defeat the enemy if it comes to all-out war. Nuclear weapons are to be used, the *NPR* says, against targets able to survive nonnuclear attacks, in retaliation for the use of nuclear, chemical, and biological weapons, and "in the event of surprising developments," which covers any remaining contingency or provocation, including preemptive strike and preventive war. In addition, nuclear force sizing is to be determined by three separate sets of contingencies. The "immediate" class of contingencies relating to "well-recognized current dangers," such as attack by North Korea on South Korea, by Iraq (and, now, no doubt Iran) on Israel, and any crisis arising out of Chinese military hostilities against Taiwan. The "potential" contingencies pertained to "plausible but not immediate" dangers sourced to "the emergence of a new, hostile military coalition against the United States or its allies," and the "unexpected" contingencies involving "sudden and unpredicted security challenges" of the kind posed by the Cuban missile crisis in 1962. The *NPR* also voiced the need for new, more handy, nuclear weapons.[98] It rang alarm bells all over the world. "We hear statements and proposals for developing low yield nuclear charges and their possible uses in regional conflicts," noted Russian President Putin. "This, to a very low bar, to a dangerous line, lowers the threshold of possible nuclear weapons use. The very approach to this problem may change, and then," he added, "it will be possible to speak of a change of strategy. In this case nuclear weapons from weapons of nuclear deterrence to the level of weapons of operational use ... this is very dangerous." The Chinese Foreign Office spokesman talked angrily of "nuclear blackmail" and vowed that China would not succumb to it, and even NATO allies protested, albeit mutedly.[99] Instead of intimidating them, the *NPR* acted as a goad to the targeted states.[100]

The U.S. Departments of Defense and Energy, on their part, enthused by a new and more proactive role for nuclear weapons and piggybacking on the eagerness of the national weapons laboratories in Los Alamos and Livermore for new projects, sought funding for the development of robust nuclear earth penetrators ("bunker busters"), for smaller, more flexible tactical weapons, and for the versatile Reliable Replacement Warhead (RRW). Elaborating on the Bush Administration's approach, William Schneider, Jr., chairman of the Defense Science Board of the U.S. Department of Defense, justified the continued utility of high-yield nuclear weapons in terms of meeting the "enduring requirement" for area destruction and for smaller yield weapons to destroy targets that, the *NPR* believed, precision conventional weapons could not. He revealed that, as part of the rationalization of the weapons inventory, out of 32 designs on the shelf for weapons to outfit future SNF, eight designs had been chosen—two designs to be optimized for each delivery system—strategic bomber, cruise missile, intercontinental-range ballistic missile (ICBM), and submarine-launched ballistic missile (SLBM), plus an additional type to be held in reserve. He also indicated that the 1992 decision by President Bill Clinton to ban nuclear tests, reversed seven years later by the U.S. Senate, had been upgraded to a policy of "conditional readiness" to resume testing at any time. In addition, he indicated that statutory authority had been accorded the concerned agencies to develop new weapons designs. Schneider explained that precision conventional strike assets conjoined to active missile and other defenses in fact meant a decreasing need for large nuclear forces, whence Bush's acceptance of smaller "operationally deployed" SNF negotiated with Putin. Among the desirable qualities Schneider implied the American weapons labs would strive to engineer into the new nuclear weapons designs, he listed low maintenance, tailored effects, compatibility with more than one delivery system, high levels of safety and reliability, the ability of nuclear weapons to be integrated into advanced conventional military operations, and the capacity of tested weapons designs to be reused with small modifications where necessary. He also talked of the United States' virtually constructing a new weapons design and production complex for "just-in-time development and manufacturing" to deal with new and emerging threats.[101] In 2006 Linton Brooks, administrator of the U.S. National Nuclear Security Agency, dilating on the modern weapons production facility (the so-called "Complex 2030"), said that as "responsive nuclear infrastructure" it will be in a position to "produce warheads on a timescale in which geopolitical threats could emerge," and clarified that the RRW program by relaxing the Cold war design constraints on maximum yield-to-weight ratios, would "increase reliability and reduce need for testing," adapt an existing design within 18 months, and produce an entirely new weapon design in 3–4 years.[102]

The most significant aspect of the new U.S. nuclear posture is the quest for smaller, cleaner, more usable nuclear weapons.[103] To realize this, the United States has over the decades invested heavily in research and development of "pure fusion" weapons now in their experimental stage. The characteristic of this genus of armament is that the thermonuclear reaction is triggered by high energy lasers or some other means. Owing to the absence of huge radioactive fallout from the fission featured in the current generation of thermonuclear and boosted weapons, the new types of area-destruction and point-destruction tactical weapons envisaged promise minimum radioactivity and little or no unintended collateral damage. Technical problems in converting the fifth generation concept into weapons, however, remain.[104] Nevertheless, the evolutionary trend line of technology is toward more militarily relevant and versatile thermonuclear weapons of the kind the *NPR* espouses, namely those that can flatten a city and, with equal felicity, a particular building in a city block. The worst outcome of regular nuclear weapons—the lingering effects of radioactivity and radioactive debris that make political decisions to use nuclear weapons nearly impossible and form such a large part of the existing "nuclear taboo,"[105] is sought to be reduced. Nuclear armaments capable of relatively low radioactivity damage are already in the American inventory. The B-61 family of thermonuclear weapons with variable yields from 300 KT to as low as 300 tons, for example, is available for use against states helping the terrorist groups and for dropping on isolated targets difficult to destroy by conventional means.[106] The low-yield weapon and the accompanying strategy for its use is already an arrow in Washington's quiver whether or not the RRW program comes to fruition.[107]

Given the complexities and risks inherent in forceful preemption, however, America is also emphasizing prophylactic measures to try to keep nuclear materials and technologies from the grasp of terrorist organizations. To this end, the U.S. government is ensuring that export rules and regulations as well as the policing system in all supplier states are tightened up. "If terrorists believe that it will be extremely risky, or impossible, to acquire weapons or materials, they may be deterred from seeking such materials," Brooks said in a September 2006 discussion at Chatham House in London. Describing this as a policy of "deterrence by denial of gains," he said it was just "another form of deterrence." Further, he warned potential state sponsors of terrorism that improved techniques in nuclear forensics now provided the United States with foolproof nuclear attribution capabilities. Should there be an incident involving the use of nuclear device by terrorists, any state that assisted in any way in the making of that device, Brooks indicated, would be identified and face condign punishment.[108] The U.S. *National Security Strategy* document of March 2006 formally spells out this new "deterrence calculus." "States that harbor and assist terrorists," it says, "are as guilty as the terrorists, and they will be held to account." However, the matter is complicated by the fact that United States' attribution capabilities are "least reliable" in the case of states—Iran, North Korea and Pakistan—offering the most active assistance to terrorist outfits.[109] Moreover, the latest wrinkle in the U.S. nonproliferation policy seeks to distinguish between "a leakage problem" that, say, Pakistan could be blamed for, and the "provider problem" posed by a North Korea, which Washington believes can only be deterred by strong and direct threats.[110] This distinction, along with Washington's tendency to soft-pedal some proliferation threats, such as that held out by Pakistan, and to overlook China's brazen proliferation activity for reasons of its national interest, brings the American approach into disrepute and prevents a universal approach to deal with the danger of proliferating nuclear WMD.

RUSSIAN REACTION

If a triumphalist America thought its initiatives in the nuclear weapons field and in the strategic arena generally would overawe potential opponents into calling it quits, it was mistaken. It has only propelled the nuclear-weapon states not allied with the United States as well as the nuclear aspirant states into firming up their stance. A revived and more confident Russia under President Vladimir Putin, with burgeoning oil revenues fueling economic growth, has indicated it is game for Cold War II.[111] Maintaining nuclear parity with the United States, modernizing its conventional military forces, and neutralizing the security advantages garnered by an enlarged NATO is the way, the Kremlin believes, that Russia will gain the international standing the USSR enjoyed. While earlier Russia seemed reconciled to its geographical and political shrinkage, President Putin drew the line on ceding ground in the military sphere because, he said, "The weak get beaten."[112] Russia's extensive Soviet-era nuclear deterrent is still formidable and its "central mission," according Dmitri Trenin, a former member of the Russian delegation to arms control talks with the United States, "remains essentially unchanged" from the Cold War days "albeit at a numerically reduced level." Further, it allows the country to be considered on par with the United States, which deflects Western pressure and prevents U.S. interference in its affairs. It led Putin to describe the country's nuclear deterrent as "the main foundation of Russia's national security."[113] Russia finds itself, however, in a tough situation. The functioning of the "new triad" and the qualitative upgrading of the American strategic nuclear forces during George W. Bush's presidency set alongside the depleting Russian strategic forces owing to inadequate investment in them, for example, have led some analysts to conclude that the United States is now in a position to launch a successful counter-force first strike. These analysts cite its markedly improved strategic strike assets (in terms of yield and accuracy), a powerful and invulnerable nuclear submarine-borne retaliatory element, and a still thin-on-the-ground but limited-use missile defense system that, therefore, makes it clear the United States enjoys "nuclear primacy."[114] The Russian analyst Alexei Arbatov's response was to posit a frightening scenario. The Soviet-era arsenal of some 3,500 warheads on strategic bombers and sea- and land-based missiles was indeed wasting away, he conceded, but its replacement with some 100 mobile and silo-based Topol-M missiles and 3–4 new nuclear powered nuclear missile firing submarines (SSBNs) of the Borei class was, he claimed, "enough to serve as a minimal deterrent but," and here was the kicker, "it will rely heavily on hair trigger alert, which is very dangerous in the age of nuclear weapons proliferation and catastrophic terrorism."[115] In trading numbers for a frighteningly thin tripwire and an implied launch-on-warning strategy, Moscow may be compensating for its weakness in strategic armaments and, at the same time, trying to enhance the deterrence value of the limited modern nuclear forces it can field, by invoking the most unstable period of the Cold War.

The paucity of modern hardware may be a problem, but the large stocks of ex-Soviet-era weapons, warheads, and delivery platforms will ensure there is no sudden drop in numbers of Russian weapons or warheads. Based on this, the 2000 *Military Doctrine of the Russian Federation* delineated a nuclear policy that included the country's SNF assuring "required damage" defined as "what would be subjectively unacceptable to the would-be attacker, so as to outweigh any potential gains from attacking Russia, and thus would be enough to dissuade the enemy from considering an attack." The document, however, referred to the low-yield nuclear weapons—the mini-nukes that the United States has put much store by—as "highly destabilizing, virtually on par with WMD proliferation."[116] However, taking into account the deterioration in Russia's conventional force structure, Moscow announced its right to retaliate with nuclear weapons in response to the use of weapons of mass destruction against it or its allies and also in case of large-scale conventional military aggression, which last was in line with the 1993 document *Basic Provisions of the Military Doctrine.* The Soviet government's 1982 commitment to "No First Use" was jettisoned. These innovations in Russian nuclear policy neatly reversed the Cold War situation when it was NATO, fearing the Soviet bloc's massed armor, which aimed to neutralize any thrust by it on the Central European front by initiating the use of nuclear weapons. These changes, Arbatov argued, were only to bring the Russian nuclear strategy in conformity with its U.S., U.K. and French counterparts.[117] Russia, like the United States, has a policy of nuclear weapon use in limited wars. The Russian nuclear strategy refers to a mission for "de-escalation of aggression through a threat of actual launching of strikes on a varying scale by using conventional and/or nuclear weapons" and "dosed" (selective, limited) combat use of some elements of the SNF. The willingness to resort to nuclear weapons is to be demonstrated by "enhancing the level of [force] readiness, conduct of exercises, and relocation of some components," i.e., by deploying SSBNs, dispersing mobile ICBMs, and moving bombers to alternate locations.[118]

The increased tension in the U.S.-Russian relations was not anticipated by the Kremlin. The Russian *Military Doctrine,* for instance, spoke of cooperating with the United States to maintain peace and stability in Europe. The break with the United States began with President George W. Bush's unilateral abrogation of the 1972 Anti-Ballistic Missile Treaty in December 2001 after failing to negotiate joint withdrawal with Russia in a deal linking concessions on missile defense with reductions in offensive strategic weapons.[119] Moscow's allergy to any kind of missile defense is because of its fear it will be used to intercept Russian missiles and facilitate a disarming first strike. To head off U.S. missile defense plans, in 2004 Russia test-fired a "hypersonic" missile that Colonel-General Yuri Baluyevsky, then first deputy chief of General Staff, claimed would make "any missile defense useless."[120] An unimpressed Washington's plea that installing an X-band radar in the Czech Republic and several batteries of anti-missile missiles on Poland's Baltic coast was to neutralize Iranian missiles coming over the azimuth, in turn, cut no ice with Russia.[121] Putin then offered the use of an ex-Soviet radar station in Azerbaijan and to cooperate closely in the installation of a system of missile defense for all of Europe,[122] but Washington failed to react to the proposal. Moscow followed up by placing its most advanced anti-missile systems, the S-300 PS, on NATO's eastern flank to counter the proposed American missile defense system and to protest the expansion of NATO by allowing former Warsaw Pact member states into it.[123] Hoping to intimidate Poland into reversing its stand, Baluyevsky, now chief of General Staff, threatened: "We are talking about the possibility of a retaliatory strike being triggered by the mistaken classification of an interceptor missile launch."[124] This threat buttressed his earlier comment that the expansion of the U.S. economic, political, and military presence in areas traditionally considered a Russian sphere of influence constituted the main security threat to Russia—a threat he characterized as more dire than the one faced by the USSR.[125] And to show that Moscow would engage in military competition if that is what Washington wanted, Kremlin allotted 5 trillion rubles (U.S. $190 billion) for its armed forces modernization in 2007–2015, which funds President Putin said would be used to "substantially enhance" Russian SNF so as "to preserve what is one of the most fundamental guarantees of lasting peace—the strategic balance of forces." This indicates that, rather than go in for a destabilizing hair-trigger nuclear situation as the Russian analyst Alexei Arbatov envisaged, Moscow intends to beef up its nuclear forces to blunt U.S. nuclear superiority. Putin declared that if the Americans spend a lot on defense to "make their house into a fortress," Russians should prepare to do the same, as the law of jungle prevails and "Comrade wolf knows whom to eat!"[126] In fact, the rift between the United States and Russia has widened with Moscow making good its threat and, on December 12, 2007, formally disavowing the 1990 Conventional Forces in Europe Treaty curtailing the deployment of conventional military hardware (tanks, artillery) and troops on either side of the divide—the basis for the post-Cold War thaw.[127] To show it means business, Russia has also threatened to walk out of the 1987 Intermediate Nuclear Forces Treaty restricting the numbers of intermediate-range ballistic missiles and other armaments with like range deployed in-theater by the United States and NATO and Russia and its partners. And, as a first step in this direction, Russia has indicated that it will dust off the Cuba option from the Cold War years of deploying strategic bombers in that country, not a great distance from the U.S. mainland.[128] With the U.S.-Russian relations dipping and the strategic competition on the upswing, the political differences are bound to increase, and the proliferation of WMD to friends and partners among the developing countries could return as means of advancing their particular national interests. These and similar developments showcase Russia's determination to regain its relevance as a great power.[129]

CHINA, THE UNITED KINGDOM, AND FRANCE IN THE NEW NUCLEAR MATRIX

The second-tier nuclear-weapon states—China, the United Kingdom, and France, incapable economically of affording the nuclear orders of battle of the kind boasted by the United States and the Soviet Union, carved out a role for themselves on the sidelines of the superpower rivalry by fielding limited strategic forces.[130] Post–Cold War, in the wake of intense domestic debate, especially in the United Kingdom, on the utility of a nuclear deterrent,[131] the British and the French governments decided that "less was enough" and settled on four Vanguard (Trident-II)-class SSBN systems and four Triomphant-class SSBNs plus an extended range air-to-ground nuclear missile (ASMPA) carried by land and carrier-based aircraft, respectively. Both the Vanguard submarines and the Triomphant vessels will carry reduced loading of multiple independently targetable re-entry vehicle (MIRV) warheads on the British D-5 ICBM and the French M-51 ICBM.[132] The British Labor Party prime minister, Tony Blair, explained that the United Kingdom would retain its nuclear deterrent as a hedge against an uncertain future and the possibility of a threat of "nuclear blackmail and acts of aggression against our vital interests by nuclear-armed opponents."[133] Faced with intense opposition from within his own party, Blair barely managed to get parliamentary approval in March 2007 for retaining an independent British nuclear deterrent and earmarking $10 billion for refurbishing the U.K. Atomic Weapons Establishment at Aldermaston and equipping it with an inertial confinement fusion facility to help design and develop the next generation thermonuclear warhead. Various justifications were offered, none more attenuated than Foreign Secretary Margaret Beckett's that the Trident option will cut the existing warheads strength by 20 percent by the end of 2007 and help meet the Article VI obligations under the NPT requiring the P-5 progressively to divest themselves of nuclear weapons.[134] By going beyond the traditional rationale for its compact nuclear force of deterring nuclear-weapon states, and conceiving of a substrategic role for it against state sponsors of terrorism, Britain has fallen in line with the U.S. official policy.[135]

If nuclear weapons as symbols of great power and an independent foreign policy applies to the United Kingdom, it applies even more to France. Unlike the British government that has sounded a bit defensive, however, Paris is thinking expansively about the probable missions for its nuclear weapons. In 2006, French President Jacques Chirac talked of nuclear weapons as not only deterring state sponsors of terrorism, preempting an adversary's "capacity to act," providing the French government with discriminate and controllable employment options, and signaling France's willingness to launch a "final warning strike" but also acting as "guarantee of our strategic supplies" of natural resources, such as oil. How exactly nuclear weapons would be used to achieve these objectives, he did not say, but stressed nuclear deterrence as the foundation of the strategy of prevention and intervention. Additionally, the traditional French policy about defenses not replacing nuclear deterrence was changed by Chirac. He contended that missile defense combined with nuclear deterrence reduced vulnerabilities. According to David Yost, some of the new wrinkles in the French nuclear doctrine amount to lowering the nuclear weapons use threshold.[136] More generally, on missile defense and in terms of dealing with "loose nukes," rogue states, transnational terrorist groups, and their WMD nexus, the new British and the

French nuclear doctrines clearly converge with the American preemption and preventive war policy.[137]

Strategic weapons development in China is enigmatic. Its nuclear program is so opaque and shrouded in secrecy, it is hard to be sure about basic things such as force size. With an estimated fissile material stockpile of some 1.7–2.8 tons, it can theoretically produce as many as 900 warheads or weapons. Reports about the actual strength of the Chinese Strategic forces, however, vary greatly. On the low side, the Chinese deterrent is supposed to comprise 30 ICBMs, 50–100 intermediate-range ballistic missiles (IRBMs) and medium-range ballistic missiles (MRBMs), and an inventory of 80–130 weapons and warheads (estimated by the Natural Resources Defense Council and the Council of Foreign Relations in the United States); in the middle range the International Institute of Strategic Studies, London, and the research wing of the British House of Commons believe China possesses some 400 weapons and warheads.[138] And on the high side, the estimate by the U.S. Defense Intelligence Agency is of an inventory of over 800 weapons.[139] Whatever the truth, the Chinese SNF are in the growth phase with increasingly higher allocations in an annual defense budget that analysts contend is touching $100 billion and "increasingly supplanting Russia as the primary benchmark for determining the size and capabilities of U.S. strategic forces."[140] Statements made by Chinese military leaders point to a hefty strategic buildup and aggressive thinking. Lieutenant General Liu Yazhou of the Peoples Liberation Army Air Force (PLAAF) in an interview declared that "Geography is destiny ... Generally when a powerful country begins to rise, it should first set itself in an invincible position."[141] To do that, China has begun by throwing out its No First Use policy[142] and to invest more and more on its strategic and power projection capabilities. Lieutenant General Michael D. Maples, Director of the U.S. Defense Intelligence Agency, said in February 2007 that he expected "China's nuclear weapons stockpiles to grow over the next ten years as new ballistic missile systems reach operational status" and in this respect mentioned three strategic long-range missiles—the DF(Dong Feng)-31 and DF-31A road mobile ICBMs and the JL(Julong)-2 SLBM. He added that China was paying particular attention to improving the "survivability" of its missiles besides "increasing the capabilities of its "theater ballistic missile force." He worried too that "China's development of a Tomahawk-class ground-launched land attack cruise missile ... will enable it to execute strikes in the Asian theater."[143] This trend is not surprising, says a 2005 RAND report, as the United States is viewed as the "greatest threat." "Credible strategic nuclear capabilities" are being sought to be developed by China, in particular to defeat any attempts at nuclear coercion or "to limit its strategic options, especially during a crisis."[144] Inducting more accurate, long-range, and mobile missiles with advanced MIRVed warheads to defeat missile defense, dispersing these missiles widely, expanding the fleet of relatively invulnerable SSBNs, and upgrading its satellite sensors and C4ISR (command, control, communications, computers, intelligence, surveillance and reconnaissance) systems for early warning are measures

China is taking[145] to escape preemptive strike the United States is in a position to mount with its Trident-II D-5 missile, the W-88 warhead, the B-2 bomber, and the stealthy AGM-129 cruise missile constituting its main counter-force capabilities, within the extant "launch cycle time of Chinese forces."[146] Further, the transition of the Chinese nuclear deterrent into a sophisticated and reliable force has paralleled changes in its strategy—"secure second strike" has given way to "limited nuclear deterrence" and capability for some counter-force targeting as a means of limiting damage. With a multi-trillion dollar economy growing at a yearly average of 6–7 percent, China is able to afford beefed-up strategic capabilities. The Chinese defense procurement budget estimated to touch $38 billion by 2010 is expected to rise to $113 billion by 2025.[147]

A Chinese analyst, Dingli Shen, warns that China's nuclear modernization and force enhancement in response to U.S. missile defense and advanced warheads and delivery systems will upset "the balance" and set off "a ripple effect" in India and Pakistan—"an outcome," he suggests, "the United States certainly doesn't want."[148] Other than the fear of a nuclear chain reaction that Beijing has tried to invoke to get the United States to negotiate a treaty to ban weapons in space and that Russia too desires, it conducted a test of its own well-developed anti-satellite system in January 2007. A land-based missile destroyed one of its own aging satellites.[149] And, it has significantly increased investments in the asymmetric cyberwar wherewithal. The 2007 U.S. Department of Defense report on Chinese military power has observed the heavy deployment of resources of all kinds to realize capabilities for "computer network attack, computer network defense, and computer network exploitation" which are "critical," according to the Peoples Liberation Army, "to achieving 'electromagnetic dominance'." In fact, to wage "comprehensive war," Beijing expects to rely on cyberwar capabilities to disrupt the enemy economy by penetrating computerized financial networks, and by introducing "logic bombs" into the adversary's nuclear command and control links. It will make first strike or any coordinated strategic operations against China difficult for the United States (or any other country) to pull off. General Robert Elder, heading the newly established U.S. Cyberspace Command tasked with protecting U.S. military data, communications, and control networks, perhaps, mirroring the Chinese intent, revealed that his Command seeks to disable adversary networks by crashing computers, especially targeting "supervisory control and data acquisition" systems allowing remote monitoring and control of manufacturing lines and civil works projects, such as dams.[150] China has reportedly tested the American cyber-defenses with as many as 1,100 attempts to steal data through December 2007 from computer networks in U.S. nuclear weapons laboratories such as the Oak Ridge National Laboratory in Tennessee.[151] If China is now or soon will be in a position credibly to preempt U.S. strategic preemption capabilities and its nuclear forces, it will be in an even stronger position to wield coercive leverage against India and Japan, both of whom it regards as traditional enemies and peer competitors in Asia. The upward rising trajectory of the Chinese strategic power may, in any case, result in nuclear dominoes, with, in the main, Japan and Taiwan—presently protected by the U.S. strategic umbrella—wondering if the United States can be banked on in any serious confrontation with China.

NUCLEAR DOMINOES IN ASIA

Japan, South Korea, and Taiwan have so far chosen not to go beyond their threshold status, less because they don't feel threatened by China and its protégé, North Korea, than because the United States has provided formal nuclear protection and pressured these countries into foregoing the nuclear weapon option with the threat of withdrawing from its security commitments.[152] This "bargain" may fail both because North Korea could disable its weapons production units without destroying the small inventory of weapons it has acquired or, for that matter, giving up its nuclear ambitions[153] and because the United States could be seen as incapable of really deterring either China or North Korea.[154]

Japan's nuclear quest can be traced to two separate efforts under the aegis of the Japanese Imperial Army and the Navy in the 1940s when sharp scientific talent hindered by lack of natural resources, such as uranium, and inter-service rivalry, led to the programs reaching a certain level during the Second World War period before stagnating.[155] The societal revulsion against nuclear weapons did not, however, stop the Japanese governments from 1945 onward from adopting a pragmatic approach. Tokyo supported the U.S. nonproliferation policy, as Morton Halperin writes, while "quietly putting Japan into a position to be able to quickly develop nuclear weapons and sophisticated missile delivery systems."[156] With an advanced nuclear research complex, enrichment facility, and large holdings of spent uranium fuel, Japan is described, by Masahiro Matsumara, as "a virtual nuclear super power" which can, if it chooses to do so, have a bomb inside of a few months and to build a nuclear arsenal "ranked only behind the United States and Russia."[157] This may happen, albeit later rather than sooner, owing to the fundamental reexamination of its security policy underway in Japan possibly resulting in that country's remilitarization in order to avoid "entrapment or abandonment by the United States" and because of the "threat-capability mismatch."[158] The political support in Japan for a reversal of its nuclear stance is both growing and becoming institutionalized.[159] Tetsuya Endo, the former acting chairman of the Atomic Energy Commission of Japan and a key negotiator for normalization of relations with North Korea, concerned with Washington's seeming inattention to Tokyo's concerns about Pyongyang's proliferation tendencies and its retaining a small weapons inventory even as its nuclear capability is disabled, was forthright. It may, he says, "result in distrust of the United States among the [Japanese] public" and has called on the government to think of ways "to deal" with the situation.[160] It isn't too much of a stretch to think that, down the line, Japan may consider it necessary to rely on nuclear weapons of its own to protect itself and safeguard its interests as regards North Korea and China if Washington is perceived as infirm in its resolve to do so.

South Korea initiated nuclear weapons work in the early 1970s only to shut it down under American pressure and sign the NPT. The subsequent peaceful orientation of its program under International Atomic Energy Agency (IAEA) safeguards did not obviate some of the South Korean nuclear scientists, described as "rogue" by Seoul, refining uranium to bomb-grade using lasers—a technically sophisticated if expensive method.[161] It suggests that its "sunshine policy" and subscription to the Non-Proliferation Treaty notwithstanding, advanced threshold countries can get around the safeguards system and quite easily cross the nuclear Rubicon.

Taiwan's situation, in many ways, resembles Japan's and South Korea's in that it is a rich nation able to afford a nuclear deterrent and has the requisite scientific and technological base to produce one. It also has the same patron, the United States, frowning on its acquisition of independent means to deter China. Beyond a certain threshold, though, and depending on whether Sino-U.S. relations warm up or become edgier, Taiwan, like Japan or even South Korea, may opt to go in for nuclear weapons.[162] The Taiwanese nuclear program is based on a heavy-water reactor imported from Canada and nuclear materials from the United States in the 1960s. Within a decade, it was near enough to the weapons threshold to prompt Washington into squeezing Taipei and shuttering that reactor.[163] Obviously the reactor was not completely nonfunctional nor was all "research" ended, because there are reports of valuable knowledge in nuclear warhead design and construction accruing to the Taiwanese.[164] The Chungshan Institute of Technology that ran the nuclear program now builds missiles (such as the 1,000-km range Hsiung Feng-2 land attack cruise missile that can reach as far as Shanghai), enabling it to produce both the warhead and the delivery system anytime the Taiwan government so decides.[165]

Vietnam has historical enmity with China, last fought a war with it in 1979, and has an unresolved dispute over island territories in the South China Sea. Like Japan and Taiwan, it is bent on preventing Chinese "bullying" and may think of nuclear weapons as providing the safety factor in case relations with China, now on the mend,[166] take a dive. Hanoi may be choosing the civilian nuclear-energy route to develop the requisite skills. At the Dalat Nuclear Research Institute, a 500-KW experimental reactor, functioning for several decades now, has been used primarily for training purposes. The policy of exploiting China's soft underbelly in Southeast Asia and Vietnam's fierce pride in keeping the Chinese out of their country for "a thousand years" by building up that country's strategic muscle, had been mooted in the mid-1990s, at a time when Hanoi offered India the use of Cam Ranh Bay naval base, among other military facilities.[167] Under the rubric of its "Look East" policy, this approach was furthered in 2002 with the establishment of the Vietnam-India Nuclear Science Center with a rotating team of Indian scientists from the Indian nuclear complexes.[168] It has been suggested that as part of this strategy the liquid-fueled short-range nuclear-capable

Prithvi ballistic missiles India will phase out should be transferred to Vietnam to equip it with a ready and reliable delivery system.[169] Considering the strategic stakes, India is forging strong military ties with Vietnam as a hedge strategy to curb China's aggressive ambitions.[170]

In west Asia, there are two reasons why Arab states will want nuclear weapons. Israel, with manifest conventional military superiority and possessing nuclear weapons, is a perennial provocation to Arab states, reminding them of their military and technological inferiority. If Iran gets the bomb, it will be the other significant motivation for the Arab countries to go nuclear by hook or by crook. For one thing Iran's strategic leadership of the Islamic nations in the region, courtesy of nuclear weapons, is anathema to the Arabs. Second, most of the conservative Arab regimes are being undermined by what has been referred to as the HISH (Hamas-Iran, Syria-Hizballah) alliance, which is also active in the politics in Iraq and in orchestrating opposition to the U.S. military presence there. And, third, the conservative regimes are worried that the uncompromising Iranian rhetoric against Israel and America's regional role is gaining ground in the Sunni Arab states and is destabilizing of the current order.[171] All the Arab nuclear aspirant countries, however, are NPT signatories and cannot openly and legally pursue their nuclear weapons ambitions. Libya tried illegally to do so, courtesy the A. Q. Khan network operating under Pakistan government aegis, but was compelled by U.S. pressure to give up its weapons program. Attempting a similar venture, Syria invited a preemptive Israeli strike. Moreover, covert means of securing the capabilities have become immensely difficult. With the tightening of the various technology denial regimes and strict export control laws and stricter implementation by the supplier states, the Non-Proliferation Treaty and the Missile Technology Control Regime are losing their porosity. With the shutdown of the A. Q. Khan outfit in 2003, there is no easy and secret way, any more, for countries and nonstate actors to obtain sensitive goods and technologies.

This has left aspirant states in west Asia with two choices, neither of them easy. They can either do as Iran has done—buy civilian-use nuclear technologies and materials under the cover of NPT from Russia, the only major supplier state willing to cut commercial deals because of the priority it accords revenue generation.[172] The civilian reactors and related technologies thus acquired can then surreptitiously be used for military purposes, allowing for an accumulation of skills and competencies and, over time, the attainment of the weapons threshold. Or, it can conditionally bankroll a friendly threshold state, as Saudi Arabia, which lacks the necessary human and technological resources, did vis-à-vis Pakistan's nuclear weapons program. In fact, among Arab states Saudi Arabia is the most determined to go nuclear. According to intelligence analysts and the Saudi diplomat and nuclear physicist who defected to the United States, Mohammed Khilewi, in the aftermath of the Arab defeat in the 1973 War with Israel, Riyadh set up a nuclear weapons project at the Al-Khurj Nuclear Research Center. It bought some 60-odd CSS-2 'Silkworm' IRBMs from China as the prospective delivery system. Start-up difficulties and the singular lack of skilled manpower and infrastructure, though, led in the 1980s to a decision conditionally to finance Pakistan's weapons program instead. The understanding was that in return for the funding—a billion dollars each for weapons development and for converting the F-16 strike aircraft to carry and fire nuclear ordnance, and 150,000 barrels of oil per day as energy grant partially to meet Pakistan's energy needs—Saudi Arabia would have access to Pakistani nuclear weapons if it faced aggression.[173]

CONCLUSION

Several factors are making for a combustible mix with a short nuclear fuse and impacting on India's security and Indian strategic interests. The reassertion by the United States and the P-5 of the nuclear weapon as the final arbiter of relations between states, the breakdown of the Non-Proliferation Treaty system, and America's aggressive defense of the *status quo,* are the main elements. The secondary factors include the nuclear black market (centered in Pakistan), failing states and regimes seeking safety in the bomb, the sometimes strained relations between nuclear-weapon states fueling tension (United States./NATO vs. Russia, Russia vs. China, India vs. Pakistan), the regional nuclear security dynamic (India vs. China; India vs. China/Pakistan/North Korea, India/Japan/South Korea/Taiwan/Vietnam vs. China, United States/India/Japan vs. China or North Korea, Arab states vs. Israel or Iran, Israel vs. Iran), colliding great-power interests (United States, China, Russia on regional and international security architecture, nonproliferation, and arms control), internal unrest in nuclear-weapon states (Pakistan) spilling over the borders into adjoining nuclear or threshold countries (India, Iran), and hyperactive and risk-taking transnational extremist and terrorist groups, exploiting the Islamic identity politics in much of West, Central, and southern Asia and trying to link up with unreliable elements in Pakistan in the hope of securing nuclear weapons or fissile material. The high levels of fear and anxiety, particularly in Asia, have led to something unprecedented, what Michael Dillon in another context calls the "intensive and extensive hyperbolicization of security"[174] and a premium on nuclear weapons as hyperbolic means of security. In the resulting nuclearization of international relations, the non-possession of nuclear weapons has become a liability for states.

The risks and uncertainties in an increasingly disoriented and unstable regional and international milieu are strong motivations for India to keep up its nuclear guard and strengthen its strategic defense. It also has other reasons to do so. A consequential thermonuclear weapons inventory is an attribute of great power and affirms its strategic independence. India's security priority is also to ensure it is not psychologically crippled in a crisis with China and require it to close the gap in terms of the reach and deliverable megatonnage of its strategic forces. If the strategic situation deteriorates vis-à-vis that country, India may be required to create a security dilemma for China of the kind Beijing created for India by arming Pakistan with nuclear missiles. This will mean assisting Vietnam and Taiwan—and any other state on China's periphery seeking to bolster its strategic capabilities—to become proficient in nuclear weapons and long-range missiles. This will be to play nuclear hardball in the manner China and the United States have done and to adopt a *realpolitik* attitude to proliferating nuclear weapon and missile technologies if it serves the national interest. Indian defense science officials, for example, angry at the double standards in proliferation, have long sought permission from the government to sell Indian missiles to countries in Africa, the Persian Gulf and Southeast Asia. "I would like to devalue missiles," said Dr. A. P. J. Abdul Kalam, then head of the Defense Research and Development Organization in 1999, "by selling the technology to many nations and to break [the Missile Control Technology Regime's] stranglehold."[175] The infrastructure for Indian nuclear strategic cooperation with Vietnam and Taiwan, for instance, may be in place.[176] As later chapters in this book will show, Pakistan is not a credible conventional or nuclear threat to India. India has, however, to ensure it is always in a position to overawe the Islamic extremists potentially presiding over a Taliban-ruled nuclear Pakistan by deploying a thermonuclear arsenal that is forbidding in both size and quality.

CHAPTER 2

Laying the Foundation: India's Nuclear and Missile Capabilities and Minimum Deterrence Concept, 1947–1998

Unlike in the first three decades of the nuclear era, an atom bomb today is neither high science, nor does it represent the most advanced technology. Any country with a civilian nuclear program is capable of making weapons and any terrorist organization able to recruit a competent physicist, a chemist, and a high explosives expert and able to procure plutonium the size of a golf ball can craft a serviceable device using fairly rudimentary equipment.[1] Globalization, moreover, has made the quest for nuclear weapons easier.[2] If the bomb is not widely available to countries that want it, it is only because the first five states to acquire nuclear weapons (P-5) established a monopoly and then preserved it with the 1968 Non-Proliferation Treaty (NPT). Promising nuclear disarmament, the P-5 persuaded the rest of the world to sign the treaty, and with severe policing measures prevented the diffusion of relevant technologies and materials. After the 1995 Indefinite Extension of the NPT, the P-5 policy of persuasion vis-à-vis the NPT signatory states seeking to break out of the treaty confines changed to that of coercion and compellence. Three countries—India, Pakistan, and Israel—that had refused to join the nonproliferation regime, were treated as exceptions.[3] The coercive behavior includes the threat by friend and foe alike to "secure" or take out nuclear arsenals and capabilities any time these threaten their interests. Thus, the Iranian nuclear facilities face preemptive destruction by the United States and Israel, the Pakistani nuclear weapons inventory is in danger of being captured and/or disabled by friendly American forces, and a similar fate may await the North Korean bombs at the hands of Pyongyang's Chinese patrons.[4]

Countries other than the P-5 found their nuclear ambitions thwarted by the arbitrary criterion in the treaty defining a nuclear-weapon state as any country that tested a device before 1967 and by its generally discriminatory nature. Of the three NPT non-signatory states, India posed the gravest challenge to this jerry-built nuclear order. By securing weapons capability early, protecting its weapon option, and eventually exercising it, India unsettled the strategic calculi of the P-5 and exacerbated the dissatisfaction with the NPT by many signatory states. Relentless criticism of the P-5 by Delhi for not delivering on the treaty's Article VI obligation to disarm was something Indian representatives had consistently harped on in the lead-up to the NPT[5] and meant that India was the wrecking ball swinging at the regime superstructure. The high level of disaffection with the treaty among the signatory states owing to the slow-go on nuclear disarmament led in 2005 to the last NPT Review Conference's ending without any consensus document or declaration. Over the years, India discovered that its potential for weakening the nonproliferation system helped leverage an easing of the U.S. pressure to join the NPT and to sign the Comprehensive Test Ban Treaty (CTBT).[6] If, despite having every motive to do so, India chose not to pull down the Non-Proliferation Treaty regime, it was because of its conservative instinct—it hoped to become part of the exclusive nuclear club.

For the prevailing global order to be maintained, it makes sense the Indian Prime Minister Manmohan Singh said to accommodate India at "the high table."[7] The trouble with bundling India with Pakistan and Israel is that it has not only made such accommodation more difficult but created a systemic anomaly and potential fissure endangering the NPT regime and the international balance of power. While all the existing great powers are nuclear-weapon states, not all nuclear-weapon states can be great powers. Whatever the criteria for the great-power tag, India makes it.[8] Conversely, the United Kingdom and France, for instance, may no longer deserve this status.[9] Pakistan and Israel are simply too small and weak to matter. To complicate things, India's attitude to the present nuclear order has been negatively influenced by the policies of China and the United States, who deliberately helped Pakistan become a nuclear-weapon state. If, as a result, Pakistan has verily turned into a strategic nuisance for India and a nuclear mischief-monger and menace to everybody else, then the threat from a China-Pakistan nexus is doubly daunting. It would be imprudent, under the circumstances, for Delhi to do other than proceed seriously with building up its nuclear deterrent and do as Beijing and Washington have done —pursue a nonproliferation policy tempered by *realpolitik* considerations in order to improve its relative position. This could mean helping, say, Vietnam augment its strategic forces, cooperating with Taiwan in the "peaceful" uses of nuclear energy, and exploring strategic measures with Japan to stifle China's expansionist ambitions, as payback for Beijing's nuclear help and missile technology assistance to Pakistan in order to strategically discomfit India.[10] In contrast to Pakistan, India is proficient in two whole fuel cycles (plutonium and uranium) and has unmatched experience in a third fuel cycle (thorium)—all indigenously developed. If the relatively puny Pakistan can create so much security chaos and peril with its proliferation activities, the potential damage to the international system a frustrated India can do if it is denied its rightful place in the world for too long is enormous.

To get a perspective on India's frustration and impatience, consider that at the time of independence in 1947 India was, in military terms, already a "great power." As the "eastern arsenal," it had supplied war materiel, including locally made armaments ranging from artillery, to armored personnel carriers, to bomber aircraft, to the victorious Allies during the Second World War and provided huge military manpower that was largely responsible for the defeat of Nazi Germany in North Africa and stopping the westward advance of the Imperial Japanese Army in Burma. Even after partition and the separation of the rump state of Pakistan, with two active airborne divisions in its order of battle (since demobilized), it was one of only five countries in the world capable of projecting power.[11] Today as a politically stable democracy, with its economy experiencing sustained growth and with the country's conventional military complemented by a small nuclear deterrent in the process of becoming a meaningful strategic nuclear force, India is on the cusp of great power. Much has been written about India's democratic polity and the economic strides it has taken. The philosophy and approach behind India's versatile high-value nuclear program and the weapons capabilities it has spawned, however, is not as well known, let alone understood.

STRATEGIC THINKING

India's first prime minister, Jawaharlal Nehru, who served until his death in 1964, appreciated early the connection between great-power status and modern military wherewithal, as well as the fact that the atom bomb was the new standard of international power. He also understood that if India was to realize its ambition, it had to have the capabilities to construct a nuclear weapon. Other than his own deep understanding of history,[12] he made the connection between the strategic attributes of the country and its nuclear imperatives. Nehru trusted the Cambridge University–trained physicist Dr. Homi J. Bhabha explicitly and handed him the charge of structuring and running a versatile, dual-use nuclear program. Nehru's strategic thinking regarding a nuclear program, however, was the result of the influence on him, ironically, of three Englishmen—Field Marshal Claude Auchinleck, the former commander-in-chief of the Allied Middle Eastern Command in the initial years of the Second World War before Winston Churchill posted him as commander-in-chief, India; Lieutenant General Francis Tuker, who commanded the famed 4th Indian Division in the North African campaign and returned to lead India's Eastern Army—the last British officer to do so; and Professor P. M. S. Blackett, the 1948 Nobel laureate in physics, who first met Nehru at the Indian Science Congress held in Delhi in 1947 and so impressed him on military issues that he was thereafter tapped for advice on defense matters.

In the transition phase leading to independence, Nehru as Prime Minister of the Interim Government in 1946 was exposed to some very sharp long-term thinking done by the British Indian Army stalwarts. Auchinleck, in Policy Note No. 16 dated July 30, 1946,[13] for instance, stunningly for a planning paper of that vintage, outlined a future force able to contend with "nuclear energy" and "guided projectiles." These developments, he ventured, made force and logistics concentrations vulnerable, and therefore massed armies obsolete. He recommended compact force structures—armored strike formations capable of fighting dispersed for offense and "fortress groups" or "defense groups" to hold territory. This sort of forward thinking was not attempted by the Imperial General Staff in London at the time and predated the "pentomic era" experiments in the United States.[14] The basic assumption in Auchinleck's Note regarding the inevitable use of nuclear weapons in future war doubtless conditioned Nehru's views about the desirability of securing such weapons for India's defense. If Auchinleck worried about the Indian armed forces at the receiving end of nuclear weapons, Tuker thought of India as a nuclear weapon power, which may be why his writings had greater effect on Nehru and shaped his geostrategics. Tuker argued that India, as a big-sized country with large "land space" had the ability to "absorb" an atomic strike and stood a better chance of surviving nuclear war than smaller states. He believed that the mountain massifs—the Himalayan ranges and the peninsular highland (the "Western Ghats"), would permit its people to "burrow" into them to escape the worst effects of radiation from atomic bombing. And, in a clear hint that India should go nuclear, mentioned the ready source of nuclear energy found "in the sands of southern India"—a reference to the monazite sands on the Kerala Coast rich in thorium which, transmuted into uranium 233, can be used in making nuclear bombs.[15] In an earlier piece penned in 1945 under the *nom de plume* "Auspex," Tuker had underlined the importance of rockets (missiles) in the new nuclear age, something Auchinleck mentioned in his Note the following year. He also stressed the value of the subcontinental landmass from the military geography point of view and the significant role India could play in maintaining peace and order in all of Australasia. India, he said, constituted, "the great axis about which the rim of any future war will be revolving," with the "rim" defined by him as stretching from New Zealand to the Maghreb. He believed the country was the natural guardian of the oil-bearing Persian Gulf region and advised "the build-up of India into a great military power" which, Tuker thought, would be "the greatest factor for peace in Asia and the Far East."[16] It was a grand vision for India that Nehru latched on to,[17] as it reinforced his own views about the country as "the pivot of Asia" and about its military value in the emerging international order.[18] Nehru hoped that India's nuclear weapon–weighted military potential would both serve to realize its great-power ambitions and obtain for it bargaining power in relations with the United States and the West.[19]

In the evolution of Nehru's thinking about nuclear weapons and the sort of nuclear capability to aim for, Blackett's impress is palpable. Blackett wove three themes—the utility of nuclear weapons, disarmament, and nuclear energy as source of electricity—into his argument which, it turned out, were dear to Nehru. Blackett, like Auchinleck, considered the atomic bomb to be a decisive weapon that had revolutionized warfare.[20] He argued that atomic bombs are not militarily useful other than for destroying "very large targets" and because such targets will "inevitably" be cities, that it is a "only a weapon of mass destruction."[21] Even so, Blackett doubted whether "a large number of atomic bombs ... will by themselves [decide] the course of future wars" and, in this context, concluded that "the problem of the control of atomic energy becomes a part of the problem of general disarmament."[22] Further, he appreciated the deterrent value of even a small number of atomic armaments,[23] albeit some time after American strategists had done so.[24] Unwilling to succumb to the reigning paranoia about the atom, Blackett championed the potential of atomic energy to improve the lot of the poorest countries. Pointing out that the difference in the per capita wealth of India or China vis-à-vis the United States was 1:20 and that the per capita generation of energy in India from other than human labor was one-sixtieth of America's, Blackett made the case for India's needing to rely on atomic energy for "cheap power." He pointed to the ample reserves of thorium that the country was too weak industrially and technologically to exploit "unaided,"[25] thereby anticipating the rationale for the U.S. "atoms for peace" program.

Blackett's sympathetic treatment of India's economic plight and his political orientation toward the atom seemed to be in sync with that of the leading scientists in India, who regarded nuclear power as an energy lifeline.[26] A holistic paradigm was still needed to pull in these various strands and it was provided by Blackett. His opposition to the United Kingdom's investing heavily in nuclear weaponization only to beget a puny force, voiced in numerous memoranda to the government in 1945–1946,[27] led to his being blackballed by the British government.[28] With the official doors slamming shut on him in the United Kingdom, Blackett's advocacy of a "neutralist" atomic policy as part of an independent foreign and defense policy struck a chord with the Indian Prime Minister. Nehru's ideas coalesced around Blackett's notions of a small, independent, affordable, nuclear deterrent that would enable India to be genuinely "neutral" in the U.S.-Soviet rivalry and to possess the strategic wherewithal for its own protection. In addition, it gave teeth to Nehru's policy of "nonalignment." The Indian Prime Minister not only hoped to empower the developing countries of the nonaligned movement with capabilities for the peaceful uses of atomic energy[29] but also actually conceived of nuclear weapon-armed India, Yugoslavia, and Egypt as a countervailing influence in the world to the militarily powerful United States and the Union of Soviet Socialist Republics–led blocs.[30] This idea was not all that far-fetched. In a 1965 television program Dr. Glenn Seaborg, chairman of the U.S. Atomic Energy Commission, in fact, placed India in the top category of countries along with Japan, West Germany, Sweden, Italy,

Canada, and Israel able to acquire nuclear weapons and rated both Yugoslavia and Egypt in the second rung of threshold countries capable of nuclear weapons but "over a longer period of time."[31]

That an Atom Bomb-capability was no bad thing to have was surmised early by Nehru. Wrote Nehru to his Defence Minister Baldev Singh in 1948: "The future belongs to those who produce atomic energy. That is going to be the chief national power of the future. Of course, defense is intimately concerned with this. Even the political consequences are worthwhile." Reflecting Auchinleck, Tuker, and Blackett's ideas, he added: "The probable use of atomic energy in warfare is likely to revolutionize all our concepts of war and defense. For the moment we may leave [this] out of consideration except that it makes it absolutely essential for us to develop the method of using atomic energy for both civilian and military purpose. This means scientific research on a big scale."[32]

The fabled pacifism of Mahatma Gandhi did not deter Nehru from embarking on an ambitious nuclear program because he was familiar with the espousal in 1921 by Mahatma Gandhi—the "father of the nation"—of the "doctrine of the sword" justifying the use of violence in self-defense and for national security alongside the latter's articulation of the ideology of nonviolence. Too much the realist, Nehru, in any case, would have rejected as impractical any talk of nonviolence as state policy even had Mahatma Gandhi lived to insist on it. Rather, persuaded by its "Janus-faced" nature, science and, in particular, nuclear science, he was convinced, would help yank the tradition-bound Indian society into the modern age and, at the same time, obtain for the newly independent country economic development and the most advanced armament.[33] It helped that Nehru's pragmatic policy orientation had civilizational sanction in the hard-edged and amoral ancient Hindu statecraft and *machtpolitik* dating back several millennia,[34] which undergirded the deeply rooted realist tradition in Indian culture.[35] It is one reason why the Indian nuclear weapons program has always enjoyed strong popular support, especially after the 1998 series of tests that brought the Indian bomb out of the closet.[36]

Revealingly, he likened the revolution wrought by nuclear energy to the revolution triggered by the invention of gunpowder which, Nehru said, had "pushed the Middle Ages away completely and fairly rapidly" and ushered in "a new political and economic structure"; it was, however, a revolution, he rued, that had passed India by, leading to the country's missing out on industrialization, becoming vulnerable, and falling victim to subsequent foreign depredations. He was determined that India would not miss out on the nuclear revolution or on reaping its political, economic, and military benefits.[37]

"THE QUESTION OF KNIVES"

A favorable constellation of personalities, circumstances, events, and international developments was chiefly responsible for establishing the dual-purpose Indian nuclear-energy program with an overt civilian impress and a covert weapons thrust. The first factor was the close personal relationship between Prime Minister Nehru and his choice as chairman of the Atomic Energy Commission (AEC) and secretary of the Department of Atomic Energy (DAE), Dr. Homi J. Bhabha. Bhabha was given the authority to organize and run the program as he saw fit. The confidence Nehru reposed in Bhabha was crucial and derived, in part, from their social compatibility and sharing the same vision of nuclear energy promoting economic progress and pushing India into the front ranks of military powers.[38] It helped that Bhabha, like Nehru, hailed from a wealthy family belonging to the Westernized Indian elite and was Cambridge University-educated, except the former as a physicist won renown for his pioneering research in cosmic ray cascades, and the latter joined the politics of the freedom movement. Bhabha structured the nuclear program around the nuclear complex in a suburb of Mumbai (or Bombay), called Trombay (which, after his death in 1966, was renamed the Bhabha Atomic Research Center—BARC) and the Tata Institute of Fundamental Research (TIFR), originally founded by Bhabha in the mid-1940s with funds from a Parsi philanthropic trust. TIFR was described by Bhabha as "the cradle of India's atomic energy program."[39] BARC today has some 4,000 scientists, five research reactors of various types, and "Dhruva"—a 100 megawatt weapons-grade plutonium producer that went critical in 1985. A second nuclear complex in Kalpakkam, near Madras, later christened the Indira Gandhi Center for Atomic Research (IGCAR) came up in the 1970s, housing some of the most sensitive projects, including the 40 megawatt fast breeder test reactor, the upscaled 500 megawatt prototype fast breeder reactor under construction, the thorium-fueled "Kamini" reactor, and the test-bed for the miniaturized enriched uranium-run power plant for the indigenous nuclear powered submarine project. The dual-use program has now grown to 17 reactors connected to the grid with installed capacity of 4120 megawatts electric with a record, as Anil Kakodkar, chairman of the Atomic Energy Commission, disclosed to the International Atomic Energy Agency in August 2007, of "270 reactor years of safe, accident-free operations."[40] Unusual for an Indian government undertaking, Bhabha managed to obtain full functional and decision-making autonomy for the nuclear program, with the nodal DAE having the freedom to set its own research and work agenda, with oversight being exercised only by the prime minister in his concurrent capacity as minister for atomic energy. Further, DAE's shared location with the AEC in Mumbai was designed to keep the dead hand of central bureaucracy (evident in the functioning of much of the rest of the Indian government) from affecting the working of the nuclear establishment. As Bhabha put it in an official April 1948 Note to the government, this arrangement eliminated any "intervening link" between DAE, AEC, and the Prime Minister.[41] In addition, the Atomic Energy Act of 1948 and the successor Act of 1962 pruned the Atomic Energy Commission to just three members because, Bhabha wrote Nehru, "Secret matters cannot be dealt with under [the previously formed 28 member] organization."[42] These acts also centralized decision-making authority in the AEC and sealed the already tight security-related procedures and institutional mechanisms. Secrecy was furthered by a system of verbal approvals and commitments amounting to a paperless regime, all of which exist to this day.[43] It helped Nehru protect the nuclear program as much from the ardent anti-nuclearists within the country as from the curiosity of foreign countries and intelligence agencies.[44] The downside of the weapons aspects of the program being shrouded in layers of secrecy and distanced from mainstream policy-making was that no stakeholders were created over the years for the nuclear weapons program among the political class, the armed forces, the policy establishment, and the Indian society at large. So much so, the fact India finally and formally obtained a nuclear deterrent in the wake of the 1998 tests —some 34 years after reaching the weapons threshold—continues to be a politically contentious issue.[45] The closed, essentially two-person, decision loop of the prime minister–cum–minister for atomic energy and chairman AEC–cum–secretary DAE that Bhabha configured, other than reinforcing secretiveness, ensured that (1) the nuclear program faced no dearth of funds during Nehru's time when the Indian economy was in a parlous state,[46] and (2) lightning fast decisions were followed up by their equally speedy implementation (bypassing, for instance, where acquisitions are concerned, the usual lengthy tendering process characteristic of other ministries). Thus, no sooner did Bhabha, chairing the 1955 UN "atoms for peace" conference in Geneva, identify for purchase the Canadian natural uranium fueled, heavy-water–moderated Nuclear Research Xperimental (NRX) reactor because of its better neutron economy and more efficient production of plutonium central to making weapons, than Nehru approved the deal over telephone.[47] The NRX, modified as CANDU (CANadian Deuterium Uranium) reactor and its improved indigenous version called INDU (INdian Deuterium Uranium) reactor, is the workhorse of the dual-use Indian nuclear program, with fifteen 220 megawatt plants currently under operation. "Homi Bhabha found in Nehru his most ardent supporter," wrote M. G. K. Menon, a former director of TIFR. "With his support . . . Bhabha translated his visions . . . in the incredibly short space of two decades, into a self-propelled and self-reliant Indian atomic energy program."[48]

If Bhabha designed the near autonomous nuclear establishment to derive maximum benefits from his personal ties with the prime minister, just as critical to the success of his plans were the international nuclear knowledge-sharing programs. This constituted the second major factor in helping India firm up its capabilities in the nuclear field fast. Whatever the U.S. motivations for the "atoms for peace" program announced by President Dwight D. Eisenhower in the UN General Assembly on December 8, 1953,[49] the announcement fostered expectations that any country seeking to develop economically needed to have atomic power or else get left behind in the race for economic development.[50] It provided the justification for the Indian program and, furthermore, helped Bhabha's thesis on the duality of nuclear energy sound reasonable. This may, in turn, have encouraged Western countries to subscribe to nuclear knowledge sharing. "As I have said, the peaceful and military uses of atomic energy are so closely knit that in fact, just as in the question of knives, it is the intention of the user which determines whether it is used for peaceful or military purposes," he said, at the Conference on the IAEA Statute in October 1956. "[A] knife on one's table could be used equally well for cutting meat or stabbing one's neighbor. The solution is not one to prevent people from having knives."[51] Having secured access, few developing countries plugged as extensively and purposefully into such programs as did India. It strengthened the Indian scientific and technological base and brought the first group of young Indian scientists up to speed on the whole range of nuclear-energy-related areas. A library was built up at the Trombay complex, its shelves stocked with data, documents, and other nuclear science and technology-related information procured under the aegis of the "atoms for peace" program from the United States. This storehouse of knowledge served as a ready reckoner for the applications aspects of nuclear energy in the initial period. Under this program, many Indian scientists and engineers gained professionally from training abroad. In addition, fairly sophisticated equipment to further research capabilities became available to India. The International Atomic Energy Agency (IAEA), formed to advance the "atoms for peace" program, began functioning by the end of the 1950s and played its part, as Bhabha acknowledged, in rendering "technical assistance" and generally "in the dissemination of scientific knowledge throughout the world" and in encouraging "laboratories in developing countries to expand their research activities."[52]

The United Kingdom, for its part, conceived of the Commonwealth nuclear program as an alternative in case the close nuclear cooperation with the United States London was seeking did not come through. However, given Prime Minister Winston Churchill's misgivings about parting with nuclear knowledge with military ramifications[53] and, at the same time, his eagerness to exercise "a guiding and coordinating influence" over the nascent Indian nuclear program resulted, as the official history of the British nuclear program records,[54] in the United Kingdom's choosing to limit the transfer of technology. Thus, other than passing along the know-how to turn uranium salts into metal, Churchill's government restricted itself to providing training to Indian scientists. Britain engaged in cooperation also because India played it tough, conditioning its membership in the British Commonwealth so important to Churchill on collaboration in the nuclear field. Bhabha threatened to go to France for reactor technology and training if London proved unwilling. In 1948, the radio-chemist Joliot-Curie had offered Bhabha heavy-water reactor technology France was developing. With the working arrangement Bhabha had sought with the United Kingdom falling through owing to London's security concerns, India signed up with France to produce a beryllium-moderated reactor, a project London, incidentally, was invited to join.[55] The relatively open international regime of scientific exchanges speedily raised the levels of scientific expertise and technical competence in India. Had the weapons purpose of the Indian program been publicized at the time, angry Western governments might have shut down access. In any event, the more the Indian nuclear establishment connected to international nuclear programs, and benefited from the knowledge-sharing schemes, the more India's, albeit civilian, nuclear program and ambitions gained legitimacy and many Indian scientists gained proficiency after their stints in the atomic energy establishments at Harwell in the United Kingdom, Saclay in France, Argonne and Oak Ridge in the United States, and Chalk River in Canada.[56]

Conjoined to this second factor was a third one, relating to Bhabha's reputation as a first-rate physicist. Friendships based on professional respect led to the positive and forthcoming attitude of the leading Western scientists and their affiliated scientific establishments toward the program Bhabha was heading.[57] With restraints on smoother information flow lifted by the Western governments, courtesy the "atoms for peace" program, Bhabha's personal ties with his counterparts in advanced countries eventuated in close interaction with them. At his invitation, renowned physicists and mathematicians, like Paul Dirac, Wolfgang Pauli, and Peter Mashak, visited the Tata Institute of Fundamental Research, taking up short-term residence there and conducting seminars in cutting-edge areas of nuclear science. Bhabha likened all such foreign inputs into the Indian nuclear program to "booster-assisted take-off." "A booster in the form of foreign collaboration can give a plane an assisted take-off," said Bhabha in a speech delivered on January 7, 1966, in Mumbai to the International Council of Scientific Unions, a month before his death in an air crash, "but it will be incapable of independent flight unless it is powered by engines of its own."[58]

India was a potentially attractive nuclear partner for foreign countries also because of its valuable natural resources, which was the fourth reason for the success of the Indian nuclear program. Bhabha bartered natural resources for nuclear technology. Thus, in return for collaboration in building a beryllium reactor, India offered to sell beryl to France. Beryllium is used as a neutron initiator in fission devices. India paid for the top-of-the-line Van de Graaf particle accelerator it bought from the United States with the thorium-rich monazite.[59] Transactions in these same monazite sands by Britain predated Indian independence. This material was shipped for use in the "tube-alloys" project—the secret British undertaking to make the atom bomb, which venture merged with the U.S.-led "Manhattan Project" in the early 1940s. After 1947, Britain hoped to have continued access to the thorium deposits in India constituting 30–40 percent of the world's total estimated reserves. Playing to Bhabha's interest, as inducement, the United Kingdom even mooted joint development of breeder reactors, a proposal that did not pan out.[60]

The breeder reactor, as the British government realized, is the key to the successful realization of the Indian energy security plan based on exploiting some 500,000 tons of thorium-rich monazite found on the southwestern coast of the country and in the central Indian plateau. "This enormous national asset," wrote Bhabha, "sets the pattern for the long range program of development of atomic energy in India."[61] His 1955 plan for three interlocked stages envisioned natural uranium-fueled pressurized heavy-water reactors (PHWRs) of the CANDU/

INDU type in the first stage, producing the feedstock for the fast breeder plutonium reactors in the second stage which, in turn, would produce the fuel loading
for the thorium reactors in the third stage and, in case the spent fuel from the
PHWRs, were used in the breeder, would beget weapons-grade plutonium.[62]
Another way to generate weapons-grade plutonium is by running the CANDU
PHWRs at "low burn-up" rate, meaning a power reactor could be switched to
the weapons mode to produce weapons-grade plutonium by simply irradiating
the natural uranium fuel for a short time in the reactor. At once promising limit-
less energy and a huge stockpile of high-quality fissile material for armaments,
Bhabha's plan met Nehru's original guideline that the nuclear program make
India self-reliant in both energy and in military security.[63]

In pursuance of this plan, in an April 1948 note sent to Nehru, Bhabha proposed making heavy water to run the CANDU pressurized heavy-water reactors
at hydroelectric plants and chemical fertilizer manufacturing units and suggested
that the heavy-water factories "should be set up for the purpose under the
Defense Ministry and put under the same security measures as the armaments
factories of that Ministry." So successful has this scheme become, India is now
among the largest exporters of heavy water in the world.[64] Bhabha yoked the
gains from "atoms for peace" to his policy of "growing science."[65] This policy
involved making scientists and engineers, fresh off training courses, responsible
for new and challenging projects, and led to "learning by doing," by trial and
error, and by hands-on project work. It was preferred by Bhabha to importing
technology on a turnkey basis. It resulted, for instance, in the indigenously
designed uranium-fueled reactor, *Apsara,* being constructed in Trombay and
going critical in August 1956 inside of 14 months[66] and in many technological
milestones being crossed.[67] A U.S. Scientific Intelligence Report dated March 26,
1958 observed that while the Indian nuclear accomplishments do not compare
with "the technologically advanced countries," "in comparison with other Asian
countries, it is impressive" and concluded, wrongly as it turned out, that "There
is no indication in government or scientific circles of a change from the traditional Indian pattern of passivity and mediation" with respect to producing
nuclear weapons.[68] Apparently unaware of the dual-nature of the Indian program, such reports may have lulled Washington into thinking that India was
not, after all, "misusing" the "atoms for peace" program.

Table 2.1 shows the Indian, Chinese, and Japanese capability levels and the
year these were reached. It points out that unlike China, which aped the American and Russian model, as have all the other nuclear-weapon states, in focusing
on securing nuclear weapons first, and accordingly, prioritizing reprocessing
and uranium enrichment, India chose the more sustainable route to the bomb.
"The establishment of a strong base in basic science and engineering has been
crucial in developing the philosophy of self-reliance—initially to absorb and
assimilate the essential elements in imported technologies," notes the official
history of the Indian nuclear-energy program, "and then, more importantly,
to develop new designs—processes, materials, components, equipment,

Table 2.1 Comparative Nuclear Benchmarks

Technology/Capability Thresholds	India	China Year	Japan
First research reactor	1956	1958	1960
First heavy-water plant	1962	–	–
First plutonium reprocessing plant	1964–65	2001 (pilot plant)	1968
First nuclear power plant (imported)	1969	1993	–
First nuclear test	1974	1964	–
First indigenous nuclear power plant	1983	1991	1969
First fast breeder reactor	1985	–	1984 (since decommissioned)
First uranium enrichment plant	1990	early 1960s	under planning

The Table reproduced from a slide presentation by Dr. M. R. Srinivasan, former chairman, Atomic Energy Commission, at a seminar on "Indo-US Nuclear Cooperation: The Emerging Debate," Delhi Policy Group and the Nuclear Threat Initiative, Habitat Centre, New Delhi, October 25, 2005.

instrumentation, and engineering systems—entirely on our own."[69] India invested in a broad-based program of scientific research and technological development, in order, explained Dr. Anil Kakodkar, chairman of the atomic energy commission, to secure "strategically important . . . core capabilities in critical areas."[70] Following Bhabha's example, the scientists took care to see that, whenever needed, the equipment secured, whether from abroad or mostly designed and developed at home, served both civilian and military ends. The heavy-water–moderated weapons-grade plutonium-producing NRX reactor secured from Canada is an instance of dual-use equipment and technology Bhabha carefully obtained from abroad. Incidentally, the NRX could also output tritium, extracted from the heavy water and used in enhancing fission yield in "boosted" weapons and in fashioning thermonuclear or hydrogen weapons.[71] A pulsed-fast "Purnima" reactor, able to vary the neutron flux, was developed in Trombay along the lines of a similar plant that Indian scientists had visited in Dubna in the Soviet Union.[72] This uniquely designed reactor with a rotating beryllium reflector, according to Dr. P. K. Iyengar, a former Chairman of AEC, "helped the bomb project because the dynamics of the system is very similar to what happens when you compress plutonium until it becomes super-critical. It tells us how much we can compress."[73] The nuclear science infrastructure developed fast together with the competence levels on a broad technological front. Consequently, the use of the infrastructure and the budgeted funds, which in the period 1954–1965 totaled $385 million and represented "0.2 percent of the estimated gross national product,"[74] was optimized. This meant that, as far as the weapons project was concerned, the financial resources channeled into the supportive nuclear science facilities and manpower training amounted to "sunk costs."

When Prime Minister Indira Gandhi asked about the cost of the device exploded in 1974, Iyengar, then head of the physics group at BARC, replied truthfully that "it had cost nothing."[75] The piggybacking by the weapons program on the larger, more versatile, civilian nuclear-energy program added only incrementally to the financial outlays and maximized efficient use of the relatively small manpower pool.[76]

The commissioning in early 1964 of the indigenously designed plutonium reprocessing plant in Trombay put India—only the fifth country at the time to have this capability, the other four being the United States, the USSR, the United Kingdom and France,[77] in a position to explode a nuclear weapon. A U.S. Central Intelligence Agency (CIA) cable dated October 24, 1964 noted that "The government of India (GOI) has all of the elements necessary to produce a nuclear weapon and it has the capability to assemble a bomb quickly."[78] How quickly? A Special Intelligence Estimate by CIA dated October 21, 1965, concluded that India "probably already has sufficient plutonium for a first device, and could explode it about a year after a decision to develop one."[79] Thus, when China conducted its first nuclear test in October 1964, India could have responded with one of its own latest by the summer of 1966 or thereabouts. Curiously, Bhabha had, some five years earlier, mentioned to Nehru the same one-year time frame for obtaining a bomb, suggesting that the pace of weapons capability acquisition by the Indian nuclear program may actually have slowed down when the Prime Minister showed no urgency. In an account of a 1960 meeting with the Indian prime minister and Bhabha, retired Major General K. D. Nichols, who was associated with the war-time Manhattan Project and was General Manager of the U.S. Atomic Energy Commission in the early 1950s, recalls that midway through it Nehru asked Bhabha, "Can you develop an atomic bomb?" Nichols records in his memoirs what happened next: "Bhabha assured him he could and in reply to Nehru's question about time, he estimated that he would need about a year to do it. I was really astounded to be hearing these questions from the one I thought to be one of the world's most peace-loving leaders. He then asked me if I agreed with Bhabha, and I replied that I knew of no reason why Bhabha could not do it. He had men who were as qualified or more qualified than our young scientists were fifteen years earlier. He concluded by saying to Bhabha, 'Well, don't do it until I tell you to'."[80] Nehru's real attitude to nuclear weapons evident here jells with his mentoring India's dual-use nuclear policy. Even if Nehru did not tell the scientists to "do it," he was certain in his mind India would go nuclear, only he was not clear just when.

Nehru's desire to green signal the weapons project waxed and waned; it shot up as early as early 1961[81] but despite the gravest provocation offered by China's initiating hostilities and winning the 1962 war in the Himalayas, he did not ultimately do so, in the main, because of the lingering aftereffects of the strong anti-bomb lobby active in the 1950s,[82] and because of his overriding views that the "peace efforts," as he called nuclear disarmament initiatives, ought to be given a fair chance,[83] that an offensive Chinese nuclear capability would not emerge for five years and, in any case, that in the interim the United States and the West would respond if China struck or intimidated India with nuclear weapons.[84] Not convinced by such views, Bhabha sought to reduce the time lag between the decision—whenever it was made by Nehru—and the program's readiness to test a nuclear device, by ordering some basic preparations.[85] For instance, he set up in January 1962 a high pressure physics group in TIFR "to study equations of state in the megabar range for designing implosion weapons."[86] With the reprocessing plant ready and the weapons threshold reached, and aware of China's preparations for a nuclear test, Bhabha found Nehru strangely unwilling to make the decision to go for the bomb. Frustrated, Bhabha spoke up publicly for the first time on January 27, 1964, on the military necessity and, more significantly, the economic logic of nuclear weapons, tellingly at the 12th Pugwash Conference. While nuclear weapons provide "absolute deterrence even against another having a many times greater destructive power under its control ... Conventional weapons," he said, "can at best enable a country to acquire a position of relative deterrence." More pointedly, China, he declared, "must always present a threat to its smaller neighbors, a threat they can meet either by collective security or by recourse to nuclear weapons to redress the imbalance in size." And, in the context of the suddenly increased defense budgets and the masses of conventional hardware being imported by the government for the Indian armed forces in the aftermath of defeat in the 1962 War with China, he made the point of nuclear weapons being a more economical alternative. Nuclear weapons, he said, were within easy reach of any country with a civilian nuclear program, and asserted that such weaponry made more economic and military sense because "the expenditure involved in [producing nuclear weapons] would be small compared with the [conventional] military budgets."[87] Nehru died in May 1964, however, and his successor, Lal Bahadur Shastri, and his advisors, none of whom were clued in to the secret weapons program, had to be educated about it. Conscious that the supposed high price tag of a nuclear deterrent is what made many people in the new dispensation wary, Bhabha addressed that issue head-on in a radio broadcast on October 24, 1964, a scant eight days after the first Chinese nuclear test. Extrapolating from figures in a paper presented at the Third International Conference on Peaceful Uses of Atomic Energy in Geneva a month earlier, which referred to a 10 kiloton (KT) device costing $350,000 and a 2 megaton (MT) weapon costing $600,000, he postulated that an inventory of 50 atomic bombs would cost under Rs 10 crore (or $13 million) and a stockpile of 50 2 MT weapons no more than Rs 15 crore (or $25 million), which costs, he implied, were eminently affordable. "The explosion of a nuclear device by China," he said, trying to bring in some urgency, "is a signal that there is no time to be lost." Absent disarmament, large countries such as India, he advised, should "get into a position of having a deterrent force." He then outlined the contours of a policy of "minimum deterrence"—a very flexible concept that has animated Indian strategic thinking ever since. "A minimum supply of nuclear weapons coupled with an adequate delivery system confers on a State," he observed, "the capacity to destroy more or less totally the important cities and industrial centers in another State. There appears to be no means of totally intercepting such an attack, and if even a small fraction of it gets through, entire cities and regions may be totally devastated. The only defense against such an attack appears to be a capability and threat of retaliation."[88] As we have seen, in Bhabha's scheme of things, the "minimum supply of nuclear weapons" India needed were 100 weapons divided equally between the low and the high end in terms of yield—10 KT and 2 MT types. Incidentally, a decade after Bhabha's death, Dr. Homi N. Sethna, then chairman, AEC, considered a small nuclear force "worse" than no force at all as it would "invite preemptive Chinese attack," and upped the desired size of the minimum deterrent to 150 nuclear weapons.[89]

Bhabha was serious about his weapons plans even as the Indian government dithered. A U.S. Special National Intelligence Estimate (SNIE) dated October 1965 noted, "early work applicable to weapons technology and design [had probably] started . . . [and] India [had] . . . expanded its electronic facilities at its nuclear establishment considerably and . . . a high explosives test facility [to design and physically test chemical explosive lenses as trigger for fission bombs, had been] set up, though both developments could be intended for other purposes than production of nuclear weapons."[90] Senior scientists working in Trombay recall that Bhabha, in fact, had approved the "non-nuclear" parts of the bomb project around the time the plutonium reprocessing unit became operational.[91] This SNIE also correctly anticipated a number of other things. It concluded that the weakening credibility of the joint U.S.-Soviet security guarantees proposed during the short (one and a half year) tenure of Nehru's successor, Shastri, as Prime Minister, would spur an Indian government decision to weaponize; "the pace and scope of the Chinese nuclear program" would be the main driver of the Indian weapons project; the Indian armed forces, fearing they would be procured at the expense of conventional military spending, would oppose nuclear weapons; there would be detonation of a device "in the next few years"; this test would use the "Plowshare" [the codename assigned the American program for "peaceful nuclear explosions"] rationale; and that the concern about the high cost especially of imported delivery systems would, in the short-term, inhibit the decision to produce nuclear weapons. The SNIE also predicted India would end up being nuclear-armed.[92] Given how diligently the Indian government had nursed the nuclear weapon option as a self-reliant means of security, the search during the Shastri interregnum for joint U.S.-Soviet security guarantee against the Chinese threat, was an aberration.[93] After this short detour, Delhi got back on the armaments track, strongly opposing concepts such as "nuclear free zones" (NFZs), posited as nonproliferation measures. Its argument since then has been consistent. In a world where "general and complete disarmament" is ruled out, the NFZ concept is "unrealistic" and, as the Indian Foreign Minister P. V. Narasimha Rao pointed out at the UN General Assembly Second Special Session on Disarmament in June 1982, legitimizes "the possession of nuclear weapons by a few Powers" leaving other states "to live under [the] professedly benign protection [of these nuclear Powers] in the guise of a Nuclear Weapon Free Zone."[94]

The first nuclear test by India in 1974 was the culmination of the Indian government's hesitant advance to weaponization using the "peaceful nuclear explosion" (PNE) as cover. The American Plowshare PNE program envisaged excavating tunnels, digging large water reservoirs, and quarrying using nuclear explosives,[95] and indicated the rationale India would use to safeguard its nuclear-energy program without discarding its peaceful pretensions. It provided both credible scientific justification and a compromise solution permitting Prime Minister Shastri to escape the onus of overt weaponization. Finding himself pulled in opposite directions by calls for testing and acquiring nuclear weapons by Bhabha and sections of the ruling Congress Party and by contrary U.S. and British advice to desist from going in for nuclear weapons on account of their being too expensive,[96] which meshed with his personal antipathy to the bomb on account of its destructiveness,[97] Shastri approved the Study of Nuclear Explosions for Peaceful Purposes (SNEPP) as a *via media* in the wake of the first Chinese test and Beijing's threat to open a second front when India was at war with Pakistan in 1965. It helped, on the one hand, to deflect Western nonproliferation pressures and, on the other hand, to assuage the pro-bomb sentiment in Parliament and the country. As a result, a motion in Parliament calling for production of nuclear weapons by the right-wing Jana Sangha Party (JSP) was defeated by a voice vote on November 27, 1964 mainly because the Prime Minister used Bhabha's acquiescing in SNEPP to silence the clamor for the bomb and postpone taking the hard decision. (Some 34 years later, the JSP's latter day *avatar*—the Bharatiya Janata Party—ordered the 1998 tests and weaponization.)

Bhabha's eagerness to conduct a nuclear test was, at one level, to showcase the advanced capabilities of the Indian nuclear program and to contrast it with the Chinese counterpart, which was relatively backward in every respect except on the weapons front and that too only because of the assistance it had received from the Soviet Union, which fact Delhi tried to highlight.[98] At another level, he saw a test as a means of matching the Chinese accomplishment, denying China any kind of political and military ascendancy in the Third World, and of raising the morale of the Indian people. With so much at stake, Bhabha did not cavil at taking help from any quarter if it was unconditionally offered. Jerome Wiesner, President of the Massachusetts Institute of Technology and formerly science adviser to John F. Kennedy, visited India in January 1965 on a mission to push U.S. nonproliferation policy goals. On being apprised by Bhabha about the Indian weapon capabilities and intent, Wiesner mooted the possibility of the United States helping out with a peaceful nuclear explosion as a shortcut to an answering Indian test. Wiesner, in a cable to the U.S. Secretary of State Dean Rusk, however, pleaded for U.S. help with an Indian PNE only if India foreswore weapons, which condition had it been proposed to Bhabha would have been instantly rejected. The fact that Bhabha pursued the matter further in Washington a month later suggests no such *quid pro quo* was broached to him by Wiesner. All Bhabha seemed to care about was that there was no real difference between a PNE and a test of a nuclear military device as evidenced in his agreeing to SNEPP, and that he wished to explore the kind of help the United States could, in fact, render. In a meeting he had with the U.S. Under Secretary of State George Ball, Bhabha expounded on the dilemma facing India and opined that while, on its own, it could design and test a device in 18 months, with "an American blueprint for a nuclear device" the job could be done in six months.[99] There is no doubt Bhabha was determined on an Indian test, the earlier the better, and welcomed any U.S. or other foreign country's help. His taking up the issue with Ball on Wiesner's say-so has been interpreted as evidence of the technical incapacity of the Indian nuclear program, this to make the larger point that, despite huge investments in it, the program had produced little of worth and, in any case, was not weapons capable.[100] This reading goes against the growing evidence of the Indian nuclear capability, which would have eventuated in the production of a nuclear bomb had the program been put on a war-footing by the government.

In fleshing out a possible U.S. role, Bhabha must have hoped to ride on the sort of thinking in Washington represented by the Secretary of State Dean Rusk who wondered "whether countries in China's shadow, such as India and Japan, could pledge never to develop nuclear weapons and whether they should depend entirely upon the American nuclear umbrella."[101] In the NATO-Warsaw Pact context, a similar American dilemma had occasioned the French *force de frappe*.[102] The opinion in the Lyndon Johnson administration was, in fact, divided between directly helping India with a design for an explosive device and transfer of some fissile material and providing a PNE device from the American inventory for firing by India.[103] Washington, however, ended up focusing on ways to keep India a nonnuclear-weapon state, whatever it took, including facilitating an Indian nonnuclear "spectacular" event, such as a space launch, to highlight India's supposed achievement in the scientific and technical fields to neutralize the political gains from the Chinese bomb. The emphasis shifted to the deleterious effects of Indian nuclear weapons. Henry Rowen, a senior official in the International Security Affairs Bureau of the U.S. Department of Defense in a secret memorandum dated December 24, 1964, after discussing the kind of nuclear forces India could go in for and their costs, and making the point that, given the paucity of financial resources, an Indian nuclear deterrent would be bought at the expense of its conventional military security and economic development, laid out the template of a distinctly adversarial nonproliferation policy directed at India. It is an approach that has held to this day, informing the American *raison d'etre* for the civil nuclear cooperation deal with India. (More on this in the last chapter.) Topping the list of the "consequences of an Indian [weapon] program," Rowen mentioned India's acquiring rocket technology and "some day [being] able to attack the United States with nuclear weapons." He also apprehended India's starting a "catalytic" nuclear war involving the United States.[104] Rowen went on to list other ill-effects of an Indian bomb, including the "reduction in [U.S.] power to influence events in South Asia and to some extent throughout the world" and about pressures for further proliferation unleashed in Asia (Pakistan, Japan, Indonesia) and Europe ("the fact that yellow and brown men are making these most modern of weapons is not likely to lead white men to decide to abstain from making them"). Given the generally good relations between the two countries, the determination that the Indian bomb was dangerous to U.S. interests was questionable, as was some of the logic used. Take the concept of "catalytic" war Rowen had postulated. Bhabha had already strongly refuted it. The "question is whether a third country possessing nuclear weapons could in a certain situation use then with the object of bringing in on its side the full nuclear capability of one of the two major powers, or whether an atomic bomb from some unidentified source exploded on a military target or city of one of the two major powers could catalyze a nuclear war," wondered Bhabha at the 1964 Pugwash Conference. "The answer to this question appears to be in the negative, for a major nuclear power could conclude from a fairly straightforward argument that such action would not be in the interests of the other major power, since the gains, if any, would be relatively small and the risk of devastation to itself very great."[105]

The Rowen document is important in that it conceived the use of the economic aid leverage to choke the Indian nuclear program. Rowen opined that the United States could plausibly oppose an Indian nuclear weapons program on the grounds that it would damage the Indian economy whose growth, he claimed, was being underwritten by the U.S. aid and that the United States was "not prepared to see [its] aid funds wasted on India needlessly devoting its scarce resources on nuclear systems."[106] The use of economic aid as nonproliferation leverage became the U.S. policy. The flip side of this policy was the serious debate it precipitated in India over the correct sequencing—whether India should not first become a hefty economic power with external aid and World Bank assistance before acquiring matching strategic military wherewithal. In any event, the two-pronged pressure of the United States threatening to withhold economic aid and limit access to World Bank credit and of the domestic lobby demanding the government prioritize development over nuclear bombs reined in Indira Gandhi's impulses in the pre- and post-1974 periods.[107]

Insulated from the hurly-burly of government decision-making and the raging public debate over whether or not the country should go in for the bomb BARC, by mid-1965, carried out tests with "high explosives to calibrate seismographs used for test monitoring" under the aegis of SNEPP.[108] This seismographic capability was improved in 1967 when, in collaboration with centers in the United Kingdom, Canada, and Australia, a seismic array station was set up in peninsular India, to detect and "read" an American megaton test.[109] The main aspects of designing the bomb proceeded at a low key, notwithstanding Bhabha's successor, Dr. Vikram Sarabhai, calling the weapons program a "paper tiger" and trying to down-gear it. Sarabhai was formerly head of the Indian Space Research Organization (ISRO) that has since the 1980s successfully developed powerful rocket systems used in long-range missiles that afford Indian nuclear weapons strategic reach.[110] His case was that the acquisition of an atom bomb by itself amounted to little without putting in place "a total defense system" and "means of delivery" and that this would involve prohibitive costs the country was in no position to bear.[111] In other words, that an Indian nuclear bomb could "existentially" deter only if there was the paraphernalia for its use, especially delivery systems. By the early 1960s, however, the Indian Air Force had the Canberra medium bomber in service—an aircraft that could have been used in a clutch to deliver an atom bomb on a one-way desperation sortie to Shanghai or on a more normal mission to hit Kunming and Chinese cities in that arc.[112] Still, if Sarabhai thought prioritizing atom bombs but not delivery systems was absurd, his preferring rockets to bombs was no less absurd.[113] He ended up alienating the powerful Trombay establishment. Dr. Raja Ramanna, director of the BARC, made an end-run around Sarabhai to get approval for testing directly from Prime Minister Indira Gandhi. The go-ahead was secured, sidelining the AEC chairman and forcing Sarabhai to reconcile to the weapons program.[114] The original core group in the weapons unit at BARC for the 1974 test comprised Ramanna, Iyengar, chief of the physics group, R. Chidambaram from the crystallography group, and S. K. Sikka from the solid state and spectroscopy group. Mahadeva Srinivasan, who resigned from service for personal reasons in 1992 as the associate head of the physics group at BARC and was responsible for some of the most critical calculations in designing the fission and boosted-fission weapons, recalls that generally, "people were involved not on the basis of designation but on the basis of specialization." "Very often," he adds, "the head of the division or group director was told not to interfere with the work and contribution of a junior [scientist or engineer], this caused a lot of heart-burn."[115] Talented scientists and engineers, busy in other projects, joined in weapons work as and when required. The absence of separation of skilled manpower and infrastructure into exclusively military or civilian spheres resulted in the cost-effective use of both.[116]

Calculations for the "equation of state" for plutonium were followed first by full discussions on the "paper designs." There was no "difficulty as such" in configuring the implosion fission device with a polonium neutron initiator, as the "basic physics was well-known." The challenges, however, were "in fabrication and assembly, in integration of the various components into a workable design." "But we had no way to find out if the data used were good enough," avers Srinivasan. "The ultimate test was going to be the final experiment."[117] The implosive chemical lens—designed by the Defense Ministry-run Terminal Ballistics Laboratory in Chandigarh—was triggered by firing a BARC-designed discharge condenser. This role in the improved fission design and in the subsequent boosted-fission and fusion weapon designs in the 1980s was performed by locally produced krytons—devices that source pre-ionization, so that the time required for development of the pulse to impact on the spherical geometry of the plutonium ball to make it super-critical, is much faster. There was some controversy about whether the 8 KT yield read by seismic stations abroad—the local sensors indicated 12 KT—was anywhere near the designed yield. According to Iyengar, 8 KT was "a respectable yield" when compared to the 10 KT Hiroshima bomb with its devastating effect, and the fact it was not "a fizzle is what mattered." Iyengar explains that "the seismic measurement gives a logarithmic relationship between explosive power and seismic disturbance, and so the error can be quite high ... Theoretically, we know that had we increased the amount of plutonium in the device, the yield would be proportionately higher." Moreover, "It could have been turned into a deliverable weapon," says Iyengar, "simply by integrating the electronics."[118] Not following up the 1974 test with more testing and an overt nuclear weapons program cost India plenty. It retarded the advance of India's nuclear weapons capability, of course, but also postponed the international system's reconciling to the altered strategic reality and India's weapons status. Worse, it raised the bar and increased the political costs of winning recognition as a bona fide nuclear-weapon state.

Why Indira Gandhi worried overmuch about the economic consequences of taking this route in terms of the withdrawal of U.S. aid and World Bank loans, is difficult to understand. The U.S. Secretary of State, Henry Kissinger, passing through Delhi after the 1974 test, had pleaded with her to only delay further testing until after the Non-Proliferation Treaty Review Conference scheduled for 1975. She obviously misread, as did her successors in government right up to 1998, the hard-nosed realism that has always propelled U.S. policy. This was ironic considering the 1974 meeting had occasioned in Kissinger considerable respect for Mrs. Gandhi's "hard-headedness," leading to his directive to U.S. government agencies to adopt "a basic policy of not pressuring the [Indians] on their nuclear weapons program."[119] Kissinger's pleading for postponement of further testing by India was as clear a sign as could be given by Washington that, after a decent interval, the United States could do little other than accommodate India as a nuclear-weapon state under the NPT. It is a reading Robert J. Einhorn, deputy assistant secretary of state for nonproliferation in the Bill Clinton administration, subscribes to. "In 1974, if Indira Gandhi had gone ahead with a weapons program, it would have been a different nonproliferation order because NPT," he said at a 2003 meeting in Delhi organized by the Pugwash Society, "came into being in 1970 and in 1974 many states were still undecided about it. By not weaponizing then, India, in effect, supported the NPT and ensured its success."[120] The 1974 test would have turned out to be "an epoch-making venture" that the nuclear scientists involved believed, "was bound to catapult India into global geopolitics,"[121] if Indira Gandhi had allowed further testing and ordered full-scale weaponization as Kissinger had expected. India would have arrived on the international scene, packing nuclear heft. It would have forced the NPT to recognize it as a nuclear-weapon state, emerged as a nuclear supplier and member of what later became the Nuclear Suppliers Group, and beefed up its position as a swing state in the Cold War, a role China appropriated for itself with Kissinger's cultivation of the "China card" to play against the Soviet Union.

In the wake of the 1974 test, the technology denial schemes—the NPT and the Missile Technology Control regime—were activated. By then the basic nuclear science research and industrial infrastructure was well established in India. It led over the subsequent 35-odd years, ironically, to perhaps the most substantive and sustained advances registered by the country in three fuel cycles based on enriched uranium-235, plutonium, and uranium-233 (derived from thorium), especially thorium utilization.[122] The sudden severance of knowledge links with the West led to an inward turning of the nuclear program, and this had ripple effects. The stewardship of the weapons project, for instance, which had been shifted during Sarabhai's tenure by Prime Minister Indira Gandhi to Dr. Ramanna, did not revert to the AEC chairman once Sarabhai's successor, Homi N. Sethna, took over. Hence, Sethna, a chemical engineer in charge of designing and erecting the plutonium reprocessing plant, had little impact on the weapons activities leading up to and after the 1974 test or, for that matter, in setting the nuclear weapons agenda.[123] A major fallout was on the size of the force that was envisaged by the Trombay establishment. Ramanna, a determined minimalist where nuclear deterrence was concerned, was satisfied that India needed no more than weapons in two digits to keep the peace with China and Pakistan. Influenced by the thinking of Robert Oppenheimer and Hans Bethe of the Manhattan Project, who opposed the nuclear buildup in America on moral grounds, he was convinced a large nuclear weapons inventory somehow would sit ill with Mahatma Gandhi's teachings on nonviolence and the country's pacifist reputation. Even more, Ramanna was concerned that a large nuclear arsenal would draw the military into the nuclear business, resulting in the scientists' losing control over the weapons program. Ramanna's distrust of the Indian armed forces ended up in his equating the possibility of the military controlling nuclear weapons with their likely misuse.[124] The consequences, Ramanna believed, would be disastrous. Thus, the blueprint for a 150 weapons-strong nuclear force mooted by Sethna and Bhabha's earlier proposal for 100 weapons, inclusive of megaton thermonuclear armaments, were jettisoned by Ramanna at BARC and later as chairman of the Atomic Energy Commission. A much smaller force with several scores of simple fission weapons and warheads was considered adequate. It fit in both with Ramanna's views on "minimum deterrence" as minimal deterrence and the stasis in which the nuclear weapons program found itself, with successive Prime ministers not approving nuclear tests to validate and improve various weapons designs.

For the Indian weapons program, 1975–1979 were the "lie-low" years when Indira Gandhi's domestic political problems snowballed into the "Emergency" rule, followed by her ouster in the 1977 general elections and the Janata Party government's coming to power. Even so, in the years immediately after the 1974 test some 25 plutonium cores for bombs were machined, with the device that was imploded serving as "reference design."[125] Under the new Prime Minister, Morarji Desai, a formidable anti-nuclearist who, from the 1950s onward when he was Nehru's Finance Minister, worked against Bhabha and the bomb both inside the ruling Congress Party circles and the government, the nuclear weapons program faced closure with the government almost accepting a non-weapon state status and international safeguards on the Indian nuclear program.[126] However, uncongenial as Desai's attitude was to the weapons program, BARC's autonomous functioning was not disturbed. It ensured the continued development of some very sensitive weapon-related technologies, none more critical than the "detritiation" technology based on "wet proof" liquid phase catalytic exchange process to obtain tritium. This radioactive hydrogen isotope is a by-product of the heavy water used to moderate the fissile material burn-up in the CANDU/INDU pressurized heavy-water reactors. The technology developed by BARC facilitated the capture of neutrons by deuterium (heavy water) atoms to yield maximum tritium, which is enriched through some 240 stages. A pilot plant was operational by the time Indira Gandhi returned to power in 1979 and revived the weapons program. Commercial-scale tritium-manufacturing plants —two or three times the size of the pilot plant—are attached to each of the eight PHWRs dedicated by the Indian government for military use. Depending on the "time component," 2400 curries of tritium are outputted by each of these reactors for every megawatt of power generated.[127] Mrs. Gandhi approved a new series of underground tests and these were scheduled for 1982, supposedly to validate several weapons designs on the shelf, including one for a "boosted fission" weapon using tritium. These tests were eventually not held because the United States again threatened to cut off easy credit. It revived the old arguments Indian economists in government had always used to oppose the nuclear weapons project, namely, that this would hurt the prospects of economic development, which worked.[128] However, the ready availability of tritium hereon means the Indian arsenal will increasingly feature boosted fission and thermonuclear weapons and, if there is a requirement in the future, neutron bombs or radiation weapons as well.[129]

The nuclear program was restarted by Indira Gandhi on her return to power, and after her assassination in October 1984 her son and successor, Rajiv Gandhi, ordered the assembly of nuclear weapons. It was during this period that a basic nuclear command and control system was also put in place. It reflected Ramanna's distrust of the military with the control of nuclear weapons being retained by the nuclear scientists and the strategic weapon system designers in the Defense Research and Development Organization (DRDO) with the armed forces, as late as the mid-1990s, not even being told about the numbers of ready weapons in the Indian arsenal or about the guidelines for their use in war.[130] And to maintain the myth of India as a nonnuclear-weapon state, a 1985 proposal, for example, to familiarize senior military officers with nuclear strategies and doctrines was rejected by then Defense Minister P. V. Narasimha Rao on the basis that such instruction would be tantamount to acknowledging India's possession of nuclear weapons.[131]

With the nuclear-weapons program in steady state, the strategic focus in the 1980s shifted to dealing with the emerging nuclear threats by nonnuclear means, and in the 1990s to the development of strategic missile systems. In 1982 and again in early 1984, Indira Gandhi considered aerial strikes on Pakistan's uranium enrichment plant in Kahuta, with the earlier operation primarily involving Israel Air Force attack aircraft staging out of Indian bases. In 1987 Rajiv Gandhi also contemplated similar preemptive action. In all these instances, the Indian government called off the strike at the "last minute" because of the feared retaliation, including counterattacks by the Pakistan Air Force F-16 planes on the Trombay complex.[132] The resumption of testing was again seriously contemplated in 1995 but, as in the past, the option was shelved because the Congress Party Prime Minister P. V. Narasimha Rao claimed there was no consensus on the need for it. The absence of tests notwithstanding, the Indian nuclear weapons program was accorded higher budgetary priority at the expense of the conventional military budget and brought up to "optimum speed." In addition, the national deterrent was "operationalized,"[133] which probably meant that "weapons were produced in numbers and delivery systems were made ready."[134]

The emergence during this time of a nuclear Pakistan spooked the Indian government and skewed Indian strategic thinking. The approach shrank along with the geographic context as the threat focus moved from China to Pakistan and the "minimum deterrence" concept was reduced by analysts in government-aided think-tanks into something called "recessed deterrence." It resembled the notions of "non-weaponized deterrence"[135] and "opaque deterrence"[136] and was based on an untenable spin given "existential deterrence" first articulated by McGeorge Bundy, President Kennedy's assistant for national security. Bundy talked of sufficient thermonuclear weapons in the armory and of being able to survive "the strongest possible preemptive attack" affording "existential deterrence," making excessive nuclear war-fighting capability the United States had acquired redundant.[137] Historian of war Michael Howard pointed out the basic flaw in Bundy's concept: "If the prospect of a nuclear war as such is an effective deterrent, the whole concept of deterrence falls to the ground; no one will believe that its adversary, or its ally, would under any circumstances use nuclear weapons."[138] Their thinking unclouded by such doubts, the votaries of "recessed deterrence" in India averred that a nuclear weapon deters simply by existing in whatever, even disaggregated, form, and that the operational status and support paraphernalia for such forces and preparedness schemes and such like are unnecessary.[139] Consistent with this belief, they argued that an untested weapon would have the same deterrent effect as a tested one, and ended up campaigning for India's signature on the CTBT and opposing the tests in 1998.[140] The Indian military brass led by former Army Chief General K. Sundarji, to the extent they evinced any interest at all, fell in behind the minimum deterrence concept that nuclear scientists such as Ramanna and civil servants such as K. Subrahmanyam were pushing. General Sundarji found hard to swallow, however, the idea that an adversary would be "deterred adequately by not being sure our bombs will not work." In a letter to a Defense science official, he cautioned that while this sort of calculation may "be right in theory," "the adversary's assessment is neither homogenous nor monolithic [and] it may vary from time to time, depending on the mindset of those who control the levers of policy making at that time. Some people . . . might need greater proof than others that the Indian nuclear weapon would indeed work." Sundarji proposed giving potential adversary states just such assurance: "A few tests might provide this proof to doubting Thomases, among the decisionmakers of our potential adversaries, our own leaders and people than our present [no testing] stance."[141] Subrahmanyam, who had retired as the head of the department of defense production, was of the view that India was "content to demonstrate capability, put basic infrastructure in place, and leave deterrence implicit and somewhat ambiguous."[142] Apprehending the diversion of national attention and defense spending away from the conventional military forces, its lukewarm attitude and tolerance for nuclear weapons never stretching beyond a thin "minimum deterrence" cover, served the military's interests. From this thinking came General Sundarji's view that 15 weapons of 20 KT yield would suffice for Pakistan and 30 of the same weapons for "even a larger country."[143] Current nuclear force-structuring plans, as we shall see in the next chapter, far exceed the limited-use, small-sized, short-legged, deterrent that Ramanna and Sundarji envisioned, even as the acquisition of strategic wherewithal and the practice of "credible minimum deterrence" encapsulated in the 1999 nuclear doctrine has made "recessed deterrence" and other conceptual mutants of minimal deterrence obsolete.

Ironically, the growing Pakistan fixation that collapsed the country's threat horizon and the inherently expansive strategic rationale for nuclear weapons as also their most credible justification, namely, China, happened just when the Indian nuclear complex was gearing up to produce advanced nuclear weaponry. Nuclear and thermonuclear weapons to counter nuclear-armed and larger conventional-military Chinese nuclear forces made sense; the "absolute" weapon as response to the nuclear threat posed by an undersized, albeit nuclear-bomb–equipped, Pakistan, was less convincing. Inevitably, Indian analysts referred to the Pakistani bomb as the military "equalizer,"[144] paying no heed to the fact that Pakistan actually enjoys virtual parity with India in deployable conventional forces, proved in the nearly yearlong eyeballing contest between the land forces of the two countries in 2002, and that this parity could have been the reason for the standoff rather than nuclear weapons possession by either country.[145] For their part, Western analysts, contemplating the limited subcontinental nuclear battle space with short missile flight times, concluded post-1998 that nuclear crisis would be the constant handmaiden of instability in South Asia.[146] By merely substituting India and Pakistan for the United States and Soviet Union in the Cold War paradigm, such prognoses miss out on the organic links between the two countries and the social and cultural constraints that exist, which have translated into severe limits on the scale and intensity of the hostilities in the past. What has eventuated as a consequence is a history and system of war between the two countries of limited aims and limited means that makes nuclear exchange improbable.[147] Unaware of this ground reality, Western analyses cause undue alarm and tend to anticipate the worst outcomes.[148] Empirical evidence notwithstanding, they refuse to perceive nuclear weapons as "domesticable" and prone to "conventionalization," resulting, as John J. Weltman has argued, in new nuclear-weapon states rapidly assimilating them "into the panoply of means that states employ to defend or advance their interests."[149]

From the late 1970s onward, the lack of strategic delivery systems that had agitated people like Sarabhai was finally addressed in two ways: by purchasing nuclear-capable aircraft from the Soviet Union/Russia (MiG-23 BN and Su-30 MKI), Britain (Jaguar) and France (Mirage 2000) with progressively longer radii of action, and by founding the semi-autonomous Integrated Guided Missile Project (IGMP) in 1968 tasked with designing and developing a range of tactical and ballistic missiles. To crown the various strategic programs, the highly secret "Advanced Technology Vehicle" program was inaugurated in 1970 to produce, with Soviet/Russian technical assistance, three nuclear-powered submarines capable of launching nuclear ballistic missiles (SSBNs), with the first unit slated for harbor trials in 2009 followed by sea trials in 2010 and fleet service by 2012.[150] The important thing about the IGMP and generally the Indian missile program is that, like the Indian nuclear weapons program spawned by a civilian nuclear-energy program, the Indian missiles are by-products of the civilian space program.[151] The first missile produced was a short-range variant of the Soviet-era surface-to-air missile, SA-2, called the Prithvi, which was first test-fired in 1988 and entered service with the army in the mid-1990s. It is nuclear capable with a range of 150 km and can deliver a 1000 kg conventional or nuclear warhead.[152] Being liquid-fueled, it is cumbersome, requires time to launch, and because its long and slow-moving Tetra truck TEL (transporter, erector, launcher) convoy is easy to spot even when on the move, it is vulnerable to a preemptive strike. Plainly a stopgap solution to deal with the immediate threat from Pakistan, it meshed with the undeclared, generally accepted, "retaliation only" strategy that was current in that decade. Assuming adequate protection during its long preparation time, the Prithvi, fired after a great deal of thought and deliberation, was thought to promote crisis stability. The Agni family of missiles meant mostly for Chinese targets use the ISRO-developed space launch vehicle (SLV-3) as the first stage.[153] The first of this type and test-fired thrice in 1994–1996, the 1500 km range Agni was a nuclear missile with the solid-fueled SLV-3 as first stage and a compact version of the Prithvi as second stage carrying a 1000 kg payload. The testing regime for the Agni missile was curtailed but the coalition government of Prime Minister H. D. Deve Gowda in 1997 firmly resisted U.S. pressure to apply closure to the project.[154] Owing to its liquid-fueled second stage offering uniform and precise burn characteristics, the missile is both maneuverable in the terminal phase—making it difficult to intercept—and highly accurate. With enough notice, it is usable in the counter-force mode and even for preemptive strike. This version of the Agni has since been replaced by an all solid-fuel missile.

CLARIFYING THE INTENTION

Western policy-makers and strategic community alike have portrayed the resumption of testing by India and its decision to come out of the closet as a nuclear-weapon state in 1998 as both unexpected and unsettling and contrary to expectations and the Indian government's pronouncements,[155] and as a result India was dubbed a "nuclear pariah."[156] The surprise is that there was this kind of reaction at all considering Indian representatives had since the 1950s consistently iterated in nonproliferation and disarmament forums that India would acquire nuclear weapons if the nuclear-weapon states did not disarm fully. Apparently, this warning—repeatedly issued over the years at the UN General Assembly, in the First Committee dealing with disarmament issues in the United Nations in New York, at the Eighteen Nation Disarmament Committee, and in the UN Disarmament Commission in Geneva—got lost in the Indian government's rhetoric on the desirability of disarmament, which was mistaken for a policy to remain a nuclear celibate. Considering the calculated Indian nuclear capability buildup, Nehru's strategy was politically to pave the way for Indian nuclear weapons as a means to even out the strategic playing field and shift the onus for India's going nuclear—whenever that happened—squarely onto the great powers. Nehru's confidante and the country's Defense Minister, V. K. Krishna Menon, spearheaded the campaign in the international circles. In a speech, for example, before the UN General Assembly in October 1954, he laid down disarmament markers. Other than declaring that measures such as the 1954 Partial Test Ban Treaty were not a substitute for disarmament, Krishna Menon asked for "general and complete" disarmament, with the elimination of nuclear weapons to be realized in lockstep with conventional military drawdowns on the basis of "equitable reduction" in terms of "quantums and qualities." This was to ensure that a world freed of nuclear weapons was not made safe for conventional war, and did not advantage states with superior conventional military might. As an interim measure, he demanded that an agreement on the nonuse of nuclear weapons—the first faint intimation of India's subscribing to the No First Use principle as a nuclear weapon power—be speedily facilitated along with an "armaments truce." He also specifically warned that if these disarmament goals were not met, India could and would acquire nuclear weapons at one-tenth the cost, given the labor and other comparative advantages it enjoyed. India could not have been clearer about what it intended to do.[157]

There was always the danger of this official Indian position that, had genuine disarmament occurred in the 1950s, India's nuclear weapons capability would have been stranded midway. In hindsight it may be seen that given the fact that the total elimination of nuclear weapons was unachievable, India was no worse off championing disarmament than not doing so, and that India benefited politically from pushing this cause and putting the great powers on the defensive, even as such advocacy did not hinder the development of the Indian nuclear weapons capabilities. India's role in the campaign for disarmament, along with its founding of the Nonaligned Movement and leading the international fight against colonialism and racism in the United Nations, won it many admirers and a following in the Third World as well as grudging respect in the West. It helped India box well above its weight in the international arena in the first two decades after independence.

However, Delhi has always seen India's interests as overlapping those of the nuclear-weapon states more than converging with the interests of countries that either had no capacity whatsoever to acquire nuclear weapons, had signed away their weapon-option by acquiescing in the NPT or, like many European countries and Japan, had forsaken nuclear weapons because of the protection provided by friendly great powers. Its nuclear policy, strategy, and diplomacy, therefore, credibly twinned the country's disarmament objectives with those of the great powers by covertly building up its nuclear weapons capability and zealously protecting it, ensuring India did not get stuck with the worst of all possible worlds—the nuclear-weapon states' failing to disarm fully and, having foresworn nuclear weapons, its being left in the strategic lurch.[158] It has also served the larger purpose of forcing a change in India's standing, in the global "correlation of forces," and in the international status quo.

CHAPTER 3

Maturing Nuclear and Missile Capabilities and Credible Minimum Deterrence Strategy, Post-1998

After the first decade and half of the nuclear program with Jawaharlal Nehru at the helm of state and Homi J. Bhabha, the scientific and the strategic visionary, propelling it, the Congress Party receded as the source of forward nuclear thinking. Instead, its policy of "keeping the nuclear option open" got calcified, turning in slow stages into a weapons-on-backburner policy as late as the mid-1990s. Starting in the mid-1960s, though, it was the right-wing Jana Sangh Party, later transformed into the Bharatiya Janata Party (BJP), that called for nuclear weapons to counter China.[1] M. L. Sondhi, a young diplomat who resigned from the Foreign Service and won election to Parliament on the Jan Sangh Party ticket, initiated correspondence with the French Air Force General Pierre Gallois, one of the main proponents of an independent nuclear force for France.[2] In a letter to Sondhi dated December 18, 1970, Gallois labeled nuclear armaments "defensive weapons," criticized the Indian government for postponing the "pivotal decision" to obtain them and the nuclear haves for successfully "brainwashing" the rulers in the nuclear threshold states, like India, with offers of "nuclear guarantee." He claimed these offers had "little meaning" and would provide only "false protection" for which the recipient country would pay heavily in terms of "independence, politically, diplomatically and economically." He commended Sondhi's proposal for a peaceful nuclear explosion as the path to nuclear weapons status but urged this former Indian diplomat not to think of Indian nuclear weapons as providing security for all of Southeast Asia (which Sondhi perhaps proposed in his letter) but only for India. Gallois went on to say it is "more rewarding [for countries] to work on atomic and ballistic [*sic*] matters than to produce machine guns, lorries and uniforms." And, he lauded the capacity of Indian nuclear weapons to stabilize the security situation in the extended region. Gallois ended the letter, astonishingly, with an offer to travel to India to help the Jan Sangh Party campaign publicly for Indian nuclear weapons "if . . . it may be useful for your combat."[3] With his writings as backdrop, it is easy to surmise that General Gallois was keen to get a nuclear India to join France in diluting the strategic power of the United States and the Soviet Union in the Cold War, believing that a grouping of unaligned nuclear-armed regional powers could leverage just such a *denouement,* something akin to what Nehru had in mind when he had conceived of the bloc of nuclear nonaligned states a decade earlier.

If Gallois sought to improve the bargaining position of nuclear France and India in the heyday of the post-1945 system, the BJP nearly thirty years later had a somewhat similar goal in ordering a resumption of nuclear tests: It wanted to enhance India's international standing as a nuclear-weapon state in what Brajesh Mishra, national security adviser to Prime Minister Atal Bihari Vajpayee in the BJP-led coalition government, described as a rapidly changing world, one in which the Soviet Union was dead, the Non-Proliferation Treaty (NPT) was extended into perpetuity in 1995, and moves were afoot to push through the Comprehensive Test Ban Treaty (CTBT) and to control fissile material production. The fact that the nuclear complex had weapons ready for testing was also an incentive. "All these things goaded us into testing," explained Mishra. "Had we waited too long, there might have been conventions, etc. that put much more pressure on India than would happen if these treaties did not come into existence." He also referred to the scientific and military reasons for testing. "The scientists were keen that what they had weaponized should be tested," he said. "You can't forever keep bombs in the basement. And, if I were from the armed forces, I'd say I don't know whether these things will work or not."[4]

The decision to test was taken on April 8 or 9, 1998, with the series of five nuclear tests scheduled for some time later that month. The tests were then postponed to May 11 and May 13 because then President of India K. R. Narayanan, was on a state visit to Brazil on April 26–27, and the Vajpayee government did not want him to answer for the tests when he was abroad.[5] In making the decision, the Vajpayee government was determined that neither the poor economic situation in the country—owing to the east Asian currency crisis in 1998 and the loss of $3–$4 billion out of the country's hard currency reserves of only $30 billion, nor the fear of economic sanctions, the sort of considerations that had influenced previous Indian governments to forego taking the nuclear plunge, would deter it from testing and weaponizing. Because he was convinced, as Vajpayee told Parliament that, "economic prosperity and security needs are not mutually exclusive," he intended to use national resources "optimally so that the nation is secure and prosperous."[6] The BJP regime was perhaps reassured by a study done by the Finance Ministry in 1995–1996 when last the government, under Prime Minister P. V. Narasimha Rao, considered testing. This study concluded that the country would be able to withstand the force of economic sanctions.[7] So sanctions were anticipated but, as the Finance Minister at the time, Yashwant Sinha says, it was hoped the United States and the West would "not go the whole hog ... in the sense that they wouldn't [economically] blockade India or prevent trade from taking place and prevent Indian dollar transactions with third countries going through American banking channels in New York," because if they had done that "we'd have had a much more difficult situation."[8] The impact of the partial sanctions—most external financing of ongoing programs, for instance, continued—were to an extent blunted by certain measures taken by the Vajpayee government, and by the initiation of the strategic dialog with the United States, involving the Prime Minister's representative Jaswant Singh and the U.S. Deputy Secretary of State Strobe Talbott. Among the actions the Vajpayee government took was the issuance in the international market in August 1998 of the "Resurgent India Bonds"—a five-year instrument bearing an interest rate of 7.25 percent, which compared favorably with the sovereign bond issues of developed countries. It was subscribed to mainly by Indians residing abroad, some $4.25 billion was collected, and it was a "great confidence booster." Combined with the half-hearted sanctions, the rupee appreciated, the economy grew by 6.5 percent in 1998–1999—an improvement on the growth rate of 4.8 percent in 1997–1998, the last year of the previous government, and the sanctions began to peter out. "It was," Sinha said, "a great tribute to holding our nerve. It brought the feel-good factor back to the economy." Sinha believes Jaswant Singh's strategic dialog with the United States was equally if not more important. India's position needed to be explained and the government realized early, he said, that "if we wanted the world to accept what we had done it was important to carry conviction with the US first. It had the desired effect."[9]

Speaking, in a sense, as much for India as he did for his own country, the Permanent Representative of Pakistan at the United Nations in Geneva, Masood Khan, declared, "In 1998, we made a transition from one strategic platform to another—from a recessed covert capability to an overt nuclear power, from 'existential deterrence' to 'credible minimum deterrence'. The 'nuclear force architecture' and security concepts of India and Pakistan became comparable to those of the *de jure* nuclear-weapon states under the Non-Proliferation Treaty. By moving from 'nuclear opacity' to a 'demonstrated nuclear capability', they became members of the nuclear club, *ipso facto*."[10] The tests, moreover, proved India had in its inventory an efficient 20 KT implosion fission weapon, an effective "tritium-boosted" fission design of 40 KT as the primary for a fusion weapon scalable, so it is claimed, to 100–300 KT, a couple of workable low-yield armaments, at least one of them fashioned out of reactor-grade plutonium of which there is no dearth in the country, but only a partially successful two-stage thermonuclear weapon. The "type testing" of weapons could have been done in discrete tests, but simultaneous triggering was preferred, even though it complicated the reading of the explosions data. This was because Atomic Energy Commission (AEC) Chairman R. Chidambaram feared, as did all the scientists at the Bhabha Atomic Research Center (BARC), that after the first test of one weapon the Indian government would buckle under Western pressure and end further testing—as had happened in 1974 when, despite approving a number of tests, Prime Minister Indira Gandhi stopped the testing after just one implosion device was exploded. The difficulty in reading the mixed data was considered a price worth paying to have the weapons program avoid getting into a limbo again and without a variety of test data to work with.[11] In any case, the hydrogen bomb design could not have been tested at full strength (100–300 KT) because the only shafts that were available were those dug many years earlier and were 100 meters deep, while the depth of the L-shaped shaft needed to be at least 300 meters. At 100 meters, it would have set off destructive seismic tremors over a large part of the surrounding countryside. Deeper holes could not have been dug because the country did not possess technology to drill below 100 meters.[12] It is the questionable success of the fusion or thermonuclear design that triggered a lively public debate about whether or not more tests are required for India credibly to claim that it, in fact, has a reliable thermonuclear deterrent.[13] R. Chidambaram held the view prior to the underground explosions that the high level of computational skills and simulation capabilities the BARC had developed had made testing redundant, that designs could be converted into reliable weapons without their having to pass through the stage of physical testing. He contended that because a lot of the staged bomb was designed on the computer and a lot of the computer simulations were verified against the available data even before the tests, and because each of the subsystems, subassemblies, and components in each of the designs was tested thoroughly, when put together these various parts would work perfectly. "We did not develop designs by tests," he said in a talk at the Indian Institute of Science in Bangalore in December 2002, "but confirmed the design validity by testing."[14] This goes against the grain of nuclear weapon designing norm where "the focal concern" of a nuclear weapons laboratory is to test, and test again in order to verify and validate designs.[15] To be able realistically to simulate the multiple explosive stages of a thermonuclear weapon, moreover, depends centrally on the richness of the test data previously collected and the computational speeds. India finds itself, however, severely limited in test data and lacks high computational speed. According to a senior DRDO official involved in the nuclear testing, some six months after the May 1998 tests, he recommended resumption of testing to the government because he was convinced that the test of the hydrogen bomb was inadequate for the purposes of developing simulation software and designing performance-capable thermonuclear weapons. He supported the official line on the test moratorium because, he said, of "functioning pressures."[16] Absent also is both a large Indian inertial confinement fusion facility, such as the American National Ignition Facility in Livermore and the French Laser Megajoule coming up southwest of Bordeaux[17] to simulate thermonuclear explosions (based on data from 210 nuclear tests France has conducted) using high-energy lasers, and the magnitude of investment in three-dimensional simulation of fusion explosions and development of complex computer codes, of the kind other nuclear-weapon states are going in for.[18]

To put India's situation in perspective, consider the most complex calculations in designing the 1974 weapon, for example, those relating to the critical "neutronics" aspect, namely, "the pre-detonation probability," "the strength of the neutron source trigger needed in order to ensure the near 100% successful initiation of the fission chain reaction," and the "neutron multiplication factor." These calculations were done not by computers but "by hand ... using equations and formulae" in the manner the pioneers in the Manhattan Project had done, reveals Mahadeva Srinivasan, the chief mathematical physicist of the weapons program. He subsequently published a series of internationally acclaimed papers on the "Trombay Criticality Formula." "The non-availability of fast and powerful computers in India during the 1970s and 1980s," Srinivasan declares, "was a blessing in disguise. I think it is fair to say that I had a better grasp of the physics of neutron multiplying systems than the American physicists of Los Alamos and Livermore of the era." If there were no supercomputers that the Indian weapon scientists could access as late as the 1980s, for Chidambaram to maintain that inside of ten years, i.e., by the 1990s, BARC had reliable even if not U.S.-level computing capabilities to simulate accurately a thermonuclear explosion, is problematic.[19] Furthermore, as *The Economist* reports, a 1990s vintage supercomputer would take 60,000 years to process all the fusion explosion test data from over 1,800 nuclear tests collected by the United States in order to simulate a full thermonuclear explosion, something more modern machines can do in only six weeks. Even so, American weapons designers at the Lawrence Livermore National Laboratory, University of California, Berkeley, and the Sandia National Laboratories in New Mexico are not sure their Reliable Replacement Warhead design can do without explosive testing.[20] With the Indian nuclear weaponeers having data from a single thermonuclear test and that too, as many Indian scientists apprehend, only a partially successful one, and nothing like the computational wherewithal available to their American counterparts, Chidambaram's controversial view that the modified fusion weapon and other designs need no further testing seems unsustainable. It obviously did not persuade Prime Minister Atal Bihari Vajpayee, who ordered the explosive tests of the weapons designs despite Chidambaram's lack of enthusiasm for this course of action. It is another matter Vajpayee then turned around and used Chidambaram's apparent confidence in BARC's simulation capability to justify the "voluntary moratorium" on testing he announced on May 28, 1998. It highlights the fact that simulation is a politically convenient justification for the Indian government to avoid making the hard decision to test or to resume testing. It affords a plausible scientific reason for not testing, thus saving the country the economic costs and rigors of automatically imposed Western sanctions. Hence, Prime Minister P. V.

Narasimha Rao latched on to the simulation option and ruled out the resumption of nuclear tests in 1995.[21] The BJP government was determined to test to "the essential minimum necessary for credible minimum deterrence" and hoped that good relations with the United States could be forged on the basis of the test moratorium as proof of Indian restraint. The test series marked the process of serious and formal weaponization. At the same time, it opened up Washington for talks to dilute the technology denial regimes in place on the basis of India's newly acquired nuclear-weapon state status.[22]

That 1995 decision, however, stirred up powerful opposition in Trombay where Chidambaram's minority view on testing was and is still anathema. BARC Director A. N. Prasad, a plutonium reprocessing specialist, was outraged enough to arrange for a "unanimous note" from the BARC Council—the highest decision-making body in the nuclear complex—to be sent to Chidambaram challenging his view on technical grounds and demanding new tests. Going a step further, Prasad briefed Arundhati Ghose, Indian representative negotiating the Comprehensive Test Ban Treaty (CTBT) at the Conference on Disarmament in Geneva in 1995, on the need for more testing by India before the government agreed to a testing ban and asked her to convey BARC's strongly held professional view and sentiment on this crucial matter to the Indian government.[23] It was one of the background reasons for the government of Prime Minister H. D. Deve Gowda's blocking the draft CTBT in 1996.[24] On the basis of the yield calculations and design parameters, moreover, Prasad believes there was a problem with the thermonuclear device tested in 1998—the boosted primary worked fine as a triggering mechanism, but the secondary package did not work as anticipated.[25] It is an assessment shared by the vast majority in the nuclear establishment. P. K. Iyengar, who as head of the physics group in BARC designed the 1974 fission device, is convinced there was only "partial thermonuclear burn," which design flaw can be remedied, he argued, only by further testing.[26] Placid Rodriguez, former director of the Kalpakkam nuclear complex, was more trenchant. "We should not," he said at a 2007 seminar, "fool ourselves that one thermonuclear test is enough."[27] A former secretary of the Ministry of Science and Technology, Ashok Parthasarathy, who began his career in the Atomic Energy Commission, contends that the testing done in 1998 is "grossly inadequate."[28] According to Srinivasan, without more tests the reliability of the 20 KT fission weapon is "100%," of the tritium-boosted design—"It will surely work, . . . there will be a bang! But the full performance of the booster part will be subject to less than 100% surety; [and] in the case of the full thermonuclear device the confidence level will perhaps be less."[29] Assuming the 1998 designs worked perfectly and do not need to be retested, there will still arise in the future a need for testing. The "regional and international situation is not static," said Prasad, "and weapons considered adequate today may require to have their yield and other characteristics changed to suit new threats and this would require more tests." He also pointed out that a ban on testing will mean that the cumulative skills in designing and producing nuclear weapons will remain at a basic level with no possibility of their advancement.[30] These and other factors may have persuaded R. Chidambaram to modify his position. In representations to the government thereafter he maintained that no testing would be needed but only "for the next ten years," meaning that by 2008 or thereabouts the Indian nuclear weapons would require an upgrade, necessitating a renewal of explosive tests to validate improved designs to keep up with the modernized armaments in other countries. Chidambaram's ambivalence led a high-powered task force appointed by the government to advise the Ministry of External Affairs in late 2007 not to sign the Comprehensive Test Ban Treaty.[31]

The uncertainty in the mind of the nuclear community about the reliability of the generally unproven boosted and thermonuclear weapons is mirrored in the trepidation of the armed services. Other than giving evidence that a new design or a variant of an old design works reliably, iterative tests can produce as much as a threefold increase in yields for the same weight. In a decade worth of tests in the United States the yields, for instance, improved by a factor of 1000, from 20 KT to 20 MT. Further, testing permits more kilotons of yield to be packed per pound of fissile material, and it helps in miniaturizing multiple independently targetable reentry vehicle (MIRV) warheads for different types of missiles.[32] Such testing also enhances the safety aspects of various weapon types and helps to study how a weapon design responds in proximity to detonation of other weapons, and for "routine optimizations" of different types of payload on numerous vectors (missiles, aircraft) and for calibrating simulation software.[33] In any case, as Kathleen Bailey, a former U.S. arms control official put it, "We should not trust that the continuing reliability of [the] nuclear arsenal can be assured using old test data . . . Testing is necessary . . . when safe, highly complex nuclear weapons designs are required for . . . high performance delivery systems."[34] The 1998 tests did few of these other things, and the data collected is plainly inadequate for the purposes of weaponizing, in particular, the partially successful thermonuclear designs, let alone newer weapons designs required for force augmentation in the future, unless the deterrence premise is that the adversary bears the risk of a non-performing Indian thermonuclear weapon. "I don't think anybody is satisfied. I mean people in the military wonder if five tests are enough for all time to come when other countries have conducted over hundreds of, even thousand, tests of thermonuclear weapons . . . They needed to do those tests, then are our computer simulations enough?" wondered Admiral Arun Prakash, who retired as chairman of the Chiefs of Staff Committee, and chief of the Naval Staff (2004–2007). "Most of us in the military don't believe it, although some of the scientists have been repeatedly reassuring us. They may have no choice . . . having signed away their option by agreeing to the unilateral moratorium on tests, which was obviously a political step. I think that was a mistake." Even when the military's doubts about unproven and untested nuclear weapons are conveyed to the government, it has had little effect. "Between a scientist and a soldier," he rued, "the politicians . . . believe the scientist."[35] General Ved Malik, chief of Army Staff in the period of the 1998 tests, recalled that Iyengar, who was then waging a relentless campaign in official circles for additional testing, met with him and gave him technical reasons why he thought the thermonuclear device did not work and more testing was needed. Troubled by what he had been told, Malik conveyed the former nuclear chief's misgivings to National Security Adviser Mishra.[36] Mishra states that the BJP government had no choice other than to believe R. Chidambaram, the AEC chairman at the time. "Who am I to go and say [these tests did not work]," says Mishra, "and . . . I will appoint a commission to enquire into whether the scientists are telling the truth or not?"[37] Then Deputy National Security Adviser Satish Chandra, however, alluded to the voluntary ban on testing as India's doing the politic thing and "joining in a moratorium observed by every one."[38] Jaswant Singh, foreign minister in the BJP government, was more candid. Prime Minister Vajpayee, according to Jaswant Singh, "was by instinct placatory" and "had from the beginning in his public stance been in support of disarmament . . . There was no bouncing off of ideas with his confidantes . . . It [the testing moratorium] was an instinctive reaction. It shows up Vajpayee in bad light. But the fact of the matter is the Indian political leadership [across the board] does not have the tradition of either great study or reflection. It has always been reliance on technicians to be guided into certain stands."[39] The "technician" in question is, perhaps, Brajesh Mishra, a retired diplomat with whom, it was rumored, Jaswant Singh had differences. Mishra, however, reveals that Prime Minister Vajpayee made decisions alone and unhesitatingly on issues he had strong views about; it is only on other issues he involved his National Security Adviser.[40]

While most scientists believe India will have to resume testing to obtain a credible nuclear deterrent, a very small minority is of the view that, in lieu of tests, "design uncertainties" can be compensated by preparing for a "bigger yield." "On thermonuclear weapons," avers a former director of BARC, "if you say you want yield 'y', I will design for two times 'y', what is the problem?" Furthermore, he points out that "even if the actual yield of a weapon is 10%, 30% or even 50% off the designed yield, it does not matter if I have pinpoint accuracy of delivery?"[41] What is really in doubt is whether a sustainable thermonuclear burn-wave can be propagated—which the 1998 tested design, according to Iyengar and others, proved it cannot, rather than whether the yield can be pumped up. In other words, the issue is one of correcting a basic design flaw, not just adding to the thermonuclear fuel, which may remain unignited. In any case, the stiff opposition by the nuclear scientists combined with the military's apprehensions about the government policy of a testing moratorium is, in the main, why two successive governments recanted or found political support eroding for their nuclear initiatives predicated on India's giving up its testing option, which resulted in the freezing of the Indian thermonuclear weapons technology at the level of a failed design. The right-of-center Bharatiya Janata Party–led government headed by Vajpayee, which had ordered the 1998 tests and overt weaponization, considered signing the CTBT, but was forced to draw back,[42] and the successor center-to-left-of-center Congress Party coalition government of Prime Minister Manmohan Singh, which promoted the civil nuclear co-operation deal with the United States predicated on India's giving up further testing, found great difficulty in mustering a majority in Parliament in support of the deal. There are over 12 untested weapons designs, [43] encompassing nuclear and thermonuclear gravity and glide bomb and warheads optimized for delivery by aircraft, land-based cruise and ballistic missiles, and ship and submarine-launched cruise and ballistic missiles, on the shelf. These failures by two ideologically disparate regimes in their attempts to enter test ban deals suggest that the Indian government is unlikely politically to risk using the permanent cessation of testing as a bargaining chip in negotiating bilateral or multilateral agreements or arms control treaties until the new and improved designs for the numerous weapons on the shelf undergo thorough underground testing to the satisfaction of the scientists and, growingly, the military services. Indeed, the Congress Party government, finding itself isolated in Parliament, turned around on the issue, and starting in 2006 has averred that India has not foreclosed the nuclear testing option. [44]

CAPABILITY GROWTH

The Indian nuclear weapons program is homegrown. That is why the United States intelligence agencies fail to pick up signs of test preparations, because they rely on traces of weapons programs from the five NPT-recognized nuclear-weapon states. [45] Like in other major countries, it is also technology-driven. The decision space on technology development—what type of weapons to design and develop, in what time frame—while rightfully in the government's strategic policy domain, owing to the disinterest of the Indian political class and the secrecy attending on the nuclear program, was expropriated early by the nuclear establishment as another aspect of the near absolute functional autonomy it enjoys. Even Raja Ramanna, the longtime leader of the weapons project and later chairman of the AEC, apparently placed the technological imperative to improve nuclear weapons above "minimum deterrence" which he advocated and believed was realized with the first test in 1974. In 1992, around the time the design for a tritium-boosted weapon had been completed but awaited testing and the development of a design for a thermonuclear weapon was revived, Ramanna wrote, "the 'ultimate' nature of modern weapons does not by itself seem sufficient for countries to give up further development of more efficient weapons." [46] He was referring to the upgrading of already advanced arsenals in P-5 countries, but he could just as well have been speaking about the Indian nuclear weapons program. The urge to obtain more sophisticated nuclear weapons technology and to see such technology as scientific and engineering challenges and hurdles to be overcome, has been a strong and constant motivator and a factor in the success of the Indian weapons designers. [47] Thus, no sooner was a basic fission design tested in 1974 than preliminary work began on a staged thermonuclear weapon with open experiments related to fusion in the indigenously designed PURNIMA-I (Plutonium Reactor for Neutron Investigations in Multiplying Assemblies) unit—the first of the fast reactors in Trombay. BARC had two reasons for doing so—to keep up with China and to develop a civilian nuclear-energy option in terms of fusion energy.[48] This hydrogen bomb project experienced a "lull" for a decade or so, according to Mahadeva Srinivasan, the former chief physicist at the PURNIMA complex, and "slowly petered out at least among the lower rungs of the scientific hierarchy." Iyengar recalls, however, that a hydrogen weapon design was ready for testing by 1982. Based on the "Teller-Ulam configuration,"[49] the design used depleted Uranium 238 as mantle to reflect gamma rays to implode the thermonuclear fuel by isotropic (or uniform) compression of tritium.[50] The project regained priority in the early 1990s after it went through the "intermediate stage" of boosted fission, but serious difficulties were still encountered. Because, as Srinivasan says, "one's confidence decreases and degree of uncertainty increases as one goes from a simple fission device to a more complex staged thermonuclear system [even if it is] through the intermediate boosted system." In terms of fabrication, the boosted design, according to Srinivasan, involved adding a concentric layer of lithium deuteride [thermonuclear fuel] around the plutonium core. Otherwise, it was not very different from the fission device. Its influence on the yield, however, was very important. As regards the reliability of the boosted design, it depends, says Srinivasan, "on what degree of reliability the designers are happy with: 70% or 90% or 99.99%?" The success of the booster design, he adds, "depends on what the temperature of the LiD-T (lithium deuteride) layer was actually achieved or calculated to be" and, in any case, can produce a yield only in the 30–50 KT range. The use of the solid lithium deuteride, instead of liquid deuterium, in the booster and the staged thermonuclear weapons suggests high-level expertise because it involves, as Herbert York, former head of the Lawrence Livermore National Laboratory, has written, "complex, multi-step, multi-branched chain-like processes . . . in the explosion."[51]

Other than as a step up from the fission weapon on the way to attaining competence in designing thermonuclear weapons, there were two other reasons for developing the boosted fission weapon. First, the scientists wanted to provide more bang for the same amount of fissile material. "Boosted fission," says Iyengar, "allows you to use the same plutonium inventory for higher yield. Any progress in the physics of explosive devices has to go on and have a fusion component—the explosive power from fusion of deuterium and tritium—and the first but more difficult step is to incorporate that in the fission device itself. Therefore, we thought of the booster." And second, they wanted to increase the "burn efficiency" of plutonium in a standard fission weapon from the maximum of 25–30 percent achievable by even the "cleverest designs."[52] Open literature offered no great help in any of the weapons-related work. Rather, the Indian scientists adopted, what Iyengar calls, "the right physics approach," using which, he said, "you can achieve anything."[53] Whether it was simple fission, boosted fission, or staged thermonuclear, in each case the Indian scientists faced three levels of difficulty. The first level was in conceptualizing a weapon in terms of physics principles and wondering how their counterparts elsewhere solved any particular problem like, say, boosting the yield. The second level had to do with transforming a concept into a workable weapon design. And the final level of difficulty concerned fabricating the "pit" or "core" for the weapon. "For example, you want to fabricate plutonium to the accuracy of a micron in radius; unless you do that, you are not going to get the experience," says Iyengar. "So you have to machine a sphere of plutonium, let us say 10 cms in diameter to an accuracy of a microgram. It has to be done by remote control in a gloved box filled with inert helium gas to prevent combustion from heat produced from machining plutonium after the plutonium and graphite are put together and heated. The French challenged me saying there would be fire; there wasn't. So the infrastructure has to be created—that is a challenge in itself." The technology developed in machining plutonium was used to develop the plutonium-carbide fuel for the fast breeder program.[54] While admitting he was out of the program by the time the hydrogen bomb design was completed and had "no direct knowledge of the 4-stage device," Srinivasan speculates that "The design would have to involve detonation of a thermonuclear burn wave in a secondary linear fusion section; this would be ignited by a primary booster device yielding 40 KT or so. The over-all 4-stage design could then have a total yield of 100 KT to 200 KT."[55] Chidambaram confirmed that the fusion weapon with "a design yield calibrated at 45 KT can go up to 200 KT without any problem."[56]

It has been known that reliable weapons with yields from low kilotons up to 20–40 KT can be developed using reactor-grade plutonium with "fissile content" of 66 percent owing to the fact that only a little more reactor-grade plutonium (16 kg) is required to reach critical mass than weapons-grade plutonium (10 kg). Richard L. Garwin, the stalwart American thermonuclear weapon designer, wrote, before the 1998 tests, that the Indian nuclear-weapon establishment was quite capable of converting reactor-grade plutonium into weapons.[57] At least one of the low-yield designs India tested on May 13, 1998, featured reactor-grade plutonium. BARC has experimented with designing weapons from this fissile material for many years. Again, it was the challenge of taming the spontaneous fissioning plutonium 240 isotope, which excited the Indian scientists. This isotope accounts for some 30 percent of reactor-grade plutonium, forms an "unacceptably high background neutron source," and can cause predetonation. Regarding the design of a reactor-grade plutonium weapon, Srinivasan only says that it is "a bit tricky" with "the technology of achieving implosion very rapidly using advanced implosion concepts" being known only to "experienced design groups."[58] India currently holds some 11 tons of spent fuel, a stockpile increasing every year by two tons, all of which, in theory, can be converted into a serviceable arsenal.[59] The capability to produce the whole range of nuclear and thermonuclear weapons from very low yield to very high yields is now available, and it is something the Indian military considers desirable. Several reasons are adduced for this, namely, the removal of any force asymmetries (China shouldn't have a weapon we don't); the enhancement of deterrent credibility and prevention of escalation (low-yield weapons will convince the adversary to restrict the nuclear exchange—should one materialize—at that yield level); and the encouragement of "graduated deterrence."[60]

The production capacity for weapons-grade fissile materials is only now catching up with the capability of the Indian weapons designers. This is relevant because the shortage of weapons-grade plutonium was one reason government officials adduced for not carrying out open-ended testing leading to fast depletion of this fissile material stock. The 500 megawatt (MW) breeder reactor under construction in Kalpakkam is expected to be operational by 2010. It will consume approximately two tons of the 11 tons of the stockpiled spent fuel[61] as its initial fuel loading with another ton of reactor-grade plutonium held in reserve, but thereafter the breeder reactor "operated under equilibrium and achieving a capacity factor of 75%" conditions could begin adding 150 kg of weapons-grade plutonium to the holdings annually.[62] Compare this with the combined output of 30 kg per annum by the military-dedicated 100 MW Dhruva and the 40 MW CIRUS reactors—both located in Trombay.[63] Or put differently, the anticipated "breeding ratio" of the 500 MW fast breeder is 1.5, meaning that within five years of its going on stream, it will produce enough fissile material for its own re-load.[64] The plan is to put up a chain of fast breeder reactors with total capacity of 2,750 MW.[65] The breeder reactors, though, may not be usable any time soon for military purposes because of the use of mixed oxide fuels, resulting in 20–30 year "doubling time" (i.e., the time taken by a breeder to produce a full fuel load to fire up another breeder). The Indian nuclear program still has to gain experience in metallic fuels that have half this doubling time.[66] Further, in addition to the three active units able to chemically reprocess 250 kg of spent fuel from the CANDU PHWRs annually, two new reprocessing plants are coming up.[67] Iyengar indicated that another two such plants are in the planning stage to raise the total reprocessing capacity in the country to 400 kg plus a year.[68] The estimated holdings of weapons-grade plutonium in India are around 445 kg.[69] As a result of the detritiation technology developed by BARC in the 1980s (see the last chapter), tritium is available aplenty—chemically separated from the heavy water in the array of PHWRs.

India also has a gas centrifuge plant in Ratnehalli near Mysore. Commissioned in the early 1990s, it enriches uranium to 30 percent primarily as fuel for the miniaturized 100 MW light-water reactors powering the ballistic missile firing nuclear-powered submarine (SSBN). The first of three of this class of boats is scheduled to join naval service by 2012.[70] The 100 MW reactors in submarines will naturally lead to their consideration as power plants for aircraft carriers. In the present plans of the Indian Navy, out of the three aircraft carriers that are to be built indigenously—the first of which is currently under construction at the shipyard in Kochi, one is going to be nuclear powered.[71] Some 60 kg of uranium 235 enriched to 30 percent will be required annually to run each of these submarine reactors. Because the ship will be refueled in 10 year cycles when the entire hull will be de-welded, each vessel, once the reactor is placed in the titanium double hull, will have to carry enough of the enriched uranium fuel, i.e., some 600 kg plus reserve component, for the entire duration.[72] According to Iyengar, some 3,000 centrifuges are working in Ratnehalli; these cascades will be progressively increased to some 10,000 centrifuges to meet the enlarged requirements of the growing nuclear submarine force.[73] Since 2003, a scheme is on to replace the older vintage "subcritical" centrifuges with the technologically more modern "supercritical" centrifuges capable of greater enriching efficiency. The components for the centrifuges built with indigenously manufactured maraging steel have been produced in-house, imported, or mostly reverse-engineered until now when, according to David Albright, "India appears to have finally developed the capability to build and operate a centrifuge plant."[74]

BARC transferred to the Defense Research and Development Organization (DRDO) the technology, for example, for the discharge condenser used in the 1974 device to fire the chemical explosives and, subsequently, the kryton chemical explosive lens-triggering technology it had developed. DRDO produced the fuzes, arming and safety devices, electronic interlocks, etc. and generated the requirements for the size, weight, and other characteristics of the warheads based on the nose-cone geometries of the various missiles and bombs to be carried by different aircraft. The DRDO Chief Dr. A. P. J. Abdul Kalam made his reputation, especially with the political class, as the leader of the Indian Space Research Organization (ISRO) team that developed the first of the Space Launch Vehicles (SLV-3) which, after Kalam was chosen to head the Integrated Guided Missile Project in 1983, was incorporated as a first stage in all the long-range Agni missiles India produced or has on the drawing board.

If surmounting scientific and technological challenges was and remains a primary motivation for those involved in the Indian strategic programs, another motivation was and is defiance of the punitive-minded United States and the West, who emerged as the villains for imposing technology sanctions on the country after the 1974 test. It is an attitude best reflected in the fighting words of Kalam, who in 1995 urged defense scientists to view the "do's" and "don'ts" as gleaned from the list of technologies sanctioned by the West as a challenge. "When the developed world says don't do that, we will do that," he declared.[75] This defiance, rooted in Jawaharlal Nehru's 1950s thinking about India as an autarchic system—a self-sufficient technology-wise self-reliant country, has provided strong motivational fuel to propel indigenous high-technology programs, particularly in the prestigious nuclear, space, and military technology areas. It continues to push Indian nuclear scientists and engineers into proving they can produce any technology to match the best anywhere in the world and accounts for the fact that many of the most critical technologies needed in many sensitive projects were developed in-country in 1974–1990 when the international technology denial regimes (Wassenar Agreement, Nuclear Suppliers Group, Missile Technology Control Regime) and economic sanctions were most punitively implemented and the "import" option was unavailable.[76] "We have been driven to a more modern technology," says Iyengar. "That is the major output from the point of view of defense preparedness."[77]

Many Western analysts are, however, unimpressed by the Indian nuclear weapons capability, for instance. "The real problem here," writes Ashley Tellis, a former adviser to the American ambassador in Delhi and one of the proponents of the India–United States civilian nuclear cooperation deal, "may be India's scientists who in their zeal for the fanciest devices imaginable, may fail to produce even simple devices that are reliable, consistent in quality and yield, and operationally adequate."[78] This begs the question: How are reliability, consistent quality and yield, and operational adequacy of nuclear weapons to be obtained by Indian weapon designers if the test moratorium adhered to by the Indian government prevents them from improving and advancing their designs? In a Carnegie monograph, Tellis has rated India's technical capability to make weapons as "low" based on the amount of weapons-grade plutonium used in fission devices, which he claims is 6 kg in the case of India vs. 3–4 kg used in weapons in "high" capability countries, such as the United States.[79] Stephen Younger, Associate Director for Nuclear Weapons at the Los Alamos National Laboratory, classifies India's weapons technology as "midlevel" without explaining why.[80] Indian weaponeers, like Srinivasan, other than saying such conclusions are wrong, do not elaborate.[81] However, A. N. Prasad makes a distinction between the nuclear parts of whole weapons systems that BARC produces and the "trickiest" nonnuclear portion of the weapon system that is DRDO's responsibility. Testing will improve the performance especially of the boosted and thermonuclear armaments in the Indian inventory, but he cannot, he said, vouch for the quality of the components and technologies in the weapons systems produced by DRDO.[82]

The nuclear weapons scientists, however, find the apathy and the complacency of political leaders to be the major roadblock. "I once talked to Prime Minister Rajiv Gandhi in 1986–87 about refining and testing new generation boosted and thermonuclear weapons such as those we had designed and were engaged in designing," says Iyengar, recalling his frustrating experience as chairman of the AEC. "Instead of saying, well, keep it up, I fully support you, he responded by saying, any way, why are you worried? We have lived with a thermonuclear China for the last 30 years, why are you in such a hurry? He then referred to the 'Action Plan' he was going to put forward in the UN, which came to nothing. This sort of attitude puts a damper."[83] It was an attitude uniformly seen in the speeches by Congress Party leaders in Parliament to debate the 1998 tests. In his *suo moto* statement on May 28, 1998, in Parliament, Prime Minister Vajpayee said: "The restraint exercised for 24 years, after having demonstrated our capability in 1974, is in itself a unique example. Restraint, however, has to arise from strength. It cannot be based upon indecision or doubt. The series of tests recently undertaken by India have led to removal of doubts."[84] In response, Pranab Mukherji of the Congress Party, for instance, leading the attack, argued that the longstanding "consensus" on "keeping the nuclear option open" was destroyed by the tests and assailed Prime Minister Vajpayee for his statement that the tests removed "uncertainty and doubt," which he argued, was tantamount to doubting the "talent" of Indian nuclear scientists.[85] Mukherji was defense minister before being appointed minister for external affairs in 2006 in the successor Congress Party government headed by Prime Minister Manmohan Singh which, however, has moderated its aversion to nuclear weapons after it assumed power in 2004. A former military chief of staff recalls that Natwar Singh, the minister for external affairs until he was replaced by Mukherji, made it a point in cabinet meetings to join the Finance Minister C. Chidambaram (no relation of the former atomic energy chief, R. Chidambaram), in opposing the financial outlays for strategic programs. Natwar Singh's case was that the country was trying to mend its relations with Pakistan and China and, in any case, that adversaries could be "de-fanged" with diplomacy, making nuclear weapons unnecessary.[86] Such views may be attributed as much to Natwar Singh's personal beliefs as to the fact that those in government and the permanent secretariat are unaware of the secret history of the dual-purpose nuclear program in its early years, which led to even Congress Party leaders sourcing their nuclear negativism, ironically, to Nehru.[87] Here Mukherji as defense minister, perhaps protecting his ministerial turf, saw to it that nuclear weapons and other strategic programs were not financially starved. The apparent disinterest of the political leadership, however, reinforced the long-standing system of the weapons program working on "autopilot," of its being run by the nuclear scientists themselves with virtually no political direction or interference. Except that Kalam and DRDO, who were brought into the nuclear decision circle in 1987–1988 by V. S. Arunachalam, science adviser to the defense minister, to facilitate better coordination in the weaponization of the nuclear designs, began becoming bigger players—a fact resented by the nuclear estate.[88] Kalam successively headed the Integrated Guided Missile Project and the DRDO before being elevated to scientific adviser to the defense minister and, eventually, President of India in 2001–2006.[89]

MISSILE MUSCLE[90]

The ISRO, like the nuclear-energy program, was founded and steered by Homi J. Bhabha in its first decade and until 1972 was controlled by the Atomic Energy Commission. At the end of the 1971 War, the threat of military intervention by the U.S. carrier task group in the Bay of Bengal focused the Indian government's mind on the country's strategic weaknesses. As part of this exercise, ISRO was separated from Department of Atomic Energy (DAE) and put under the new Department of Space (DoS). ISRO continued to share many traits with DAE, specifically the civilian-cum-military nature of their technology-driven programs and the fast-track approach to acquiring the requisite technology and competence. Imported rocket and satellite technologies provided the seedbed for indigenous design and development capabilities, and ISRO graduated quickly from the sounding-rocket stage to space launch vehicles lofting light satellites and, by 2005, cryogenic engine-powered heavy-lift vehicles able to launch indigenous surveillance and communications satellites in polar and geosynchronous orbits. A number of "spy" satellites[91] are transmitting militarily useful sub one-meter imagery and with a footprint covering the extended southern Asian region, including Tibet and the eastern approaches, and most of the Indian Ocean area. ISRO provided the rocket and other technologies and trained manpower for the military-dedicated Integrated Guided Missile Program (IGMP) started in 1983.[92]

Like BARC, where nuclear scientists began working on thermonuclear designs after the 1974 simple fission test, the rocket engineers in IGMP, even as their Agni long-range missile "technology demonstrator" was at the design stage in 1985, just as ambitiously embarked on producing a full-scale missile able to carry a 1000 kg payload 1100 km. This shortened the development and delivery time of the 1500 km Agni-II first tested in 1992 and saved the public exchequer over $300 million (Rs 1200 crore). The first IGMP product was the Prithvi 150 km short-range ballistic missile (SRBM), which was hurried from design to full-scale development. With an optional 20 KT nuclear warhead, it was considered sufficient to deter such nuclear threat as was posed by Pakistan in the 1980s and 1990s. While it has tested accuracy, it is not popular with the military owing to the operational limitations imposed by its liquid fuel configuration—the time taken to fuel up the rocket, the inability to keep the corrosive rocket fuel in the tank for very long, etc.[93] These missiles equip the Army's 333 Missile Group (run by the artillery directorate), but do not constitute either a conventional or nuclear-ready force. As they can carry conventional HE (high explosive) warhead as well, some 200 of these missiles are being retained for dual conventional-nuclear use in short-range contingencies.[94] It is another matter that because sensors may not be able to detect the nature of the warhead, Pakistan might respond at the first hint of an incoming Prithvi missile.[95] India may be better off without this missile in its inventory and use its removal from the Indian order-of-battle as a confidence building measure to reassure Pakistan.[96]

The 1500 km Agni-II extended range medium missile, which initially had combined solid fuel–liquid fuel stages, was equally rapidly developed with readily available missile technologies for any immediate strategic crisis involving China. This Agni-II could hit fair-sized cities in the provinces of Sichuan and Yunnan adjoining India and, if properly vectored, reach the Chinese seaboard around Hainan. On the down side, it took a half-day to ready for launch[97] and was clearly a weapon for use in the interim if the need arose until its solid fuel variant and other longer-range, more reliable, missiles became available. This is now the case. India today has an all solid-fuel suite of Agni missiles. The 700–900 km Agni-I medium-range ballistic missile (MRBM) with closed-loop inertial guidance was developed inside of a year, controversially, at the behest of Jaswant Singh, foreign minister and for a short while also defense minister in the Vajpayee government, who espied a "missile gap" vis-à-vis Pakistan. DRDO scientists were puzzled because they felt the 150 km Prithvi and its variants, under development, for the air force (250 km) and the navy (350 km) took care of the Pakistan threat. The "mission priority" accorded Agni-I by the government meant a diversion of the efforts of the design team at the Defense Research and Development Laboratory (DRDL) in Hyderabad from the long-range missiles, including an intercontinental-range ballistic missile (ICBM). The rocket engineers saw this as a move to mollify the United States. Jaswant Singh was then in a "strategic dialog" with the U.S. Deputy Secretary of State Strobe Talbott, and, perhaps, felt pressured by the American into agreeing to a "strategic restraint" regime,[98] and thus projected the Agni-I development as evidence of self-restraint. Jaswant Singh implicitly acknowledges U.S. pressure to curtail long-range missile development by India, saying "The [U.S.] concepts and doctrines of national interest is that no country except the P-5, who were considered within the corral, as it were—should have nuclear technology capable of being converted to weapons and ICBM . . . that would cause damage to the American territory and the people." It illustrates what he called America's "fortress mentality" and adds, "This was a rather artificial fortress they had created around themselves of which essentially the Non-Proliferation Treaty (NPT) and the Comprehensive Test Ban Treaty (CTBT), the Fissile Material Cutoff Treaty (FMCT) and the Missile Technology Control Regime (MTCR) are parts."[99] In any event, the Agni-I development delayed the testing and induction into service of the 2500–3000 km Agni-III intermediate-range ballistic missile (IRBM) by 4–5 years and disrupted the planned progress of the follow-on 5,000 km Agni-IV IRBM-project by a year, and postponed the development phase of the intercontinental–range ballistic missile. The design for the 30 m-long ICBM with diameter of 2.5 m has been frozen. Conceptualized in 1998 as a three stage 10,000–12,000 km-range missile with liftoff weight of 130–150 tons and payload capacity of 2–3 tons, it is expected to deliver as many as eight MIRVed warheads, each of 125–150 KT yield and accuracy of 1 km at extreme range (vs. 25 m for the MX missile, for example). The first stage is to be built with maraging steel and the latter two stages are all-composite. Kalam, as science adviser to the defense minister, secured an initial outlay of $800 million (Rs 3200 crore) for the ICBM project. DRDL, followed up with an ICBM-specific plan costing $2.5 billion (Rs 10,000 crore) over 10 years, which was presented to the Vajpayee government. It consisted of 16–18 ICBMs plus full site preparation (silos).

During his short tenure in the defense ministry, Jaswant Singh also agreed to an autonomous program, separated from DRDO, dedicated exclusively to long-range missiles. What was originally mooted in a 1999 DRDL paper was an independent "strategic weapons directorate" responsible for designing, developing, and manufacturing long-range long-endurance weapons systems for the "strategic security" of the country. The idea was to combine the nuclear weapons unit in BARC, the nuclear-powered submarine ("Advanced Technology Vehicle") project, and the missile design and development complex, including 12 of the 54 DRDO laboratories, and testing and production facilities. Despite Prime Minister Vajpayee and Defense Minister Jaswant Singh's backing this plan, bureaucratic politics resulted instead in the formation in 2002 of a separate organization —the Advanced Systems Laboratory (ASL) in Hyderabad but within the DRDO to produce the Agni MRBMs and IRBMs and the ICBM. As part of the long-range missile program, a plant to produce solid fuel for missiles with the right burn rate and specific impulse has been established in Jagdalpur in Jarkhand province. A distinct long-range missile program was desired by the Agni missile design and development teams because of their unwillingness to be tainted by association with the DRDO's Integrated Guided Missile Program whose consistent failure in producing battlefield and tactical missiles is proving to be a serious embarrassment to DRDO, Defense Ministry, and the government.[100] Soon after the formation of ASL, at a high-level meeting called by National Security Adviser Brajesh Mishra and attended by the three military chiefs of staff, $1250 million (Rs 5000 crore) was sanctioned to develop and deploy Agni-I and Agni-II—both mounted on multiunit Tetra truck TEL, to prepare their respective launch sites, and to speed up the 3000 km Agni-III IRBM. The extended range 5000 km Agni-IV was authorized by the government in 2006. All the long-range Agni missiles have flex nozzles on their main rocket engines and a bank of eight vernier motors—two each to control the pitch, roll, and yaw—in the nose cone firing compressed oxygen during the terminal phase of their descent for nose down final target orientation. It is a design innovation the Indian missile designers are particularly proud of, as it enables both precision targeting, with accuracy claims of 500–600 m at maximum range, and compensates for any kinks in the composition and burn characteristics of the indigenously made solid fuel. In addition, all the Agni missiles can execute "porpoise" maneuvers in the terminal phase by opening and closing their flaps, to evade ballistic missile defenses.

Like BARC in relation to nuclear weapons where, as A. N. Prasad recalls, "the government set the Department of Atomic Energy no tasks, oversaw no military developments"[101] and left it to the scientists to decide on weapons quality and characteristics, a core group within ASL in weekly brainstorming sessions conceptualized the whole series of missiles—their mission, range, special parameters, and, most significantly, the payload attributes, as prelude to the design and development stage. Thus, Agni-I has been optimized by weight and size, for 20–30 KT warhead, Agni-II for 90–150 KT warhead, and the Agni-III for as much as 300 KT warhead. Agni-III—with diameter of 2 m is, moreover, configured to carry three MIRVed warheads with total deliverable destructive tonnage of nearly one megaton, and the ICBM payload can be as many as eight MIRVed thermonuclear warheads and decoy warheads. The MIRVing technology, DRDO officials claim, has been developed independently of ISRO's proven satellite package orbit insertion technology. MIRVs represent a sharper more demanding technology, which cannot tolerate deviation in the "velocity of injection" of more than 0.1 m per second compared to the permissible 5–8 m per second for satellites that will still keep them within the acceptable orbit zone. Other than a small but significant part of the total MIRV system, the technology has been ready for actual testing since 2005. It has not been sent aloft on a missile only because of organizational inertia, and the present dispensation at ASL sticking with the monolith warhead as a safe option needing no further proof of its efficacy. Agni-I and Agni-II, moreover, are also MIRV-able. Released at one second intervals, during which time the missile travels between 4–5.5 km, the IRBM's elliptical target area for three planned MIRVed warheads has been calculated to be 50 km by 150 km. The nose cone is made of carbon-carbon composites able to withstand very high temperatures when reentering the atmosphere at 8 km per second. The first and the second stages, molded from "eroding" polymeric composites, enables the missile to shed weight as it progresses to target. The 5000 km Agni-IV is designed to carry a monolithic 1 MT or as many as eight decoy and 100 KT thermonuclear warheads, as is the ICBM. The design and development processes of the ICBM proceeded during the Vajpayee years at a slower pace than originally planned in order not to give offense to the United States and China.[102]

With the advent of the Congress Party government, however, this project virtually ground to a halt before official hints of its revival surfaced in 2007. After a failed first test-firing of the 3500 km Agni-III in May 2006 because of a defective heat shield, the DRDO Chief M. Natarajan in the wake of the successful test flight of the missile the second time around, in April 2007 announced that the follow-on 5000 km, 1.5 ton payload-carrying Agni-IV would be quickly achieved by "miniaturizing systems of Agni-II" and squeezing a third stage into the 16 m-long missile. He also indicated that an ICBM was well within India's ability to produce and only awaited a government decision.[103] ASL scientists believe an ICBM can become operational within six years of a government decision. Four seaborne nuclear missiles are under development: The 350 km Prithvi carried on warships is in its final stages of testing before induction. The 650–700 km K-15 Sagarika submarine-launched ballistic missile (SLBM), to be embarked on the locally built SSBN, was test-fired several times from a pontoon moored 50 m underwater off the coast in the Bay of Bengal. It had a full system test launch in February 2008. The missile reportedly came out of the canister, broke water, and the rocket engines fired, but thereafter certain things went wrong and will need to be corrected.[104] The most difficult leg of the strategic triad—the seaborne missile, is almost ready for use.[105] The sea-launched missile has been a laggard, in the main, because of the inordinate delays in the SSBN program. Planned as part of the SSBN package, it ended up being pushed back, repeatedly deprioritized. It was only in the late 1990s that design and development of the K-15 began in earnest, but the really potent 6000 km SLBM is some years away from fruition, especially because many of the most critical technologies on the 700 km missile have still to be proven.[106] With this India's missile program "guided by a clear strategic vision" has "assumed a self-sustaining character".[107] A longer-range 5000–6000 km SLBM is the follow-on to the K-15, able to reach any Chinese target from a Bay of Bengal firing point. The navy expects the latter missile, designed, like the Agni-IV, to carry eight MIRVs to be available by 2012–2015. It will enable each of the Indian SSBNs with 12 vertical launch tubes to fire as many as 96 warheads.[108] The SLBMs are being developed by a separate team in a parallel program to the Agni long-range land-based missiles at the Advanced Systems Laboratory, Hyderabad. By its very nature, the K-15 program is a test-bed for many new missile technologies and design features making these SLBMs more sophisticated than the land-based Agni missiles. If the competitive relationship between these two programs is replaced by cooperation, the more innovative SLBM features could be transferred to the Agni missiles and the quality of Indian missiles generally improved.[109] However, delays in implementing designs into production will persist. This will be so, said V. K. Saraswat, director of air defense systems, DRDO, because the U.S.-led technology-denial regimes necessitate the development locally of each and every technology and the designing and fabricating of each component needed in every missile system.[110] India also has the 300 km Brahmos supersonic cruise missile (SCM), produced with Russian collaboration, and can deliver a conventional warhead. A 20 KT fission warhead is being specifically designed for it by BARC and optimized for the Russian Amur-class type of diesel submarines the Indian Navy expects to acquire.[111] This SCM is also to equip the six Scorpene diesel submarines acquired from France, the first of which will join the navy in 2012[112] as well as the navy's fleet of missile-destroyers.

Until 2002–2003, the high firewalls between the nuclear weapons program and ASL prevented the optimization of nuclear missile designs. Now there is very close cooperation and coordination. Thus, for example, S. K. Sikka, as head of the thermonuclear weapons project, was asked to change the size parameters of a weapon for a certain Agni missile by a mere 5 cm to exactly fit the missile configuration—because changing the missile size even minimally would require massive redesign and development work resulting in a delay of 3–4 years. After some quick calculations, Sikka readily agreed to change the dimensions of the weapon in question. This level of cooperation and coordination is a great improvement on what existed when R. Chidambaram headed AEC. Apprehensive about secrets leaking out, Chidambaram refused to part with any information about the nuclear weapons and provided only limited scaling data which left the missile design teams "no wiser" and required them, as a senior rocket engineer put it, to "take what DAE said on faith, design [missiles] on that basis, and hope for the best." The consequence is that none of the missiles has been tested with its nuclear warhead in the nose cone, though there have been tests with dummy warheads. According to former Pakistani army chief, General Jehangir Karamat, India and Pakistan have both used conventional warheads on missiles for "training and integration purposes" and to test "combat readiness and assignment to designated operators."[113] The Indian missiles are also, it is said, insufficiently "ruggedized." Unlike in Russian missile systems, say, where ruggedization means tolerating a bigger diameter than exactly specified, thereby increasing a missile's capacity to carry a heavier payload, in Agni missiles that margin of tolerance is less.

One of the vexed issues ASL has had to resolve pertains to the number of test-firings needed before a missile is deemed safe and reliable enough for entry into service. It concerns the political sensitivities of the Indian government determined to minimize regional and international friction and to economize on cost. Each test launch has a price tag of Rs 20–30 crore and involves the use of satellites, downrange telemetry systems, Indian Navy ships, etc. Ideally, Indian rocket engineers would like to carry out a large number of tests and point to the American MX ICBM, which was flight tested some 80 times. The Russians are understood to test-fire a missile type 10–20 times, which, from the Indian point of view, is still considered too many and too expensive. In 2002 a panel chaired by a former chairman of the ISRO, R. Kasturirangan, concluded on the basis of statistical analysis of failures of major systems, subsystems, and components and their performance in static tests that two to three consecutive successful test-firings would meet the standards of reliability and affordability.[114] The three-test standard, for instance, mandates that Agni-II be tested at 700–950 km, 1300–1500 km, and 1800–2000 km, and Agni-III at 1000–1200 km, 1800–2200 km, and 2800–000 km (using the rule of thumb that a missile can hit targets from one-third its range to extreme range) in order to generate precise parametric flight data to build up the confidence of the missileers and the military end-users.

THE DOCTRINAL THRUST

In the interregnum between the 1974 and the 1998 tests, while there was some high-quality analysis justifying a nuclear armed stance for India, there was little substantive, leave alone sophisticated, thinking done on what the country's nuclear strategy should be and why. This was because successive governments in Delhi owned up to no nuclear weapons or any related program, nor did they express any interest or even desire to secure the nuclear-weapon-state status for the country. The supposedly self-explanatory concept of "minimum deterrence," because it seemed moderate, limited, and reasonable, served as a device to, at once, legitimize an immanent nuclear arsenal,[115] deflect inconvenient questions, and obviate more serious thinking on the subject. Vajpayee claimed that this concept reflected the urge for self-defense, which his deputy prime minister, L. K. Advani, explained amounted to "Deterrence [as] defense" and added that nuclear weapons prevent "diplomatic coercion . . . [something] we would not like to be subjected to."[116] This only embroidered the notion of "minimum deterrence" that Homi J. Bhabha, the visionary founder of the Indian nuclear program, had talked about. Brajesh Mishra, national security adviser to the prime minister, announced that the Indian nuclear weapons "are not country-specific but . . .

aimed at providing us the autonomy of strategic choices in the best interest of our country, without fear or coercion in a nuclearized environment."[117] Since then the husk around the concept had grown even as the kernel within had withered. In the intervening years, when strategic theory and principles were reduced to easily remembered maxims, slogan substituted for analysis, as the pioneer nuclear theorist, Bernard Brodie, had warned in the late 1940s, would happen in such circumstances.[118] In any event, with India's long-time attachment to the slogan of "minimum deterrence" in mind, the Western assumption until the 1998 tests that in case India acquired nuclear weapons, it would be content to remain a "small nuclear power," was understandable.[119] All such formulations of "minimal deterrence" became obsolete, however, with the 1998 tests. This was realized by some American analysts, who wondered if the official "credible minimum deterrence" (CMD) doctrine denoted some or all of the following things: sufficiency of a small arsenal, nuclear weapons held in low-readiness state and at low levels of alert, renunciation of war-fighting, and counter-value targeting. They also concluded that the CMD concept was a departure from and "more demanding" than the minimal deterrence notion it was assumed had been animating Indian nuclear policy until then.[120] It was the informed view of other Western analysts, seemingly confident of their knowledge of Indian strategic programs, that the "de-alerted, de-mated" nuclear posture and, hence, the Indian preference for a "force in being," was for keeps rather than just the initial phase in a "staged strategic buildup."[121]

Also pushed into oblivion by the 1998 tests was the then atomic energy chief R. Chidambaram's belief that computer simulation capability made physical testing redundant. The underground explosions to verify and validate tritium-boosted and staged thermonuclear weapon designs as also low-yield weapon designs using reactor-grade plutonium, and the steady accretion in the capability to design and manufacture nuclear weapons and missiles (analyzed in previous sections) indicate that both BARC and ASL have marched to the drum of their own expansive agendas, which were far more ambitious in their implications than anything the political leaders, the government, and government-connected strategic thinkers had seriously contemplated, with the threshold for minimal deterrence having been passed long ago. For example, Ashley Tellis' doubts about India's being able to reprocess 55–60 kg of plutonium a year, which reprocessing capacity he regards as necessary for it to realize the 400 weapons or warheads-strong strategic force by 2030,[122] was a benchmark that, according to Iyengar, has already been reached.[123] It is not surprising then that as early as 2004 Indian defense ministry officials talked of plans for a nuclear force with 300–400 weapons.[124] The government's conceptualization of "credible minimum deterrence" has gradually been brought into sync with the country's burgeoning nuclear weapons and missile capabilities.

Having declared the country a nuclear-weapon state in 1998, the Indian government felt compelled to make its nuclear status credible. It meant finally getting serious about nuclear weapons, dealing in specifics, allocating budgetary resources, and forming new organizations for the purposes of planning, controlling nuclear assets, detailing strategy, implementing programs, and for oversight.[125] The armed services and DRDO too began thinking strategically. With the nuclear weapons–related activity conjoined to short-term, medium-term, and long-term planning being done by a number of agencies, the nuclear policy is beginning to put on flesh and the strategic programs have acquired direction. Drafting a doctrine was the first step. The Indian government formally authorized the newly founded National Security Advisory Board (NSAB) to produce a nuclear doctrine. It just so happened that the military and DRDO, on their own initiative, had embarked on their separate doctrine-writing ventures, at the same time. By the time the NSAB draft was submitted in 1999, the government also had in hand the military's doctrine paper produced by the joint services Defense Planning Staff—the precursor organization to the Integrated Defense Staff—and the doctrinal scheme outlined by Dr. Abdul Kalam, heading DRDO.[126] The NSAB doctrine provided the *raison d'etre* for Indian nuclear weapons, the basic guidelines for force structuring, and the framework for a policy and strategy of "credible minimum deterrence." It encompassed the two key characteristics of nuclear policy that Prime Minister Vajpayee had already announced in Parliament on May 28, 1998, namely, "minimum deterrence" and the "No First Use" (NFU) principle, which were generally considered as highlighting India's attributes as a "responsible" nuclear-weapon state. In order to be seen as promoting "transparency" and responsible behavior, the government over the years kept the weapons thrust of the nuclear program under cover, announced a moratorium on testing, and released the NSAB draft doctrine for public scrutiny. It also played down the country's steadily growing strategic nuclear and missile capabilities and the readiness aspects of the nuclear forces. It hid the costs of obtaining nuclear armaments, delivery systems, and the support infrastructure, like command and control, in the budgetary allocations of the Department of Atomic Energy and DRDO.[127] This was done, said Jaswant Singh, because of the "global climate" and "management of policy." "One has to balance," he said, "the view [that some level of opacity will have to be maintained] by the reality of managing the entire global assault with sanctions and so on" by reinforcing the country's image as a "responsible" nuclear player.[128] Whatever the compulsions of the government, the NSAB doctrine drafters were focused on elasticizing the minimum deterrence concept. The idea of "credible minimum deterrence" around which the doctrine crystallized with its emphasis on the credibility of the deterrent, has proved useful. It afforded doctrinal sanction and rhetorical cover of minimum deterrence for bulking up and qualitatively upgrading the nuclear forces at any time. Particularly relevant in this regard are Sections 3 and 4 of the draft doctrine. Section 3 calls for nuclear forces to be "effective, enduring, diverse, flexible, and responsive" and moots the strategic "triad" of bombers and "mobile land-based missiles and sea-based assets." Section 4 requires the deterrent to be credible, effective and survivable especially against "surprise attacks" and "a first strike" and to be able to "endure repetitive attrition attempts" and still retain "adequate retaliatory capabilities for a punishing strike, which would be unacceptable to the aggressor."[129] It is difficult to interpret these provisions—pertaining to credibility and survivability, the crucial variables—in the doctrine, however they are read, as other than sanctioning sizable and progressively more modern nuclear forces.[130] As retired air force chief, Air Chief Marshal S. Krishnaswamy correctly noted: "The credibility improves day by day, and this improvement is asymptotic, you don't know when you'll reach the required level of credibility."[131] Indeed, the NSAB document meets Henry Kissinger's criterion of a good strategic doctrine, namely, that it provide "for the widest range of challenges and to the extent that the marginal case is in fact, an unusual situation."[132] The draft doctrine was made public by the Vajpayee government despite opposition from the NSAB members and the armed services, who protested that this would result in Western pressure on the government to scrap some of the more expansive clauses in it and to restrict the size and quality of the proposed "credible minimum deterrent."[133] This, in effect, is what happened.[134] The military's version ordered by General Ved Malik, chief of army staff and chairman, chiefs of staff committee, was drawn up from the point of view operationalizing the deterrent in a nuclear contingency. "We were concerned," he stated, "with how to make a weapon in its de-mated state operational, with the procedures and the time-frame within which the cores would be inserted into the weapon, etc."[135] The DRDO variant was closer to the literal notion of minimum deterrence and included the assembly time of weapons systems, the erection time of missiles, and so on, that strictly speaking, do not belong in the doctrine.[136]

The nuclear doctrine formally adopted by the Indian government on January 3, 2004 took the NSAB document *in toto* and incorporated some practical ideas gleaned from the military's version and the DRDO document.[137] To bring it on par with Western policy, the Vajpayee government also attached to it the provision for nuclear retaliation in response to attack by chemical and biological weapons. This addition to the nuclear doctrine, according to Satish Chandra, deputy national security adviser, was simply to keep that option open and to make it known to those contemplating the use of chemical weapons (CW) and biological weapons (BW) against Indian targets, that the retaliatory attack could be nuclear. In addition, the government formalized an elaborate nuclear decision-making apparatus revolving around the National Security Council, as well as a nuclear command and control system and the National Command Authority. New institutions were established, including the Strategic Forces Command (SFC)—to control, deploy, and use nuclear weapons, to structure strategic nuclear forces, and to plan for nuclear operations and nuclear contingencies —and the Strategic Policy Group (SPG) in BARC to liaise with the government and the military and to contribute to the overall policy and plans. Deliberately kept out of the nuclear decision loop until a few years ago, the Indian military has sidestepped into it with a retired three-star rank officer appointed in the prime minister's office—the nuclear decision-making core—and placed in charge of the Special Projects Group dealing with the nuclear policy and posture. This officer, among other things, coordinates with the SFC, SPG, and Armed Services headquarters.

Most importantly, the organizing theme of nuclear deterrence was overhauled. Prior to 1998, nuclear security was dealt with by political leaders vaguely promising massive destruction and by the strategic community repeating the officially sanctioned phrase "minimum deterrence" as if that explained everything. The inexactness of this communication mirrored the state of the thinking, with the concept being perceived differently by influential persons. To the late Dr. Raja Ramanna, representing the view of the nuclear establishment of the 1970s, it meant a number of nuclear weapons in low two digits controlled by the scientists with the military kept as far away from the arsenal as possible. To the former chief of the army staff, the late General K. Sundarji, who as commander of the College of Combat in the 1980s authorized the first set of "Combat Papers" dealing with a nuclearized security environment, it amounted to an inventory of as few as 45 weapons to take care of any and all strategic threats.[138] To K. Subrahmanyam, the civil servant who ran the government-funded Institute for Defense Studies and Analyses (IDSA) for almost two decades and, after the 1974 test, popularized "minimum deterrence," it translated into a somewhat larger inventory (60 weapons) capable of deterring "nuclear blackmail" defined as "the threat of use." Except Subrahmanyam, intellectually the most fertile, presented his retaliation only notion as a more sedate and responsible alternative to the Cold War "theology" of nuclear war-fighting that emphasized huge stockpiles of ready-to-use weapons. More questionably, he maintained that (1) "large thermonuclear weapons" being "essentially war-fighting weapons," India could do without them, and (2) the doctrine of nuclear deterrence would "decay over the next couple of decades for sheer lack of utility of the nuclear arsenal"; in that event, that India can save money and stay secure with a small strategic force.[139] The Indian nuclear doctrine and the present force structuring plans go much beyond the small, finite, deterrent notions entertained by those like Ramanna, Sundarji, and Subrahmanyam and are closer to the criteria for a deterrent force espoused by Bernard Brodie, to wit, that a large force may be required "to guarantee even a modest retaliation," that deterrence is "a relative thing" varying with the "degree of motivation which the enemy feels for our destruction," that "if deterrence fails we shall want enough forces to fight a total war effectively," and that "our retaliatory force must also be capable of striking first [in which case] its attack had better be, as nearly as possible, overwhelming to the enemy's retaliatory force." Brodie further advised that because the absolute effectiveness of retaliatory response is essential, it "allows for no breakdowns ever" and nuclear forces will have to be "maintained at a high pitch of efficiency and readiness [which should be] constantly improved."[140]

Another aspect of the deterrent that Subrahmanyam underlined, namely, that Indian retaliation is not time critical, that it could be ordered as late as a couple of days after receiving a nuclear strike, has also been bypassed by the readiness schemes implemented by the Strategic Forces Command designed in part to obviate the possibility of what is perceived by the military as weak-willed political leadership succumbing to external pressure and calling off retaliatory strikes altogether. In view of the government's operationally restraining the military, inclusive of instructions not to cross the "line of control" in the 1999 Kargil War with Pakistan, a former army chief doubted that "in a nuclear war [the Indian government] would be able to resist international pressure [to stop an Indian counter-strike]. I have my very serious doubts," he said, "that we would really be allowed to respond [with nuclear weapons]."[141] Subrahmanyam's conceiving of a time delay for nuclear retaliation led to his long-time deputy at IDSA, Jasjit Singh, to conceive of "recessed deterrence" premised on disaggregated nuclear weapons that could be assembled for launch well after the country had absorbed a nuclear strike.[142] This concept found some traction at a time when India had not formally weaponized. Ramanna, Subrahmanyam, and Jasjit Singh also shared the view that more testing was unnecessary because even an untested nuclear device, they believed, is capable of existential deterrence—a view an otherwise nuclear minimalist General Sundarji contested.

Post-1998, while Vajpayee's moderate instincts defined the limits of his government's "minimum deterrence" policy, many of his cabinet colleagues understood that the testing of the thermonuclear weapon and the immanence of long-range missiles had irrevocably changed the shape of strategic policy. They understood, for example, that "minimum" was not minimal, and nuclear deterrence could not be inherently confined to the subcontinent. Even the shadow foreign minister in the opposition Congress Party, Natwar Singh, realized the situation had changed radically. "Sticking to an anti-nuclear stand," he said, "becomes counter-productive once the objective reality has changed."[143] The concept of "credible minimum deterrence" married the old idea of "minimum deterrence," reflecting moderation and mirroring policy continuity, with "credible," promising gain from future growth in the nuclear forces. "Credibility," elaborated Jaswant Singh, "has to be both to the satisfaction of the country that is evolving the policy, constructing it, and the direction in which it is aimed . . . and it is not simply military. You have a huge arsenal but all of it can be so tied in a system of lock and key, that people really mock at it rather than fear it." This last is an argument against a de-alerted, de-mated Indian deterrent. Deputy National Security Adviser Satish Chandra during those years expounded on the "credible" and "minimum" aspects of the nuclear policy some more. "The view was taken by the government," Chandra said, "that though we are against an arms race and don't want to expand our weapons systems infinitely, we want to have weapons that are sufficiently varied, and we need to have an underwater [launch] capability." The reigning sentiment according to him was "that if we must have a deterrent it bloody well be credible." He added that "the point was also taken [by the government] that the deterrent was to be not 'minimum credible' but 'credible minimum' with emphasis on credibility."[144]

The United States wanted the size and the other attributes of the "credible minimum deterrent" spelled out. The U.S. Deputy Secretary Strobe Talbott, in the strategic dialog, repeatedly pressured his Indian opposite number, Jaswant Singh, to define the Indian requirements in terms of force size, sought to pin him down on the numbers. This, according to Jaswant Singh, "had, unfortunately, become central to the determination of both credibility of deterrence and the definition of minimum." It was an issue that remained unresolved. As Jaswant Singh says, "There's no fixity to minimum, there cannot be, because it is a variable, in technological terms, in terms of physical numbers, it is a variable in terms of the launch capacity." He cautioned, however, that the "elasticity" in the CMD concept, while "not a license for unbridled proliferation in Cold War terms, [had] sufficient leeway within [its] confines" to "enable the country to formulate a policy to meet the challenges of the times" and to protect India's strategic interests, which he equated with its "civilizational reach." This will mean, he conceded, the country's eventually acquiring a "commensurately large arsenal."[145] Vajpayee's National Security Adviser, Brajesh Mishra, reinforced the point made by Jaswant Singh. "The credible minimum deterrence concept is a very flexible concept," says Mishra. "It has been misunderstood with more emphasis on the world 'minimum' than on 'credible'. He went on to explain: "We had a certain threat scenario then and decided what we needed generally—Pakistan, China, and we don't want the USS Enterprise coming again. But we could not have decided then what it is going to be like 10 years, 15 years, 20 years from now. And so the governments will keep on either increasing or decreasing [the force size and quality] depending upon what is happening around us and in the world generally." He added: "We gave instructions about a certain number of weapons, a certain mix [of nuclear and thermonuclear weapons], as we saw it then. Timeframe-wise, the way it works is that today I see the situation this way. Tomorrow, if certain events take place, the force size, quality and mix can change. These changes can happen any time. It is left to the government of the day to decide what to do and how to define credible minimum deterrence."[146]

The expansive strategic policy outlines of the BJP government generated plans for what a former commander-in-chief (CINC) of the Strategic Forces Command, described as a "staged strategic build-up" of the nuclear forces, in the first instance, to the 200 weapons and warheads level.[147] This figure, Air Marshal Ajit Bhavnani, who retired as the vice chief of the air staff after pulling a stint as CINC, SFC, said, "is not static, the deterrent has to keep increasing in size, because for any force-sizing you have to consider what the enemy has and what you have. So even though we may say we don't have a first use policy, and have very good dispersion and survivability, we will need to build up our strategic forces in an evolutionary manner. Thus, the number of missiles will keep increasing, the number of bases will keep increasing."[148] It suggests that what is in the cards is development of the deterrent to whatever level may be required in the future by changes in the threat scenarios, with the aim eventually of achieving near or at least notional parity with China as the basis for "equitable security." It is a prerequisite, as the communist bloc saw it in the Cold War, for "peaceful coexistence between states with different social systems."[149] Keeping the country's nuclear and thermonuclear forces modern and technologically upgraded is, in any case, a must for deterrence to be credible and will mandate bigger financial outlays. "As deterrence is over the moment a nuclear weapon is used," Air Chief Marshal Krishnaswamy cautioned, "so we'll have to spend a whole lot of money and we'll have to keep improving the [weapons and missile] technologies, because today's model [of weapon and delivery system] has got to be changed, and we will be operating in an environment in which we may not be able to test, making it that much more difficult, and trying to remain credible is going to be that much harder requiring that much more money, research and people."[150] Many apprehend, however, that the reactive nature and defensive mind-set of the Indian political leadership could still become a factor in how force-structuring plans ultimately pan out. The issue will be, said Admiral Prakash, one of "not what we can do to [the enemies], but what they can do to us. Then the calculation will be, if the enemy has 50 warheads, say, he will take out 40 targets in India. For the Indian force to be credible, our deterrent must exceed the number of targets he can physically knock out . . . , exceed the number of targets he can neutralize."[151]

In contemplating credible minimum deterrence, the highest echelons of the military have serious doubts whether in a nuclear crisis political leaders will display the will to use nuclear weapons, which, as far as they are concerned, is central to the credibility of the national nuclear deterrent. This concept, argued, General Malik, has "both a physical and psychological content . . . One is the strategic wherewithal and its state of readiness to do what is intended for them to do. The other is the psychological side—the will of the nation reflected in the will of the government . . . I am afraid the political will is the problem." It is a worry echoed by Air Chief Marshal S. Krishnaswamy. In case of deterrence breakdown, "the will to use" nuclear weapons will come to the forefront. "If that political will is not there or it is weak, will it not," he wondered, "affect the capability and the understanding and, down the line, the will to put down a chunk of money, resources and so on to [build up the deterrent]?"[152]

If the Indian nuclear deterrent is not likely to be low-quality or small-sized, support for the NFU too may be mainly rhetorical and for an abstract principle, rather than something that in reality will be permitted to crimp India's options. Political leaders shy away from talking about the practicability of NFU. Military men voice what they consider its shortcomings. "NFU may be sensible policy," said Air Marshal (Ret.) Vinod Patney, member of the National Security Advisory Board who, while in service, was regarded as an offensive-minded air force commander. "But even a sensible policy cannot be allowed to become a millstone around our neck. In case the other side is not being sensible . . . In that case, if our hands are twisted to an extent that we have no other option, then we should give the NFU the go-by."[153] According to Admiral Prakash, NFU is "incompatible" with the Indian government's position that nuclear weapons are political instruments, and not meant for war-fighting. "As political instruments, the best use of our nuclear weaponry would be to persuade, compel, or coerce a recalcitrant adversary, *without having to use force,* to either comply with our wishes, or desist from pursuing a particular course of action inimical to our interests," he explained. "However, in order to obtain such compliance, *the threat of use of nuclear weapons, no matter how subtle, subliminal, or understated, has to be held out.* By forswearing 'first use', we obviously cannot hold out such a threat. Therefore, we are denying ourselves the advantage of using nuclear weapons as political instruments and relegating them exclusively to the 'second strike' role of uncertain efficacy. The self-imposed condition of NFU thus obviously undermines our deterrence, for some illusory moral advantage of very dubious value." Prakash also wondered "what would be the NFU policy worth, if we were faced with incontrovertible evidence that an adversary was on the verge of launching a decapitating-disarming nuclear first strike against India?"[154] A chief of the Army Staff, who retired not too long ago, speaking in background, was of the view that "the potential to preempt" should be introduced into the NFU concept. He suggested that the government change the definition to say "that NFU is fine as long as India is convinced that the other side is not going to use a nuclear weapon. The moment we have any evidence or apprehensions or such appreciation that there is even the remotest possibility [of a first strike by an adversary], it would take all necessary action in its national interest" including preemptive strike. He also pointed out that the NFU policy imposed additional costs in terms of dispersion and "pre-location of weapons."[155] It appears the Strategic Forces Command has succeeded in convincing the political leadership to think along these lines. "Time and again it is emphasized for us that we have a no first use policy and we would stick by it," said Air Marshal Bhavnani. "But in a nuclear situation, if one has to change the scenario I guess we have the capability to do that, the options are there, the contingencies are there." Regarding these contingencies, he said, "If we know that the enemy is going to launch and all the preparations are being made, when we are clear in our minds that we have the inputs, the intelligence that they are going to launch at any moment, then . . . we feel it is better that the NFU need not be followed, that we should strike before we get struck." Bhavnani revealed that the "Strategic Forces Command have wargamed this contingency numerous times. In the gaming," he said, "we always assumed we are in NFU situations . . . But...if the war situation is briefed to be in a position where the enemy is going to launch very soon, and we know that if we don't take action, we'll be destroyed, then we'll act."[156]

Brajesh Mishra, national security adviser to Prime Minister Vajpayee, was against imposing any kind of "strategic restraint" on the Indian nuclear forces and negatived the giving of assurances that Talbott was seeking in his dialog with Jaswant Singh. Quite apart from wanting to cap its nuclear force size and quality, Talbot was keen that India sign the Comprehensive Test Ban Treaty (CTBT), agree to a moratorium on fissile material production, and refrain from deploying its nuclear weapons. "Mr. Jaswant Singh was very clearly aware of the thinking and of the view of the prime minister and the government," said Mishra, "that we would not go for the test moratorium being converted to CTBT or for a moratorium on fissile material production. [And as regards deployment] that this is something for us to decide about what to do and how to do it . . . We said we were not going to agree to any restraint on the development of missiles and, in fact, to any nuclear restraint other than what is in our interests." As far as Mishra was concerned, in South Asia if any restraint was needed Pakistan would have to supply it as India had done its bit with its No First Use declaration.[157] Lacking any maneuvering room, his main aim in his discussions with Talbott, recalls Jaswant Singh, was "to keep talking in generalities, string the Americans along" and with this purpose in mind offered the American a conciliatory "National Statement" from the Indian Parliament. "There's no such thing as a national statement that was ever produced [but] it bought us time." However, such ruses to keep the United States interested and engaged required making small concessions, such as adiverting for a time the missile effort from the long-range Agni-IIIs and Agni-IVs into producing the 700–900 km Agni-I missile that, from a military standpoint, was unnecessary. The dialog led eventually to the Next Steps in Strategic Partnership (NSSP) and paved the way for the far-reaching "Defense Framework Agreement" that the successor Manmohan Singh regime signed with the United States on June 28, 2005, and the Joint Statement presaging the deal for "civil nuclear cooperation" that it agreed to less than a month later.[158]

By the time the coalition government led by the Congress Party under Prime Minister Manmohan Singh assumed power in May 2004, the strategic programs, according to Natwar Singh, the Minister for External Affairs in the new dispensation until his resignation from the post in 2006, had acquired "momentum." "You have a nuclear program, so you have to keep it up," he explained. He recalls his cabinet colleague, Pranab Mukherji, who was defense minister until he replaced Natwar Singh in the Foreign Office, likened the growing nuclear arsenal to paste squeezed out of a tube that could not be pushed back in, and the country had to make the best of it.[159] All these signs indicate that the Bharatiya Janata Party government's credible minimum deterrence policy has been supported by the successor Congress Party regime but, perhaps, more passively and with less conviction.[160]

OPERATIONALIZATION OF THE DETERRENT

Until 2001 or so, there was no great urgency in building up the deterrent. By that time, however, international attention on the smallness of the extant Indian arsenal[161] prompted the government to divert many of the dual-purpose CANDU/INDU pressurized heavy-water reactors into the low burn-up mode to produce weapons-grade plutonium, resulting in the plummeting of power in the grid from these plants. This is the path that has been continued in order to stock up on fissile material, so that an early Fissile Material Cutoff Treaty does not catch the country short. Since then, the stock of weapon-usable plutonium has increased and it is expected that by 2010–2012 there will be fissile material enough for some 200-plus weapons.[162] The capability to design, develop, and bring on-line nuclear weapons and missiles is fine, but the deterrence payoff in a situation where other states have ready or near-ready nuclear forces is meager unless the weapons and missiles are operationalized. The usability of a nuclear arsenal is dependent on its preparedness, and the extent and quality of the support structures, like a properly delineated National Command Authority, secure and redundant command and control links, ready launch sites, and workable measures to increase survivability or, conversely, reduce vulnerability in relation to weapons storage, security, and mobility. "Nuclear threat (and hence deterrence)," avers a former Indian Air Force (IAF) chief, Air Chief Marshal Anil Tipnis, "cannot be created through a potential; weapons have to be up and standing, particularly so if the other side has that position. Between adversaries there cannot be differential in readiness."[163] This is a sentiment uniformly shared by the senior echelons of the Indian military. It is widely felt that for an operationally acceptable level of nuclear force readiness, the de-mated posture is a liability. It was only after the nuclear-laced 1999 War and the 2002 crisis that the military's uneasiness with a, perhaps, "politically correct" but operationally hazardous posture began to be appreciated by the government. Indeed, CINCs of various military commands believed that such a posture is a reflection of the Indian government's tendency to give way under the slightest pressure from powerful countries, such as the United States. After 2002, prodded by the military, the government agreed to a modified nuclear de-mated posture. It has not satisfied the armed forces, which still is concerned that unless nuclear retaliation is instantaneous, deterrence will fail. "I have very serious doubts that because of international pressure we would be able to respond [to a nuclear strike]. But if we are going to respond, how much time will it take? The response would have to be within minutes, the worst can be half an hour. The [inability to have this short reaction time] is a problem," said an ex-chief of the Army Staff.[164]

One of the things pushing the Indian military into demanding higher readiness and, generally, a more responsive nuclear infrastructure is the fact that the Indian deterrent seems to be a step behind Pakistan, especially with regard to the integration of nuclear weapons in the conventional military system. This is because the Pakistani system of the army as the sole custodian of the processes of nuclear weapons production and of the extant nuclear arsenal, had a head start relative to its Indian counterpart where democratic functioning and multiple actors involved in implementing the nuclear policy, has made for a zigzagging progress.

Unlike in India, the army is both in charge of Pakistan's nuclear military program and responsible for planning, actual use of nuclear weapons, and for downstream activities. Its "tight grip" has brought coherence among "the military planners, operators and scientific bodies" and allowed the military, according to Pakistani Army Major General Ausaf Ali, director (operations and plans),

Strategic Plans Division, General Headquarters, Rawalpindi, speaking at a March 2007 seminar held in Bahawalpur in Pakistan's southern Punjab region, to "train strategic forces with a great deal of secrecy and compartmentaliza-tion."[165] The creation of the Strategic Plans Division (SPD) within the Pakistani General Headquarters, Rawalpindi, as the secretariat for the National Command Authority, has centralized all planning, implementation, and day-to-day nuclear force maintenance functions (such as safety and security of weapons). The nuclear weapons systems may be in de-mated condition, but it is only the SPD that carries out the mating procedures, readies the system for launch, and fires the missile or orders an aerial nuclear bombing sortie—compared to many play-ers at each stage in the Indian arrangement, which last increases the chances of miscommunication and miscues. With only one organization there is, as this Pakistan SPD officer claimed, less likelihood of foul-ups and makes for more uniform thinking and more motivated strategic forces. It also results, he said, in better planning and continuity over time in strategic visioning, strategizing, decision-making, and in the establishing of a unitary work ethic and standard of performance. In addition, it ensures high levels of secrecy. SPD's 8000–10,000-man cadre, led by 50 officers chosen from the three armed services in Pakistan is, for instance, carefully selected after rigorous psychological testing. Once in, all members of the SPD cadre come under what Ausaf Ali called "cradle-to-grave oversight," which applies to all military, scientific, and engi-neering personnel involved in the nuclear program. These personnel, after they retire, are put on retainer and continue to be under surveillance. So tight is the security and the effort to minimize the chances of sensitive information being leaked, sneaked out, or otherwise passed on to foreign countries, every trip abroad by any SPD staffer, or even by scientists of the Pakistan Atomic Energy Commission to the International Atomic Energy Agency in Vienna, has to be cleared by the SPD and all meetings with foreigners have to have prior approval and are monitored. Such measures apparently come within the ambit of strict professionalism and the institutionalization of best practices, which Ausaf Ali said "enhances Pakistan's nuclear deterrence."[166] At the very least, the Pakistani nuclear setup eliminates uncertainty over what the strategy is and how deterrence will be practiced in any situation. To duplicate such a system in every detail in India is infeasible. The main aspects of comprehensive control of the entire nuclear decision chain dealing with issues ranging from weapons specifications and development to weapons use as per the Pakistani model, in Ausaf Ali's words, of "management of nuclear capability" is, in fact, sought to be replicated in the prime minister's office.[167] This conforms to the prime minister being clearly identified in the doctrine as the only person authorized to order nuclear weapon use.

The SFC was to have been established in 2001, but it was delayed by three years, according to a former CINC, SFC, because of the Vajpayee government's "fear of sending wrong signals of aggressive intent." In the first few months, the Command was one only in name—it had no office space, no staff, no support structures. And, because of its presumed role in nuclear war planning, there was friction with the Integrated Defense Staff (IDS) Headquarters that had, until then, been doing the job. The SFC soon obtained all the papers and documentation from IDS and got to work. On a priority basis, it drew up a strategic targeting list, identified appropriate sites for storing nuclear cores and weapons systems and the emplacement of the vectors, and worked on nuclear weapons use plans on the basis of three distinct scenarios concerning Pakistan, China, and the China-Pakistan nexus. To hew to the No First Use pledge and "to avoid escalation," SFC devised plans for conventional Indian strikes at the stage of "pre-attack or at-attack posture" by precision guided munitions fired from aircraft and artillery. There is confidence in SFC that satellite-based sensors will provide credible evidence of any nuclear strike preparations by regional adversaries. Fleshing out of such plans for dissuasion are the responsibility of the Armed Services Headquarters. SFC has also assigned nuclear weapons with different yields for different targets, but 100 KT thermonuclear weapon will be the basic armament in part because it has emerged as an international standard.[168] At least one former CINC, SFC, was of the view that low-yield tactical nuclear weapons were not needed as these would require their integration into the conventional military organizations, and command and control would become attenuated. And, given the two-key scheme for launch, any breakdown or destruction of communications links, in effect, would result in nonuse of these presumably forward-deployed weapons, or worse.[169] Others, however, such as retired Air Marshal Patney, disputed that nuclear weapons could be separated into tactical and strategic categories. He avers that "All nukes are strategic in nature" and adds that "the credibility of our deterrent will be much greater if we have low yield nuclear weapons. These will be required . . . if we do not wish the escalation to go up too high . . . When one talks of rationality, the credibility is that much better if we say we have a range of options from which we can choose. It is not flexible response or anything," he clarified, "but a standard operating procedure we have probably worked out about when we require what weapon to retaliate with."[170]

The cumbersome six-stage alert system that was originally instituted has been refined to four stages of readiness—fourth stage to the first stage of alert. In that order, the lowest (fourth) stage involves arming the weapon, the next higher stage dispersal of the armed weapons to avoid destruction by a counterforce first strike. The penultimate stage is the mating of the weapon to the delivery system/launcher, and the final stage has control over the ready-to-fire weapon passing completely over to the military user for triggering. After the 2002 mobilization crisis, the new wrinkle is that, in step with the launch of Cold Start operation (more on which in the last chapter)—conceived as an automatic conventional military riposte to a major conventional or subconventional provocation, nuclear forces too automatically step into the first stage of alert to avoid compromising the use of the weapon if the crisis escalates to that level. The nuclear scientists and DRDO engineers are involved up to the third stage of readiness. "Too many agencies in the firing loop could lead to dissonance. [In reducing the six stages of readiness,] the problem was between BARC and DRDO than between the two of them and the military. We only wanted," said General Malik, chief of the army staff in 1997–2000, "that when final orders are given that the military be in charge at that time."[171]

A former CINC, SFC, delineated three types of targeting schemes—counter-force, counter-value, and something "beyond counter-value" involving decapitating strikes on the adversary's apex decision-making body—call it "counter-value plus." It designated weapons with different yields for these targets—low and medium yield for counter-force or small counter-value targets and large-yield armaments for indiscriminate attack. This resembles the concept of "proportional dissuasion" postulated by Pierre Gallois.[172] It has many votaries in the Indian military. Air Marshal Patney talks of a nuclear force comprising "x number" of low-yield weapons (up to 20 KT), "y number" of medium-yield weapons (90–100 KT) and "z number" of high-yield weapons (of 250–300 KT plus) as ideal to practice "graduated deterrence."[173] Rear Admiral Sir Anthony Buzzard conceived this deterrence concept and said that it removes the possibility of an adversary misinterpreting the threat of "massive retaliation" as "bluff" and that it was "advantageous politically, militarily and economically."[174] The SFC started out by measuring deterrence vis-à-vis China in terms of the range of the Su-30 MKI fighter-bomber. Steady accretion in the quality of the nuclear forces since then with the induction of long-range Agni-II and Agni-III missiles is resulting in the force looking eastward. By 2009 sizable nuclear assets will be available for employment against China.

The land-based Prithvi, Agni-I, and Agni-II missiles, under the army's supervision, are directly controlled by the Strategic Forces Command. The naval and air force units, like aircraft squadrons and ships and submarines, are dual-tasked and will remain with the parent service right up to the time in a crisis when they are assigned specific strategic nuclear missions and come under command of SFC, and await the go signal from SFC before they can launch their nuclear ordnance. The decision to use nuclear weapons will in turn be communicated by the prime minister through the National Security Council to the chairman of the Chiefs of Staff Committee, who, in turn, will pass on the orders to CINC, SFC, and down the line. Aware of the requirement for a "decentralized command" in nuclear operations,[175] the system of subordinate commanders having the triggering authority has been elaborated and kicks in should the Indian leadership be eliminated in a surprise "bolt from the blue" attack. In such as situation the nuclear triggering authority routinely devolves to subordinate commanders in the context of the generalized approval to use nuclear weapons having already been secured.[176]

The Indian deterrent is increasingly acquiring a strategic outlook in which Pakistan as a credible threat features less and less. For starters, the military's dissatisfaction with the Prithvi SRBM has eventuated in the decision to phase it out, but slowly. The strategic nuclear order-of-battle will feature all-Agni missile forces. Agni missiles in all range classes, including the 700–900 km Agni-I MRBM will, moreover, be progressively equipped with the 100–300 KT thermonuclear warhead, with the 100 KT as basic fusion weapon. This decision was made because hydrogen warheads use less fissile material, are lighter in weight, and offer "more bang for the buck" than either fission or boosted-fission weapons. Once the 5,000 km Agni-IV and the high-priority 6,000 km SLBM to be carried by the Indian SSBN are procured, the nuclear triad against China will become truly functional.[177]

A little belatedly, perhaps, and behind Pakistan in this respect, the procedures and processes to handle nuclear weaponry and implement deterrence decisions are being formalized with the compilation of the "Red Book." This manual for nuclear war and contingencies is being finalized by the newly created Special Projects Group attached to the National Security Adviser's Office in the prime minister's secretariat. Headed by a deputy national security adviser, a separate secretariat has been set up in the prime minister's office to become, as alluded to previously, a "full function" counterpart of Pakistan's Strategic Plans Division, including as the agency to perform staff functions for the National Command Authority. Other than informing nuclear weapons handlers what to do and when in a nuclear crisis or war, the Red Book will lay down the interface protocols for agencies—the Department of Atomic Energy, DRDO, and SFC—in the nuclear firing loop. It will also flesh out the four-stage alert system, define in greater detail the roles and responsibilities of each player at each stage, and delineate what is required of those in the designated chain of command down to the delivery system managers and weapons firers. Additionally, the requirements and the criteria for psychological profiling of personnel guarding and preparing the nuclear weapons for use and in triggering weapons are now being spelled out, as are the parameters for drawing up Qualitative Requirements for nuclear and thermonuclear weapons and delivery systems by the Strategic Forces Command. The Strategic Projects Group also began nuclear target analysis in 2007 to supplement what the Strategic Forces Command had already done. This exercise will help to decide *inter se* targeting priorities and to assign targets to the constituent elements of the strategic triad.[178] The new organizational "innovations" happened only after one of the armed services' chiefs of staff repeatedly complained to Prime Minister Manmohan Singh and Defense Minister Pranab Mukherji in 2005–2006 that the Indian nuclear deterrent was "hollow," and highlighted facts such as the de-mated nuclear weapon components lying around in open hangars, the absence of a secure command and control net, and an insubstantial Strategic Forces Command. His warning that the country faced "double jeopardy" with adversary states taking India's nuclear declarations and threats of massive retaliation seriously but satellites passing overhead providing no supporting evidence of any such capability, was especially effective. Further, this service chief also slammed the "sub-standard benchmarks" set by the government for the country's strategic forces, and pleaded for the deterrent to be qualitatively beefed up and in quantity.

This previously sorry state of affairs was confirmed by Satish Chandra, the former deputy national security adviser. "If you have weapons and they are not well developed, they are inviting an attack," he said, "and that's what I was worried about."[179] In any event, the Manmohan Singh government became attentive for a while, made a few critical decisions, and ordered some corrective measures, before its interest subsided again under the weight of its preoccupations mainly with surviving as a patchwork coalition regime.[180] To buttress its claim that the military, in fact, participates in nuclear decision-making and otherwise to mollify the military brass, an Apex Group was formed in 2005. Consisting of the national security adviser to Prime Minister Manmohan Singh, M. K. Narayanan; the former chairman of the AEC, R. Chidambaram, appointed as science & technology adviser to the prime minister; the chairman, Chiefs of Staff Committee (CoSC); and the cabinet secretary, the senior-most bureaucrat in government, this group runs mostly on Chidambaram's scientific judgments. Many of these judgments are controversial, and the military disagrees with a number of them. For example, his insistence that simulation can adequately replace testing in designing and developing new weapons designs is highly controversial.[181] These are obstacles in the path of smooth operationalization of the nuclear deterrent and indicate the basic problem that military men uniformly believe afflicts strategic policy-making in the country, namely, the disinterestedness of the political class generally. It is a trait that is turned into a policy liability by the civil servants forming the permanent secretariat in the government. They are uninformed on strategic issues but the politicians rely on them. "The political leader," said Admiral Arun Prakash, former chief of the Naval Staff, "is so preoccupied with petty politics—regional, caste, constituency, with winning the next elections, the time available to him even when he is holding cabinet rank is so small, it is not adequate for him to apply himself to [national security and strategic] issues. Therefore, he goes by the advice of the bureaucracy. But bureaucrats have their hands full with routine work . . . and they don't have any depth of knowledge."[182]

This weakness, many senior military officers are convinced, affects the implementation of deterrence policies. Considering how distanced the political leadership is from strategic issues, "When the time comes to use nuclear weapons or to practice deterrence, you need political skills and ways of handling the situation—we have got to be much more sophisticated than we are today," says Air Chief Marshal Krishnaswamy. "Where is the time for politicians and . . . how much do they know? How much are they going to practice that fine art of using [nuclear weapons] in a dialog in whatever manner to show that our deterrence is credible?"[183] And, in a cascading fashion, this knowledge gap, many fear, will end up hurting the nuclear deterrent. "Strategic forces," Air Marshal Ajit Bhavnani said, "understand how much deterrent force we should have, how many times we should test what system, how many missiles should be available, that's the crux of the issue where we happen to have a little bit of void in pushing the nuclear deterrent becoming more operational. The issue," he continued, "is the gap in understanding between those at the helm of power in the political system and in the bureaucracy—who think the [military] services want everything in a hurry. But the fact is unless we push, it doesn't happen."[184]

Ashley Tellis, in a detailed 2000 RAND study written partly on the basis of the access he had to Indians shaping the nuclear policy at the time, celebrated India's de-alerted, de-mated nuclear posture as a "force in being," something particularly suited to stabilizing the supposedly tremulous security situation in South Asia.[185] Military commanders admit that initially the political leaders were a bit wary of changing the de-alerted, de-mated posture that had won them encomiums. However, harsh reality and practical considerations changed that. "It has been time consuming for the political bosses to understand what's a de-mated situation, what's a mated situation, why we should have a mated situation and when a de-mated situation," observed Air Marshal Bhavnani, guardedly. "But once they were made to understand, we are now in a good situation. This level of understanding was achieved because of interactions between the Strategic Forces Command and the Prime Minister's Office." Part of the Indian nuclear force remains "de-mated" but a portion of the deterrent is in near-mated condition and almost operational. "It is a need-based situation and capability, and depending on our threat perception," said Satish Chandra, "we will keep our weapons systems ready or de-mated. The point is we haven't anywhere said that we are not going to de-mate."[186] Indeed, in many respects the three stages of "de-mating" nuclear weapons—the pit from the warhead, warhead from the weapon system, weapon system from the intended launcher/delivery platform—is notional. Many nuclear missiles and other types of nuclear ordnance are colocated with air and naval bases. In 2003, the British Broadcasting Corporation reported that the "reaction time" for launching Indian nuclear weapons was between 6 and 8 hours and at most 12 hours.[187] With the SFC streamlining the processes, this reaction time, it may be logical to surmise, has been vastly improved upon since then.

Indian nuclear weapons systems have sophisticated electronic interlocks and firing codes and there is a "two man" rule for arming and launching nuclear weapons. To the extent that nuclear operations against Pakistan are conceived as a follow-on to conventional hostilities, it is something the military system believes it is prepared to handle even with fairly basic readiness levels and nuclear support infrastructure. Designated squadrons of the low-flying relatively short-range Jaguar fighter-bomber, trained for 20 KT nuclear bomb-drops since the mid-1980s, were and are still considered adequate to initiate preemptive or retaliatory nuclear action against Pakistan, and generally to deter and dissuade that country. Two hundred Prithvi SRBMs, some with 20 KT warheads, are the ready missile option.[188] Even so, the operationalization of the Indian nuclear deterrent suffers in comparison to the counterpart Pakistani force in the main because, as George Perkovich has written, the Pakistani Army, unlike the Indian government, "treats its nuclear arsenal as a usable vital military instrument, and so establishes doctrine and operations to be able to deploy this arsenal quickly and decisively. [The] preparation to use nuclear weapons necessarily entails risks that could be seen as part of the proliferation *problematique.*"[189] All the same, the Indian nuclear forces are getting sharper, necessitated by their transition from being largely Pakistan-oriented to coping seriously with a more dangerous and far more strategically capable adversary—China.

The newer Mirage 2000 and Sukhoi-30 MKI are optimized to deliver higher-yield boosted fission and thermonuclear bombs at longer range, mostly against Chinese targets. The manned aircraft option for strategic delivery is sought to be enlarged with the IAF likely to obtain the Russian Tu-160 Blackjack super-sonic strategic bomber. Having traditionally favored short-range tactical aircraft to planes capable of operating at great distances from base, the IAF woke up to its strategic capability void only when, starting in the late 1990s, the Indian Navy sought to acquire the Russian Tu-22 Backfire strategic bomber first offered by the Soviet Union in 1971 ostensibly for maritime reconnaissance but actually to appropriate the manned strategic bombing role for itself.[190] The deal for the Backfire bomber broke down, however, because the requirement for the small numbers of this plane did not warrant the construction of the necessary but inor-dinately expensive servicing and maintenance facility. Russia refused to consider the Indian Navy's proposal to make the deal economically viable and allow its own fleet of Tu-22s to be also serviced at the Indian facility.[191] Alive to the possibility of the other services poaching on its turf, the IAF has since made plans to lease-buy small numbers of the Tu-160 supersonic strategic bomber air-craft from Russia.[192]

The seaborne deterrent too is taking shape, with the indigenous SSBN sched-uled to go to sea by 2010, around the time the brace of Akula-II SSNs (nuclear-powered hunter-killer submarines) contracted for in 2004, begin to be delivered to the Indian Navy, with the initial lease of these boats for ten years.[193] The SSBNs, once underway, become autonomous nuclear missile firing platforms. An ultra-high frequency communications net is already up and the commander of the submersible, with his targeting list, will be given only the go signal, with actual use of his nuclear weapons inventory being left to his discretion in time of war.[194] Admiral Prakash hinted that "An airborne command post with a trail-ing antennae emitting extra-low frequency signals in case of breakdown of nor-mal communications, and such other devices to make this system triple or quadruple redundant, so that our submarines are safe" may be in the pipeline. "After all," he said, "We have developed nuclear weapons use procedures for our ships carrying nuclear weapons and our diesel submarines are already using certain types of communications, so we marry the two and come up with the nec-essary protocol. Failsafe lies in redundancy. So we have two or three levels of [ship-to-shore] communications." There are, however, considerable naval forces available to fire nuclear missiles. "In the navy, the normal notice for a ship to get underway is '*x*' number of hours and that doesn't change; where there are gas turbine engines, it is a matter of minutes," he said. "Earlier we used to wait for a warning period and get a certain preparatory time in which we loaded up with missiles, rockets, torpedoes and ammunition. Now we decided that a certain amount of weaponry will always be on board and the magazines are full, so when the first lot of ships sail out, they are carrying some armament. When the second lot of ships go out they are carrying the full armament. I suppose the air force is doing the same thing, and now that they have the air-to-air refuelers, the aircraft can be based (if needed) in the deep south, get airborne, refuel, and fly directly on a mission."[195] This readiness scheme, presumably, is as much for delivery systems carrying conventional weapons as for nuclear weapons.

The Agni-I, like the Prithvi SRBM, is a Tetra-truck-mounted road-mobile MRBM and has entered service in the army's Missile Groups 334 and 335.[196] The Agni-II land-based long-range missile is rail mobile—an option to make the force "more variegated"[197]—with launchers fitted on flatbed railcars and formed into trains and run, with armed protection, on the vast Indian railway network along the lines of the Russian SS-24 Scalpel ICBM. At least one, possibly two, missile trains are already operating and more are in the offing.[198] Each launcher has a three car system, inclusive of power and command/control, radar and firing unit, and additional cars as living space for the crew. Owing to the paucity of rolling stock, however, the outfitting of these groups with the Agni missiles is behind schedule.[199] It is possible the unavailability of flatbed railcars is an excuse the Manmohan Singh government has used to observe, what one of its ministers called, "self-imposed restraint" vis-à-vis long-range Agni missiles.[200] This delay has not affected the reaction time of rail-based missiles, which is reported as 15 minutes.[201] In any case, land-based and submarine-borne missiles require Satellite-Based Surveillance and reconnaissance (SBS) system to keep tabs on troop movements, missile placements, and airbases in the neighboring regions. The first of the military-use satellites sent up in 2001 has been replaced by Cartosat-1 in 2005, one meter resolution for imagery capable Cartosat-2 a year later, and 0.7 m resolution capable 2A to achieve orbit by late 2008, and subsequent launches in the Cartosat series with 0.5 m resolution will provide deep reconnaissance and strategic targeting capability.[202] The imagery capability is sub-one meter resolution, with the raw data being processed by a new organization—DIPAC (Defense Imagery Processing and Analysis Center) in Delhi, and a satellite-control facility set up in Bhopal in Central India.[203] In fact, the plan is for a constellation of seven satellites by 2014 in geosynchronous orbit for 24/7 real-time coverage of southern Asia. It will also realize an India-centric global positioning system to be called the Indian Regional Navigational Positioning System, able among other things to provide midcourse guidance to ship or submarine-fired cruise missiles. The first of the satellites in this program, estimated to cost $250 million (Rs 1,000 crore), will be launched by 2009.[204]

In order to explore more secure deployment modes for missiles, a 2003 DRDO study concluded that the rail-mobile systems were increasingly vulnerable to modern surveillance, mobile target seeking, tracking, and strike technologies. Going back to General Sir Francis Tuker's advice to the Indian government in the late 1940s about mountain massifs providing ideal shelter from nuclear strike (see previous chapter), the option of basing missiles in tunnels excavated in mountain sides was studied and recommended.[205] Two such mountain tunnel complexes in the eastern Himalayas have since come up. Many of the 2500–3000 km Agni-III and the 5000 km Agni-IV IRBMs, and once it is serviceable, the ICBM, are likely to be deployed in these tunnels. More such complexes are under construction. Not everyone is convinced the tunnels make the missiles within them invulnerable. The tunnel complexes can be detected by satellite and thermonuclear bombs can seal the mouth of the tunnel, airfields can be hit and rail-mounted missiles detected and destroyed, said Admiral Prakash by way of counting the advantages to prioritizing SSBNs as primary means of deterrence and strategic reaction.[206] Silo-basing for IRBMs and ICBM has also been approved. Russian and French companies briefed the Defense Ministry officials and the Integrated Defense Staff some years back on the silo technology they were willing to sell. Security concerns led to a decision to rely on indigenously developed design, which led to delays. This silo technology is being utilized in an extended shape to house the main nuclear National Command Authority (NCA). The design for a deep underground elongated box-like structure has been finalized, long years of debate on whether it should rest on massive springs to absorb the thermonuclear detonation shockwave, was resolved and work has begun with the completion date around 2010–2011. Two smaller alternate command, control, and communications (C3) centers to replicate the main NCA capability for fallback purposes are also under construction.[207] Even so, there are no guarantees against deep boring weapons capable of exploding tens of meters underground and able to collapse the firmest reinforced concrete and steel constructions. Until the three deep bunkers become operational, the NCA is operating out of makeshift premises and will be vulnerable to attack. In the interim, there is a complicated regimen for the final nuclear use authority—the prime minister to be spirited away by the underground metro railway in Delhi to an outlying station and from there flown out by helicopter to a safe and secure command center.[208]

There is one other problem to do with the communications technology itself. All the semiconductors and integrated circuits (ICs) used in the nuclear communications network have to be hardened to withstand electromagnetic pulse (EMP) effects of nuclear explosions. The need for EMP-hardened chips has created a dilemma for Indian designers similar to that created by the foreign silo technology. Security demands indigenization, but if DRDO is to produce reliable high-quality EMP-hardened ICs, it will take time and cause delays that the SFC finds unacceptable, as it directly impacts on the quality of operationalization of the nuclear forces. The alternative the SFC has mooted is to buy the ICs from Russia or, preferably, Israel,[209] hope the military specifications and other details are not divulged by the chosen supplier to third countries, and to replace these ICs with homemade items in the C3 architecture as and when they become available.[210]

However much the Indian government might want to keep nuclear weapons–related infrastructure and decision-making sealed and separated from the conventional military system, strong interface and integration is required, especially as nuclear weapons use (whether against Pakistan or China) is being thought of as part of a continuum. Disjunctions could cause severe problems if conventional war leads to nuclear weapons–use situations. Such an interface is an imperative for a number of reasons, such as properly managing the de-mated components stored on or near air bases. The aircraft squadrons for nuclear missions have been identified, but short of imminent nuclear operations, remain under the command and control of the Indian Air Force (IAF). The crosscutting authority lines complicate the nuclear command and the training for nuclear contingencies. Initially there was resistance to colocation of numerous depots where de-mated nuclear weapons systems are stored with air and naval bases, because the IAF and naval commanders worried that their bases would attract preemptive nuclear strikes. Elsewhere, the storage sites are in crowded urban areas separated from the delivery systems deployed at a distance from the cities.[211] Practice drills have indicated that, given the chaotic Indian city traffic and crowded roads, in a crisis the mundane task of transporting nuclear weapon components to where the delivery or launcher systems are located, could become a logistics nightmare. "In the best of times," observed Admiral Prakash, "India is a controlled anarchy. If you superimpose on that a nuclear explosion, you can imagine the roads, transport, communications, etc., it will be a very difficult situation."[212] This problem is being addressed by increasingly shifting nuclear ordnance and land-based missiles to remote sites in the hinterland. The other aspect of the still minimal level of conventional-nuclear military interface has to do with the fact that, unlike in Pakistan where the Strategic Plans Division is manned by a separate, specialist, carefully selected and trained cadre, in India officers from the three military services man the Strategic Forces Command on a rotational basis, preventing the emergence of a cadre of nuclear specialists. This staffing system also keeps alive the inter-service rivalries because officers posted to SFC have their subsequent career postings managed by the parent service. Moreover, with more people serving in SFC and reverting to their original armed service, the chances for information leakage and lapses increase.

The process of familiarizing the military personnel with the nuclear weapon systems has encountered problems as well. Courses were started in 2004 by BARC for naval and air force officers, but initial difficulties were encountered —for example, at the deployment stage when the army personnel, especially at the level of junior commissioned officers and other ranks who generally have lower educational standards at recruitment, were being familiarized with the missile and nuclear warhead systems.[213] At yet another level, acquiring land from provincial governments for missile launch sites and other strategic forces support installations is tricky business because displacing farmers from hinterland agricultural areas is considered politically risky as it can lead to voter alienation at the grassroots level.[214] Such obstacles, inherent in a democracy, are "speed-breakers" and, according to Air Marshal Bhavnani, impact the strategic forces "in the sense that military men want to hasten the process . . . But [the political leaders and the bureaucrats] prefer checks and balances to ensure the military does not overstep the line."[215] Accretion in the effectiveness and efficiency of nuclear forces is apparently perceived as in some way empowering the military and this is sought to be prevented by bureaucratic and other means. It is an attitude that can be sourced to the traditional mistrust of the military by the Indian political leadership, which is now virtually institutionalized. "It is a reflection of the distrust of the military, a reflection of misplaced fears," observed Admiral Prakash. "Actually it reflects the irresponsibility of the government than anything else. For deterrence to work, the armed forces have to be deeply involved in nuclear policy matters and decision-making."[216]

The NSAB drafters of the nuclear doctrine had debated nuclear retaliation for chemical and biological weapons (CW/BW) use. Difficulties in ascribing blame to any state for attack by CW/BW means led to its omission in their paper. Some five years later, the government padded the NSAB nuclear doctrine with this provision, convinced that linkages between the weapon and the user or host country could be established and the origins of the aggressor CW/BW traced. To enable this to happen, says Satish Chandra, deputy national security adviser in that period, "systems were developed, mechanisms were put in place, for purposes of establishing the fingerprint of anyone doing anything." The National Technical Research Organization (NTRO), which was formed, was assigned this task. As an apex technical intelligence organization, its principal focus, clarifies Chandra, is to "finger-print what was coming from where" in the nuclear sphere and to develop nuclear forensics, keep track of developments in the extended region, and to give advance warning.[217]

The Indian Army's vast armored and mechanized formations with strength of some 3,000 tanks, including the ex-Russian T-90 and the T-72S tanks and armored combat vehicles and armored personnel carriers, are inherently capable of fighting in a radioactive milieu in a "hatch-down" mode and constitute the cutting edge of the Cold Start doctrine envisaging three strike corps ready for war in a matter of hours. Some units of the strike corps are being equipped to operate in radioactivity-contaminated battle zone, with nuclear, biological, chemical (NBC) warfare protection suits, radiation decontamination units, and other paraphernalia. As many as 60 NBC warfare-related items developed by DRDO have been handed over to the army in a nearly $750 million (Rs 3,000 crore) program to make the land forces NBC capable. So far, however, this program has covered little more than a brigade-sized group. Other equipment, such as remotely controlled air and land vehicles with NBC sniffers and sensors and vests impregnated with nano-silver particles to decontaminate biological agents, are under development by DRDO.[218] Most of the Indian naval ships are capable of sealing themselves and venturing into an area where nuclear weapons have been used.[219]

The flip side of operationalizing the nuclear forces are preparations to minimize the effects of nuclear attack on cities, on nuclear power plants, and generally to deal with nuclear disasters. After 9/11 and an assessment of various external and internal threat scenarios and on the basis of a "Design Basis Threat analysis," a new "multi-layered security system" encompassing "integrated physical protection for nuclear facilities and materials—during use, storage, and transport" was established, according to a report on the presentation by K. Raghuraman, from the Department of Atomic Energy. Regular technical reviews and audits of the physical protection systems are carried out, he said at a 2005 international workshop, to ensure "they are functioning properly and maintained appropriately."[220] The natural uranium fuel-run, heavy-water moderated, pressurized water (CANDU) reactor—the workhorse of the Indian nuclear program, in any case, is recognized for its safety features that make it "resistant" to attack and sabotage, such as "double-domed containment" structures, four feet thick concrete walls, automatic microprocessor-driven reactor shutdown systems for reactor control and protection, and high coolant-to-power ratio.[221] Leakage of radioactivity, moreover, is prevented by what are regarded as foolproof switching and multiple control systems. Even so, DRDO has been tasked to produce systems for surveillance, detection, protection and decontamination to ward off radioactive disaster. The larger civil defense program includes schemes to train doctors and paramedics, to stockpile potassium iodate as antidote to overexposure to radioactivity, and, in a crisis, to get the 80 identified "response centers" across India to deploy some 180 "quick response" teams. In addition, in March 2006 the Manmohan Singh regime asked every ministry and department of government and all provincial governments to draw up standard operating procedures (SOP) to deal with nuclear disasters.[222] The National Disaster Authority, headed by ex-Army Chief General N. C. Vij, and his deputy, a former director of the BARC, B. Bannerjee, is responsible for planning disaster relief and all civil defense efforts. However, nuclear disasters may be particularly difficult for the Indian government and its agencies to handle,[223] considering that their record of disaster management is not inspiring.[224]

CONCLUSION

The capability growth with respect to nuclear weapons, missiles, and delivery platforms like SSBNs and the manner and direction in which the deterrent is being operationalized, have made the thinking of the nuclear grandees like the late Raja Ramanna obsolete. Small nuclear forces have a tendency, as Albert Wohlstetter noted, to become bigger and more potent because the high research and development costs and the learning-curve effects lead to lower unit costs as the forces grow. Unit costs also decrease because the deterrent "to be stable in the face of changing technologies cannot be technologically static."[225] In the May 1998 parliamentary debate on the tests, Ramanna urged India to have "the strength of a giant but not use it like one" and urged that nothing be done to harm the "reputation we have built up of nonviolence."[226] Under pressure to cope with harsh reality, India's nuclear policy has, however, discarded the baggage of self-abnegation and denial it had carried for a long time. Still, expectations of "responsible" behavior are sought to be used to constrain India. Thus, the Indian government is asked, for example, to exercise Jawaharlal Nehru's kind of "sportsmanlike nationalism,"[227] whatever that means considering that Nehru was the progenitor of the India's Janus-faced nuclear program. In addition, a former George W. Bush administration official, Xenia Dormandy, advises India "to put its own requirements second." Until it "shows an ability to do so more regularly and on more vital issues," she adds, "India's reputation as a responsible stakeholder will be tenuous."[228] This raises the question whether India is being asked, unreasonably, to adhere to a higher standard of international behavior than are other major powers. And, realistically, whether in a world of "offensive realism,"[229] it is even feasible for India alone to stay its hand in the nuclear and strategic spheres at the expense of its national interest.

The Indian nuclear deterrent is finding its strategic bearings; the Strategic Forces Command, its feet; and the conventional military services, a role for nuclear weapons as shield behind which to prosecute limited conventional wars —all developments the five major nuclear-weapon states have experienced. The higher comfort level with nuclear weapons has led to the armed services willing to fund certain dual-purpose strategic programs out of their budgets. Thus, the army established the Prithvi and Agni-I and Agni-II regiments out of its budgetary allocations and, as the senior service, has expressed its willingness in the future to proportionately share in the costs of other strategic-use assets and paraphernalia jointly utilized by the three services.[230] The growth in national resources generally and the substantial and substantive advancements since 1998 in converting latent strength into growing muscular strategic forces are enabling India to become, if not a nuclear "Godzilla" as opposed to a nuclear "Bambi,"[231] then, in time, to at least belong to the nuclear Godzilla family. Even so, the official rhetoric is still defensive and yesteryear. After a former service chief of staff complained about the continuing shortfalls in certain categories of strategic forces, Prime Minister Manmohan Singh's National Security Adviser Narayanan soothed him by saying that the official policy of "an amorphous and diffuse deterrent" was adequate; this when the Indian strategic nuclear forces are not any more either amorphous or diffuse.[232]

CHAPTER 4

Southern Asia: Limited War, Potential Nuclear Crises, Indian-U.S. Nuclear Deal

Conventional wars have predated nuclear weapons by many millennia but are linked by the belief that escalating conventional military hostilities between two nuclear-armed states will, beyond a point, prompt the use of nuclear weapons by the losing side. Since 1945, this has led to tension between the impulse to fight conventional wars to a finish and the fear of pressing the conventional military advantage gained on the battlefield too hard lest nuclear weapons come into play. The debate on limited war in the nuclear era has revolved around when this point is reached and continuing with conventional military operations becomes counterproductive.

India is confronted by two nuclear-armed neighbors; the major threat posed by China and the minor threat by Pakistan. To complicate matters, these two countries are bound together by strong security ties resulting in the latter's helping the former acquire nuclear weapons and missiles and a semblance of conventional parity with India. China has transferred large quantities of military hardware, including main battle tanks, artillery, ships, and combat planes.[1] Pakistan, moreover, is also assisted, episodically, by the United States, to shore up its conventional military capability with advanced weapons systems, such as the F-16 aircraft, the Harpoon anti-ship missile,[2] and its nuclear weapons-related facilities.[3] It is a unique constellation of threats that led the Indian Defense Minister Pranab Mukherji in June 2005 to say that India suffered from a "security deficit." "India faces peculiar security challenges," he declared. "We live in a dangerous neighborhood, few other countries in the world face the full spectrum of threats to their security as India does, from low intensity conflicts to an unfriendly nuclearized neighborhood. Our response to such an environment has been anything but militaristic."[4] Militaristic or not, India is taking adequate strategic and conventional military precautions as the situation it confronts with China and Pakistan mirrors two different Cold War conflict systems. With China it is rivalry at the strategic level, like the contest between the United States and the Soviet Union, and with Pakistan it is, in the main, a conventional military face-off with nuclear overtones, like the one in Central Europe between the nuclear weapons-backed conventional forces of the North Atlantic Treaty Organization and the Warsaw Pact. In southern Asia these conflict systems are smaller in scale, with India involved in a subtle strategic tussle to thwart China's plans to establish dominance in the extended region, and the strong, nearly equal, deployable conventional military forces of India and Pakistan keep the peace in the nuclearized environment. The United States is the key "off-shore balancer"[5] with a threefold objective. It is eager to befriend India—"a new global power" to contain China in Asia, incentivize India's entry into the existing nonproliferation regime, and, simultaneously, freeze the Indian thermonuclear weapons technology at the stage of a failed design. It is also keen to ensure that Pakistan remains a steadfast ally in the war against international terrorism being waged in its tribal North-West Frontier Province and Afghanistan and keeps its nuclear weapons, materials, and technology away from Al-Qaeda and Taliban terrorist organizations active in that country. In addition, without seeming to support either India or Pakistan, the United States seeks to exercise "pivotal deterrence" to prevent Pakistan from being militarily overwhelmed by India[6] or getting too close to China.

DEALING WITH PAKISTAN

As discussed in Chapter 2, owing to intimate links of kinship, religion, ethnicity, and shared social norms and culture, as well as the growing domestic electoral clout of the Indian Muslim population—the second largest in the world after Indonesia—and the demands of "secular politics," the Indian government has domestic political compulsions to exercise enormous self-restraint in fighting Pakistan.[7] It has resulted in wars that are limited in aim, scope, casualties, and destruction, restricted in geographic space and time, in the eschewal of counter-city/counter-value strikes, and in the intensity of operations.[8] India-Pakistan conflicts, in effect, resemble communal riots occurring now and again in South Asia—localized affairs marked by the sudden spurt of Hindu-Muslim violence and its equally early termination.[9] With the advent of nuclear weapons in the region, what has changed is that the language of confrontation and strategy now reflect the concepts and the confusions of "deterrence."

The military geography especially of India-Pakistan wars is not unlike that of the Central Front in Europe post-1945, in that the wealth-producing, population-rich, industrial and agricultural belt and the political heartland of Pakistan is close to the border. Had hostilities broken out at the height of the Cold War, NATO and Warsaw Pact armies concentrated in that region would have "slugged it out." NATO would have sought to halt the expected breakthroughs by the massed East bloc armored forces assisted by Russian "frontal aviation" by as much conventional defense as could be mustered before NATO tactical nuclear weapons came into play. This was the strategy till the 1980s when the "air-land" capability to strike behind the forward edge of the battlefield to destroy the follow-on Warsaw Pact forces and support infrastructure afforded the West the means to widen the nuclear firebreak. The intruding forces, stranded in hostile territory, would have been destroyed in detail and the onus for nuclear use would have passed to the aggressor. Thus, war was sought to be limited to conventional military operations with the use of even tactical nuclear weapons, if not made redundant, postponed in the exchanges in the hope that a cease-fire would ensue before the redlines were crossed.[10] Pakistan's "strategic corridor" is within 20–30 km of the forward-positioned Indian forces along the border. What is significant is that, notwithstanding the vulnerability of its major cities and towns in this strip of land and the absence of conventional "air-land" military capacity for deep penetration and sustained operations inside Indian territory to arrest an Indian advance, Pakistan has selected a nuclear strategy, like the later NATO strategy, that distances itself from the precipitate use of nuclear weapons. Lieutenant General Khalid Kidwai, the head of the Pakistani Army's Strategic Plans Division, the secretariat for the nuclear National Command Authority, some years back described four redlines—India conquering "a large part of [Pakistani] territory," destroying "a large part either of its land or air forces," proceeding "to the economic strangling of Pakistan," or pushing "Pakistan into political destabilization or creat[ing] a large scale internal subversion."[11] Significantly, each of the thresholds is qualified by the word "large," leaving the Pakistani Army lots of room for interpretation, maneuver, and actions short of nuclear weapon use and suggests that Pakistan is loath both to give up the first-use threat and to initiate a nuclear exchange that can end in its destruction, whence a fairly relaxed Pakistani definition of the tripwire. The fact that Pakistan lays so much store by its nuclear weapons at all in its confrontation with India is blamed by many senior Indian military men on the Indian government's reluctance to let the world know about the true state and quality of the country's nuclear forces. "The fog [surrounding] our weaponization and delivery states, [made worse by] enunciation of our policy and our posturing," said retired Air Chief Marshal Anil Tipnis, "are allowing the Pakistan military to brandish the view that 'nuclearization' of Indian and Pakistan has taken away India's option of conventional war on Pakistani soil." As a corrective he counsels that India's posture "needs to be that Pakistan cannot think of a nuclear response to an Indian conventional offensive because the consequences would be unacceptable, that it would be like jumping from the frying pan into the fire."[12]

The record of India-Pakistan wars in the pre-nuclear era, in fact, suggests that even when the disparity in conventional forces favored India, its military forces did not or could not cut through the built-up Pakistani antitank defenses in the heavily defended and valuable Punjab sector, nor advance very deep in the open desert terrain into Pakistan. Today with the gap in deployable troops and armor narrowed, Indian forces are even less able, realistically speaking, to affect "large" breakthroughs in terms of capturing Pakistani territory or destroying Pakistani forces and therefore to start a nuclear war.[13] Moreover, because "economic strangling" in terms of a naval blockade or cutting off of the shared Indus River waters is not an action that would be contemplated short of the traditional self-restraint not being observed, and because "internal subversion" is something Pakistan has practiced more widely and effectively in Kashmir and elsewhere in India than India has done in Pakistan,[14] a nuclear flare-up as envisioned by the Pakistani military seems improbable. Indeed, the traditional India-Pakistan conflict system geared to wars of "maneuver" to achieve attrition of the adversary's fighting capabilities rather than "annihilation," has remained intact after the two countries became nuclear-weapon states.[15]

Defined by political objectives, "limited" and "unlimited" wars, the German historian Hans Delbruck observed, require two quite different strategies—the strategy of exhaustion (*Ermattungsstragie*) and the strategy of annihilation (*Nierwerfungsstrategie*).[16] In the subcontinent, because the latter strategy was never in the cards, it is the strategy of exhaustion, entailing maneuver and force-on-force attrition warfare, that has been refined over the years. The most recent perturbations—the 1999 border war in the Kargil region of Kashmir and, some two years later, mobilizing for war without war—in fact, illustrate the strategy of mutual exhaustion, preferably without initiation of hostilities, and a rapid return to *status quo ante*. Delhi could have reacted to the surreptitious occupation of Indian territory in 1999 or of the Pakistan-supported terrorist attack on Parliament in December 2001 with, say, immediate retaliatory air strikes on supply depots and force concentrations in the Pakistani part of Kashmir in the first case and punitive aerial strikes on terrorist training camps in that same region in the other instance, as was recommended by the Indian Air Force theater commanders.[17] Such a reaction would have been justified and perceived as appropriate, proportional, and non-escalatory. The Indian government instead chose to grind it out by ordering the army to oust the Pakistani intruders with slow-paced infantry action, and, on the latter occasion, to merely "mobilize" for war. Prosecuting infantry operations when the air force was available for swift retribution meant needless military casualties but also a widening of the firebreak between the Indian conventional military action and the Pakistani nuclear tripwire. And ordering "general mobilization for war" without actually going to war guaranteed exhaustion of forces arrayed to fight but compelled to stay on alert for months together. Since 1998, the new element is Delhi's readiness to contemplate nuclear action if Pakistan ups the ante. This was evidenced in the raising of the readiness level of the nuclear forces in response to Pakistan's threat of first use, in 1999[18] and again in 2002.[19] It was part of a deliberate but indirect Indian strategy of intimidation, not excluding "preemptive" nuclear use. It was meant to impress the U.S. government about the Indian resolve to settle matters forcefully by conventional means and, if necessary, to escalate to the nuclear level or to retaliate with nuclear armaments if Pakistan chose to use nuclear weapons.[20] India's compellance measures or "coercive diplomacy" apparently worked and the Pakistan government was persuaded to back down and, in January 2002, formally to distance itself from jihadi terrorism as well.[21] One motivation for working on Islamabad through Washington is the awareness in Delhi that "loss of face" and other cultural factors make it harder for Pakistan to back down in the face of Indian warnings than to heed American advice and friendly pressure.[22] As a result, the emergence of the United States as a " 'front-line circuit-breaker' for conflict and escalation"[23] and keeper of the peace in South Asia may be the unintended outcome of India's and Pakistan's going nuclear.[24] This Indian strategy is spawned by a utilitarian approach: if it works, it is fine; the concern being with advancing, peacefully if possible, the status quo aim of freezing the line of control (LoC) in Kashmir into the international boundary between India and Pakistan.

The Indian Army, however, was unimpressed by this indirect strategy. The operational restraint imposed on it by the government was interpreted by the military brass as succumbing to external pressure. A former chief of army staff was livid that the government had insisted on "a policy of defensive defense" which, he said, prevented the Indian forces from crossing the LoC even for limited tactical purposes during the 1999 Kargil War. It is a restraint that remained during the 2002 crisis with the armies of India and Pakistan staring across the border at each other. "It is a very unusual way of fighting a war, especially in the case where we are the aggrieved party," he said. "So, if in a conventional war there is so much of pressure, then in a nuclear war what kind of pressure would there be on India not to respond decisively?"[25] India's apparently successful indirect compellance strategy, combined with its unwillingness to consider any kind of a "strategic self-restraint system" (in terms of freezing the size of nuclear arsenals, foregoing missiles and missile defense, etc.[26]) that Strobe Talbott was trying to get Jaswant Singh to agree to, and Pakistan's assessment of a growingly adverse balance of forces, have led Islamabad to reconcile itself to reality. Pakistan sought such a restraint regime as an equalizer, as symbolizing strategic parity to complement the near-parity obtained in the conventional military sphere. On March 6, 2006, President Pervez Musharraf acknowledged that "Pakistan unlike India does not harbor any ambitions or regional and global status" and defined a more sober role for the country's nuclear weapons, namely, maintaining a level of "defensive deterrence."[27] It has resulted, as General Jehangir Karamat, the Pakistani Army chief who preceded Musharraf, has written, in "a noticeable thaw" in India-Pakistan relations.[28] More significantly, Pakistani officials, including Musharraf, have since iterated that their country faced no threat from India.[29] In the composite talks proposed by Musharraf,

Pakistan even jettisoned its historical demand for plebiscite, and mooted "demilitarization" of Kashmir and "joint control" of the disputed province. India agreed to a thinning out its military presence once the level of terrorist activity declined, but rejected the concept of joint control. It also approved the Pakistani proposal for an accord on the free movement of people, unhindered trade and economic relations, cross-investment, and repatriation of profits across partitioned Kashmir. This approval was given, however, on the basis of appropriate residence verification and travel documents amounting, in effect, to Pakistan's acceptance of the LoC as border. The successor civilian coalition government of the Pakistan Peoples Party and the Muslim League (Nawaz) has gone a step further, seeing trade and economic relations with India as means of resolving disputes.[30]

While charges are still traded about Pakistan's instigating terrorist activity in India and India's assisting malcontents in Pakistan, these other developments have played a part in the emergence of a new and more relaxed security paradigm in South Asia. At its center is the reassurance provided Pakistan by nuclear weapons; it now feels more secure and less driven to bellicosity[31] and finds it easier to reconcile to the inherent disparities with India that are widening owing to the sustained high rate of Indian economic growth. The economic gap is translating into conventional military and nuclear prowess Pakistan cannot hope to match. It has made for metastability in the region.[32] Accounting for 72 percent of the population, 72 percent of the region's land space and, by the late 1990s, 75 percent of the wealth produced in South Asia,[33] India in the new century is in a decisively better situation. Its estimated gross domestic product (GDP) of $1.09 trillion by the end of 2007 was more than 10 times that of Pakistan's $106.3 billion—which figure, incidentally, is less than a quarter of the market capitalization ($466 billion) of the Mumbai Stock Exchange.[34] Unsurprisingly, the Indian defense expenditure is five times that of Pakistan,[35] a differential that is likely to increase along with India's economic growth rate's accelerating at a pace that will permit its GDP to equal the United States' by 2050.[36] The widening economic and resources gap renders the prospect of Pakistan as a serious competitor, let alone rival, to India meaningless and militarily and economically unsustainable.[37] The sheer inequality also reduces to near zero the possibility in the future of all-out conventional hostilities in South Asia; a nuclear exchange is more remote.[38] The Pakistani political establishment has apparently realized that it is futile to challenge India and that its policy of precipitating military hostilities and then threatening first use of nuclear weapons has boomeranged.[39] The Pakistani Army may still be in denial, however. A lead editorial in the Pakistani newspaper, *The Daily Times,* stated the issue baldly. "This 'equal of India' spiel is fine," it said, "if it is meant to refuse dictation but dangerous if it is avowed as a strategic doctrine."[40] This belief of equality in fact—rather than in international law, which is indisputable—has resulted in repeated Pakistan-instigated crises that have led to greater willingness by India to use progressively more forceful means and to shed its nuclear inhibitions.[41] And, it has heightened the exasperation felt by Washington, which is expected to provide protection to the provocateur—Pakistan and, in the process, generate ill-will for America in India.[42] Hence, even a minimalist border conflict with India has the potential to engender unbearable economic, political, military, and diplomatic costs for Pakistan. It is this apprehension that has triggered change in Islamabad's brazenly risk-acceptant approach to actively fomenting insurgency in Indian Kashmir and terrorism in the rest of India. However small the possibility of full-fledged war, it may still be useful to deconstruct the Indian strategies for conventional operations in a nuclear environment, for nuclear exchange, and for dealing with the breakdown of "credible minimum deterrence" with a view to gaining insights particularly into the Indian military's thinking. In a crunch the Indian government has usually gone by the military's "professional" advice.

How to wage conventional war without resorting to nuclear weapons remains the central dilemma of the nuclear age given, what Pierre Gallois called, "the inflexible logic of the atomic era," to wit, that the actual use of nuclear weapons is unacceptable.[43] Certain parameters of conflict were established early in the nuclear age. The "deliberate hobbling" of the power of nuclear weapons required, as Bernard Brodie observed in 1959, the maintenance of strategic forces "at a very high pitch of effectiveness for the sake only of inducing the enemy to hobble himself."[44] As noted in the last chapter, a sizable portion of the Indian nuclear forces are deployed in notionally de-mated condition. With the induction into service of nuclear submarines, a force of nuclear missiles will be available for instant use. A nuclear arsenal makes it all the more necessary to have strong conventional military capability just so nuclear defense, as Henry Kissinger reminded us, "becomes the *last* and not the *only* recourse."[45] In any event, conventional war in the nuclear age is "stable" because neither side, Thornton Read argued, "will be compelled to use [nuclear weapons] in order not to concede overwhelming advantage to the opponent by allowing him to strike first."[46] Both India and Pakistan have strong, nearly matching, general purpose forces with a record of fighting each other but in wars of extremely limited scale and with limited objectives and intensity of operations. Pakistan has realized that with a *modus vivendi,* stability has been obtained. In such a situation, no great advantage accrues to the side starting the war because the other country can react quickly and, as Thomas Schelling speculated in the early 1960s, "there is little to be lost by waiting a little" and thereby minimizing "the likelihood that a small war would escalate into general war or that an untoward act would trigger it."[47] In this respect, the slow, studied, pace of Indian preparations for war have been helpful in delaying its onset and, if one started anyway, in keeping it small. Especially pertinent to India, Morton Halperin theorized that the side with no map-changing in mind would be less inclined to "expand the scope of its military operations" than the state seeking territorial adjustment. If each side was persuaded that the other was not interested in territorial aggrandizement "the danger of explosion into central war will be substantially reduced." He further noted, "flexible and moderate battlefield objectives of the two sides are likely to be most conducive to the stabilization, contraction, and termination of a local war."[48] These and other surmises about limited war found in the Cold War deterrence literature were premised on the fact of the rival U.S.-led and Soviet-headed military alliances and economic blocs being nearly equal in most respects. India's choosing to restrict wars against Pakistan for reasons of organic links—close social and cultural ties, and for domestic political reasons[49]—should not be confused for "equality" between the protagonists—a mistake analysts often make. Indeed, by any criterion, the inequality between India and Pakistan is at once manifest and growing conspicuously. In this context, to assume that the nuclear deterrence system relevant to the near equal Cold War blocs applies to the absolutely unequal India and Pakistan is to skew the analysis. The nearest analogy from the Cold War years would be to isolate the United Kingdom with its "independent deterrent" or France and its *force de frappe* from the U.S. strategic umbrella and pit it against the Soviet Union in a nuclear confrontation in Europe. It conveys the nuclear military problem *in extremis* facing Pakistan in an actual nuclear war. In an exchange, India may lose a city or two, but Pakistan would, for all intents and purposes, cease to exist. It is the sort of predicament the British or the French government would have faced in a nuclear crisis in the Cold War— if the United States and rest of NATO had kept out of the fray—of taking out parts of Moscow and one or two other Russian cities only to find Britain or France destroyed.[50] Pakistan may have acquired nuclear weapons but their deterrent or dissuasive power is entirely at the sufferance of India.

Appropriately, Pakistan has made clear its intention not to compete with India in the strategic sphere in terms of size and quality of its nuclear forces.[51] Elaborating on Pakistan's doctrine of "minimum credible deterrence" requirements, General Karamat writes, "To ensure minimum credible deterrence, Pakistan's effort will be to achieve determined and quantified goals and thereafter concentrate on qualitative upgrades." As part of this strategy of "acting in a responsible manner and with maximum restraint" Pakistan, he reveals, will not pursue "weapon for weapon" matching nor produce missiles beyond, what he calls, "a sufficiency level," with this level being periodically reviewed and deterrence needs generally revised upwards in case India goes in for missile defense.[52] He indicates the kind of nuclear force disparity Pakistan can live with. For "planning purposes," he says, it is "reasonable" for Pakistan to assume India will have 2:1 advantage in nuclear warheads/weapons and 3:1 advantage in missiles and nuclear capable aircraft.[53] An even wider gap seems to be acceptable to the Pakistan armed forces. General Mirza Aslam Beg, the Pakistani Army chief responsible for giving a powerful impetus to the country's nuclear weapons program in the 1990s, stated categorically that because of its "fragile economy," Pakistan cannot afford a nuclear arms race and that Pakistan is "content" with the "minimal deterrence that has been achieved both in the nuclear field as well as in delivery systems." "Pakistan's strategic parity," he explains, does not lie in equaling Indian nuclear forces in every respect, and that India's obtaining thermonuclear weapons makes no difference to the country's minimal deterrence stance.[54]

Pakistani nuclear planners seem convinced that the "balance of terror," as Alva Myrdal said, does not require a "balance of deterrence," even less a "balance of deterrent forces."[55] Intriguingly, General Karamat mentions that strong Pakistani conventional forces are necessary "to deter, and in case of deterrence failure, defend and destroy aggression."[56] In this statement, conventional forces, not nuclear weapons, are conceived as the ultimate means of defending the country and stopping aggression. Karamat's reference to deterrence failure pertains obviously to the country's nuclear forces failing to deter an Indian conventional attack because the nuclear and delivery wherewithal was not available for operational use, or because faced with a "go/no go" decision the Pakistan National Command Authority balked—unable or unwilling, for fear of consequences, to order a nuclear strike or retaliation. This is important, as we shall see, when analyzing the nuclear weapons use options open to Pakistan in an unrestrained war with India.

With the nuclear taboo as background, the Indian Army has tried to work around the dilemma of conducting conventional war without triggering a nuclear exchange. It alighted on the Cold Start doctrine, a latter-day version of the Warsaw Pact strategy of "swift advance [with] the ability to attack from a standing start."[57] The strategy, spawned by the frustration experienced by the armed forces during the 2002 crisis, makes war imminent upon serious provocation being offered by Pakistan. Believing it had lost credibility after the Indian political leadership first ordered mobilization and then failed to flag off a punitive campaign, the Indian military wanted to institutionalize automaticity of response in strength, which is what Cold Start envisages. The basic idea is to have a ready mobile and lethal force with integral logistics capable of mounting an offensive, with combat air cover, which needs virtually no preparation time. The Indian Cold Start strategy of at least getting one of the three strike corps—II Corps (the other corps being I and XXI) off the blocks fast, is designed to skirt danger while exploiting any tactical opening or opportunity that presents itself. It has to quickly find, as Albert Wohlstetter, one of the pioneering theorists of nuclear war said of the Soviet war plans in Europe, "a level and kind of attack large enough to be useful, but small enough to be well below the threshold risking . . . nuclear retaliation."[58] Apart from the Cold Start tag and an enlarged carry-along logistics suite, in its essentials there is little new in this operational scheme compared to what the Indian Army has been practicing since the massive 1987 mobile warfare exercise—Operation Brasstacks. The difference is in the greater sophistication, lethality, and large and precision destructive power of long-range self-propelled artillery, tank guns, and Indian Air Force aircraft in the ground support role.[59] The blueprint for operations by the Indian strike corps has always been in the general direction of Sukkur-Rahim Yar Khan in the desert sector which, compared to the Punjab front, is thinly defended and where the terrain is helpful for rapid advance by armor. The novel aspect is the conversion of the formerly defensive holding formations into pivot corps with some offensive capability. Instead of staying put, these pivot corps are expected to initiate the attack before the strike corps get into action and otherwise to add to the forward momentum and support the operational tempo established by the fast-moving lead elements. It falls short of being "dominant maneuver" because of the inability to sustain an offensive to create decisive advantage. This fact defines the limits of Cold Start's objectives and an Indian conventional capability tailored for small fast-paced high-intensity wars.[60]

The Indian military and the Indian Army, in particular, conforming to the strategy of "wounding, not annihilating" the enemy, plans reactive wars on the basis of goals well short of what the Pakistani Army could possibly perceive as endangering the survival of the state—the one and only credible nuclear tripwire. As General Karamat puts it: Pakistan's "nuclear and missile forces will respond to a nuclear or missile attack, or for a response if aggression threatens survival, that is, *in extremis* as a last resort."[61] He is repeating what Pakistani Army stalwarts have been saying for many years: that the bomb offers protection only against further "bifurcation" of the country by India.[62] However, total war and destruction of Pakistan has never been the military aim of the Indian armed forces.[63] Rather, the Indian operational goals have been and continue to be definitely of a tactical nature—capturing a nodal point, occupying an oil depot, silencing a communications hub, destroying a concentration of enemy armor, passing around the adversary's strong points (leaving their elimination to the follow-on forces, possibly, the pivot corps), surrounding an enemy formation, crossing a river or antitank obstacle—anything to tip the tactical balance against Pakistan and pressure it into ending the hostilities on Indian terms. All operations aim to stop short of bisecting that country by cutting Pakistan's jugular—the north-south line of (rail and road) communications on the Indus connecting Peshawar with Karachi. And, in any case, this depth of penetration also defines the theoretical (as different from actual) maximum distance to which the Indian strike forces can advance. There is a limit to the amount of logistics the armored and mechanized formations can carry into battle, even factoring in a fairly thin on-the-ground mobile logistics support chain fetching up the forward pre-positioned stores to the advancing units. The movement by armor and mechanized forces in the desert is in the context of the inevitably slow progress owing to the tank-on-tank "slogging matches," infantry and artillery duels in the Punjab, and even slower advance by the infantry in the mountains, where the objective is to capture and hold the crest line.[64] In fact, the Indian Army's operational logistics planning is on the basis of 20 km/day of contested advance in the desert, 5–8 km in the Punjab, and 1–2 km in the Kashmir mountains.[65] India-Pakistan conflicts have averaged 10 days. Thus, on paper, in a war, the Indian military can at most advance 200 km in the desert, 50–80 km in the plains, and 10–20 km across the line of control in Kashmir. In real-life operations, however, Indian penetrations have never exceeded 80 km in the desert (1971), 20 km in the Punjab (1965), and 3 km in the mountainous region (1965).

Now let us take the scenario the former Pakistani Army chief, General Karamat, believes could lead to a nuclear conflagration. Without mentioning any prior Pakistani provocation, he talks of a limited venture by Indian forces across the LoC à la Kargil. This, he says, could precipitate removal of "all restraints on Pakistan for full support of the freedom struggle inside Kashmir," which, in turn, would "cross Indian thresholds with unpredictable results."[66] The most revealing aspect about this statement is that the Pakistani response to an Indian conventional military offensive across the LoC is not, as might have been expected from a narrow reading of General Kidwai's redlines and the bandying about of Pakistani threats of first use, a nuclear riposte but an increase in the level of material support to the jihadi terrorists and Islamic militants active inside Indian Kashmir and the deployment of its Special Forces to organize "resistance" against the aggressing Indian troops inside Pakistan.[67] By Karamat's reckoning, Pakistan can try to deter the superior Indian military prowess by its considerable conventional military forces; failing which, it can try to distract the Indian military effort by revving up the insurgency in Kashmir and discomfiting the Indian forces deep inside Pakistani territory by contingent use of its special forces. It would thus appear that Pakistan's officially delineated nuclear redlines are very flexible indeed and will take a lot in terms of Indian military initiative and effort to cross. Karamat's point that Pakistan can fire up the insurgency in Kashmir is a double-edged sword. India can always reciprocate by stirring up the anti-Punjabi sentiment in the Sindh province of Pakistan and exploit the nationalist movements in Baluchistan and Baltistan—the northernmost region of Pakistani Kashmir. Given the brittle nature of the Pakistani polity, such covert Indian intervention would cost Pakistan much more than the activation of "sleeper cells" by the Pakistani Army's Inter-Services Intelligence agency would hurt India. Thus, other than in the conventional and nuclear military fields, India also has the upper hand in promoting mass discontent in Pakistan. Further, treating the LoC as cease-fire line, which is what Musharraf claimed it was in 1999, could lead to India's prosecuting low-key but sustained operations by Special Forces working in tandem with the regular forces deployed along the border to push the LoC toward Pakistan. In 2002, after swift aerial strikes in retaliation for the terrorist attack on Parliament, targeted intelligence actions would have fetched far better returns than doing nothing. Actions such as these to pay back Pakistan by the same coin, moreover, do not require India to cross over into overt military hostilities or escalate. Pressure generated on Pakistan by such actions is more likely to convince Pakistan to accept the LoC as international border and to desist from fanning the insurgency in Kashmir.[68]

To return to another nuclear war scenario, this one an extensive war-gaming exercise undertaken by the U.S. Naval War College (NWC) in May 1998. It dealt with a situation datelined 2003 in which the increase of civil unrest and terrorist activity in Kashmir is capped by a shoulder-fired missile bringing down a transport aircraft carrying senior cabinet ministers and the Indian Army chief, whereupon the Indian Army launches an operation with the publicly avowed and limited purpose of taking out terrorist camps and infrastructure across the LoC.

Pakistan does not respond immediately but, after a short interval, mounts a retaliatory offensive thrusting 50 km into Indian territory. Indian forces react by cutting across the Thar desert and getting into position to sever Pakistan's north-south lifeline. In this sequence, Pakistan next explodes three nuclear weapons against the invading Indian Army formations and the rail hub in Jodhpur. Even as the UN Security Council debates these developments, the game ends with India's firing a dozen nuclear weapons at Pakistan's nuclear infrastructure, leaving 15 million dead. The rapporteur of this exercise notes, laconically, that at the debriefing stage, those playing Pakistan protested they would have sued for peace before getting to the point of using nuclear weapons.[69] This series of NWC war games suggest the kind of preconceived notions of India-Pakistan wars as nuclear tinderbox current in Washington and animating Western security communities generally. Such war games by U.S. military institutions, predictably, fan the talk and paranoia of Kashmir as a nuclear flash point in American policy circles and worldwide. In crisis situations, this leads to hurried missions by senior American officials to Delhi and Islamabad purportedly to calm the Indians and Pakistanis itching for a nuclear fight when, in fact, India has never fought a "total war" with Pakistan even with conventional weaponry. The Indian government is usually a little bemused by the intensity of the American desire to "defuse" the crisis,[70] but Islamabad is jaunty and welcoming, both because such U.S. interest provides evidence of the "geostrategic relevancy" with which nuclear weapons have supposedly endowed Pakistan in the new century[71] and because it inspires confidence that the United States will save it from its follies by wielding "pivotal deterrence" against India. General Karamat acknowledges as much, saying that "an overt ... military offensive" by India against Pakistan "does not make sense," among other things, because of "the cooperative relationship that both India and Pakistan have with the US."[72] If the American war gamers had only listened to those playing Pakistan decision-makers, which no doubt included a few South Asians, and allowed the game to proceed along the lines they suggested, the U.S. Naval War College might have had more realistic war games that ended tamely, as have most India-Pakistan conflicts.

There is a set pattern to India-Pakistan wars: Pakistan offers provocation (guerilla activity in Kashmir—1965, strike on Indian air bases—1971, occupation of Indian territory in Kargil—1999); India reacts with tough measures (a determined thrust across the Punjab border toward Lahore—1965; sustained assault by land forces against East Pakistan leading to the collapse of the Pakistani defense enabling a blitzkrieg to capture Dhaka—1971; an operation to retake the Kargil heights clandestinely occupied by Pakistan troops—1999), and after the initial exchanges of attacks and counterattacks, Pakistan forces wilt under pressure of the heavier military mass, and the two sides agree to a cease-fire and, following the post-war accord, restore the *status quo ante* (with Delhi even returning militarily valuable points, which international law permitted India to retain in the disputed Kashmir area—like the Haji Pir salient in 1965—captured at considerable human cost). As the 1999 Kargil war shows, this pattern was not altered by Pakistan's possession of nuclear weapons. In any event, the talk emanating from the Pakistani Army chief and president of the country, Pervez Musharraf, in the 2002 crisis, for instance, of "offensive defense" coupling the country's conventional military might and its nuclear assets to push India on the defensive, is more a "feel-good" strategy providing grist for academic speculation than something realizable on the ground. In the 2002 eyeballing contest Pakistan typically played hard but could not hide a weak strategy. In an interview to the *Washington Post* newspaper during the crisis, Musharraf started out by expressing confidence that in case of deterrence failure, Pakistan would unleash its "offensive defense" capabilities. He next raised the possibility of the situation spinning out of control but quickly reassured the intended American audience that "we will never reach [the] stage" of nuclear weapons use before pleading, with a hint of desperation, for U.S. intervention. Americans "are the only ones who can help. They must help," he said. "They must bring normality here. They must resolve this dispute. And they must ensure balance in the region."[73] Musharraf was apparently not convinced that bluff and bluster alone would suffice if India was determined to coerce Pakistani compliance, especially if the United States hesitated to play the role Islamabad had assigned it. Pakistan's seeking U.S. protection in 2002 coincided with the Indian government's seriousness about building bridges with America and the perceived benefits to this policy from impressing Washington with a public show of restraint that additionally buffed up its image as a responsible nuclear-weapon state.[74] Pakistani rulers have always worried about how to get a third party— the United States or China—to commit itself to a rescue act. India has solved the problem for Pakistan by simply not acquiring the endurance to fight long wars to a decision.

As previously discussed, factors relating to shared ethnicity, language, religion, kinship, social norms, and culture mandate relatively harmless wars of maneuver, rather than a war of annihilation. Perhaps, as a result, the tendency to pull punches is built into the system of logistical support available to the Indian military. The fact that India cannot fight wars lasting more than 10–15 days is not by accident, but a deliberate policy choice which, incidentally, is mirrored on the Pakistani side as well.[75] The Indian armed forces can use their budgetary allocations to build up their capacity to fight long-duration wars by filling what are called "voids"—the unmet requirements of war materiel—the maintenance spares and stores, ammunition and shells and reserves of petroleum, oil, lubricants (POL). Instead, they choose to invest in new weapons platforms— tanks, guns, aircraft, and ships—to keep the Indian military technologically up to date. Further, the largest quantum of capital defense spending (26–32 percent) continues to be on armor, a combat arm with a great history but dim future, with a good part of these funds tasked for replacing a good main battle tank (T-72S) in service with a still newer MBT (T-90), with other mission capabilities suffering neglect.[76] However, there is no matching concern for augmenting stocks of spares and shells for tank guns, etc. In 1993–1994, the "voids" or the unmet requirements of spares, POL, and ammunition and shells for armor and artillery for the army amounted to some $100 billion (Rs 40,000 crore), which figure currently has, perhaps, crossed the $300 billion (Rs 120,000 crore) mark. Because newer MBTs are more and more expensive, progressively fewer of the latest tanks are inducted into the armored formations, and ever larger numbers of the older tanks are decommissioned or mothballed.[77] Unbalanced defense expenditure means there is, for instance, no worthwhile capability for offensive actions on the Tibetan plateau against China and, considering its prime maritime location, relatively meager sea denial and sea-control assets (both these missions now consume only around 15 percent of the defense budget). Similar strategic myopia has eventuated in the Indian Air Force's having great aerospace pretensions but, owing to its preference for short- to medium-range fighter aircraft that fill its inventory, no strategic reach.[78] The tradeoff between force modernization and war-fighting stamina—the ability to fight wars at intense rates of fire for long periods of time—necessitates the stockpiling of vast amounts of spares, of ammunition and shells, and of POL. Discounting for the nonce the social, political, and cultural reasons for limiting wars, the absence of immeasurably scaled-up logistics wherewithal for sustained long-duration military operations is why India cannot fight other than limited conflicts with Pakistan or any other country, for that matter, and why the so-called "wars" between India and Pakistan invariably end in an impasse or peter out to a draw (1947–1948, 1965). Thus, the 1965 War, for example, ended with Pakistan having less than a week's worth of stores left at the time of the cease-fire and India no more than ten days of spares to draw on.[79] And, in 1971, an all-out push in East Pakistan was possible only because war materiel was conserved owing to operations against West Pakistan being restricted to holding ground.[80]

One consequences of prioritizing defense acquisitions at the expense of sustained war-fighting ability is that India has a powerful land force but with short legs and little stamina. Where Cold Start is concerned, there may be three strike corps available for offensive operations. In reality, there is combat hardware and spares sufficiency to equip and operate only one strike corps at full tilt at any given time—the showpiece II Corps. Even at full strength, its attacking mass cannot take this Corps very far, which calculation was the basis for Pakistan's thinning out its defenses in the desert sector and confidently concentrating its Army Reserves—North and South, at the "chicken's neck" to threaten Indian Kashmir during the 1987 Operation Brasstacks. It was the first of the big Indian Army war exercises emphasizing mobile warfare, which the Pakistan military apprehended was cover for an offensive war.[81] It is also the reason for Pakistani Army's confidence in holding off an Indian Cold Start offensive, which is dependent on too many things going right and whose thrust can be blunted by Pakistani armor working inside the decision-action time cycle of the Indian forces.[82] To illustrate the point of the limitations of the Indian offensive capability, in the annual war games featuring the strike corps in the desert, most of the modern equipment and stores are typically decanted from other formations in the army to bring it up to full combat strength for the exercise period in order to create a good public impression of the army's war-fighting capability. "In these exercises," reveals Lieutenant General Vijay Oberoi, former vice chief of army staff, "the entire army's latest equipment is poured into one divisional level formation. It is showing off [to project] a picture [that] sufficient stuff is available to all." This corps is also given a high-technology sheen with the newest high-technology systems DRDO is developing being featured—even though these may be years away from induction into service.[83] For rapid advance of armor, Cold Start relies on combat aircraft to clear the path. Fighter cover for such an advance will become more difficult with the induction into the Pakistani Air Force service of five Swedish SAAB 2000 Aerial Early Warning and Control Systems, enhancing its capability for pinpoint interception of intruding aircraft.[84] However, close air support is a role the Indian Air Force is not enthused about and does not plan or train its pilots for.[85]

None of these aspects of the India-Pakistan wars or India's (and Pakistan's) actual war-fighting prowess are ever plumbed by Western analysts examining Cold Start. Intent on embroidering the nuclear flash point theme, such analyses tend to use the paper strength and paper plans of the Indian military as the basis for the usual frightening conclusions. Thus, even though the Indian Army commanders are only talking about reconstituting the armor, mechanized infantry, and self-propelled and towed artillery units in the three strike corps into eight integrated battle groups (IBGs), a recent alarmist thesis makes its case on the basis that these IBGs are already in the Indian order-of-battle. With this capability as baseline, it first retails all the usual reasons (fog of war, geography, and battlefield initiative) why India-Pakistan hostilities will spiral into nuclear conflagration. After scrutinizing a number of Indian Army war games, the article confidently asserts that 3–5 IBGs can be launched within 72–96 hours for "shallow" penetration of 50–80 km inside Pakistan, that such limited operation would escalate into a full-scale conventional war and eventually nuclear exchange and, therefore, that Cold Start is bad for regional peace and stability.[86] Actually, considering the record of international conflicts in the period 1946–1976 when nuclear weapons did not prevent conventional military escalation,[87] the Cold Start strategy actually would have a good chance of succeeding if there were adequate logistics support.

Much interest and literature has been generated about why nuclear war is imminent or inevitable in the subcontinent. Such prognoses, constructed on the record of the incendiary threats and counter-threats of nuclear weapon used by Pakistan and India in the lead-up to the recent crises, seem entirely unmindful of one of the paradoxes of the nuclear age that Hans Morgenthau detected in the mid-1960s. "The very purpose of threat and counter-threat," he wrote, "is to prevent the test of actual performance from taking place." He warned that "the plausibility is bound to be affected [negatively] by repetitive threats of nuclear war." Indeed, this last may already have happened with Pakistan's oft-repeated threats of the use of nuclear weapons being taken less and less seriously with each new crisis. Morgenthau went on to assert that deterrence works best when the "psychological capital of deterrence" is not expended, but if it is, as in the case of Pakistan, and "the policy of deterrence is close to bankruptcy," conventional war of the kind Cold Start envisions becomes a viable option if "the stakes . . . are small enough to make defeat or stalemate acceptable without recourse to nuclear weapons."[88]

Displaying innate caution—the hallmark of Indian foreign and military policy—Defense Minister George Fernandes, speaking in the aftermath of the 1999 Kargil War, said, "War remains a possibility among nuclear-weapon states below the nuclear threshold. But the danger of escalation to nuclear exchange should make us rethink about initiating even a conventional war."[89] India may not initiate even a conventional war. There is no mystery, however, about the way India will react once a conventional war is thrust upon it leading to nuclear weapon use by the adversary. In all conceivable India-Pakistan war scenarios, the critical hump that conventional hostilities have to go over before the possibility of nuclear weapon use by Pakistan becomes plausible is the Pakistani Army's inability to stanch an Indian attack or counterattack that is in full flow. Despite all that is known about how warily Pakistan has behaved in the wars with India once its initial moves were thwarted or met with stiff Indian reaction and how rationally Islamabad has acted in carefully backing out of its nuclear threats in the past, with statements by responsible senior Pakistan government and military officers that a nuclear conflict is improbable, let us for the purpose of analysis assume that Pakistan, in fact, ends up initiating nuclear weapon use for whatever reasons. Then consider what happens thereafter. Former Indian Army Chief General Ved Malik recalled discussions within the Chiefs of Staff Committee and with the National Security Adviser Brajesh Mishra in 1999–2000 in which the military made its preference for using nuclear weapons "to take out strategic value—cities and economic targets"—very clear.[90] It is on this basis that his successor, General S. Padmanabhan, talked to the press in January 2002 at the outset of the last crisis about the kind of nuclear retaliation Pakistan could expect if it pushed the nuclear button. Responding to the numerous nuclear threats held out by political and military leaders in Pakistan, presumably to deter a punitive Indian conventional military strike across the LoC in response to the terrorist attack on Parliament, General Padmanabhan warned that "If anyone uses nuclear weapons against India, Indian forces, Indian assets at sea, Indian economic or human interests, the perpetrators of that particular outrage will be punished so severely, that their continuation in the fray will be in doubt." The vice chief of army staff until September 2001, Lieutenant General Vijay Oberoi removed all doubts about what the Indian military understood by way of "minimum deterrence": No first use, but should Pakistan initiate nuclear weapons use then "massive retaliation . . . irrespective of the type or yield of the nuclear weapon used by our adversary." He amplified that Pakistan's use of nuclear weapons on Indian forces on its own territory would beget the same massive retaliation response.[91] In one sense, such talk can be dismissed as a robust view held by military men of the kind that, for example, General Eugene E. Habiger, one-time commander of the U.S. Strategic Command, voiced, namely that deterrence "is the potential for a massive, unambiguous and totally devastating 'gut shot' provided by a diversified and survivable force."[92] What Padmanabhan and Oberoi said at the time conformed to the Defense Minister Fernandes' understanding on this matter. Referring to the likelihood of a nuclear exchange, Fernandes had said in December 2001 that while India could absorb hits, "Pakistan would be finished."[93] There is always the danger, though, as Kissinger said, that "identifying deterrence with maximum power" will tend "to paralyze the will."[94]

The unusual thing about India's proposed reaction is that the side with the conventional military edge is also the one threatening massive retaliation, which is contrary to the Cold War experience. One explanation for this is that the Indian military is heartily sick of not being allowed by the government to carry out its operations to the planned objective, which falls short of sundering Pakistan, instead of having to engage in periodic and truncated conflicts which, time and again, have ended up, as the Indian military sees it, putting the game back on the same start-line. However loudly the doctrine of massive retaliation is proclaimed, it is possible that when faced with going maximal in response to, say, Pakistan's nuclear tactical bombing of an Indian tank squadron inside its territory where the loss of life is perceived to be small, the Indian Prime Minister will, to start with, only approve a tit-for-tat strike on Pakistani forces. After 2004, when the Congress Party coalition government assumed power, the political thinking may have veered in this direction. "Whether we will actually retaliate in a massive way [to tactical use of nuclear weapons by the enemy on its own side of the border] . . . is not very clear. . . . I'm not sure that such action will be approved," said Air Marshal Ajit Bhavnani, former commander-in-chief (CINC), Strategic Forces Command.[95] Equally, Air Marshal Vinod Patney, ex-CINC, Western Air Command of the Indian Air Force, said India will have to remove any doubts that putative adversaries may entertain that "even if one-odd [nuclear] weapon is fired there is no likelihood of a riposte because [of the belief that] in case of a riposte the end of the war will signify a much worse status quo [for India] rather than the mere absorption of first strike." The Indian response, he continued, need not be total but has nevertheless "to be hard-hitting . . . even if the incoming strike misses or they say sorry, we made a mistake! Whatever the case might be, we have to respond otherwise our credibility will suffer terribly."[96] The Indian armed forces' view of how best to deal with Pakistan is colored by what occurred in the recent past. "After all, what happened when we were deployed in 2002?" asked a former army chief rhetorically before answering it himself. Pakistan, he said, took, "our conventional superiority—whatever little exists, as of no value. [The Pakistani attitude was] 'I have a nuclear weapon, what will you do to me? You try something and I will nuke you. So you can keep sitting, I know you don't have the guts to move'." In a tense environment, he continued, there are two ways of dealing with a nuclear-armed adversary: "one way is the use of brute force and the [enemy] does not come near you. The second way, you have force which you are not inclined to use under the normal circumstances and you'll use it only when you are compelled to use and other people in the world know that you have [nuclear weapons] and better not take you to that threshold when you'd be forced to use [them]." The second he implied is the Indian way. He is convinced, however, as is the vast majority in the military, that the former method is more effective.[97]

Obviously, in the Indian nuclear decision-making milieu the prospective tipping point is the abnormal circumstances created by an adversary's first use of nuclear weapons, because it is easier to react than to act. In this respect, India's No First Use policy is a boon because it simplifies decision-making and removes the ambiguity of response. According to Air Chief Marshal S. Krishnaswamy, former Air Force chief and member of the National Security Advisory Board, "There is no great difficulty involved in responding to a nuclear strike by ordering a response; it is then just a matter of launching any other big weapon, that is easy." Deciding in any situation to fire nuclear weapons first will be difficult, he said, and referred to the post-9/11 attempt by the Indian Air Force to get approval from the government for a policy to shoot down a menacing passenger aircraft—it went nowhere. "If ordering an aircraft to shoot down a civilian passenger plane is so difficult, how much more difficult is it going to be," he wondered, "to make a decision to [initiate the use of] nuclear weapons?"[98]

Nuclear war may be unthinkable but it is not impossible.[99] Limited nuclear war is even more problematical primarily because, as an official in the Nixon and Reagan Administrations reportedly put it, it is like "limited pregnancy—there is no such thing."[100] Much of the deterrence literature generated during the Cold War, including on limited war, was predicated on the two sides in the nuclear conflict being of equal size with parity in nuclear military resources and capabilities. It led Herman Kahn to postulate 44 steps in the escalation ladder, with the two sides, in theory, being able to trade blows of equal intensity on each step as the hostilities progress in a supposedly orderly fashion to ever higher rungs of destruction until both the parties finally dissolve in "spasm or insensate war."[101] Few such concepts are transferable whole to the India-Pakistan context, in the main, because of the sheer inequality between the two countries. At a fundamental level, the inequality translates into both the capacity to inflict pain as well as to bear pain. For any quantum of nuclear destruction measured in deliverable kilotonage/megatonage, India will be able to bear the pain and resulting human, economic, and material losses better even as it sinks Pakistan. The issue in a nuclear war is which side survives with more of its people and cities escaping with comparatively less damage. With this as criterion, wrote Paul Nitze, a stalwart American Cold War nuclear policy-maker, one or the other side could "win decisively."[102] Few Pakistani Army officers have publicly acknowledged their nation's nonexistent nuclear-war-waging-qua-destruction-absorbing capacity, and neither it seems have analysts in the American strategic community. For example, Peter Lavoy talks about the close links between Pakistan's strong conventional deterrent and nuclear arsenal as lending credibility to its strategy of "escalation dominance at all rungs of the military ladder." He completely disregards Pakistan's manifest incapacity to survive "repeated attritive" attacks (to borrow a phrase from the published Indian nuclear doctrine). It is one thing in a nuclear crisis to demonstrate resolve,[103] quite another thing in a live nuclear-fire situation for Pakistan, with weaker conventional forces, smaller less-lethal nuclear weapons inventory,[104] and enormous disparity in resources of all kinds, to maintain "escalation dominance." On what basis Lavoy thinks Pakistan can manage this is not clear. Retired Pakistani military officers and high-ranking civilians, who presumably know better, seem less reticent in saying their country stands little chance. If Pakistan, "a smaller military power . . . in desperation [used] nuclear weapons in its defense," India would retaliate, writes Air Marshal M. Asghar Khan, an ex-Pakistani Air Force chief, and within minutes reduce three or four Pakistani cities to rubble. "Pakistan would, as a result," he added, "be mortally wounded whereas India would be damaged to a much lesser extent and would still survive as a nation."[105] Along the same lines, Abdul Sattar, former Pakistani foreign minister, admitted that "Pakistan considers nuclear capability as an insurance against intimidation and aggression. It cannot contemplate use of nuclear weapons for any aggressive purpose or for war-fighting, aware that a nuclear exchange could entail annihilation."[106] He does not, however, consider the consequences to Pakistan if it starts a nuclear affray even as a purely defensive reflex by, say, nuclear-bombing Indian forces inside Pakistan.

Many deterrence theorists wonder if dropping small-yield weapons on tactical targets would "warrant" total war.[107] Such skepticism is fine in case the adversary can impose equal costs, which can induce caution. It does not hold, however, when the enemy is small and unlikely to survive a first retaliatory salvo.[108] This is the main reason the quality of Pakistan's nuclear weapons and missiles is of little consequence. For instance, will the Chinese M-9 MRBM with the Pakistani strategic forces make other than a marginal difference to the outcome of a nuclear exchange with India? Does it really matter all that much that this nuclear missile is accurate or, because of its lightweight materials and propulsion systems, that it is virtually undetectable by radar, or that equipped with fins and vernier motors on its nose cone it has endo-atmospheric maneuverability?[109] Given Pakistan's manifest disadvantages, the American defense analyst Michael Lind hypothesized during the 2002 crisis that Pakistan could use "nuclear weapons symbolically" by bursting a bomb on the ocean or on the Indian side of the Thar Desert.[110] This may give the Indian government pause for thought, but it is hard to see what good it will do. According to the tripwire definition, Pakistan may go in for such symbolic detonation only after the Indian forces have made deep inroads into its territory to get somewhere in the vicinity of the Karachi-Peshawar line of communications. Even if such explosion has the desired effect of halting Indian armored advance, it is unlikely to coerce them into withdrawing; more likely it will result in these forces digging in, firming up their defense at that point in the line of advance. In geographic terms, this is about the extent to which the Indian Army has always planned to advance anyway and the Indian forces will still be in possession of a big slice of Pakistani territory. Indeed, the Indian Army's Cold Start plans hope to confront the adversary with impossibly difficult choices at every turn, leaving it to Pakistan to escalate the hostilities to the nuclear realm, confident that India has the upper hand. This is exactly what some Pakistani military analysts fear and is the situation with which, they imply, Pakistan will not be able to cope.[111] The idea of Cold Start seems to be to sharpen the dilemma for Pakistan about when to use nuclear weapons to the point that they are not used at all. Senior Indian Army commanders, having decided on a relentlessly offensive-minded Cold Start policy relying on armored and mechanized forces to break through the defenses and to break out, have even discarded the use of the lightweight prefabricated nuclear fallout shelters. These anti-radiation shelters were debated in 1999–2002 as a "preventive measure"[112] providing protection for troops in advancing units. If used extensively, however, these shelters were criticized as constituting a "nuclear Maginot Line" around which the adversary's armored forces could make an end-run after threatening nuclear use to immobilize the now hunkered down lead Indian elements, and embarking on a counteroffensive of their own.[113]

The other disincentive to converting huge army formations for operations in nuclear, biological, chemical (NBC) warfare environment is the complexity and the costs involved.[114] Not only does the protection paraphernalia "take a chunk out of the army budget," it is "hard to decide how much is needed and whether it is worth it," said Lieutenant General Oberoi. "If it makes sense to have one brigade's worth of [NBC] equipment, why not five brigades' worth? And if you mean to equip the whole army, would that include rear area units? If not, why not?"[115] The questions about their utility boils down to the uncertainty of their use. The commanders are not sure how to utilize the NBC-warfare-enabled unit in war. Should it be in the vanguard of the strike forces, in that case what is the guarantee Pakistan will drop a bomb in the area the brigade is deployed? Should it be held in reserve, waiting for the Pakistani first strike on the battlefield before rushing to the spot, in which case, to do what? This unit could fight through but, with its cumbersome decontamination equipment and soldiers in heavy anti-radiation apparel, the brigade would be impeded in its movement and utility, and slow the advance. Such doubts have led to a policy of not enlarging the number of army units in the nuclear war-fighting role beyond the existing one brigade-sized group equipped for operating in an NBC milieu. The more effective course of action, according to the consensus view, is for the strike corps to take the losses and for the surviving units to skirt, rather than go through, the radioactive danger zones, and continue rolling forward.[116] This is what is practiced in war exercises. It may end up in "broken-backed" warfare but it will be on the opponent's land and with the enemy on the defensive. The trouble for Pakistan is that once a nuclear exchange is ignited, the certainty is that Indian nuclear counterattacks will end it. This explains the care with which

Pakistan has delineated its redlines and why General Karamat has stressed a mainly conventional response to Indian conventional military ingress. Should Pakistan at any point in time decide to go nuclear, it will suffer disproportionate destruction in the first wave of Indian nuclear counter attacks and, were Pakistan to up the ante with strikes on symbolic and major value targets in India, such as Delhi, Mumbai, or major industrial complexes such as the large petro-chemical complexes at Vadodra or in the border town of Jamnagar, whose replacement cost is immeasurable, national extinction. Between equal or near-equal states, a strategy of limited retaliation and limited use of nuclear weapons is credible because, like the United States and the Soviet Union in the Cold War, both sides had large, well-protected second-strike forces and, in theory at least, could trade nuclear blows at the tactical or theater levels without escalating to the next higher rung of the escalation ladder.[117] In South Asia, it does not matter how well-protected Pakistan's retaliatory forces are—something its nuclear planners stress, because even as they reach down to fire the last few surviving missiles, India will still have many more nuclear assets available for employment. "We will be able to swamp the Pakistani air defenses and strategic forces," asserts Air Chief Marshal Krishnaswamy. It will become irrelevant when, where, why, and in what circumstances Pakistan initiated the nuclear conflict or even what yield of weapons Pakistan used; the fact of first use of nuclear weapons by Pakistan will be enough reason for all the restraints to come off. The Indian government may have to choose between massive retaliation and "controlled retaliation," with the former option simplifying the "judgement required of the decisionmakers," and the latter being a nuanced, "more difficult" approach.[118] In either case, "a slow motion nuclear war" could unfold with attacks and counterattacks launched at a leisurely pace.[119]

Then again, with decreasing "reaction times" on both sides, the nuclear exchange could get into high gear fast. In either case, with the country having been struck by nuclear weapons, the Indian government is unlikely to display qualms about falling in with the military's plans for deliberate escalation to the war-terminating offensive to reduce Pakistan. It may be unrealistic for Pakistan to expect that, in the thick of a nuclear exchange, some friendly big power will intervene against India. Other than making sympathetic noises, China did not do that in the 1965 and 1971 wars; with India's long-range nuclear missiles, it is even less likely to adopt such a course of action. The United States may try its utmost to dissuade both countries from crossing the nuclear use line, but once this line is crossed the premium will be on the United States to disengage,[120] or to do nothing.[121] Nor does it seem a particularly good idea for Pakistan to mix warheads—conventional, decoy and nuclear—on its missiles, something General Karamat claimed a small nuclear force needs to do "to create or increase unpredictability."[122] The uncertainty about the warhead means that in an unstable situation the side that sees missiles being fired is unlikely to wait to see what kind of warhead impacts before reacting. The retaliation will likely be "launch on warning" or "launch under attack" and for the reasons General Karamat adduced in one of his writings. India's use of missiles with conventional warheads on "air bases and facilities" in the 2002 crisis could have precipitated, he wrote, Pakistani use of nuclear missiles, thus "Even without intent, a conventional air strike can cause damage that signals . . . that a redline has been crossed and a response is warranted."[123]

In the India-Pakistan context, it may well be that India has gradually come to accept the Russian Cold War concept of "single escalation boundary,"[124] intent as it is in communicating to Islamabad that once this boundary is crossed, a predictable chain of events will follow ending in a cataclysm for Pakistan. Recent studies have thrown light on how, in the recent past, nuclear-threat-laced India-Pakistan crises and contingencies played out against the nuclear backdrop. These have detailed the manner in which events unfolded and about which side did what and when, and how the proceedings stopped short of, or swayed away from, the actual trading of nuclear blows, and provide insights into nuclear risk and crisis management.[125] The premise here is that the bigger country with the bigger forces can absorb and, therefore, survive nuclear damage better than a smaller resource-poor less well-endowed nuclear-weapon state and that this fact ultimately will deter the smaller state from committing suicide just because it fears death—suicide being the core belief of the "massive destruction" school of nuclear deterrence.[126] The critical thing is not what happens before a nuclear first use but what happens afterward. Any which way the situation is analytically sliced, the result—its utter destruction—is inescapable for Pakistan. Assuming rationality on the part of the small state attacker and the big state responder, this end-state should deter the Pakistani Army from willfully pushing conventional hostilities over the nuclear edge.

The certainty of a series of war-ending Indian actions is, first, because the notion of "limited nuclear war" itself is untenable. "A nuclear bomb is political weapon when it is used as a deterrent, but a weapon of war once deterrence breaks down," says Air Marshal Patney. "Where's the question of limiting its use in war?"[127] It is a view of nuclear weapons commonly found among the senior officers in the Indian military and is akin to the sentiments of military men elsewhere, such as that of a member of the U.S. Joint Chiefs of Staff who said, "It's nonsense to think you'd shoot two or three missiles and get on the telephone and say, 'How'd you like them apples?' . . . That's bullshit. Most of the people who come up with these ideas have never been in a war."[128] Second, tailored retaliation to keep the conflict limited is improbable because distinguishing what kind of weapon was used in the utterly confused situation at any given moment in an ongoing war will be difficult. If a city is targeted, the horrific results will spur the launching of a series of strikes that will be fatal for Pakistan. India, in any case, will be inclined to believe the worst and respond accordingly. Bernard Brodie correctly concluded in the late 1950s that "the use of any kind of nuclear weapon greatly increases the difficulties in the way" of limiting war, for one thing because, "it is much easier . . . to distinguish between use and non-use of nuclear weapons than between the use of, say, a 10-kiloton atomic weapon and a weapon two or three times as large."[129] Third, because the first nuclear hit will convulse Indian society and surprise the Indian political leadership by its violation of the hoary "code of conduct" of restrained war-fighting that has imposed virtually no hardship on the people. It is a code, one of the most respected Pakistani soldiers, the late Lieutenant General M. Attiqur Rahman, said ruled out nuclear war between the two countries.[130] With this code breached, the Indian government will feel compelled to act in a seriously puni- tive vein. "As far as [India is] concerned," said Air Chief Marshal Krishnasw- amy, "we'll not stop until we are satisfied with the amount of retribution, and it won't be small. I believe that once we retaliate, Pakistanis will not have anything to strike with, it will all break down for them."[131] There is bound to be a high level of fatalities on both sides because counter-force strategy will become indis- tinguishable from counter-city or counter-value targeting, owing to the fact that in South Asia, nuclear infrastructure and nuclear assets are often located within or just outside metropolitan areas.[132] Given the density of populations in Indian and Pakistani cities, the effects of fission weapons will be just as bad as those of fusion weapons.[133] Fourth, because by this stage the Indian government will be inured to pressure by powerful third countries trying to save Pakistan, there will be no stopping India's meting out what it sees as just punishment. After all, besides the destruction caused by the Pakistani first strike, the cost of break- ing the nuclear taboo and setting the precedent for nuclear weapon use cannot but be very high. Heavy reparations after the nuclear exchange will, of course, be exacted. Moreover, when a lot is believed to be at stake, India has shown it can stand up to great powers as happened when the USS Enterprise Task Group steamed into the Bay of Bengal in December 1971 but could not stay the Indian land, air, and naval forces from overrunning the Pakistan military in what is now Bangladesh. "The Americans were wrong when they brought in their fleet [in that episode]," recalled a former Army chief, "because they felt Indians could be dissuaded. But India reacted differently."[134] Fifth, the idea of limited nuclear war is indefensible because, as even U.S. analysts concede, any egregiously pro- vocative action in the future—and Pakistan's nuclear first use would surely amount to this—will cross the prevailing "threshold of [the Indian] willingness to tolerate Pakistani attacks."[135] Finally, a nuclear death blow to Pakistan is cer- tain because there will be ample moral sanction for such action owing to the for- bearance India has always shown in dealing with Pakistan; the accumulated moral capital can be used by Delhi to dampen criticism. "Like the water building up behind a dam, the longer India waits to retaliate against its enemies, the greater the flood will be," wrote Stephen P. Cohen, the South Asia security expert at Brookings Institution, in the wake of the 2002 "mobilization war," "but it will be a morally just flood."[136]

Nuclear terrorism can spark a nuclear conflict directly if, having secured a Pakistani nuclear weapon or nuclear materials to jerry-build a radiation diffusion device, jihadis set it off on Indian soil. The 10 battalions of Indian Special Forces lack the training and the wherewithal to preempt such threat.[137] A preemptive strike by special forces of advanced countries against nuclear terrorists in Pakistan could end up initiating an India-Pakistan nuclear exchange. The Indian chief of the army staff, General Deepak Kapoor, has talked about "nuclear bombs falling into the hands of jihadis [being] used for anything, even to start an international conflict."[138] An American/Israeli special forces mission to capture and disable Pakistani nuclear weapons in order to prevent Islamic extremists taking hold of them could,[139] be disastrous. "Our policy of deterrence is India-specific," former Pakistani Army chief, General Mirza Aslam Beg warned. "No matter who comes for us, Israel, the United States or India, we will take on India. If someone is thinking of taking on Pakistan they should know we will take on India."[140] If Pakistan makes good on General Beg's threat, the prospect is for an intentional catalytic war, giving a twist to Pakistan's deterrence strategy of holding India hostage to the good behavior of third states. Even if this scenario materializes, it will be only another prospective case in which Pakistan uses a nuclear weapon first. It will neither alter the subsequent events nor the absolute certainty of Pakistan's destruction. The United States government is apparently determined to forestall any nuclear terrorist threat from Pakistan. Apart from the placement of Nuclear EXplosion Team (NEXT) and other U.S. Special Forces in Pakistan, Washington is also seeking a hand in the country's strategic decision-making by direct interface with the Pakistan National Command Authority to preempt extreme situations from developing—such as terrorist capture of nuclear weapons and even first use of nuclear weapons in a conflict by Pakistan.[141] In a notional sort of way, nuclear weapons targeted at India, like the conventional military wherewithal, help the Pakistani Army legitimize its role in Pakistani society. The Indian Foreign Secretary Shivshanker Menon is, however, of the view that the Pakistani Army does not any longer need the India threat to justify its hold on power. "To me this does not seem a sufficient explanation," he said. "The Pakistan Army's dominance over Pakistan's internal political space has now lasted for so many years, and is so complete, that it seems no longer to need an external threat to justify its rule."[142]

Then there is the issue of India's erecting a limited missile defense. It will not be as destabilizing as many Pakistani strategists believe, even though it could result in the augmentation of Pakistan's nuclear missile forces.[143] Choosing to disregard the fact that missile interdiction technology is still to mature and is inordinately expensive to boot,[144] the Indian government has decided to go in for an indigenous missile defense with coverage restricted to the Delhi capital region.[145] (More on the Indian missile defense system in the next section.) True, even a limited missile defense can complicate Pakistan's first-strike calculus, lend credibility to India's threat to escalate an underway conflict, and undermine Pakistan's confidence to retaliate.[146] By reducing, however minimally, the chances of a successful first strike, the Indian missile defense may reinforce Pakistan's tendency to be cautious. In the discussion so far, the *problème stratégique* for Pakistan is obvious. As long as the nuclear weapon is not used, it can be seen as compensating for Pakistan's weaknesses—conventional military inferiority and lack of strategic depth.[147] However, when it comes to actual nuclear conflict with India, a bigger more powerful state in every respect, what will obtain is not mutual extermination, but extermination of the smaller, weaker, country. "First strike uncertainty," perhaps, explains why Indian and Pakistani decision-makers will hesitate when it comes to deciding on nuclear weapon use.[148] Behind this uncertainty is the fact of lopsided consequences and hugely unfavorable "exchange ratio"—for a certain level of nuclear ordnance expended, the level of destruction will be massive and unbearable for Pakistan and grievous but absorbable by India. This fact undercuts Pakistan's threat of nuclear first use—the pivot of its deterrence/dissuasion philosophy. In any event, the Pakistani threat is "serious" without being "credible."[149] Pakistani Army Lieutenant General (Ret.) Asad Durrani at a March 2007 international conference touched on this distinction. "Despite Pakistan having nuclear weapons, why did it withdraw from Kargil in 1999?" he asked, and supplied the answer: in crisis, countries are, he said, "self-deterred" because "caution and fear of consequences" take over.[150] An Indian threat of first use, on the other hand, is credible without being serious. A threat of first use by India is credible because it is physically in a position to mount a first strike and take the losses from Pakistani retaliation, but it is not serious because it makes no sense for it to start a nuclear war and, historically, has never started a conflict or waged "total war" with Pakistan. Thus, Pakistan's belligerent talk of first use only ends up proving the truism the French nuclear strategist General Andre Beaufre articulated that superpowers alone can afford an offensive deterrent; other nuclear-weapon states have to make do with using their deterrents defensively,[151] and in Pakistan's case, ultra-defensively. That said, Pakistan's policy, like India's, is based on deterrence by punishment, which is generally believed to be more credible and therefore efficacious than deterrence by denial.[152] Pakistan's actions to first provoke a Cold Start operation capable of achieving only small goals and then to threaten to unleash its nuclear weapon as punishment for this reaction, which will only fetch it state-ending losses in return, is not credible. Even as means of fueling uncertainty, such a declaratory pose has limitations.

Uncertainty qualifies as risk depending on one's interpretation of probability; but probability, as the psychologist Gerd Gigerenzer has noted, is dictated by the degree of belief in the outcome, the propensities of the actors involved, and the frequency of a certain recurring pattern of behavior.[153] The belief in the inherently limited nature of war India and Pakistan have engaged in, buttressed by the empirical record of the way the India-Pakistan conflicts have unfolded in the past, suggests enormous caution and risk-aversion on the part of the two governments as well as the two militaries once hostilities have begun. In this context, India's Cold Start and, for that matter, Pakistan's, albeit attenuated, threat of first nuclear use, amount to little. "Neither Indian nor many Pakistani commanders are comfortable taking risks. There is far too much at stake!" writes Pakistani Army Brigadier (Ret.) Shaukat Qadir. "It is for this reason most of all that I . . . consider it unlikely that [the Cold Start] concept might actually be tried."[154] Among the stakes Qadir, perhaps, has in mind, is the Pakistan military's vast economic interests. The Pakistan military's agricultural and industrial holdings account for 7 percent of the country's GDP and fully a third of the heavy manufacturing. The army owns nearly 12 percent of all land in the country, 59 percent of all rural land, including 65 percent of the total acreage in the agriculturally fertile Punjab and, as of 2002, 5.53 percent of the non-financial companies operating in Pakistan, 3 percent of the financial companies, and 3.62 percent of all companies active in the economy.[155] It affords the Pakistani Army what the Pakistani defense analyst Ayesha Siddiqa called "financial autonomy."[156] It is understandable, therefore, that the Pakistani military would want conventional wars with India to remain small and for nuclear conflict to never occur. It can, however, console itself with the fact that in the absence of the punitive power of its nuclear weapons—seen as "an economical hedge" against the obsolescence of its conventional military capabilities—India's advantages would have been "magnified."[157]

If Pakistan is not a credible strategic threat, the dedication and seriousness with which it has built up its nuclear forces and associated infrastructure is proving the model for the Indian strategic planners to emulate. In an implied acknowledgement of Pakistani nuclear accomplishments, several developments in that country are cueing Indian deterrence policy and nuclear force planning measures. Thus, for instance, the annual rate of production of 14 M-9/M-11 (Shaheen-I/Shaheen-II) missiles plus an additional three units under manufacture at any given time in Pakistan is the sort of production figure the Indian Agni (II and III) program is gearing up to surpass. Further, based on extensive gaming and simulation, and on intelligence relating to Pakistan's nuclear inventory and strategies, a number of conflict scenarios have been worked on as a means of calibrating force structuring options. These scenarios also inform the process of preparing and fine-tuning targeting schemes undertaken by the Strategic Forces Command. One of these short-term scenarios goes something like this: Pakistan mounts a counter-force first strike with as many as 36 warheads, which will degrade 20 percent of the Indian nuclear assets and severely disrupt the still basic command and control system. A much-delayed but sizable Indian retaliation will still leave in tact some 20 percent of the Pakistani nuclear weapons for counter-retaliation purposes. What Indian planners are worried about is a situation arising before, say, 2012, by which time the Indian strategic force is expected to become substantive with meaningful numbers of Agni-II and Agni-III missiles, the first of the SSBNs, the two Akula-II SSNs, and possibly a squadron of Tu-160 strategic bombers in service, and a secure and reliable C4I2SR (command, control, communications, computers, intelligence and information, surveillance and reconnaissance) system on-line. Until then, the Indian nuclear deterrent will be dependent mostly on aircraft nuclear sorties embarked from half a dozen major air bases. Preemptive strikes on these bases could seriously hinder Indian retaliatory capability. In that event, a counter-city, counter-value response becomes mandatory. Once the deterrent is substantially up and a large-enough force of missiles takes the field along with some 200 warheads and weapons, with another 100 warheads and weapons held in reserve as force strength, Indian nuclear planners will have the choice of a more nuanced targeting approach coupled with a "flexible" or "graduated" response strategy that can accommodate a collateral damage-limiting counter-force reply. The third point of reference is Pakistan's fissile material production capacity. Pakistan's building the Khushab-I (100 MW) and Khushab-II (300 MW) plutonium reactors with Chinese assistance will vault that country's production of fissile material, even as India has yet to build a second Dhruva plutonium reactor sanctioned in the mid-1990s. The anxiety is sharpened by the prospect of a Fissile Material Cutoff Treaty being readied for signature anytime soon. If an FMCT is signed before 2012, India's stockpile of weapons-grade plutonium will, from a military viewpoint, be unable to support the buildup of the national deterrent. India could always decide not to sign the treaty and face international ire or, in the worst case, shift to designing and developing nuclear weapons with reactor-grade plutonium using the fairly large holdings of spent fuel after, of course, sequestering a part of it needed to fire up the breeder reactors once these come on-line. The issue will then pertain to the quality and reliability of these weapons. The most troubling thing in this evolving milieu, according to military officials, is the lassitude of the Indian government. If India is unable to match Pakistan in the focused and accelerated development of its nuclear forces, imagine the problems India will face in a nuclear crisis with China. This thought is beginning to motivate the Indian strategic programs and provide them with fresh impetus.[158]

India's security gaze, in any case, is shifting eastward and, in time, Pakistan will become a sideshow. Proof of this shift is in the military hardware being purchased from the United States with onerous conditions attached to the sale. Washington's permission for the use of these weapons systems against China is implicit, but their use against Pakistan is barred. The amphibious warfare ship (the refurbished USS Trenton) in service with the Indian Navy,[159] is the first of the major American military systems in Indian employ; the C-130J Hercules transport aircraft have been contracted for; the F-16 or the F-18 could follow, should either of these warplanes be selected by the Indian Air Force, to constitute its fleet of 126 medium-range multi-role combat aircraft. The modern P-8 maritime surveillance plane is also in the pipeline along with a host of lesser hardware and technologies. American capital weapons and surveillance platforms are meant to beef up the Indian military for the coming strategic competition with China.[160]

TACKLING CHINA

Nuclear weapons are thought of as necessary to dissuade Pakistan—the "brother enemy"[161]—but to deter China is a more complicated business because China poses a multifaceted and comprehensive threat. Involving a nearly

4200 km-long unresolved border and clash of economic, geopolitical, and security interests in the Indian Ocean region and in Asia, the potential here is for a big war, very different from the squabbles India may face with Pakistan. The differences in culture, ideology, and political and economic systems add to the piquancy of the immanent contest between these two Asian giants in the process of becoming great powers, with China way ahead in this race. As a study by the Institute of Defense Analysis observed, "China has been the threat against which India structures its military capabilities. China is also the major power against which India seeks parity of esteem."[162] India is fundamentally disadvantaged, however, by its belief that peace begets security when China works on the opposite premise that security begets peace.[163] In trying to buy peace with China, Delhi has sometimes compromised security. When facing adversaries, Beijing has never wavered in firming up its security. It has violently pacified its western provinces, Tibet and Xinjiang, with "strike hard" campaigns ruthlessly to end Tibetan and Uyghur Muslim dissent and eviscerate their freedom movements,[164] and it has firmed up its periphery in central Asia and Southeast Asia by connecting natural resource sites with transportation and energy grids to manufacturing centers in China.[165] Its agile diplomacy offering economic aid, military assistance, and generous terms of trade in accordance with its philosophy of "getting rich together," have coopted these countries into a Greater China co-prosperity sphere. To the extent that India still has traction with the Association of South East Asian Nations (ASEAN), for instance, it is because of the visceral fear China inspires in these countries and their hope that the countervailing power of India in the region will balance the strategic situation to their individual and collective benefit. "Whether it was ASEAN, Japan or South Korea, we were always aware of the fact," recalled Yashwant Sinha, the minister for external affairs in 2002–2004 in the Bharatiya Janata Party government, "that all these countries and countries elsewhere looked to India to balance the growing influence of China on them. ... They themselves came to us and told us that they wanted us to do something so that there's balance between China and India."[166] In southern Asia, China has expanded its military presence, played the 'Pakistan card' against India by bulk transfers of conventional armaments and nuclear missile-arming of that country to rivet Indian attention to the subcontinent, and implemented its "string of pearls" strategy[167] in the Indian Ocean to protect its "seaborne oil lifeline" carrying over 76 percent of its total petroleum imports from west Asia, Africa, and Latin America.[168] By these means it has also obtained air, naval, and telecommunications bases and military presence flanking India in the Bay of Bengal and the Arabian Sea. Its development of the deep-water port at Sittwe on the Myanmarese coast adrift of the Malacca Straits, in the Maldives, and at the entrance to the Straits of Hormuz at Gwadar in Pakistan, means the Indian Navy cannot expect to remain unchallenged in these waters for long. China has also all but preempted India's "Tibet card" by, in effect, brutally eliminating the native Tibetans and Tibetan culture from Tibet.[169] It has constructed missile bases on the Tibetan plateau and built the Qinghai-Lhasa railway, enabling it to quickly reinforce its forces. It has boxed in India from all sides with Pakistan in the west, Tibet in the north, and Bangladesh in the east, and weaned away a reluctant Myanmar (which bears historical animus to China) with transfers of military hardware and massive infrastructure projects, even beating India to Myanmar's oil and gas reserves. This happened as Delhi dawdled, complained about the human rights situation, and almost "lost" Myanmar. In the past few years, the course has been reversed and India has tried to mend its relations with the military junta in Yangbon, providing armaments and rail and road projects to improve connectivity and trade links with the Arakan coast.[170] It will, however, take a sustained effort to dilute the Chinese influence there, as in the rest of Southeast Asia.

What has kept India off-balance is China's sophisticated multi-pronged strategy that is at once silk gloved and iron fisted. It seeks increased trade and commerce and cooperative actions with India to deal with the "bullying" by the United States and the West on issues relating to the UN Framework Convention on Climate Change, an international regime of international trade and tariffs,[171] and military-to-military links. Simultaneously, it keeps the border dispute with India on the boil by reneging on principles of demarcation it had agreed upon,[172] frequent armed forays into Indian territory,[173] operations across the "line of actual control" (LAC)—as the unresolved border with China is called—to destroy unmanned Indian Army installations such as posts and bunkers,[174] protests against Indian troop movements,[175] petulant statements on some issue or the other such as the one reproaching the Indian Prime Minister for visiting the Indian border province of Arunachal Pradesh falling within China's claim line,[176] to which the Indian government responded softly. Illustrative of China's dual approach were two stories published on the same day in December 2007 in an Indian newspaper. One report referred to Beijing's satisfaction with the first-ever Sino-Indian war games recently held in Kunming and expressed its desire for more such joint military exercises in the future; the other story revealed that the Peoples Liberation Army troops had physically sought to prevent the construction of an all-weather road by India on its side of the LAC in northern Sikkim by rolling boulders onto it.[177] In the competition for energy and other natural resources, China has been unscrupulous. It has undercut contracts Indian companies had to prospect for and to develop onshore and offshore oil and gas deposits with third countries and sought to push Indian firms out of Sudan, Siberia, and Kazakhstan.[178]

Plainly, the Indian government is baffled, unable to make up its mind on just how to counter China and has settled on a policy as an *International Herald Tribune* story put it of "competing without offending."[179] Emblematic of this cautiousness are the annual Ministry of Defense reports. In 1998–2007, these reports expressed concern about China's rising defense budget, its aggressive posture and military buildup in Tibet and along the Indian border, and the strengthening of its strategic strike forces. The 2008 version of the report, however, far from saying anything critical, hailed China as an "important player in global affairs" and lauded its efforts at "improving bilateral relations with neighboring countries at economic, diplomatic and military levels."[180] The Indian government is apparently hoping that the burgeoning trade—$24.9 billion in 2006, expected to grow to $60 billion by 2010[181]—and the prospective emergence of "Chindia" as a powerful global economic entity,[182] will motivate Beijing to ease up rather than seed conflict with India. Many financial experts, however, fear that a collision of interests and friction will emerge, not "Chindia."[183] To reduce its risks, part of Delhi's policy seems to be to "free ride" on the apprehensions of the United States, in particular, and secondarily Russia and Japan, about China[184] and to partake of such measures as they may take singly or jointly to contain it. This hedge strategy could become victim of separate deals these states could cut with Beijing, leaving India dangerously exposed.[185] The more the Indian government has emphasized economic relations as the foundation for peace unleavened by a realist perspective on where these relations are headed and how China is unilaterally deriving benefits and the longer India goes without an answering Indian military counter, the more it has hurt vital Indian national interests.[186] China has already displaced the United States as India's biggest trade partner. It is, however, an unbalanced neocolonial-type trade with India mainly exporting coal, minerals, gems, and such and importing light manufactures and engineering goods, and Beijing enjoying a surplus balance of payments.[187] China's mercantilist policies deliberately to cut off competition by flooding markets with cheap goods, to sever Indian access to foreign oil and gas, and to undermine India's economic reach and influence starting in the latter's backyard are not a surprise.[188] In this context, cooperation can easily slide into conflict. The military is not at all sanguine about the steeply rising Sino-Indian trade, with Admiral Arun Prakash calling it a "Trojan Horse," which together with "the inherent opacity of the Chinese system, combined with our lack of analytic inputs, renders any . . . prognostication of their intentions at best, an educated guess."[189]

Great powers have always used foreign economic policy as instruments to signal their intentions and to achieve their strategic ends.[190] Twenty-first century China is no different in this regard, but what its foreign economic policies in southern Asia and the extended Indian Ocean region are telegraphing is its determination to expand Chinese interests by whittling away at India's strategic space and imperatives.[191] In these circumstances, simply offering strengthened economic relations as inducement without insisting on a resolution of the boundary question or showing willingness to take up China's military challenge and to begin pushing on the Tibet issue, as a former Foreign Secretary Kanwal Sibal put it, is to let China profit from India's diffidence.[192] The appeasement of China has been decried by the main opposition, right-wing Bharatiya Janata Party,[193] but the Congress Party government has not deviated from its placatory attitude. It is a mental makeup mirrored in the conciliatory statement by the Army chief, General Kapoor, who admitted, for instance, that Indian troops too intruded into Chinese territory, in effect, sharing the blame with China for the violation of the *de facto* border, and implying that because the undemarcated border was a political issue it had to be resolved politically.[194]

India will need more than political and diplomatic heft; it will require strategic military wherewithal to even out the playing field with China. In conventional military terms, India is a peer-competitor but in the strategic arena, only a distant regional competitor with China. When the strategic threat is so obvious, why has India not invested the necessary resources in military effort and wherewithal and in intelligence paraphernalia to assess and counter China? In the main this is because of the dominant thinking of the Ministry of External Affairs that is rooted in the era of Jawaharlal Nehru and his conviction about China as a generally benign power combined, curiously, with what retired Major General Ashok Mehta calls, "the psyche of a defeated country,"[195] as a result of the military debacle against China in the 1962 War. This view shapes India's China policy, not concerns about China as a powerful and growing menace.[196] "The Foreign Office is usually very circumspect about issues relating to China," says a former senior official in the external intelligence agency—Research and Analysis Wing (RAW). "There seems to be an unwritten principle that Chinese sensitivities are more important than ours. Those who hold hardline views . . . end up being sidelined. The current motto is 'We have to be magnanimous'."[197] The Directorate of Military Intelligence (MI) in the Army Headquarters limits itself mostly to gathering information about the prevailing situation on the border, resulting, over the years, in the military's intelligence threat horizon being progressively shortened to tactical level concerns. As long as there are no signs of military buildup in Tibet for an imminent war," said a former additional director general in Military Intelligence at the Army headquarters, "the thinking is there is no threat from China!"[198] "The Military Intelligence looks at only the military aspects of the problem and is, therefore, limited to that extent. [They] were always reluctant to share their intelligence with the Research and Analysis Wing. MI do not do political analyses and thus are never able to develop the complete picture," says a former director of RAW, Vikram Sood. Sood recounts that RAW "was at one time considered to be among the best informed intelligence agencies for the coverage of China. Its coverage was based on both humint [human intelligence] and technical inputs and covered military and political intelligence." RAW fell out of favor with the Congress Party government of Manmohan Singh, he adds, because "its closer-to-reality forecasts and assessments [were] taken to be too grim and pessimistic."[199] With the Congress government perceived as friendly and bending backward to accommodate its interests, Beijing may have been emboldened continually to raise the level of provocation in the belief that this exercise is cost free. The Indian government's strangely passive, excessively timid, and defensive mien is tantamount, writes a former Indian diplomat, to its "groveling" before China.[200] Basic disagreements within the policy establishment about China's strategic mind-set and thinking as it applies to India and about the strength of Chinese strategic forces are making for an institutional incapacity to plumb that country's record of conflict, and its strategic culture and intent. It has resulted in initiatives mooted to countervail China or Chinese influence being stopped in their tracks by the dominant view of not giving "unnecessary offense."[201]

What, in fact, drives China's strategy? Deliberate opacity, secrecy, paranoia, covert buildup, and decisive use of force are, according to Ralph D. Sawyer, historically the hallmarks of Chinese military thought and policy. Ideology and traditional statecraft militate, he says, toward a policy stressing *realpolitik* and ruthlessness, typified by the minister for national defense in 1993–2003 General Chi Haotian's statement that "The ruthless have always won and the benevolent have always failed."[202] Among the other notable characteristics of the Chinese military is its "cult of defense"—even the most aggressive military actions, including surprise attacks, are justified in terms of "self-defense."[203] On the basis of deconstructing six of the 23 territorial disputes involving military hostilities, M. Taylor Fravel concludes that China usually resorts to force when its relative bargaining power is declining. Specifically, he notes that China initiates military hostilities when an adjoining country's military capabilities begin to match or to surpass its own, and "where the strength of [Chinese] claims [are] weak." These criteria explain why Tibet and its traditionally undelineated border with India became the flash point for war in 1962,[204] and could again trigger military conflict. Using the Fravel criteria, moreover, hostilities are inevitable because India's relative bargaining position vis-à-vis China's is bound to improve in the strategic arena to complement the rough balance existing in the conventional military sphere. This last notwithstanding, the informed view is that the Indian Navy and the Indian Air Force are superior in both equipment and skills to their Chinese counterparts.[205]

The basic problem is with the Indian Army's unwillingness to enhance its capability—some 10 Mountain Divisions—beyond fighting defensive positional wars in the mountains. Even this capability is hobbled by rank bad infrastructure on the Tibet border. Absence of a road network connecting rear areas to the forward posts make it impossible logistically to support sustained action, speedy mobilization and concentration of forces, and rapid reinforcement of the forward line in operations. Worse, the Chinese have the terrain advantage of "fighting downhill." The Indian Army has for a long time now asked for at least 2–3 new Light Mountain Divisions equipped with missiles and howitzers for exclusively offensive operations on the Tibetan plateau to take the fight to the Chinese. The army would ideally like to have 2–3 such "strike" divisions in each of the three sectors—Western, Central, and Eastern for a total of 6–9 divisions for offensive capability across the Himalayas. Lacking this strike element, the Indian Army is stuck with adopting a defensive posture; waiting for something to happen rather than having the wherewithal to take initiative.[206] Army commanders repeatedly ask for the Air Force to train with Army formations in ground support missions, but the IAF seems uninterested.[207] In the border clashes with the Chinese forces, such as the one in 1986, the IAF did not help out, perhaps because of its distaste for other than independent operations and perhaps because it is convinced the

Indian government will not allow use of combat aircraft even in a defensive war in the mountains, as it did not in 1962.

Another aspect of India's offensive capability are the 5–6 battalions of the paramilitary Special Frontier Force (SFF) led by officers from the Army's Special Forces, but manned exclusively by Tibetan exiles. The SFF is meant for deep penetration and sabotage activities against Chinese military targets inside Tibet working in parallel with army offensive operations across the front. The SFF has been reduced, though, to doing guard duty on the border. The Indian government has neither sanctioned the new light divisions the Army has been asking for and any other offensive capability in the mountains, nor addressed the difficulties the army faces in maintaining the forward posts which, lacking roads connecting them to rear areas, have to be supplied from the air. In most cases, the nearest motorable road is between 50 and 100 km behind the line of important mountain passes along the long border occupied by Indian troops. The government's view until now has been that a border road network will only facilitate the Peoples Liberation Army (PLA)'s drive to the plains, with the aggressing Chinese land forces utilizing it.[208] Further, the Army presence on the Tibet border has been thinned out with many of the Mountain Divisions being "dual tasked" for counterinsurgency operations in Kashmir and deployment on the line of control with Pakistan since the early 1990s.[209] In light of the government's policy of mollifying the Chinese, the Army's underplaying the China threat, therefore, makes sense. If it has only a bare-bones capacity to hold off the Chinese Peoples Liberation Army across the Himalayas, it is prudent for the Indian Army not to provoke the enemy into starting a conflict and, as in the 1962 War, again show up its weaknesses. Whence the refrain heard in Army circles that there is no threat from China in the "near term," which is like the horizon—a receding phenomenon, always far-off and, therefore, requiring no immediate countereffort or capability. Thus, Lieutenant General Vijay Oberoi, the former vice chief of the army staff: "As Deputy Director General, Military Operations, dealing with China, I produced the first paper in 1989 on why I thought a shooting war with China was unlikely and that there is no threat from China in the 'near term'. After five years, as Additional Director General, Military Operations, I again said there was no near term threat from China. As the Vice Chief again I said there was no danger from China in the near term!" He went on to justify his stance by imputing to China a non-aggressive intent. "In occupation of Tibet," he said, "the Chinese could have built up their forces there from a relatively thin presence, but did not." Based on this observation, he is equally sure that "China will not use nuclear weapons" against India.[210]

China seems happy with India's policy of self-abnegation and does not need to rattle its nuclear saber. It is India that will have to be more forceful in wielding its nuclear forces to deter China's egregiously provocative policies. The ex-chief of the Army Staff General Ved Malik recalls that as vice chief he included in the Army's 9th Plan document in the mid-1990s "a paragraph in it that said we should develop strategic weapons as early as possible." On being asked by the then Army Chief General Shankar Roy-Chowdhury about the reasons for this insertion General Malik explained, he says, that "unless we develop these weapons, our equation with China would remain an asymmetrical situation with great disadvantages to India ... China could coerce us diplomatically and even in small skirmishes on the border, or where the situation can go up to the warfighting stage, as happened in 1962. I was for removing the [nuclear] asymmetry, because then, obviously, there would be a threshold that would limit conventional fighting." Malik further elaborated that "The constant theme the army voiced with the government was if you need to resolve the border dispute do so soon because the strategic gap between India and China is increasing, and we need to develop our strategic capability, and that if you remove this [nuclear] asymmetry, we would get close to Chinese capabilities."[211] Apparently, the Bharatiya Janata Party government of Atal Bihari Vajpayee, apart from its other motivations, heeded such entreaties, especially by the Army, the senior armed service, when green-signaling the 1998 series of tests and a policy of nuclear weaponization.

Having secured a nuclear arsenal, how then is India to use it against China? Malik, who served two terms on the National Security Advisory Board, is of the view that the doctrine of "massive retaliation" is relevant for use against China as well. "Massive retaliation against China means," he says, "we would do major damage to them in terms of value-based targets, basically cities within the arc of aircraft range."[212] This hews to the Cold War model in which the weaker side depends on nuclear weapons to deter the stronger adversary from exploiting its conventional military weakness. With nuclear missiles joining the nuclear order-of-battle in numbers, the aircraft will retain a secondary manned bomber role. Indian aircraft in the conventional role or for nuclear delivery advantages India insofar as IAF fighter-bombers taking off from the plains can carry a higher fuel-fraction for longer range or less fuel but bigger payload. It is a military edge India has never used against China in the numerous border skirmishes or in the 1962 War, in the latter instance because of fear of escalation and wrong appreciation of Chinese air power.[213] The manner in which military operations have been conducted against China smacks of the trademark risk-averse attitude and wariness displayed by the Indian government and raises questions whether in a crunch Delhi will summon the will to threaten use of nuclear weapons, and, if such a threat were made and were disregarded, whether it would have the gumption to deliver on the threat. In the most celebrated action so far against any Chinese military intrusion into the Indian side of the disputed border in Somdurong Chu in the Walong sector of the eastern border in 1986–1987, the very forceful commander of Indian Army's IV Corps immediately brought in heavy artillery and rained down intense and sustained fire on the PLA unit, significantly, not with the aim of obliterating that Chinese encampment or vacating the aggression, but merely to show that the Indian Army could fight. "This incident ... in which we went very aggressive surprised the Chinese and their response to our reaction was subdued," remembers Lieutenant General

Oberoi.[214] Indeed, it was after this experience that a chastened Deng Xiaoping is supposed to have commented to his colleagues that China "cannot any longer take a chicken knife to a bullock," meaning, that while India was a "chicken" in 1962 and was dealt with easily, a quarter of century later it had grown into militarily the much heftier "bullock" and required a different strategy to subdue it. As a consequence of this aggressive show of Indian resolve, China sought *rapprochement* with India; Prime Minister Rajiv Gandhi was invited by Deng to visit Beijing in 1987.[215] The lesson that China respects power and forceful actions to safeguard its interests will get India respectful treatment by the Chinese was, however, lost on the Indian government and Army. Instead, the 1986 success was seen as facilitating a dialog to obtain normal, mutually beneficial, relations while remaining oblivious to China's two-pronged policy. Its one prong has used the excuse of an unresolved border to put constant military pressure on India and, in the Indian Ocean, to collapse its strategic space and to diminish its political and military influence in the littoral and the extended region. The other policy prong has held out the promise of benefits from open economic relations and co-operation to forestall the attempts by the United States and the West to obtain unequal international treaties relating to climate change, environment, and system of trade and tariff and prevent a gang-up by India and the United States.

The disparities between India and China notwithstanding, the strategic situation as regards these two countries is heading toward a "deterrence deadlock"[216] (compared to the deterrence dead-end Pakistan has reached with India). Whatever the look of government's public foreign policy, Indian strategic deterrence capabilities against China are being built up unobtrusively. The connection between national power and nuclear weapons and delivery systems with reach, is now well understood, as also is the threat from China. "It is one of tenets of the post–Cold War world era," states the Indian Navy's Maritime Doctrine (IMD), "that the ability of a nation to adopt a truly independent foreign policy/posture is inexorably linked with [its] strategic capability," which the doctrine elsewhere defines as "an independent nuclear/missile capability." The doctrine refers to Pakistan's "hostile attitude" and "China's growing influence in the region" as having "the potential of upsetting the strategic balance and adversely affecting the security of India." After alluding to China's "conscious maritime resurgence" marked by its Navy's transiting from brown water to a blue water force with its (Xia-class and newer Jin-class) SSBNs and (Shang-class) SSNs and its interest in acquiring aircraft carrier capability, it points out that China's exclusive economic zone (EEZ) of 2.6 million sq km is only slightly bigger than India's EEZ stretching over 2.01 million sq km. The IMD then gets to the nub of the issue: India, it says, "sits astride [the] major commercial routes and energy lifelines"—the so-called 8 degree and 9 degree channels, which "puts us in a favorable position to control the choke points," namely, the Hormuz Straits seeing oil traffic worth over $200 billion pass through it annually, and $60 billion worth of annual trade in traffic through the Malacca Straits and, more pointedly, that "China's trade and oil demand [are] growing at 10% per annum."[217] Clearly the ability to strangle

China's seaborne trade and oil traffic and disturb the economic growth propelling its strategic ambitions, is the key. It is viewed as a very sharp Damocles' sword to hang over Beijing's head to ensure it behaves, acts within the limits of Delhi's tolerance.[218] From this can be surmised the thrust of Indian strategy.

If China has a disputed border to pressurize India, India aims potentially to try to throttle Chinese ambitions in the Indian Ocean and have the capacity to create at will even bigger problems for China ranging from nuisance-level actions, such as cutting off of oil and trade traffic, to nuclear retaliation and, with its forward presence in the Andaman Islands, prosecuting naval actions east of the Malacca Straits. The most prestigious acquisitions underway are meant to bolster such capability. The Indigenous SSBN, to enter fleet service by 2012, is to be supported by two nuclear-powered hunter-killer submersibles—the ex-Russian Akula-IIs, and a total of 20–24 diesel SSK hunter-killer submarines that will carry nuclear warheaded Brahmos cruise missile and other missiles—six French Scorpenes, and 10 operational Russian Kilos (that will be phased out by 2020)., There are also prospective plans to add several Amur-class-types—this Russian submarine was short listed before a decision was made to float a global tender. The slow-going SSBN, with top speed of 2–3 knots is expected to stay silent, with minimal movement in and around its main and proximate firing points, and have its thermonuclear MIRVed missiles cover the strategic end of the conflict spectrum. The SSBN-SLBM is regarded as the fail-safe option for massive or graduated retaliation against China, once the nuclear wire is tripped. "[T]he impossibility of calculating at what stage in a conflict [SLBMs] will be used," says the IMD in making its case for the SSBN, "can make it difficult for the aggressor to gamble rationally on achieving gains through aggression."[219] The Akula-II SSNs are to prowl the surrounding seas looking for Chinese SSBNs and SSNs. With dash speeds of 20–25 knots, they can trail and strike Chinese submersibles should they manage to steal into the Indian Ocean via the Western Australia route. They can also catch up with, shadow, and in war take out Chinese warships and merchant marine, including, presumably, bulk carriers, using ordnance such as its Type-65 wake-homing torpedoes with "one-shot kill capability."[220] The SSKs with 8–10 knot speeds are meant for shallow water anti-shipping and anti-submarine operations; placed near the choke points, they can detect and are meant to deter the Chinese Xia-class and Shang-class submarines from venturing past the Malacca and Sunda Straits and into the Indian Ocean.[221] It is expected that the Indian SSBNs, SSNs, and SSKs will also carry a land-attack version of the Brahmos missile, which is being planned.[222] The ex-Russian aircraft carrier, Gorshkov, under refurbishment for service with the Indian Navy and set to join it in 2011–2012, along with its escort flotilla, can be expected to take the surface fight in the littoral or the high seas to the Chinese Navy. After two decades of studying the carriers Melbourne and the Varyag bought from Australia and Russia respectively, the Chinese navy has not put together or operationalized a carrier. A carrier-vessel is expected to materialize but not before 2018–2021.[223] And it will take an additional two decades for it to be properly integrated into fleet operations—time enough, the Indian Navy feels, to establish its strategic dominance.[224]

The Chinese Navy, perhaps aware of the ease with which India and other countries can disrupt its energy Sea Lines of Communications (SLOCs), is building up a major force presence centered on its new submarine base in Sanya at the southern tip of Hainan Island, complete with tunnels into the cliff on the seaward side to permit its nuclear submarines to berth inside them.[225] This maritime approach to restraining Chinese strategic nuclear capability has enough latitude to allow for India's China policy to swing back to a less forgiving stance.[226] Notwithstanding this, the realization of the strategic triad remains the main goal. Admiral Richard Mies, then CINC, U.S. Strategic Command, talking in 1999 of the "unique attributes that enhance deterrence and reduce risk" of each leg of the triad, said ICBMs provided "prompt response," SLBMs "survivability," and bombers "flexibility." He also remarked that the triad enables a variety of strategic plans and "a wide range of options" to facilitate an appropriate response, "rather than [an] 'all or nothing' response."[227] What the strategic maritime approach has done is accord priority to the seaborne nuclear forces as the cutting edge of the triad while continuing to invest in land-based missiles. To complete the triad, negotiations are ongoing to try and procure a small fleet of Tu-160 strategic bombers from Russia on a lease-buy basis.[228]

The policy to obtain credible maritime strategic deterrence of China, in the first instance, leaves the acquisition priorities and the ultimate strength of the nuclear weapons inventory and air- and land-based delivery systems open-ended. For one thing, the size of China's strategic forces is not clear. The estimates of the numbers of Chinese nuclear warheads and weapons range from as few as 80–130 nuclear weapons[229] to as many as 800-odd nuclear weapons by the U.S. Defense Intelligence Agency.[230] The low figures are calculated on the basis of numbers of operational delivery platforms in Chinese military service estimated by the U.S. intelligence agencies.[231] For obvious reasons, this is a fallible criterion and does not, among other things, account for the weapons and warheads held in reserve by the Chinese nuclear complex and the PLA's strategic nuclear combat arm—the Second Artillery Corps. For Indian force planning purposes, prudence has dictated an assumption of a median figure for the Chinese inventory of some 500 nuclear weapons as a number to steer the growth of the Indian deterrent beyond the present level of 200 weapons and warheads and another 100 weapons in reserve. Hence, an eventual inventory of 400-plus weapons in the Indian strategic triad—a force level the Defense Ministry has supported as noted in the last chapter, is taking hold. It is premised on the conviction shared by important sections of the government that whatever the public face of policy, nuclear force structuring decisions ought to be made on a "near worst case" basis.[232] It underscores the anxiety about China and the uncertainty attending on a slew of combustible issues possibly spawning conflict. Besides the unresolved border, there are four main issue areas that could trigger war.

Potentially the most dangerous issue is the possible diversion by China of the Yarlung-Tsangpo River in southern Tibet northward at the great bend before it enters the Indian state of Arunachal Pradesh as the Brahmaputra River, on which the entire economies of the northeastern states and Bangladesh rest. Chinese dams on other major rivers originating in the Tibetan plateau, like the Mekong and the Salween, are endangering whole ecosystems and economic life of states downstream, and Thailand, Vietnam, Cambodia, and Myanmar have taken umbrage and protested. After a series of massive and environmentally unsound works that China has showcased, such as the Three Gorges Dam, Chinese engineers are proposing to divert the Yarlung-Tsangpo to meet the water requirements of the arid north of that country and to also reinforce the notion of Chinese sovereignty over Tibet. Beijing refuses to consider a joint river monitoring mechanism with India and does not share details about the water flow or about its plans for the various rivers its shares with adjoining countries.[233] During his January 2008 state visit to China, Prime Minister Manmohan Singh sought an accord preventing the damming or diversion of this river but Beijing resisted, promising only "protection and rational use" of the river water.[234] This has not eased the Indian government's concerns. Any attempt by China to in any way seriously deny or divert the Yarlung-Tsangpo will provide India, a lower riparian country, with a *casus belli* under international law.

The second issue is the continuing program of material assistance and "soft" help in terms of technical advice from visiting Chinese scientists to Pakistan's nuclear weapons program. Since the mid-1990s, there have been reports about China upgrading the Pakistani arsenal by transferring technology for boosted weapons to Islamabad.[235] Because China's nuclear arming of Pakistan was to keep the latter in strategic lockstep with India, the next step for Beijing, given India's thermonuclear weaponry, would be to begin passing designs and materials for hydrogen weapons. If this happens, there will be pressure on Delhi to remove its self-imposed shackles and cooperate with other countries on China's periphery to beef up their nuclear and other strategic armaments programs, putting India and China on a collision course.

The third issue relates to Tibet. The matter of the "independence" of Tibet transcends the autonomy of the region that Beijing is willing to concede and that the Dalai Lama, the spiritual and temporal head in the Buddhist lamaist system, has announced he is ready to accept. There is a serious schism developing in the Tibetan community between the younger generation of Tibetans inside Tibet and in the exile community in India and the Dalai Lama–led "Tibetan government in exile" based in India. The young "freedom fighters" are unwilling to countenance anything short of an independent Tibet,[236] this even though development has come to their land and the standard of life of people has improved.[237] If India's relations worsen with China, a future Indian government may be tempted directly to help the budding Tibetan armed struggle, and develop it as leverage, with its assistance going much beyond its role in the late 1950s when it joined the United States in a covert war against the communist Chinese in Tibet.[238] The center set up in the 1950s in northern India to train Khampa gue-rillas for the Tibetan revolt—the so-called "Establishment 22"—is still run-ning.[239] In answer to Indian interference in Tibetan affairs in the 1950s, China initiated a policy of arming and assisting secessionist movements in the seven tribal states in India's northeast. It is, perhaps, not a coincidence that just as the exiled Tibetan community in India was making plans, starting in 2006–2007, to embarrass Beijing in the lead-up period to the 2008 Summer Olympics—that Delhi did nothing to discourage—the incidence of border violations and aggres-sive troop movements on the Tibetan side by the Chinese military went up along with the increase in Chinese assistance to Indian northeastern rebels and, more worryingly, the homegrown Naxalite-Maoist guerillas now active on the Deccan plateau and in Central India.[240] The Indian government has safeguarded its options of intervention because, despite intense Chinese pressure, it has declined to accept Tibet as "historically part of China."[241] Because Delhi's recognition of Chinese claims over Tibet rest on genuine "autonomy" for Tibet and, implicitly, protection of its unique culture and religion, anything less can be deemed as unacceptable and reason to support the Tibetan cause. It is likely that the extent to which India will stay its hand in Tibet in the future will be a function of Beij-ing's show of restraint.

The fourth issue that can possibly instigate a conflict are natural resources and energy interests.[242] Predatory actions by China to corner oil and mineral rights in Africa, in particular, has incensed the Indian government. The China National Petroleum Corporation (CNPC), in recent years has riled the Indian public sector firm Oil and Natural Gas Corporation (ONGC) by, time and again, beating it on bids to prospect for oil and gas and to develop the fields in distant parts of the world. ONGC was bested in 2005 by Chinese companies in the $4.2 billion take-over of PetroKazakhstan and in the $1.4 billion sale of an oil field in Ecuador. ONGC and CNPC went up against each other for the control of an oil field in Thailand and in the $2 billion deal in Nigeria, and the former wound up the loser in both cases. China's oil market of 6.7 million barrels per day (mbd), moreover, is far more attractive to Western oil majors who are therefore willing to cut Chi-nese oil firms in on prospecting deals than India's oil market, of a little over 2 mbd. A first attempt at cooperating in the oil sector led to a successful Sino-Indian joint bid for a Syrian oil field. Analysts do not, however, see this as a har-binger of more cooperation. A clash of interests and cultures ensures that.[243] In fact, more, not less, conflict may be in the offing because India is seeking to become a big player on the international energy scene quickly and, for that pur-pose, ONGC is acquiring stakes in foreign oil companies and aggressively pro-specting for oil and gas all over the world.[244] It is also planning to invest $300 billion in oil exploration, a good portion of this sum in acquiring foreign licenses, in 2008–2016, starting with $450 million in Venezuela.[245] The Indian government is serious about accessing the raw materials in African countries and organized an India-Africa summit in Delhi in March 2008 and, by way of incentives, doubled credit to some $10 billion and offered a duty-free preferential market access to exports from African states.[246] As discussed earlier, the Indian Maritime Doctrine envisages the Indian Navy role as protecting the sea routes carrying oil to meet 70 percent of the country's energy needs and, at the same time, holding China's vulnerable sea lines of communication at risk.

In each of these potential cases of conflict, whatever the actions of the Indian air and land forces, a powerful Indian sea denial capability will come into play to squeeze the Chinese oil and trade lanes in the Indian Ocean, even as the SSBNs will ensure a safe and secure retaliatory punch should China choose to escalate to the nuclear level. The Indian military, however, is mindful of the country's limitations in facing up to China, starting with the resources allotted defense. Despite the "steepest hike" since independence that raised the Indian defense budget in 2008–2009 to $26.4 billion and a plan to spend $30 billion in 2008–2012 to modernize the armed forces, these spending levels pale before Chinese defense expenditures.[247] In March 2008, Beijing announced "a double digit increase [17.8%] in defense spending for the 20th year running" amounting to some $40 billion.[248] The actual level of China's defense spending is routinely estimated at three times the publicly stated figure;[249] in 2008 that would roughly be $120 billion. While the Indian economy is galloping along, growing at an average of some 7 percent annually, it is outpaced by its Chinese counterpart, which has been on a rocketing growth curve, clocking 9 percent-plus rate since the early 1980s. Beijing has been investing heavily in upgrading its power projection, conventional war-fighting, and strategic capabilities[250]—new solid fuel land- and submarine-launched missiles and anti-satellite weapons—and in the support infrastructure pertaining to signals intelligence, electronic warfare, and cyber-warfare.[251] So much so, China is fast emerging as a serious threat to the United States,[252] which makes it doubly threatening to India. The resources gap is beginning to put distance in the strategic and theater-level military capabilities between China and India and to make for stark options in a nuclear crisis with China.

As the weaker party in the strategic dyad, India is doing predictable things, such as lowering the nuclear threshold. China can quickly build up its conventional military strength in Tibet—from the existing 8–10 Border Guard Divisions to 20 full PLA divisions and to 44-odd divisions (but over two campaign seasons) because of the newly constructed Qinghai-Lhasa railway.[253] According to an official working on strategic plans, if Indian satellites pick up evidence of this, Indian nuclear weapons will automatically be armed as the first stage of readiness.[254] The forward-deployed surface combatants and submarines will work alongside the offense-capable Sukhoi-30 MKI combat aircraft that are replacing the old MiG-21 air defense planes in eastern India. A number of new air fields and supply depots are under construction to host the Sukhois, which will be tasked to neutralize the Chinese air forces based in the Lanzhou and Chengdu Military Regions, including all of Tibet and southern China. Of the eventual Su-30 force of 190 aircraft, 149 will be permanently deployed to deal with the Chinese threat. In tandem with aerial tankers, the Sukhoi aircraft will also function as the nuclear bomber leg of the strategic triad until the Tu-160s enter service.[255] And, more routinely, Su-30 squadrons will patrol the expanse stretching southeastward to Malacca in fulfillment of the "expeditionary role" assigned them by the new Indian Air Force doctrine.[256] The expansive use of Su-30s and air power generally is prompted by the fact that while IAF aircraft taking off from the plains will be able to carry an optimized weapon and fuel load, Chinese planes taking off from the high altitude bases on the Tibetan plateau will face quite severe performance penalties in terms of limitations on takeoff weight. It will reduce their range and fighting abilities and otherwise undermine what senior Chinese Air Force Lieutenant General Liu Yazhou, in another context, called "the fighting strength" of a military force, which he said can be judged by "attacking distance, advancement speed and destroying power."[257] Based on detailed intelligence, officials in the highest ranks of the national security decision-making are, however, convinced that the Tibetan plateau-based Chinese missiles[258] are not as reliable or accurate as they are made out to be, and point to this deficiency as the reason for Beijing's seeking to establish a close-in maritime military presence in the Indian Ocean region to increase its margin of safety.[259]

One of the ways for a defensive-minded country to inject uncertainty into an adversary's nuclear attack calculus is to build a missile defense system. Missile defense (MD) was first presented to the government by DRDO in 1997. The justification for it was found in the No First Use principle. "The system is particularly necessary for our country due to the No First Use policy," averred V. K. Saraswat, chief controller (research & development) at DRDO. "We will not know if any missile coming in has a conventional warhead or a nuclear warhead. We need a system to take on this threat. It is a defensive posture that will not affect the military balance."[260] In a 2007 briefing to the military, Saraswat talked of a missile defense system that will be activated by 2017, cost $5.5 billion (Rs 22,000 crore), and cover the entire country. However, the Indian government has approved the erection of a missile defense system only to protect the Delhi capital region and has authorized $1.75 billion (Rs 7000 crore) for the project. The system also promises to deal with the cruise missile threat by placing aerostats with look-down radars along the approaches to the country.[261] A single MD battery is expected to protect 200 sq km of area, with the system predicated on "hit to kill" technology with guarantee of interdiction due to two interceptor missiles being fired at different points, at altitudes of 80 km and 15 km, in the terminal phase of the enemy missile trajectory, according to Saraswat.[262] Tested twice in 2006 and a third time in December 2007, the system is based on the Israeli Green Pine Long Range Tracking Radar (LRTR) upgraded to give 30–40 percent better "target classification and identification" and with detection range of 600 km. An additional 5–6 tests of the system are slated, and the provisional deployment date for this system is 2011.[263] Fifty of the Green Pine LRTRs will be the backbone of the system and, plugged into the existing air defense radar network, will be able to track 25 incoming missiles at a time and launch 15 interceptor missiles. "The electronically scanned phased array active radars," writes Vice Admiral (Ret.) A. K. Singh, "provide for interceptor guidance in real time, with closing velocities of 5 to 7 km per second." The system will have a range of 2000–2500 km and an upgraded variant as much 5000 km.[264] Missile defense technology is still evolving, and there is no evidence that even the United States has acquired or can, any time soon, install a foolproof MD.[265] The importance of the Indian missile defense system, whatever its intrinsic worth, even with U.S. technology inputs,[266] is less that it will provide a viable defense against ballistic and cruise missiles than that it will put pressure on China and change the "strategic dynamic."[267]. Beijing is already apprehensive about American missile defense systems covering Japan and Taiwan in Asia. The prospect of a missile screen stretching in an arc from Japan to India cannot but have a salutary effect on China's abrasive policies. If China responds by enlarging its missile forces, it has to worry that the United States, Japan, and India will likely react by building up proportionately, leaving China no safer than before; and if it does not react, it becomes strategically more vulnerable. It is a dilemma Indian nuclear policy-makers would like to push China into facing.

China's strategy for preemption is thought of by PLA as means to make the "enemy's will to waver." The follow-on actions dictated by its strategy of active defense does not acknowledge, writes Larry M. Wortzel, "differences between offense and defense . . . and sudden 'first strikes' in campaigns as well as 'counter-attacks in self-defense' into enemy territory are part of the doctrine."[268] With the availability of large numbers of weapons and missiles, the PLA Second Artillery Corps has moved from "minimum deterrence" to "limited deterrence" and a stabilizing counter-force targeting stance.[269] This is only a precursor to the Indian strategic triad developing in the same way. Until it achieves "notional parity" with China in strategic forces,[270] however, a high level of readiness and a strategic targeting scheme based on destroying China's wealthy southeastern and eastern seaboard from Hainan to north of Shanghai suggests itself because, other than Beijing with its symbolic value, Chinese leaders will be loath to have the economic dynamo in the country destroyed.

With a lot at stake, what are the situations the Indian military sees as involving nuclear weapons use by China? Air Chief Marshal (Ret.) Anil Tipnis and Admiral Arun Prakash, for example, both believe that China would consider going nuclear on two counts—if it sees, in Tipnis's words, "Pakistan's integrity under severe threat from an Indian offensive" and "in the event of Sino-Indian hostilities . . . if the Indian air offensive against Chinese military forces and infrastructure or communication links—rail, road, oil pipeline in Tibet causes overwhelming attrition."[271] China's riding to the nuclear rescue of Pakistan, as has been discussed, is a possibility only if it is assumed that China will not mind nuclear strikes on its cities. The second scenario, in fact, is what is exercising the military. "Faced with a serious conventional military setback [in hostilities with India] China," Admiral Prakash speculated, "may resort to nuclear first use, initially at the tactical level. More complex scenarios can also be conjured up, wherein China may resort to first use, to ease pressure, ... or to punish those providing assistance to Tibetan/Uyghur insurections in the so-called Tibet Autonomous Region and Xinjiang."[272]

A war game conducted by retired Brigadier Arun Sahgal, formerly director, net assessment, Integrated Defense Staff, was based on just such a scenario. In a series of games played at the Army War College, India and China were posited as engaging in a military modernization race resulting in the Indian policy of "strategic assertion as a sequel to Rising China." Setting the scene for the war game was the increased naval activity in the Indian Ocean in 2021 leading to an Indian maritime surveillance plane being shot down by the Chinese. In response, the Indian Navy sinks a Chinese frigate. China demands compensation; after consulting with friendly countries, India refuses whereupon three missiles are fired into the sea offshore of the Eastern Naval Command headquarters at Vishakhapatnam. Frenetically paced buildup of conventional land and air forces in Tibet is detected. Even as India is trying to mobilize international opinion on its side, Chinese forces, as per their doctrine of surprise and "shock power" to catch "the enemy unprepared," attack the easternmost Indian province of Arunachal Pradesh in force. India hits back deep inside Tibet with its air force at PLA force concentrations and military infrastructure causing considerable damage. China readies its nuclear missiles for launch. The United States, having failed to broker peace but provoked by China's preparations to engage in nuclear combat, enters the fray. Every time the game was played it progressed smoothly to the point at which China was prepared to escalate from conventional to nuclear hostilities. In the majority of the games, the U.S. intervention as mediator and India's rescuer was accepted as both critical and necessary, perhaps because of a realistic assessment of India's chances in a nuclear confrontation with China, at least in the foreseeable future.[273] "China is a large power [and] even with our nuclear weapons, I don't believe we are protecting ourselves against China by ourselves. In the time frame up to 2025, China cannot be taken on individually," said retired Air Chief Marshal Krishnaswamy. "If you take on China, India will need the help of other great powers . . . We have to go for a regional solution, a coalition of friends, by bringing other countries—South-East Asian States, Japan and Australia—into it." The main strategic security pillar he implied would still be the United States, a country India can strategically rely on in a serious contingency with China, because, he claimed, it "has stood" by its commitments with its allies in the past.[274] However, the credibility of commitment by the United States with "an uncertain military clout"[275] or of coalition defense may not survive Beijing's upping the ante because of its belief, as expressed by General Liao Xilong, director of general logistics and member of the powerful Central Military Commission, that "whoever possesses a stronger nuclear capability will be able to control the process of war."[276] If India does not speedily close the gap in the size and quality of its strategic forces, which gap can in a crisis be psychologically debilitating, China with its "stronger nuclear capability" will hold the whip hand.

INDIAN-U.S. NUCLEAR DEAL

In the twenty-first century, with the power in the international system moving to Asia,[277] the U.S.-Chinese rivalry has taken front stage and the American policy of "congagement" combining containment and engagement articulated by the U.S. ambassador in Afghanistan, Zalmay Khalilzad, in 2000[278] has become the prime variable from which individual Asian states take their bearings. This rivalry has none of the tone, tenor and tensions of the Cold War superpower fight. There are, moreover, two other consequential players, namely India and Japan, on the scene which can tilt the scale one way or the other, depending on the issue. In an era of tenuous balancing, China cannot afford to alienate India or Japan overmuch, because an India-Japan-United States economic and military bloc will be difficult for it to overcome. Likewise, the United States would be foolish to rub India the wrong way or to take even its steadfast ally, Japan,[279] too much for granted for fear of a possible emergence of an India-China-Japan grouping.[280] Given the deep differences this last seems less feasible, however, than the India-Japan-United States partnership. In the Asian balance, what India and Japan do singly and, more importantly, together becomes crucial,[281] with or without the United States weighing in on their side.[282] There is a hard military edge to the relations between India and China and Japan and China, notwithstanding increased trade links and periodic attempts at easing bilateral relations, because of historical bitterness and clashing interests. With China perceived as the common danger by the other three Asian powers, if the United States is counted as one,[283] a lesser relationship, like that between the United States and Pakistan, for instance, which had strategic significance in the post-1945 world,[284] has slipped down in importance in terms of the larger geopolitics and is less of the grit in the machine of warmed-up Indo-U.S. relations. For the United States, it is now more important to balance China in Asia with nuclear-armed India's help than to balance India in South Asia with nuclearized Pakistan's help. Having been the key balancer in the subcontinent for a long time, its policies, such as the one on "civil nuclear cooperation," as we shall see, still has that residue of the "pivotal deterrer" in it. U.S. policy-makers, however, continue to envision America as providing overarching security against China and being the supreme balancer in Asia as a whole and within its various regions. Deputy Assistant Secretary of Defense James Clad made this dual role plain. The U.S. involvement with India, he said, was "to make it clear that there is an equilibrium in Asia, that no particular country should behave as if it is predominant."[285] As long as the United States retains its military dominance in Asia and the world, its influence in Pakistani politics, and its focus on terrorism,[286] the Pakistan-China axis will be strategically muted. It is an end state Delhi would like to prolong by cementing a strategic relationship with the United States but on equitable terms. It was fortuitous for the prospects of such a relationship that the regional and international power trends resulted in what one U.S. nuclear scientist, the late Wolfgang K. H. Panofsky, called the "nonproliferation nonchalance" of the U.S. government.[287] This was central to realizing an Indian-U.S. *rapprochement*. The trouble is that the attitude of Washington has not relaxed enough for relations to get over the nuclear hump.

The furious finger-wagging at India by Washington on account of the 1998 nuclear tests was followed by President Bill Clinton's "demonstration of good faith" in holding Pakistan responsible for the 1999 Kargil War. That, according to Brajesh Mishra, the National Security Adviser at the time, was seen by the Bharatiya Janata Party coalition government of Prime Minister Atal Bihari Vajpayee as the "window of opportunity to normalize relations."[288] Normalization of relations with the United States meant "persuading the Americans to recognize India as a nuclear-weapon state in some way or the other," recalled Yashwant Sinha, the finance minister in the early years of that government and later minister for external affairs. The recognition, albeit indirect, of India's new nuclear status was to be obtained by seeking cooperation in three sensitive but cognate technology fields—civilian nuclear, civilian space, and dual-use high-technology, such as supercomputers. The Next Steps in Strategic Partnership (NSSP) was conceived as the instrument. In nuclear cooperation, remembers Sinha, "we progressed beyond talking about safety norms, export controls, and all that," but the process got stuck on certain U.S. proposals, such as the one for separating the civilian and military parts of the nuclear-energy program. "Our rejection [of such proposals] was absolute," he asserted. "We were not prepared to pay a heavy or substantial price for it." The Indian government's hopes that the continuing sanctions on the Indian Space Research Organization would be lifted, were also belied, and on the issue of unhindered high-technology trade, there was little progress. "By the time we demitted office, there was nothing concrete that had been achieved," Sinha confessed, "except we engaged [the Americans] in a dialog [conducted by Jaswant Singh and Strobe Talbott] to try and build on it as early as possible. This was difficult ground we were treading. There were no easy or low-hanging fruit we could pluck." However, goodwill had been generated, for instance, when Prime Minister Vajpayee in 2003 seriously considered the deployment of an Indian Army division in Iraq, which did not happen because, among other things, of the Indian government's reluctance to put this peacekeeping formation under U.S. military command.[289]

The elections in 2004 saw the Congress Party coalition assume power, with the communist parties in the country providing it the required majority in Parliament. This coalition with the communists meant that the incoming government of Prime Minister Manmohan Singh was on short reins, with the allies on the left in a position to enforce their diktat and prevent any ideologically abhorrent policy. The Indian prime minister, nevertheless, chose to make the deal for "civilian nuclear cooperation" with the United States the defining policy initiative of his government, knowing full well it would stutter once the communists cried stop. It will suffice here to analyze its pros and cons to get an idea of just why this deal has been so controversial in India and why it has the potential for poisoning Indo-U.S relations. Prime Minister Manmohan Singh was influenced by two stark facts: because of the misassessment in the 1990s by the Department of Atomic Energy of the requirements of natural uranium, the Indian civilian nuclear-energy program was facing short-term shortages of this material.[290] India has 10,000 MW worth of natural uranium in identified sites but it has remained in the ground. Even a crash program of mining and milling the mineral into "yellow cake" will take several years to come on stream. What motivated Delhi to obtain this deal was also the belief that with imported natural uranium fueling the civilian power plants, indigenous uranium would be freed up for the weapons program.[291] The other fact was that the shortfall in energy production threatened to impair Indian economic growth. Despite the diseconomics of nuclear energy, the deal, in the short term, envisaged the purchase of "yellow cake" from abroad to run the indigenous reactors and the import of light-water reactors as a double-pronged method to increase electricity production.[292] This was the basic motivation fueling the desire for a nuclear compromise with the United States and, by extension, the 45-member Nuclear Suppliers Group.

In the Joint Statement signed by Prime Minister Manmohan Singh and President George W. Bush on July 18, 2005, dealing with the proposed civilian nuclear cooperation, the latter affirmed "that as a responsible state with advanced nuclear technology, India should acquire the same benefits and advantages as other such states" and that "he will work to achieve full civilian nuclear-energy cooperation with India" and for this purpose "seek . . . to adjust US laws and policies . . . and . . . work with friends and allies to adjust international [technology denial] regimes to enable full civilian nuclear-energy cooperation and trade with India." Manmohan Singh, for his part, iterated that "India would reciprocally agree that it would be ready to assume the same responsibilities and practices and acquire the same benefits and advantages as other leading countries with advanced nuclear technology, such as the United States." And among the "responsibilities and practices," he listed separating the Indian nuclear-energy program into civilian and military parts, "taking a decision to place" the civilian nuclear facilities under International Atomic Energy Agency (IAEA) safeguards, "signing and adhering to an Additional Protocol" to ensure stricter enforcement of the safeguards regime, "continuing India's unilateral moratorium on nuclear testing," "working with the United States for the conclusion of a Fissile Material Cutoff Treaty (FMCT), refraining from transfer of enrichment and reprocessing technologies" to nuclear states that do not have them, and promising "adherence to the Missile Technology Control Regime (MTCR)."[293]

Clearly, the phrase "state with advanced nuclear technology" in the Joint Statement attributed to President Bush refers to India's nuclear weapons capability and, to that extent, achieved the aim of an indirect U.S. acknowledgment of India's status as a nuclear-weapon state. As far as the United States is concerned, India has to earn the "same benefits and advantages" enjoyed by the nuclear Non-Proliferation Treaty–recognized nuclear-weapon states by doing certain things and making certain legal commitments. What follows are succinct criticisms leveled at each of the important undertakings by the Indian Prime Minister, which supposedly will burnish India's image as a "responsible" nuclear-weapon state.[294] (1) The deal is predicated on India's not testing again. This is ensured by India's right to test being rendered thin and theoretical by the disincentives (such as the cessation of fuel supply for light-water reactors India hopes to buy from the United States, Russia, and France and, generally, the ending of all nuclear cooperation) packed into the enabling U.S. laws. Preventing India, or any other country deemed a "nuclear non-weapon state" under the Non-Proliferation Treaty, from testing, according to John Holum, senior adviser at the State Department in the second Clinton Administration, will "arrest" their "ascent up the nuclear learning curve." In India's case, this will mean that the decisive weaponry in the Indian inventory will remain permanently unproven and unreliable.[295] As discussed in Chapter 2, the 1998 test for the thermonuclear weapon design succeeded but only partially and will require more rigorous explosive testing; computer simulation alone will not suffice even if it is in tandem with an inordinately costly full-aspect inertial confinement fusion facility capable of replicating fusion reactions on a small scale for the purpose of designing weapons—were India to obtain one. Without more tests, India's nuclear weapon technology will be frozen at the level of a failed hydrogen bomb design and a 20 KT fission device. This will curtail the psychological and military potency of the Indian deterrent, hurt its credibility, undermine the country's great-power ambitions and, faced with progressively more modern nuclear armaments in the Chinese inventory, hollow out India's nuclear strategy and options. (2) Bifurcation of its nuclear-energy program into civilian and military sections will at a stroke destroy the unitariness and cohesion of the broad-based dual-use nuclear-energy program that has allowed, in terms of both cost and effort, for economical use of the human and material resources, which are in short supply. (3) Putting civilian facilities under permanent IAEA safeguards means that in case the deal breaks down for any reason, the fuel supply will cease and pricey imported reactors will be a dead investment. The Manmohan Singh government, moreover, was extremely chary when asked about "corrective measures" in the safeguards agreement permitting the withdrawal of the nuclear facilities from the IAEA safeguards regime and for good reason. Any categorical assertion that India would under any circumstances exercise that option would antagonize Washington and prevent the fruition of the deal.[296] The NPT-recognized nuclear-weapon states are permitted to move nuclear facilities in and out of the safeguards net as serves their purposes. If India is being accorded, albeit indirectly, status of a nuclear-weapon state, should the same right to India not follow? (4) Implicit in the obligation to "work with the US for the conclusion" of the FMCT is acceptance of an American time frame for the treaty to come into effect; it expressly denies India the freedom to stretch the treaty negotiations until India's interests are served—the tactics it adopted interminably to extend the talks over the Comprehensive Test Ban Treaty (CTBT) before bailing out. The reason it serves India's purposes to delay an FMCT is because it has still to build up a sufficiently large stockpile of fissile material to allow the growth of the nuclear deterrent to respectable size, as the other four principal nuclear-weapon states and China have done. It will cap the number of weapons and war-heads the Indian nuclear force can have. (5) Adhering to the MTCR restrictions has nothing at all to do with anything nuclear, and should be no part of the deal. Insofar as it relates to missiles as nuclear delivery systems, the trouble is, other than passing nuclear weapons designs and technologies to Pakistan, China has also equipped it with accurate missiles. China apparently violates at will treaties it signs. In order to deal with such a lawbreaker, the threat and policy of militarily discomfiting it in like manner by equipping its adversaries with strategic where-withal is a powerful tool to check Chinese excesses. It is leverage India, pru-dently, should nurse. The Joint Statement also promised increased transfers of dual-use technology, something the previous Bharatiya Janata Party government had sought as a means to end the technology "apartheid." This begs the question of how high the technology would have to be to satisfy Delhi, considering coun-tries jealously guard their most advanced technologies. If cutting-edge dual-use American technologies are, by their very nature, going to be unavailable to India and other vendor states are ready to sell technologies of less than the cutting-edge level anyway, then why constrain the country by such deals?

In the wake of the Joint Statement, a "separation plan" was drafted by the Indian government in consultation with Washington. The original scheme mooted by the predecessor Bharatiya Janata Party for designating only a couple of nuclear reactors as civilian was rejected by the United States. By the time a list acceptable to Washington was finalized in March 2006, two-thirds of the Indian nuclear-energy program had migrated into the civilian category. The research resources were hitherto available for the military nuclear program were by these means methodically rendered inaccessible for weapons designing purposes. Indian scientists warned that such division of the nuclear program into civilian and military sections would end in international supervision of Indian nuclear research projects and would be subject to external approval. Eight of the 22 CANDU/INDU reactors were set aside for the production of weapons-grade plu-tonium and tritium; this entailed 14 CANDU/INDU reactors becoming suddenly unavailable to produce the fissile material. It eliminated the "surge capacity" for weapons-grade plutonium and tritium production. Because "islanding" of certain parts of the Bhabha Atomic Research Center was difficult, as part of the separa-tion plan the government offered to close the CIRUS plutonium producing reac-tor—reducing the weapons-grade plutonium production capacity by a third.

Scrutinizing the above list of do's and don'ts, the U.S. intention was obviously to give a lease of life to a creaky nonproliferation system rather than to negotiate a new nuclear order with many more nuclear-weapon states, one that would result in the relative decline of American strategic standing and power. By insinuating India into the NPT regime, the Unites States calculated that it would tame the one country which, remaining outside, had the greatest potential to wreck it. Pakistan, Iran, North Korea, and other aspirant countries are relatively small and manageable and can be coerced or cajoled into remaining below the threat threshold. Conceding a hollow and conditional recognition as nuclear-weapon state to an India defanged by the nuclear deal and without materially changing the international nuclear pecking order, therefore, must have appeared to American policy-makers as a small price to pay for so large a nonproliferation dividend and retention of the U.S.-favored international balance-of-power system. It explains the hard canvassing on its behalf in Delhi by other than George W. Bush administration officials; Democratic Party influentials, like Senator Joe Biden, Jr., chairman of the Senate Foreign Relations Committee, and former Deputy Secretary of State Strobe Talbott. It also explains the heavy bipartisan support (76 percent of the votes) in the U.S. Congress for this deal-enabling legislation—The Henry J. Hyde United States-India Peaceful Atomic Energy Cooperation Act of 2006.[297]

The Hyde Act tightened the screws on India, imposed more onerous terms and conditions, and closed off India's escape routes. For instance, it strengthened the "no testing" predicate of the deal, permitted only so much uranium fuel to be stockpiled for the civilian CANDU/INDU reactors as to meet their "operational requirements," mandated the return of all nuclear materials, but not the radioactive spent fuel, in case the deal broke down at any point in time, insisted that the White House ensure that the Hyde Act provisions would dictate all NSG transactions with India, and emphasized the permanency and intrusiveness of the international safeguards. It expressly prevented the transfer of any nuclear technology relating to uranium enrichment and heavy-water production. Such limits on nuclear technology were ironical because the former director of the Los Alamos National Laboratory, Siegfried S. Hecker, testified on April 20, 2008 to a subcommittee of the U.S. Senate Committee on Appropriations, "whereas [technology] sanctions slowed progress in nuclear energy, they made India self-sufficient and world leaders in fast reactor technology. While much of the world's approach to India has been to limit its access to technology, it may well be that today we limit ourselves by not having access to India's nuclear technology developments. Such technical views should help to advice the diplomatic efforts with India."[298] And, it required India's Iran policy to reflect American concerns. Most of these provocative provisions in the Hyde Act are alluded to or included in some form or the other in the 123 Agreement and the "India-specific" safeguards agreement. In India, the opponents of the deal pointed out that according to the government's own Planning Commission study, by the year 2035, the addition of electricity into the grid from 20 imported reactors and from CANDU/INDU reactors put up at the rate of one unit every 5–7 years, would still amount to only 5–6 percent of the total electricity produced in that year. This is only a marginal improvement on the current 2–3 percent of energy produced in the country from nuclear power plants. Further, importing light-water reactors was one way of diverting India from the "plutonium economy," which can more easily be used for military purposes, to the "uranium economy," and Indian public investment into enriched uranium fueled-imported reactors rather than into the development of the breeder and thorium reactors. These latter programs, as discussed in Chapter 2, based on exploiting the plentiful thorium reserves in the country, promise genuine energy independence but suffer from inadequate funding. It was stressed that the Hyde Act legalized the severance of nuclear cooperation at any time for any reason by the United States if it believed that ending it served its interests. The Manmohan Singh government attempted to retrieve lost ground by, for instance, negotiating an "India-specific" safeguards agreement with the IAEA inclusive of a provision allowing India to take undefined "corrective measures" in case the deal breaks down. This phrase will enable India, it is said, to withdraw from the safeguards agreement altogether.[299] It is obvious that, in order to enable the deal to go through, the two sides have agreed to disagree and to paper over their differences. There are grave doubts, however, about the Indian government's having been shown any laxity by the IAEA. In the so-called "India-specific" safeguards agreement, there is mention of "corrective measures" but only in the preamble with no articles to to indicate the Indian response if the nuclear cooperation ends at any time in the future for whatever reasons. The text of the agreement, however, is not as ambiguous about the safeguards-in-perpetuity clause, following up the preambular mention with provisions to operationalize the safeguards regime. It suggests a hollowing out of the "corrective measures" concept and, specifically, of the possibility that India will be able legally to withdraw its civilian nuclear facilities from the safeguards net. Worse, the safeguards text read in conjunction with the restricted document GOV/1621 leads to an interpretation that the provisions in the Hyde Act would apply. This the entire political opposition, ranging from the communist parties to the right-wing Bharatiya Janata Party, has found unacceptable. As a result, the ruling Congress Party coalition government may have won a generalized vote of confidence of the majority in parliament on July 22, 2008 but not a consensus on whether the nuclear deal is good for the country. This did not dilute the political opposition to the deal.[300] Ideally, the communist parties would like to terminate the deal; the leader of the Bharatiya Janata Party L. K. Advani has promised to "renegotiate" the nuclear deal and, failing which, to scrap it. Advani also proposed an enactment by parliament of an Indian counterpart of the Hyde Act, though how this would neutralize the impact of the American law he did not say.[301] In this equation India is the favor seeker and Washington in a position to dispense favors but on its terms. The United States acknowledges India's nuclear-weapons capabilities and, hence, recognizes de facto the country's nuclear-weapon state status and has tried to ease the Nuclear Suppliers Group trade guidelines, while remaining well within the confines of the Hyde Act in terms of the proscribed technology transfers. In return, India agrees to hew to some very onerous conditions, such as those on safeguards that are not applicable to *de jure* nuclear weapon states. The bulk of commentators in the press and the electronic media supported the government position but were unable to refute any of the technical and strategic arguments made against the deal. Stalwart Indian nuclear scientists charged that energy from coal and hydroelectric power plants would be far less expensive than that from imported reactors bought at the cost of foreign and strategic policy freedom, that the deal would weaken India's nuclear military capabilities and indigenous nuclear technology research and development, and that the safeguards would be in perpetuity..[302] Their case was countered by speculations about how the deal would pave the way for strategic cooperation, transfer much needed advanced technology in various fields, and generally brighten up the country's economic prospects with the inflow of American investment. These outcomes are realizable, however, even without the nuclear deal.[303] Indeed, geostrategic compulsions, convergence of liberal values, and increasingly symbiotic economic linkages will ensure that.[304] This still leaves a niggling worry about what America values more: nonproliferation rigidity or seriousness in containing China? Because if it is the latter, then it makes ample strategic sense to enable India to acquire the same level of thermonuclear and long-range missile clout so it can, in coalition with other Asian states, more credibly reign in Chinese ambitions. Surely, this serves the U.S. interests better than trying to hobble India strategically or singly taking on China.

The larger issue is something else. Assuming the 123 Agreement and the safeguards agreement do, in fact, implicitly acknowledge India's changed nuclear implicitly status, the question is: Should India be content, as the Australian strategic analyst Sandy Gordon has argued, merely with its recognition as "a 'responsible', but not fully 'legitimate' nuclear weapons state" within the existing nonproliferation regime?[305] Would it not have been more sensible and prudent for India to distance itself from any treaty obligations-qua-policy hindrances? This would have preserved its freedom of action and three-pronged leverage potentially to (1) use proliferation as a *realpolitik* device, in a tit-for-tat way strategically, for instance, to arm fearful states on China's periphery, (2) become a genuinely independent system balancer, and (3) manipulate its growing economic, political, and nuclear presence in the world to undermine the existing global NPT order and, thereby, to push the United States and other nuclear states with large arsenals to think "minimum deterrence" and to begin negotiations for a new, more equitable, nonproliferation system in which all countries are limited to, say, at most 200–250 weapons.[306]

The Manmohan Singh government and the George W. Bush administration erred in politically making too much of the nuclear civil cooperation deal, which was, ironically, seen by both the nonproliferation lobby in the United States and the nationalist strategic enclave in India as wrongheaded and requiring the payment of too high a price.[307] Indeed, this deal could turn out to be a sugarcoated poison pill for Indo-U.S. relations. Given that the issue facing the Indian nuclear weaponeers is when (not whether) to resume testing, and the question confronting the government is how best to tackle the deal-ending consequences that will follow, and considering that the many benefits from the deal promised India are unlikely to be realized in the short to medium term, a scapegoating of the United States if the deal turns sour or does not fulfill the raised expectations is on the cards. Moreover, the role of money, middlemen, and the controversial manner in which the "trust motion" endorsing the deal was railroaded through parliament has cleaved the polity down the middle.[308] Any future coalition government involving either the right-wing Bharatiya Janata Party or the left parties will feel politically compelled to call off the deal or to water it down to nothing. In that situation, India could well be stuck with the worst possible outcome—no imported reactors, no meeting of energy shortfalls, and no cost-free way of invoking the "corrective measures" clause and pulling the Indian civilian facilities out of the IAEA safeguards. In any event, the nuclear deal may turn out to be more serious than a "hiccup," as Bruce Riedel, a former CIA officer and adviser on Middle East and South Asia to three U.S. presidents, sees it.[309] It could hurt the burgeoning Indo-U.S. relations deeply, turning out to be more serious than either Delhi or Washington anticipates.

Notes

INTRODUCTION

1. Robert D. Blackwill and Albert Carnesale, eds., *New Nuclear Nations: Consequences for US Policy* (New York: Council on Foreign Relations Press, 1993).

2. For a detailed historical-theoretical analysis of the evolution of the Indian nuclear program, and India's nuclear thinking and minimum deterrence policy, see Bharat Karnad, *Nuclear Weapons and Indian Security: The Realist Foundations of Strategy,* 2nd ed. (New Delhi: Macmillan India Ltd, 2002, 2005).

3. For recent books along these lines, see George Perkovich, *India's Nuclear Bomb: The Impact on Global Proliferation* (New Delhi: Oxford University Press, 2000); Ashley J. Tellis, *India's Emerging Nuclear Posture: Between Recessed Deterrent and Ready Arsenal* (Santa Monica: RAND, 2001); Michael Krepon and Paul Gagne, eds., *The Stability-Instability Paradox: Nuclear Weapons and Brinkmanship in South Asia* (Washington, DC: The Henry L. Stimson Center, June 2001); Michael Krepon, Rodney W. Jones, Ziad Haider, eds., *Escalation Control and the Nuclear Option in South Asia* (Washington, DC: The Henry L. Stimson Center, November 2004); Sumit Ganguly and Devin T. Hagerty, *Fearful Symmetry: India-Pakistan Crises in the Shadow of Nuclear Weapons* (New Delhi: Oxford University Press, 2005); and S. Paul Kapur, *Dangerous Deterrent: Nuclear Weapons Proliferation and Conflict in South Asia* (Stanford, CA: Stanford University Press, 2007).

4. Ashley J. Tellis, *India a New Global Power: An Action Agenda for the United States* (Washington, DC: Carnegie Endowment for International Peace, 2005).

CHAPTER 1

1. Pierre Goldshmidt, "Nuclear Renaissance and Non-Proliferation," Lecture at the 24th Conference of the Nuclear Societies, Israel, February 19–21, 2008, http://www.carnegieendowment.org/files/nuclearsocieties_2-19-081.pdf.

2. T. V. Paul, "Power, Influence and Nuclear Weapons," in *The Absolute Weapon Revisited: Nuclear Arms and the Emerging International Order,* ed. T. V. Paul, Richard J. Harknett, and James J. Wirtz (Ann Arbor: University of Michigan Press, 2000).

3. A group of former armed forces chiefs from the United States, Britain, France, Germany, and the Netherlands, including General John Shalikashvili, the former Chairman, U.S. Joint Chiefs of Staff, and Field Marshal Lord Inge, the ex-Chief of the British Defense Staff, deemed nuclear "first strike" as an "indispensable instrument" to stop the spread of nuclear weapons. See Paul Dibbs, "Nuclear Warfare Stepped Closer," *Sydney Morning Herald,* February 11, 2008.

4. That many nuclear powers will make for a more stable world is something Kenneth Waltz and Martin Van Creveld have argued. See, respectively, *The Spread of Nuclear Weapons: More May Be Better,* Adelphi Paper 171 (London: International Institute for Strategic Studies, 1981), http://www.mtholyoke.edu/acad/intrel/waltz1.htm; and *Nuclear Proliferation and the Future of Conflict* (New York: Free Press, 1993).

5. The policies and actions of the United States and the North Atlantic Treaty Organization members in balkanizing Yugoslavia is a case in point. See Raju G. C. Thomas, ed., *Yugoslavia Unraveled: Sovereignty, Self-Determination, Intervention* (Lanham, MD: Lexington Books, 2003).

6. Ibid.

7. See Derek D. Smith, *Deterring America: Rogue States and the Proliferation of Weapons of Mass Destruction* (Washington, DC: The Brookings Institution, 2006).

8. Phillipe Le Billon, *Fuelling War: Natural resources and armed conflict,* Adelphi Paper 373 (London: International Institute of Strategic Studies, 2005).

9. Kurt M Campbell and Michael O'Hanlon, *Hard Power: The New Politics of National Security* (Cambridge, MA: Basic Books, 2006).

10. It has been argued that strong Cold War alliances reduced the incentives for nuclear proliferation. See Michael Mandelbaum, *The Nuclear Revolution* (Cambridge, UK: Cambridge University Press, 1981), pp. 159–166, and Lawrence Freedman, *The Evolution of Nuclear Strategy* (New York: St. Martin's Press, 1983), pp. 283–289.

11. Colin S. Gray, "Nuclear Weapons and the Revolution in Military Affairs," in Paul et al., *Absolute Weapon Revisited,* p. 117.

12. In the 1950s, Henry Kissinger, for instance, regarded a nuclear proliferated world as both natural and inevitable with "secondary powers" acquiring nuclear bombs from "the constantly growing list of countries which will possess a nuclear armaments industry." See his *Nuclear Weapons and Foreign Policy* (New York: Harper & Brothers, 1957), p. 14.

13. Robert S. Litwak, "Non-Proliferation and the Use of Force," in *Ultimate Security: Combating Weapons of Mass Destruction,* ed. Janne E. Nolan, Bernard I. Finel, and Brian D. Finlay (New York: The Century Foundation, 2003), pp. 75–76.

14. See Larry A Niksch, *North Korea's Nuclear Weapons Program,* Updated August 27, 2003, CRS Brief for Congress, pp. 6–7, http://www.fas.org/.

15. Helene Cooper, "North Koreans Agree to Disable Nuclear Facilities," *The New York Times,* October 4, 2007; Wyn Q. Bowen, *Libya and Nuclear Proliferation: Stepping*

Back from the Brink, Adelphi Paper 380 (London: International Institute of Strategic Studies, 2006)

16. Israel aerially attacked an under-construction nuclear reactor of possibly North Korean origin, usable in a potential Syrian weapons program. See David E. Sanger and Mark Mazzetti, "Israel Struck Syrian Nuclear Project, Analysts Say," *The New York Times,* October 14, 2007. For a concise take on Syria's nuclear program, see Campbell and O'Hanlon, *Hard Power,* pp. 221–222.

17. For a policy statement by the George W. Bush administration about preventing Iranian nuclear weapons, see Under Secretary of State John R. Bolton's remarks to the Hudson Institute, Washington, DC, on August 17, 2004, http://www.state.gov/t/us/rm/35281. htm. See "Iranian Progress Toward Developing Nuclear Weapons," updated April 20, 2007, http://www.milnet.com/Iranian-Nuclear-Chronology.htm for the case that Iran will definitely go nuclear, and for analysis that suggests Iran may acquire capabilities, not nuclear weapons, see *Iran: Nuclear Intentions and Capabilities,* National Intelligence Estimate, November 2007, National Intelligence Council, http://www.dni.gov/press_ releases/20071203_release.pdf.

18. Harold Brown, "New Nuclear Realities," *The Washington Quarterly,* 31, no. 1 (Winter 2007–08):20.

19. David Rohde, "Foreigners redefine Taliban's extremism," *International Herald Tribune,* October 31, 2007.

20. See the record of the U.S. Congressional Hearings on "A. Q. Khan Nuclear Wal-Mart: Out of Business or Under New Management," by subcommittees of the House Foreign Affairs Committee, June 27, 2007, http://www.fas.org/irp/congress/2007_hr/ aqkhan.pdf.

21. On Islamic religion, culture, society, and state being antagonistic to, and sparking conflict with, their Christian, Jewish, Hindu, and Buddhist counterparts, see Samuel P. Huntington, *The Clash of Civilizations and the Remaking of World Order* (New York: Simon & Schuster, 1996). Huntington's thesis gains credence from inflammatory statements by the leaders of the Al-Qaeda terrorist organization calling for jihad against the Christian Crusader West and Jewish Israel. See Robin M. Frost, *Nuclear Terrorism After 9/11,* Adelphi Paper 378 (London: International Institute of Strategic Studies, 2006), pp. 56–62.

22. President George W. Bush was apprehensive that the U.S. war on terror would be seen by Muslims as war on Islam. See "President Discusses War on Terror at National Endowment for Democracy," October 6, 2005, http://www.whitehouse.gov/news/ releases/2005/10/20051006-3.html. On the issue of whether Islam condones terror, see Bernard Lewis, *The Crisis of Islam: Holy War and Unholy Terror,* (New York: Random House, 2004). And for the case that antiterror war is war on Islam, see Enver Masud, *The War on Islam,* 4th ed. (New Delhi: Tara Press, 2007).

23. Herman Kahn long ago warned that the use of nuclear weapons in local wars could motivate frightened regional states to acquire these weapons. See his *On Thermonuclear War* (Princeton, NJ: Princeton University Press, 1960), p. 479.

24. One such speculative analysis featured, other than the calculi of the five NPT-recognized nuclear weapon states, only the strategic uncertainties created by a few newly nuclear-armed regional powers. See Keith B Payne, *Deterrence in the Second Nuclear Age* (Lexington, KY: The University Press of Kentucky, 1996).

25. This disaffection with the NPT resulted in the last NPT Review Conference held in New York, May 7–27, 2005 ending without a consensus document or declaration. It has

been called "the biggest failure in the history of the treaty." For an elaboration of the reasons why the Conference failed, refer to Harald Muller, *The 2005 NPT Review Conference: Reasons and Consequences of Failure and Options for Repair* (Stockholm: The Weapons of Mass Destruction Commission, Report No. 31, undated), http://www.wmdcommission.org/files/No31.pdf.

26. Rebecca Johnson, " 'Do as I Say, not as I Do': From Nuclear Non-Proliferation to Counter-Proliferation" in *Arms Control After Iraq: Normative and Operational Challenges,* ed. Waheguru Pal Singh and Ramesh Thakur (Tokyo, New York, Paris: The United Nations University Press, 2006), pp. 69–72. Its is a view that is now spreading across the Atlantic. See Douglas Hurd, Malcolm Rifkind, David Owen and George Robertson, "Start worrying and learn to ditch the bomb", The Times, June 30, 2008.

27. See George P. Schultz, William J. Perry, Henry Kissinger, and San Nunn, "A World Free of Nuclear Weapons," *Wall Street Journal,* January 4, 2007 and their "Toward a Nuclear-Free World," *Wall Street Journal,* January 16, 2008. Regarding the British view, refer to Douglas Hurd, Malcom Rifkind, David Owen, and George Robertson, "Start Worrying and Learn to Ditch the Bomb," *The Times* (London), June 30, 2008.

28. George Perkovich, Joseph Cirincione, Rose Gottemoeller, Jon B. Wolfstahl, and Jessica T. Mathews, *Universal Compliance: A Strategy for Nuclear Security,* Draft (Washington, DC: Carnegie Endowment for International Peace, June 2004).

29. J. D. Crouch, "Special Briefing on the Nuclear Posture Review," January 9, 2002, http://www.globalsecurity.org/wmd/library/news/usa/2002/us-020109-dod01.htm.

30. Perkovich, Cirincione, Gottemoeller, Wolfstahl, and Mathews, *Universal Compliance.*

31. Sisir Gupta, "The Indian Dilemma," in *A World of Nuclear Powers,* ed. Alastair Buchan (Englewood-Cliffs, NJ: Prentice Hall, 1966), p. 59.

32. Avery Goldstein, *Deterrence and Security in the 21st Century: China, Britain, France, and the Enduring Legacy of the Nuclear Revolution* (Stanford, CA: Stanford University Press, 2000), p. 1.

33. For an amplification on this theme, see Bharat Karnad, "Security and Sovereignty," in *Globalization and Environmental Challenges: Reconceptualizing Security in the 21st Century,* ed. Hans Gunter Brauch, Ursula Oswald Spring, Czeslaw Mesjasz, John Grin, Pal Dunay, Navnita Behera Chadha, Bechir Chourou, Patricia Kameri-Mbote, and P. H. Liotta (Berlin, Heidelberg, New York: Springer-Verlag, 2008).

34. Dean Wilkening and Kenneth Watman, *Nuclear Deterrence in a Regional Context* (Santa Monica: RAND, 2006), pp. 31–58. Iran in late November 2007 unveiled a new, nearly 2000-km-range missile, designed to reach Israel and U.S. bases in the Middle East. See "New Missile Can Hit US Bases: Iran," AP, *The Times of India,* November 28, 2007.

35. For an assessment of the Nuclear Posture Review, see Roger Speed and Michael May, "Assessing the United States' Nuclear Posture," in *U.S. Nuclear Policy: Confronting Today's Threats,* ed. George Bunn and Christopher F. Chyba (Washington, DC: The Brookings Institution, 2006).

36. Jean du Preez, "The Impact of the Nuclear Posture Review on the International Nuclear Nonproliferation Regime," *The Non-Proliferation Review,* 9, no. 3 (Fall-Winter 2002).

37. Johnson, " 'Do as I say, not as I do'," p. 57.

38. Vladimir Putin, " ' US has overstepped its borders in every way'," (extracts from Putin's speech at the Munich Meet on Security Policy), *The Asian Age,* February 13, 2007.

39. Mitchell B. Reiss, "The Nuclear Tipping Point: Prospects for a World of Many Nuclear Weapons States," in *The Nuclear Tipping Point: Why States Reconsider Their Nuclear Choices,* ed. Kurt M. Campbell, Robert J. Einhorn and Mitchell B. Reiss (Washington, DC: Brookings, 2004), pp. 1–17.

40. Henry Kissinger, *Diplomacy* (New York: Simon & Schuster, 1994), p. 608.

41. The chapter with this as title in Albert Wohlstetter, Thomas A. Brown, Gregory Jones, David C. McGarvey, Henry Rowen, Vince Taylor, and Roberta Wohlstetter, *Swords from Plowshares: The Military Potential of Civilian Nuclear Energy* (Chicago and London: The University of Chicago Press, 1997), pp. 126–150.

42. Kenneth Waltz, *The Spread of Nuclear Weapons: More May Be Better,* Adelphi Paper 171 (London: International Institute of Strategic Studies, 1981); Martin Van Creveld, *Nuclear Proliferation and the Future of Conflict* (New York: The Free Press, 1993).

43. Muller, *The 2005 NPT Review Conference,* p. 16.

44. Ibid. Japan, Brazil, Argentina, South Africa, Indonesia, Egypt, and Nigeria are identified as "middle powers" on pp. 15–16.

45. This was reflected in the April-May 2008 meeting of the preparatory committee for the next NPT Review Conference to be held in 2010. States of the Nonaligned Movement, led by Indonesia and joined by Iran, severely criticized the Indian-U.S. civil nuclear cooperation deal and asked for the strictest observance of NPT norms barring an NPT-recognized nuclear weapon state (the United States) from transferring any nuclear technology and materials to an NPT non-signatory state (India). See Pranabdhal Samanta, "Egg on both UPA & Left faces as NAM and Iran slam nuclear Deal," *The Indian Express,* May 6, 2008.

46. Gilinsky's statement in Farah Zahra, " 'Flexible Response' and Security," *The News* (Islamabad), December 6, 2007.

47. Karl F. Inderfurth and Bruce Riedel, "A U.S.-Indian Partnership against Nukes," *International Herald Tribune,* November 27, 2007. Inderfurth was U.S. assistant secretary of state for South Asia and Riedel, special assistant to the president for Near East and South Asian Affairs, during the Clinton presidency.

48. This is precisely what many Pakistanis fear. Refer to Naeem Salik, "US Strategy to Combat WMD Should Worry Pakistan," *The Friday Times* (Lahore), May 5–11, 2006. Salik is a retired Brigadier-General formerly with the Strategic Plans Division—the secretariat for Pakistan's nuclear command authority.

49. See Pervez Hoodbhoy, "A State of Denial," *International Herald Tribune,* January 17, 2008, and Zaigham Khan, "Mullahs and the bomb," *The News* (Islamabad), January 22, 2008. But the Pakistan government has gone out of its way to reassure the international public that its nuclear weapons program and posture is immunized against Islamic extremism. See Peter Wonacott, "Troubled Regime Tests Level of Religious Zeal in Nuclear Scientists," *The Wall Street Journal,* November 30–December 2, 2007.

50. "President Bush Visits National Defense University, Discusses Global War on Terror," The White House, Washington, D.C., October 23, 2007, http://www.whitehouse.gov/news/releases/2007/10/20071023-3.html.

51. Quotes from Kennan's famous 1947 "X article" published in *Foreign Affairs,* in "Kennan and Containment, 1947" http://www.state.gov/r/pa/ho/time/cwr/17601.htm.

52. For a critique of the neoconservative thinking driving this strategy, see Francis Fukuyama, *After the Neocons: America at the Crossroads* (London: Profile Books, First South Asian edition, 2007).

53. President Bush's speech at http://www.whitehouse.gov/news/releases/2002/06/20020601-3.html.

54. Ramesh Thakur, "Managing the Nuclear Threat after Iraq: Is It Time to Replace the NPT Paradigm?" in Singh and Thakur, *Arms Control After Iraq,* p. 3.

55. According to the latest U.S. intelligence estimates, which reversed the 2005 findings, Iran shut down its nuclear weapons program in 2003. See Mark Mazzetti, "No Arms Program in Iran, U.S. Finds," *International Herald Tribune,* December 5, 2007. Despite this assessment, President George W Bush held out the threat of U.S. preemptive strike or attack by Israel. See "Iran Still a Danger to the World, All Options on Table: Bush," Reuters, *The Indian Express,* December 5, 2007.

56. Kalevi J. Holsti, "The Use of Force in International Politics: Four Revolutions," in Singh and Thakur *Arms Control After Iraq.*

57. Regarding difficulties in implementing the policy of democratizing foreign polities that require social and political engineering, refer to Fukuyama, *After the Neocons,* ch. 5.

58. Having burnt its fingers in Iraq and Afghanistan, Washington has apparently decided to slow down its democratizing impulse in central Asia. See C. J. Chivers, "U.S. Revises Plans in Central Asia," *International Herald Tribune,* February 4, 2008.

59. Consider, for example, the foreign policy agendas of the various Republican Party and Democratic Party presidential candidates for the 2008 elections published in *Foreign Affairs* issues of July/August 2007, September/October 2007, and November/December 2007.

60. Campbell and O'Hanlon, *Hard Power,* pp. 238–241.

61. Charles A. Kupchan and Peter L. Tubrowitz, "Dead Center: The Demise of Liberal Internationalism in the United States," *International Security,* 32, no. 2 (Fall 2007).

62. "Russia Warns US on Missile Defense," AP, *USA Today,* June 21, 2007.

63. Fukuyama, *After the Neocons,* pp. 111–113.

64. The political-military venture in Iraq has, through the end of 2007, cost the United States $1 trillion, with the bill going up by $3–$4 billion monthly. Source: Senator Barack Obama, Debate between Democratic Party Presidential candidates on CNN television, January 21, 2008.

65. Thom Shanker, "Gates Calls Iran a Threat Even without Weapons," *International Herald Tribune,* December 10, 2007.

66. The India-Russia-China Triangle was first mooted by the Indian Prime Minister Jawaharlal Nehru in the 1950s. See Bharat Karnad, "India's Weak Geopolitics and What To Do About It" in *Future Imperiled: India's Security in the 1990s and Beyond,* ed. Bharat Karnad (New Delhi, Viking, 1994), pp. 34–41. The idea was revived in the 1990s by the Russian Foreign Minister Georgiy Primakov. See Iwashita Akhiro, "Primakov Redux? Russia and the 'Strategic Triangles' in Asia," http://src-h.slav.hokudai.ac.jp/coe21/publish/no16_1_ses/09_iwashita.pdf. The U.S. National Intelligence Council has more recently espied the possibility of such a 'Triangle' emerging by 2015. See National Intelligence Council, "A Dialogue About the Future with Non-Government Experts," http://www.dni.gov/nic/NIC_home.html.

67. Fukuyama, *After the Neocons,* pp. 90–91.

68. Commander-in-Chief, U.S. Central Command, Admiral William Fallon, pooh-poohed the possibility of a preemptive strike on Iran's nuclear installations, saying "the continuing stories . . . just keep going around and around that any day there will be another war, which is just not where we want to go." He admitted that the U.S. forces were already

stretched thin on the ground. See Demetri Sevastopulo, Daniel Dombey, and Andrew Ward, "U.S. Strike on Iran 'Not Being' Prepared," *Financial Times,* November 12, 2007.

69. "IRGC Commander Warns of Tsunami-like Response to Any Attack," *Tehran Times,* November 24, 2007.

70. " 'New Iran Missile can Reach Israel, US Bases'," AFP, *The Asian Age,,* November 28, 2007.

71. Jason T. Shaplen and James Laney, "Washington's Eastern Sunset," *Foreign Affairs,* 86, no. 6 (November/December 2007).

72. Dimitri Simes, "Losing Russia," *Foreign Affairs,* 86, no. 6 (November/December 2007).

73. See Roger W. Barnett and Stephen J. Cimbala, *Asymmetrical Warfare: Today's Challenges to US Military Power* (Dulles, VA: Potomac Books, Brassey's Inc., 2003) and Ivan Arreguin-Toft, *How the Weak Win Wars: A Theory of Asymmetric Conflict* (Cambridge, UK: Cambridge University Press, 2006).

74. See his "The Dispensable Nation," *International Herald Tribune,* August 8, 2007.

75. Edward N. Luttwak, "Toward Post-Heroic Warfare," *Foreign Affairs,* 74, no. 3 (May/June 1995).

76. The U.S. Secretary of Defense hoped that some 10 brigades would return home by the end of 2008. But military leaders in the field oppose a too hasty reduction of troops; they fear this may jeopardize the security and political gains made in Iraq. See Demetri Sevatopulo and Stephen Fidler, "Pentagon weighs Iraq troop levels," *Financial Times,* December 18, 2007.

77. "Kremlin: Russia to revise military doctrine to respond to growing role of force in world," AP, *International Herald Tribune,* March 5, 2007.

78. Robin Frost, for example, discounts the possibility of even efficiently run terrorist outfits being able to muster the necessary expertise and resources required for building an "improvised atomic device." See his *Nuclear Terrorism After 9/11,* pp. 25–40.

79. Pakistan President Pervez Musharraf, in a BBC Radio 4 interview, warned of just this happening in case political instability occurs from his departing the scene in Pakistan and the Pakistan military loses control over nuclear weapons. See "Nuclear Assets Safe in Army's Hands, says Musharraf," *The Daily Times* (Islamabad), November 18, 2007.

80. Matthew Bunn, *Securing the Bomb 2007* (Cambridge, MA, and Washington, DC: Project on Managing the Atom, Harvard University and Nuclear Threat Initiative, September 2007), pp. 6–8.

81. Dr. Khan confessed that he took the blame for transferring nuclear technology to Iran, North Korea, and Libya in order "to save Pakistan." See "Dr Khan Says He Confessed to Save Pakistan," *Dawn,* April 8, 2008.

82. For the first detailed and comprehensive account of the U.S. government's role since the late 1970s in Pakistan's covert nuclear weapons program and in helping Pakistan's Dr. A. Q. Khan-run nuclear black market become a revenue-earner for the Pakistan army, see Adrian Levy and Catherine Scott-Clark, *Deception: Pakistan, the United States and the Secret Trade in Nuclear Weapons.*(New York, Walker & Co., 2007). The deliberate policy of ignoring Pakistan's proliferation activities is also detailed in David Armstrong and Joseph J. Trento, *America and the Islamic Bomb* (Hanover, NH: Steerforth Press, 2007).

83. The complicity of the U.S. State Department in Pakistan's covert program of nuclear arming was first revealed by Senator Larry Pressler in the mid-1990s. See his

"The Restraint of Fury: US Nonproliferation Policy and South Asia" in Karnad, *Future Imperiled,* pp. 202–203, 206–210.

84. Ibid; p. 210.

85. Levy and Scott-Clark, *Deception,* p. 204.

86. "Remarks by the President to Students and Faculty at the National Defense University," Washington, DC, May 1, 2001, http://www.whitehouse.gov/news/releases/2001/05/20010501-10.html.

87. Thakur, "Managing the Nuclear Threat after Iraq," p. 13.

88. "Naysayers Refuse to Budge on Deal," *The Times of India,* December 5, 2007.

89. Michael Chossudovsky, "Cover-up or Complicity of the Bush Administration? The Role of Pakistan's Military Intelligence (ISI) in the September 11 Attacks," Center for Research on Globalization, Montreal, November 2, 2001, http://www.globalresearch.ca/articles/CHO111A.html.

90. B. Raman, "The Al Qaeda Empire in Pakistan & Spurt in Terrorism in Kashmir," Paper No. 554, South Asia Analysis Group, New Delhi, November 26, 2002, http://www.southasiaanalysis.org/%5Cpapers6%5Cpaper554.html. Raman, a highly regarded analyst on Pakistani affairs, retired from the Indian external intelligence agency—RAW (Research and Analysis Wing).

91. Robin Wright and Glenn Kessler, "U.S. Brokered Bhutto's Return to Pakistan," *The Washington Post,* December 28, 2007.

92. Jonathan Schell, "Bush, Pakistan and the Bomb," *International Herald Tribune,* November 16, 2007.

93. Thakur, "Managing the Nuclear Threat after Iraq."

94. Rajiv Gandhi, "A World Free of Nuclear Weapons," at the United Nations General Assembly, New York, June 9, 1988, http://www.indianembassy.org/policy/Disarmament/disarm15.htm.

95. For reasons why, from the U.S. point of view, disarmament may be impractical and imprudent, see Brown, "New Nuclear Realities," pp. 17–18.

96. "Remarks by the President to Students and Faculty at the National Defense University."

97. Crouch, "Special Briefing on the Nuclear Posture Review."

98. "Nuclear Posture Review [Excerpts]," http://www.globalsecurity.org/wmd/library/policy/dod/npr.htm.

99. The international response to the NPR in du Preez, "The Impact of the Nuclear Posture Review," pp. 70–71.

100. For the angry reaction of the former Iranian President and known moderate, Ali Akbar Hashemi Rafsanjani, see Philipp Bleek, "Nuclear Posture Review: Outlines, Targets, Contingencies," *Arms Control Today,* April 2002, http://www.armscontrol.org/act2002_04/nprapril02.asp (accessed July 2005).

101. See his "A 21st Century Role for Nuclear Weapons," *Issues in Science and Technology,* Spring 2004, http://www.issues.org/20.3/schneider.html.

102. Linton Brooks, "The Future of US Nuclear Weapons Stockpile," 2006 Arms Control Association Panel Discussion, Washington, DC, January 25, 2006, http://nnsa.energy.gov/news/979.htm

103. "US Nuclear Weapons Policy: Dangerous and Counterproductive," Backgrounder, Union of Concerned Scientists (Undated but put on its Web site possibly in late 2005 or 2006), http://www.ucsusa.org/global_security/nuclear_weapons/us-nuclear-weapons-policy-dangerous-and-counterproductive.html.

104. Hisham Zeffirri and Arjun Makhijani, "Pure Fusion Weapons?" *Peace Magazine,* January-February 1999, http://archive.peacemagazine.org/v15n1p24.htm.

105. George H. Quester, *Nuclear First Strike: Consequences of a Broken Taboo* (Baltimore: The Johns Hopkins University Press, 2005), ch. 1.

106. "Nuclear Weapons," http://www.isanw.org/facts/weapons.html.

107. The U.S. Congress cut funding for the development of the new reliable replacement warhead, directing the Bush Administration to come up with "comprehensive nuclear weapons strategy for the 21st century." According to the spokesman for the Department of Energy, this meant using the nuclear weapons already in the stockpile but with "full life extension." See Walter Pincus, "Nuclear Warhead Cut From Spending Bill," *The Washington Post,* December 18, 2007.

108. Linton Brooks, "Countering Nuclear Terrorism," Remarks at Chatham House, London, September 21, 2006 at http://nnsa.energy.gov/news/print/1192.htm. Attribution or "nuclear tagging" is possible because "current fissile material processing techniques leave unique chemical traces that make traceable the fissile material coming from not only a particular processing facility, but each run at each facility." See Anders Corr, "Nuclear Terror and the Blind-Side Attack: Deterrence Through Nuclear tagging," September 3, 2006, http://www.people.fas.harvard.edu/~corr/site.

109. Caitlin Talmadge, "Deterring a Nuclear 9/11," *The Washington Quarterly,* 30, No. 2 (Spring 2007):28.

110. David E. Sanger and Thom Shanker, "U.S. Revamps Its Deterrence Policy for the Terrorist Age," *International Herald Tribune,* May 9, 2007.

111. Russian President Vladimir Putin has used military maneuvers to signal his readiness to up the ante. As a follow-up to its strategic bombers overflying the North Sea, on February 9, 2008 these Russian warplanes flew over the U.S. nuclear aircraft carrier, Nimitz, in the western Pacific, and in another case Moscow announced that bombers would fire missiles into the Atlantic as part of Russian naval exercises. See "Russian Bombers to Test-Fire Missiles in Bay of Biscay," *TimesOnline,* January 22, 2008, www.timesonline.co.uk/tol/news/world/europe/article3230615.ece; and Bruno Waterfield, "Russia Threatens Nuclear Attack on Ukraine," *The Daily Telegraph,* February 13, 2008.

112. Quote in Pavel K. Baev, "Russian Preventive Strikes—Options and Capabilities," *Eurasian Daily Monitor,* The Jamestown Foundation, September 14, 2004, http://www.jamestown.org/publications_details.php?volume_id=3069&article_id=2368497.

113. Dmitri Trenin, *Russia's Nuclear Policy in the 21st Century Environment,* Proliferation Papers, (Paris: Institut francais des relations international, Autumn 2005), pp. 7–10.

114. Keir A. Lieber and Daryl G. Press, "The Rise of US Nuclear Primacy," *Foreign Affairs,* 85, No. 2 (March/April 2006); David S. McDonough, *Nuclear Superiority: The 'New Triad' and the Evolution of Nuclear Strategy,* Adelphi paper 383 (London: International Institute for Strategic Studies, 2006).

115. Alexei Arbatov, "Cutting a Deal," *Foreign Affairs,* 85, No. 2 (March/April 2006), p. 154.

116. Trenin, *Russia's Nuclear Policy in the 21st Century Environment,* pp. 10–11, 13.

117. Quotations from the Russian documents in Alexei Arbatov and Vladimir Dvorkin, *Beyond Nuclear Deterrence: Transforming the U.S.-Russian Equation* (Washington, DC: Carnegie Endowment for International Peace, 2006), pp. 58–59.

118. Ibid, Quotations from p. 59.

119. Nikolai Sokov, "US Withdrawal from the ABM Treaty: Post-Mortem and Possible Consequences," *CNS Reports,* James Martin Center for Nonproliferation Studies, December 14, 2002, http://cns.miis.edu/pubs/reports/2abm.htm.

120. "Russian Hypersonic Missile?" AP, February 19, 2004, http://forum.keypublishing.co.uk/archive/index.php?t-21605.html.

121. "Russia Warns US on Missile Defense."

122. Konstantin Kosachev, chairman of the foreign affairs committee of the Duma, wrote that "any attempt to build [a missile defense system] without Russia automatically means [it] is being built against Russia." See his "Shield or Sword?" *International Herald Tribune,* April 8, 2007.

123. Vladimir Radyuhin, "Russia Deploys Advanced Anti-Missile Systems near NATO's Eastern Borders," *The Hindu,* April 24, 2006.

124. "US Could Trigger Russian Strike," AFP, *The Sunday Times of India,* December 16, 2007.

125. "Kremlin: Russia to Revise Military Doctrine."

126. Quote in Vladimir Radyuhin, "Putin calls for strong army", *The Hindu*, May 11, 2006.

127. Stephen Fidler and James Blitz, "Putin Suspends Arms Control Treaty in Worsening of Relations with US," *Financial Times,* December 3, 2007. General Baluyevsky, in fact, accused the Western countries of turning "an arms control agreement into an instrument to achieve political aims." See "US Could Trigger Russian Strike."

128. Peter Finn, "Russian Bombers Could Be Deployed to Cuba," *The Washington Post,* July 22, 2008, online at http://www.washingtonpost.com/wp-dyn/content/story/2008/07/22/ST2008072200062.html.

129. Robert Skidelsky, "Vladimir de Gaulle," *The Daily Times* (Islamabad), December 13, 2007.

130. John C. Hopkins and Weixing Hu, *Strategic Views from the Second Tier: The Nuclear Weapons Policies of France, Britain and China* (Edison, NJ: Transaction Publishers, 1995).

131. Rebecca Johnson, Nicola Butler, and Stephen Pullinger, *Worse than Irrelevant? British Nuclear Weapons in the 21st Century*(London, Acronym Institute for Disarmament Diplomacy, 2006).

132. Goldstein, *Deterrence and Security in the 21st Century*, pp. 228–238.

133. See the Foreword by Prime Minister Tony Blair to the Defense White Paper *The Future of United Kingdom's Nuclear Deterrent,* December 2006, pp. 6–7, at http://www.fco.gov.uk/Files/kfile/WP%20Final.pdf. 2007.

134. "UK Vote on Trident Renewal," The Acronym Institute, March 14, 2007 at http://www.acronym.org.uk/uk/Trident_reaction.htm.

135. *The Future of the British Nuclear Deterrent*, Research Paper 06/53 (London: Library, House of Commons, 3 November 2006), pp.23–24 at http://www.parliament.uk/commons/lib/research/rp2006/rp06-053.pdf.

136. David Yost, "France's New Nuclear Doctrine," *International Affairs,* 82, No. 4 (2006):712–713.

137. Bruno Tertrais, "A Comparison Between the US, UK and French Nuclear Policies and Doctrine," February 2007, at http://www.ceri-sciences-po.org; Braxton D. Rehm, "French Nuclear Strategy in an Age of Terrorism" (Monterey, CA: Naval Post-Graduate School, December 2006).

138. *The Future of the British Nuclear Deterrent,* p. 21.

139. Hans M. Kristensen, Robert S. Norris, Matthew G. Makinzie, *Chinese Nuclear Forces and US Nuclear War Planning*, Federation of American Scientists/NRDC, November 2006, p. 36 at http://www.fas.org/nuke/guide/china/Book2006.pdf.

140. Jeffrey Lewis, "The Ambiguous Arsenal," *The Bulletin of Atomic Scientists*, May/June 2005.

141. Interview with Lieutenant General Liu Yazhou, PLAAF, in *Heartland: Eurasian Review of Geopolitics*, No. 1 (2005), online at http://www.eheartland.com/_lib/_docs/2005_01c_China_America_The_Great_Game.pdf.

142. Major General Zhu Chenghu, Dean of China's National Defense University, warned that in case the United States intervened in a crisis over Taiwan, Beijing "will have to respond with nuclear weapons." See Stephanie Lieggi, "Going beyond the Stir: The Strategic Realities of China's No First Use Policy," December 2005 at http://www.nti.org.

143. See his statement to the U.S. Senate armed services committee on February 27, 2007 at http://www.fas.org/irp/congress/2007_hr/022707maples.pdf.

144. Keith Crane, Roger Cliff, Evan Medeiros, James Mulvenon, and William Overholt, *Modernizing China's Military: Opportunities and Constraints* (Santa Monica: RAND, 2005), p. 200.

145. Ibid, p. 202–203.

146. Keir A. Lieber and Daryl G. Press, "U.S. Nuclear Primacy and the Future of the Chinese Deterrent," *China Security*, Winter 2007 at http://www.wsichina.org/cs5_5.pdf, pp. 72–75, 77–79, 82–83.

147. Crane, et al., *Modernizing China's Military*, pp. xxiv, 202.

148. Dingli Shen, "Upsetting the Balance," *The Bulletin of Atomic Scientists*, July/August 2007, p. 37.

149. William J. Broad and David E. Sanger, "China Tests Anti-Satellite Weapon, Unnerving US," *The New York Times*, January 18, 2007.

150. John Schwartz, "Preparing for a digital Pearl Harbor: Ominous forecasts, but. . .," *International Herald Tribune*, June 25, 2007.

151. John Markoff, "Cyber Attack on U.S. Arms Lab Has Link to China," *International Herald Tribune*, December 10, 2007.

152. By overstating Japan's readiness to make a nuclear bomb in the wake of China's first nuclear test explosion in 1964, Prime Minister Eisuku Sato managed formally to obtain nuclear protection from the United States. See Bennett Richardson, "Nuclear Question Still Nags at Japan," Christian Science Monitor, November 6, 2006 at http://wwwcsmonitor.com/2006/1106/p)6s01-woap.htm.

153. The U.S. Assistant Secretary of Defense for Asian and Pacific Security Affairs-designate, James Shinn, doubted whether North Korea would give up its nuclear ambitions no matter what. See "US Defense Nominee Unsure if NKorea Will Give Up Nuclear Ambitions," *The Korea Times*, December 19, 2007.

154. Michael Moran, "Will Nukes March across Asia?" October 15, 2006, Council on Foreign Relations at http://www.cfr.org/publication/11731/will_nukes_march_across_asia.html.

155. Robert K. Wilcox, *Japan's Secret War: Japan's Race Against Time to Build Its Own Atomic Bomb* (New York, Marlowe & Co., 1995).

156. See his "The Nuclear Dimension of the U.S.-Japan Alliance," The Nautilus Institute, Undated (but probably, 1998–1999) at http://www.nautilus.org/archives/library/security/papers/US-Japan-4.html, section 4.

157. Refer his "Prudence and Realism in Japan's Nuclear Options," November 10, 2006, online at http://www.brookings.edu/opinions/2006/1110japan_matsumura.aspx.

158. William E. Rapp, *Paths Diverging? The Next Decade in the U.S.-Japan Alliance* (Carlisle Barracks, PA: Strategic Studies Institute, Army War College, January 2004), pp. v, 7–13.

159. See Andrew Mack, "Japan and the Bomb: A Cause for Concern?" *The Asia-Pacific Magazine,* No.3 (June 1996) at http://coombs.anu.edu.au/SpecialProj/APM/TXT/mack-a-03-96.html; and Richard Tanter, "Japan, Heisei Militarization and the Bush Doctrine," October 28, 2004, *Policy Forum Online,* Nautilus Institute at http://www.nautilus.org/fora/security/0442A_Tanter.html.

160. Tetsuya Endo "Define Steps to Verify North's Denuclearization," *The Asahi Shimbun,* December 26, 2007.

161. David E. Sanger and William J. Broad, "South Koreans Say Secret Work Refined Uranium," *The New York Times,* September 3, 2004.

162. Taiwanese fears about their country's security requirements being dictated by the U.S. national interest in having stable relations with China were stoked recently when Washington decided against selling the F-16 combat aircraft in a $5 billion deal. The American assessment, according to Commander-in-Chief, Pacific Command, Admiral Timothy Keating, was that "there is no pressing, compelling need for [it] at this time." See Kathrin Hille, "Taipei Ends Pursuit of $5bn US Jets Deal," *Financial Times,* July 20, 2008.

163. For a whole bunch of declassified U.S. government documents pertaining to intelligence assessments and the evolution of the United States policy toward Taiwan's nuclear program, and decision to pressure Taipei to abandon the weapons route, see "US opposed Taiwanese bombs during 1970s." See William Burr, ed., National security Archive Briefing Book No. 221 at http://www.gwu.edu/~nsarchiv/nukevault/ebb221/index.htm.

164. James Galants and Shivan-Ju Chen, "Bubble-Tea Diplomacy: The Nuclear Solution to Taiwan's International Recognition," Center for Advanced Defense Studies, August 2006 at http://www.c4ads.org/files/cads_report_bteadiplo_aug06.pdf.

165. Wendell Minnick, "Taiwan President Denies Nuclear Weapons Research," *Defense News,* October 20, 2007 at http://www.defensenews.com.

166. Donald Greenlees, "From Tanks to Trade: A New Road for Ex-Foes," *International Herald Tribune,* December 14, 2007.

167. Bharat Karnad, "India's Weak Geopolitics and What To Do About It," in *Future Imperiled,* pp. 50, 53–56.

168. Bharat Karnad, *Nuclear Weapons and Indian Security,* pp. 541–542.

169. Bharat Karnad, "Vietnam as India's Force-Multiplier," *The Indian Express,* October 3, 2005.

170. "India-Vietnam Military Ties Taking Shape," *The Indian Express,* December 18, 2007.

171. Barry Rubin, "Iran's Nuclear and Syria's Iraq Adventures," *The Middle East Review of International Affairs (MERIA),* 11, No. 4, December 2007.

172. Russia stopped fuel delivery for the reactor it has helped build in Bushehr that many apprehend will be used for weapons purposes by Iran because of disagreements, not over nonproliferation laws, but payments. With the financial dispute resolved, the supply of enriched uranium was resumed. See "Iran Receives Nuclear Fuel in Blow to U.S.," *The New York Times,* December 18, 2007.

173. "Saudi Arabia profile," SIPRI at http://www.sipri.org/contents/expcon/cnsc2
sau.html.

174. Michael Dillon, "The Security of Governance," in *Global Governmentality: Governing International Spaces,* ed. Wendy Larner and William Walters (London: Routledge, 2004), p. 82.

175. Quote in Richard Speier, "U.S. Satellite Space Launch Cooperation and India's Intercontinental Ballistic Missile Program," in *Gauging US-India Strategic Cooperation,* ed. Henry Sokolski (Carlisle Barracks, PA: Strategic Studies Institute, Army War College, March 2007), p. 197.

176. See "India helping Taiwan with Nuke Project, Report Claims," *Taiwan News,* November 9, 2007 at http://www.taiwansecurity.org/TN/2007/TN-091107.htm (accessed November 2007).

CHAPTER 2

1. Frank Barnaby, *How to Build a Nuclear Bomb and Other Weapons of Mass Destruction,* (New York: Nation Books, 2004), pp. 68, 121–123.

2. Mitchell Reiss, "A Nuclear Bargain: Atoms for Peace 2.0," in *Nuclear Asia: US Policy in an Age of Proliferation,* NBR Analysis, 18, No.2, National Bureau of Research, March 2007, p. 20.

3. Kennedy Graham, "From Deterrence to Compellence: Doctrinal Implications of the Iraq Crisis" in *Arms Control After Iraq: Normative and Operational Challenges,* ed. Ramesh Thakur and Waheguru Pal Singh (Tokyo: United Nations University Press, 2004), pp. 40–46.

4. For U.S. concerns about Pakistan's nuclear arsenal, see Paul Kerr and Mary Beth Nikitin, *Pakistan's Nuclear Weapons: Proliferation and Security Issues,* Updated November 14, 2007, CRS Report for Congress. Regarding Beijing's plans to capture North Korean bombs in case of escalating unrest within that country, see "China Plans to Secure N Korea's Nuclear Arsenal," AFP, *The Times of India,* January 9, 2008.

5. For example, the Indian Ambassador Badr-ud-din Tyabji at the 1965 IAEA General Conference said: "The Indian view was that the way to stop the further spread of nuclear weapons was not so much to prevent more countries from acquiring them as to make those countries which already had them give them up." Prime Minister Indira Gandhi criticized the NPT in the UN General Assembly in October 1968, thus: "The problems of insecurity cannot be solved by imposing arbitrary restrictions on those who do not possess nuclear weapons, without any corresponding steps to deal with the basic problems of limiting stockpiles in the hands of a few Powers. How can the urge to acquire nuclear status be controlled so long as this imbalance persists?" See "Statement by the Indian Representative Badr-ud-din Tyabji at the Ninth IAEA General Conference, 23 September 1965" and "Statement by Prime Minister Indira Gandhi in the UN General Assembly, 14 October 1968 (Extract)" in *Nuclear India,* Vol. II, Documents, ed. J. P. Jain (New Delhi: Radiant Publishers, 1974), pp. 169, 219–220.

6. Prior to the conference in 1995 that ended in the Indefinite Extension of the Nonproliferation Treaty, for instance, Washington cut a deal with Delhi—the United States would ease off the nonproliferation pressure if India reduced its effort in mobilizing opposition among the ranks of the nonaligned and Third World signatory states. Revealed in personal communications from Ambassador Prakash Shah, who was Indian Permanent

Representative at the UN Headquarters in New York, 1994–96, this was confirmed by Ambassador Arundhati Ghose, Indian Representative at the Disarmament Commission in Geneva during the negotiations on the Comprehensive Test Ban Treaty.

7. Prime Minister Singh used this phrase in reference to membership in the UN Security Council at a joint news conference in Delhi with the visiting British Prime Minister Gordon Brown, which membership Britain supports. See "Brown Backs India's Bid for Security Council seat," *Hindu,* January 22, 2008. But it holds equally for India's membership in the club of NPT-recognized nuclear weapon states.

8. Gregory F. Treverton, Seth G. Jones, *Measuring National Power,* Conference Proceedings (Santa Monica: RAND, 2005), p. ix.

9. Sir Henry Tizzard, Science Advisor to the British Defense Minister, for instance, keeping in mind economic difficulties and resource scarcity, urged the government in an official Note in 1949 to refrain from a nuclear weapons program because the United Kingdom, he wrote, is "not a Great Power and never will be again." See Margaret Gowing, *Independence and Deterrence: Britain and Atomic Energy, 1945–1952* (London and Basingstoke: Macmillan, 1974), p. 229.

10. China reasoned that after India's dismemberment of Pakistan in 1971 and its nuclear test in 1974, a nuclear weapon-armed Pakistan would help resist Indian expansionism better. See John W. Garver, *Protracted Contest: Sino-Indian Rivalry in the Twentieth Century* (New Delhi: Oxford University Press, 2001), p. 327.

11. Regarding India's position as the prime legatee of the British Empire in South Asia, its quite considerable military contribution to the Allied cause during the Second World War, and its potential as the balancer of power in Asia, see A. Martin Wainwright, *Inheritance of Empire: Britain, India and the Balance of Power in Asia* (Westport, CT and London: Praeger, 1994).

12. That Nehru was an accomplished historian is evident from his writings, in particular two books: *Glimpses of World History* (New Delhi: Jawaharlal Nehru Memorial Trust and Oxford University Press, 2004), which astonishingly, was written by him as a series of letters in the late 1920s to his daughter Indira [later, Indira Gandhi, after her marriage to Feroze Gandhi], while incarcerated in a British jail for his involvement in the freedom struggle, and *Discovery of India,* 11th Impression (New Delhi: Jawaharlal Nehru Memorial Trust and Oxford University Press, 1991, originally published 1946).

13. The Note is reproduced in full in John Connell, *Auchinleck: A Biography of Field Marshal Sir Claude Auchinleck* (London: Cassell, 1959), pp. 840–846.

14. See A. J. Bacevich, *The Pentomic Era: The US Army Between Korea and Vietnam* (Washington, DC: National Defense University Press, 1986), and John J. Midgley, Jr., *Deadly Illusions: Army Policy for the Nuclear Battlefield* (Boulder, CO, and London: Westview Press, 1986).

15. Lieutenant General F. S. Tuker, "Nuclear Energy and War," *USI Journal,* January 1946. Tuker, incidentally, edited this premier Journal of the Indian military in the 1920s.

16. Auspex [F. S. Tuker], "India's Strategical Future," *USI Journal,* April 1945.

17. For Nehru's very Tuker-esque vision of India's strategic importance he presented before the Constituent Assembly on March 8, 1949, see Jawaharlal Nehru, *India's Foreign Policy: Selected Speeches, September 1946–April 1961,* 2nd reprint (New Delhi: The Publications Division, Ministry of Information and Broadcasting, Government of India, 1983), p. 22.

18. Sarvepalli Gopal, *Nehru: A Biography,* Vol. II (New Delhi: Oxford University Press, 1979), p. 59.

19. See Nehru's instructions to India's ambassador-designate to China, K. P. S. Menon, on November 17, 1946 in *Selected Works of Jawaharlal Nehru,* Vol. 1, ed. Sarvepalli Gopal (New Delhi: Orient Longman, 1972), p. 543.

20. P. M. S. Blackett, *Fear, War and the Bomb: Military and Political Consequences of Atomic Energy* (New York and Toronto: Whittlesey House, McGraw Hill Book Co., Inc., 1949), pp. 1–2.

21. Ibid., p. 49.

22. Ibid., pp. 2–3.

23. P. M. S. Blackett, "America's Atomic Dilemma" in his collection of previously published essays, *Studies of War: Nuclear and Conventional* (New York: Hill & Wang, 1962).

24. See Bernard Brodie, ed., *The Absolute Weapon: Atomic Peace and the World Order* (New York: Harcourt, Brace & Co., 1946).

25. Blackett, *Fear, War and the Bomb,* pp. 7–8, 99–100.

26. Dr. Homi J. Bhabha, whom Nehru chose to run the Indian nuclear energy program, in his letters dated as far back as March 1944 seeking funds for setting up the Tata Institute for Fundamental Research in Bombay from the wealthy Sir Dorabjee Tata Trust, in fact presumed that nuclear energy would be "successfully applied for power production" in India and talked of the Institute he was seeking to found as the seedbed for the expertise required to man such a power program. See G. Venkataraman, *Bhabha and His Magnificent Obsessions* (Hyderabad: Universities Press, 1994), p. 141. Nehru, in his first major address on Science in 1947 at the Indian Science Congress, referred to atomic energy helping make India "self-reliant."

27. For the text of Blackett's Memorandum—"Atomic Energy: An Immediate Policy for Great Britain," see Gowing, *Independenece and Deterrence,* Appendix 8, pp. 194–206.

28. Blackett's advice was debated but eventually discarded by Whitehall with a contemptuous noting on the File: "Should stick to science." See David Dilks, *Retreat From Power: Studies in Britain's Foreign Policy of the Twentieth Century,* Vol. II, *After 1939* (Basingstoke and London: Macmillan, 1981), p. 130.

29. The Department of Atomic Energy, Government of India, prepared a paper, with Bhabha's help, on the peaceful uses of atomic energy that Nehru planned to discuss at the first Conference of Afro-Asian States in 1955 in Bandung. See Ravinder Kumar and H. Y. Sharda Prasad, eds., *Selected Works of Jawaharlal Nehru,* Vol. 28 (February 1–May 31, 1955) (New Delhi: Jawaharlal Nehru Memorial Fund, 2001), p. 207–209.

30. Dr P. K. Iyengar, former Chairman Indian Atomic Energy Commission, recalls Al-Ghabilie, the French-trained radio-chemist heading the Egyptian atomic energy program, telling him of Nehru's agenda, something communicated to Al-Ghabilie by Egyptian President Gamal Abdel Nasser; interview with Iyengar, September 2000. Indeed, Bhabha was persuaded by Nehru to visit Yugoslavia in 1956, apparently for discussions on nuclear issues and probably also to judge the quality of that country's nuclear program. See Nehru's letter dated July 29, 1956, reproduced in Venkataraman, *Bhabha and His Magnificent Obsessions,* pp. 179–180.

31. Glenn T. Seaborg (with Benjamin Loeb), *Stemming the Tide: Arms Control in the Johnson Years* (Lexington, MA, and Toronto: Lexington Books, D.C. Heath & Co., 1987), p. 250.

32. Quote in Raj Chengappa, *Weapons of Peace: The Inside Story of India's Quest to be a Nuclear Power* (New Delhi: HarperCollins Publishers, India, 2000), pp. 71–72.

33. In his Presidential address to the 34th session in Delhi of the Indian Science Congress held on January 3, 1947, Nehru talked of Hiroshima as creating "inevitably a great deal of excitement. It seemed to me to herald all kinds of enormous changes, constructive as well as destructive." It produced, he noted, "a conflict in people's mind" about ends and means, and observed that "Science has two faces like Janus" and "both [the destructive and constructive aspects] have gone on side by side and both still go on" and that "apart from the bomb aspect of it, we are obviously on the threshold of a new age in the sense of enormous power resources being put at the disposal of humanity and the community." See *Jawaharlal Nehru, Years of Struggle: Selected Readings,* compiled by Arjun Dev (New Delhi: The National Book Trust, 1989), p. 169.

34. The hyper-realist ancient Hindu *machtpolitik* emphasizes conciliation (*sama*), material aid and assistance (*dana*), sowing dissension in the ranks of the adversary (*bheda*), and force (*danda*) as the means of statecraft to be used depending on the prevailing "balance of forces" and the "conjuncture of circumstances." It extols the virtues of covert warfare (*kutayuddha*), suggests prosecuting "total war" (*sammukayuddha*) against a fearsome foe, and, when all other diplomatic and military instruments fail, recommends the use of what, from their description, appear to be weapons of mass destruction—their terrible effects vividly detailed in the four ancient Hindu texts, the Vedas, and, in particular, two of them, the Rg Veda and the lesser Dhanur Veda (dealing exclusively with armaments). The ultimate aim of the ruler or state, according to these texts, was to become the *vijigisu* (the most powerful entity) and the center of gravity (*nabhi*) of the balance of power system (*mandala*). For a succinct analysis of this traditional statecraft and Vedic *machtpolitik,* see Bharat Karnad, *Nuclear Weapons and Indian Security: The Realist Foundations of Strategy,* 2nd edition (New Delhi: Macmillan India Ltd., 2002, 2005), pp. 3–29. For a Western take on Kautilya's theory of the *mandala* as paradigm for international relations, see George Modelski, "Kautilya: Foreign Policy and International System in the Ancient Hindu World," *American Political Science Review,* 58, No. 3 (September 1964). Around 322 BC, Kautilya, adviser to Emperor Chandragupta Maurya, codified, among other things, the undated Vedic precepts on statecraft in the form of advice to the king in a text called *Arthashastra.*

35. A study on Indian cultural values, carried out under UNESCO aegis, based on opinion polls of the Indian elite, the nonelite segments of society, and students conducted in the mid- to late 1960s, concluded that the majority believed that (1) State power is coercive, (2) nonviolence is useless, (3) war between states in the prevailing international system is "inevitable," (4) the peaceful solutions of India's disputes with Pakistan and China are doubtful, and (5) a unilateral nuclear disarmament policy is irrational. Disregarding the students who were polled, it indicates just how little Gandhi's philosophy of nonviolence influenced the thinking of a generation that had experienced Mahatma Gandhi firsthand. See T. K. Unnithan and Yogendra Singh, *Sociology of Non-Violence and Peace: Some Behavioral and Attitudinal Dimensions* (New Delhi: Research Council for Cultural Studies, India International Centre, 1969).

36. Seventy-six percent of the people polled after the 1998 tests expressed strong support for India's policy of going overtly nuclear. Paul R. Dettman, *India Changes Course: Golden Jubilee to Millennium* (Westport, CT: Praeger Publishers, 2001), p. 60.

37. *Jawaharlal Nehru, Years of Struggle,* pp. 169–170.

38. For Bhabha's views, which he shared with Prime Minister Nehru about science as a tool for social and economic development and progress, his fulsome praise for Nehru, and on the difference between the "administration of science" and administration in other

fields, see his lecture on "Science and the Problems of Development" reproduced in C. V. Sundaram, L. V. Krishnan, and T. S. Iyengar, *Atomic Energy in India, 50 Years* (Department of Atomic Energy, Government of India, August 1998), pp. 254–271.

39. " 'Development of Atomic Energy in India', Talk by H. J. Bhabha over All India Radio, 3 August 1964" in *Nuclear India,* vol. II, p. 146.

40. See his speech at the 51st General Conference of the IAEA on September 19, 2007, reproduced in *The Indian Express,* September 21, 2007.

41. Venkataraman, *Bhabha and His Magnificent Obsessions*, pp. 145–147, 173–176.

42. K. S. Parthasarathy, "Bhabha's dream comes true," *The Tribune* (Chandigarh), February 1, 2008, online edition at http://www.tribuneindia.com/2008/20080201/science.htm. Parthasarathy is former secretary, Atomic Energy Regulatory Board.

43. See interview of Dr. R. Chidambaram, Chairman, AEC, in the 1990s, carried in Sundaram et al., *Atomic Energy in India,* p. 193.

44. For details of the domestic opposition Nehru's nuclear energy program faced, see Karnad, *Nuclear Weapons and Indian Security,* pp. 199–208. The U.S. Central Intelligence Agency, for instance, had no prior knowledge of the Indian decision to test in 1974 and again in 1998. The CIA admitted early that "It is unlikely that we would immediately learn of the Indian decision to proceed with a weapons program, but we probably would have advance indications of the first detonations." The "advance indications" no doubt refers to detection of test preparations by satellite sensors. See "India's Nuclear Weapons Policy," Special National Intelligence Estimate, Central Intelligence Agency, dated October 21, 1965, at http://www.gwu.edu/~nsarchiv/NSAEBB/NSAEBB187/IN09.pdf.

45. Minister for External Affairs Pranab Mukherji in the Congress Party-led coalition government, defending the civil nuclear cooperation deal with the United States in December 2007, said in Lok Sabha (the Lower House of Parliament) that the political consensus of keeping "our options open" but not weaponizing was breached by the 1998 tests. Quoted in Brahma Chellaney, "Pro-Deal but Anti-Deterrent," *The Asian Age,* January 5, 2008.

46. "Anxious as we are to economize and save money," his Government, Nehru told Parliament, had never "ever refused any urgent demand of the Department [of Atomic Energy] or come in the way of its development for financial reasons." This was in reply to the debate in the Lok Sabha (Lower House of Parliament) on the DAE budget on July 24, 1957. See *Jawaharlal Nehru's Speeches, 1953–1957,* Vol. 3, 3rd edition (New Delhi: Ministry of Information and Broadcasting, Government of India, 1983), p. 515.

47. Interview with Dr. P. K. Iyengar, former Chairman of the Atomic Energy Commission, September 2000.

48. See M. G. K. Menon and Manju Sharma, "Nehru and Science," in *Jawaharlal Nehru: Centenary Volume,* ed. Sheila Dikshit, K. Natwar Singh, G. Parthasarathi, H. Y. Sharada Prasad, S. Gopal, and Ravinder Kumar (Delhi: Oxford University Press, 1989), pp. 363–364.

49. In a meeting held in Bermuda on December 4, 1953, Eisenhower outlined his "atoms for peace" program to the British Prime Minister Winston Churchill and French Premier Laniel. The U.S. president said his "atoms for peace" program would help reduce the Soviet fissile material stockpile, dampen the extant "hysteria" about the atom bomb, lessen international tension, give the countries of Asia and Africa a "stake" in the East-West conflict by offering scientists worldwide the nuclear knowledge and fissile material to use for "practical purposes," and afford people everywhere cheap nuclear power, even

"to run tractors," and do all this without in any way compromising U.S. military options in Korea and elsewhere. See "Memorandum of Conversation," December 4, 1953, at http://www.eisenhower.utexas.edu/dl/Atoms_For_Peace/Binder4.pdf. Michael Berletta reveals that the United States meant to use the "atoms for peace" program as cover for its nuclear arms buildup. See his "Pernicious Ideas in World Politics: 'Peaceful Nuclear Explosions'," paper presented at the American Political Science Association Meeting, August 30–September 2, 2001, pp. 4–5, at http://www.cns.miis.edu/.

50. Berletta, "Pernicious Ideas", p. 4.

51. "Statement by H. J. Bhabha at the Conference on the IAEA Statute, October 19, 1956" in *Nuclear India,* Vol. II, p. 71.

52. "Statement by H. J. Bhabha at the Fifth IAEA General Conference, October 2, 1961," Ibid, p. 107.

53. Churchill responded to Eisenhower's "atoms for peace" proposal with skepticism and warned, as the "Memorandum of Conversation" notes, it was not possible to enjoy the "blessings" of nuclear energy without "suffering from the disadvantages of its curses." The U.S. president reacted by agreeing that there was the risk of the spread of dangerous knowledge. See note 49.

54. Gowing, *Independence and Deterrence,* pp. 332, 419–420.

55. Ibid, p. 331.

56. Sundaram et al., *Atomic Energy in India,* p. 35.

57. Bhabha recalls, for instance, being advised in 1962 by Leo Szilard to establish a microbiology laboratory at TIFR, which advice was accepted. Ibid, p. 261.

58. Bhabha's speech "Science and the Problems of Development," Ibid, p. 259.

59. Dr. Iyengar recalls that during a 1958 visit with Bhabha to Columbia University in New York, they were shown the Van de Graaf particle accelerator. Bhabha evinced an immediate interest, and the U.S. government bartered it for monazite. Interview with Dr. Iyengar, June 7, 2007.

60. Gowing, *Independence and Deterrence,* pp. 338, 434–435.

61. " 'Importance of Plutonium in India's A-Power Plans', Article by H. J. Bhabha, February 1965" in *Nuclear India,* Vol II, p. 163.

62. For Bhabha's three stage plan, see "Energy: A Strategy for Growth of Electricity Generation in India" at the Department of Atomic Energy Web site, http://www.dae.gov.in/publ/betrlife/energy.pdf.

63. Karnad, *Nuclear Weapons and Indian Security,* p. 179.

64. Parthasarathy, "Bhabha's Dream Comes True."

65. Bhabha, "Science and the Problems of Developmen,t, pp. 254–275.

66. On the *Apsara* reactor project, see Sundaram et al., *Atomic Energy in India,* pp. 19–20.

67. For an analysis of the growth of the Indian nuclear establishment and weapons capabilities, see Karnad, *Nuclear Weapons and Indian Security,* pp. 179–196. Also refer to George Perkovich, *India's Nuclear Bomb: The Impact on Global Proliferation* (Berkeley and Los Angeles, University of California Press, 1999), pp. 13–59; Chengappa, *Weapons of Peace,* pp. 88–103; and the official history of the nuclear energy program— Sundaram et al., *Atomic Energy in India,* which gives the basic information on the Indian nuclear energy program, but reveals little about the weapons project.

68. "Indian Nuclear Energy Program," Scientific Intelligence Report, Central Intelligence Agency, March 26, 1958 at http://www.gwu.edu/~nsarchiv/NSAEBB/NSAEBB187/IN01.pdf.

69. Sundaram et al., *Atomic Energy in India,* p. 38.

70. "Evolving Indian Nuclear Programme: Rationale and Perspectives," Lecture by Dr. Anil Kakodkar at the Indian Academy of Sciences, July 4, 2008, p. 1. Text available at http://www.dae.gov.in/lecture.htm.

71. Dr. Jeremy Whitlock, Canadian Nuclear FAQ at http://www.nuclearfaq.ca/cnf _sectionF.htm#x1_2.

72. Sundaram et al., *Atomic Energy in India,* pp. 25–26.

73. Interview with Dr. Iyengar, December 23, 2007.

74. See "India's Nuclear Weapons Policy," p. 5

75. Interview with Dr. Iyengar, December 23, 2007.

76. Dr. R Chidambaram has called the country's nuclear weapons program "the most economical in the world" and "one of the most cost-effective ones in the world" because "it followed the civilian program [u]nlike in all the other nuclear weapon states, which did the military program first and then came on to the civilian side." Interview in *Hindustan Times,* August 10, 2007.

77. "Development of Atomic Energy in India, Talk by H. J. Bhabha over All India Radio, 3 August 1964," in *Nuclear India,* Vol. II, pp. 147–148.

78. "Indian Government Policy on Development of Nuclear Weapon," Intelligence Information Cable, Central Intelligence Agency, October 24, 1964 online at http:// www.gwu.edu/~nsarchiv/NSAEBB/NSAEBB187/IN05.pdf.

79. "India's Nuclear Weapons Policy," p. 1.

80. Maj. Gen. K. D. Nichols, U.S.A.. (Ret.), *The Road to Trinity: A Personal Account of How America's Nuclear Policies Were Made* (New York: William Morrow and Company, Inc., 1987), p. 352.

81. "India's Potential to Build a Nuclear Weapon," American Intelligence Assessment, July 1988, Central Intelligence Agency online at http://www.gwu.edu/~nsarchiv/ NSAEBB/NSAEBB187/IN34.pdf.

82. Karnad, *Nuclear Weapons and Indian Security,* pp. 199–208.

83. Chengappa, *Weapons of Peace,* p. 82.

84. "Indian Government Policy on Development of Nuclear Weapon."

85. The chairman of the AEC in the 1990s, Dr. R. Chidambaram, revealed that "some work had been done on" designing the 1974 explosive device prior to his joining that project in 1967. See his interview of September 24, 1996 in Sundaram et al., *Atomic Energy in India,* p. 183.

86. "India's Nuclear Weapons Program: On to Weapons Development—1960–1967" (last changed March 30, 2001) online at http://nuclearweaponarchive.org/India/ IndiaWDevelop.html.

87. " 'Safeguards and the Dissemination of Military Power', Paper Presented by H. J. Bhabha to the 12th Pugwash Conference on Science and World Affairs, 27 January–1 February 1964" in *Nuclear India,* Vol.II, pp. 139–140.

88. "Broadcast by H. J. Bhabha over All India Radio on United Nations Day, 24 October 1964" in *Nuclear India,* Vol. II, pp. 158–161.

89. Karnad, *Nuclear Weapons and Indian Security,* p. 263.

90. "India's Nuclear Weapons Policy," p. 2.

91. Interview with Dr. Iyengar, June 7, 2007.

92. "India's Nuclear Weapons Policy," pp. 5–7.

93. Karnad, *Nuclear Weapons and Indian Security,* pp. 254–258.

94. "Disarmament: An Urgent Concern, P. V. Narasimha Rao, Minister for External Affairs, India, Statement made at the UN General Assembly Second Special Session on Disarmament on June 11, 1982" online at http://www.indianembassy.org/policy/Disarmament/disarm12.htm.

95. In the "Plowshare" Program, 1958–1975, The United States conducted 27 tests involving 35 separate detonations; see "Plowshare Program," Executive Summary, U.S. Department of Energy, Nevada Operations Office, online at www.osti.gov/opennet/reports/plowshar.pdf.

96. For the elaborate, persistent, and ultimately successful campaign mounted by the U.S. government to convince Prime Minister Shastri about the sheer diseconomics of India's going nuclear, a public campaign was launched with a paper leaked to friendly Indian government officials featuring cost figures extrapolated from the French nuclear program, which the U.S. Secretary of State Dean Rusk knew to be exaggerated and irrelevant to the Indian situation; see Karnad, *Nuclear Weapons and Indian Security,* pp. 258–265.

97. "Statement by Lalit Sen, Parliamentary Secretary to the Prime Minister and Intervention by Prime Minister Shastri in the *Lok Sabha,* 14 December 1964 (Extracts)" in *Nuclear India,* Vol. II, p. 162.

98. Briefed by Bhabha, the Parliamentary Secretary to the Prime Minister said in Parliament: "[I]t is quite evident that the know-how about the making of the bomb may be got by China in a ready-made form." See "Statement by Lalit Sen, Parliamentary Secretary to the Prime Minister and Intervention by Prime Minister Shastri," p. 162.

99. Karnad, *Nuclear Weapons and Indian Security,* pp. 252–253.

100. George Perkovich, *India's Nuclear Bomb,* pp. 93–96.

101. Dean Rusk, *As I Saw It,* as told to Richard Rusk (New York & London: W.W. Norton & Co., 1990), p. 342.

102. Wilfrid L. Kohl, *French Nuclear Diplomacy,* (Princeton, NJ: Princeton University Press, 1971).

103. Perkovich, *India's Nuclear Bomb,* pp. 91–98.

104. H. S. Rowen, "The Indian Nuclear Problem," Draft, December 24. 1964, online at http://www.gwu.edu/~nsarchiv/NSAEBB/NSAEBB187/IN07.pdf.

105. "Safeguards and the Dissemination of Military Power," pp. 141–142.

106. Rowen, "The Indian Nuclear Problem."

107. Karnad, *Nuclear Weapons and Indian Security,* pp. 286–288, 312–314.

108. "On to Weapons Development—1960–1967," see note 46.

109. Interview with P. K. Iyengar, June 7, 2007.

110. Dinshaw Mistry, "The Geostrategic Implications of India's Space Program," *Asian Survey,* November/December 2001.

111. Apropos Indian nuclear weapons, Sarabhai at a press conference said that "those who have studied military strategy would . . . agree that paper tigers do not provide security, that is you cannot bluff in regard to your military strength." See "Press Conference of Vikram A. Sarabhai, 1 June 1966 (Extracts)" in *Nuclear India,* vol. II, pp. 178–180.

112. Karnad, *Nuclear Weapons and Indian Security,* pp. 265–266, 271.

113. Brajesh Mishra, National Security Adviser to Prime Minister Vajpayee remembers how P. N. Haksar, Principal Private Secretary to Prime Minister Indira Gandhi, chastised Sarabhai for favoring rockets/missiles at the expense of the bomb, by saying: "What are you going to put atop the rocket—*diwali* sparkler?" Interview with Brajesh Mishra, April 25, 2007.

114. Ibid, pp. 293–305.

115. Email interview with Dr. Mahadeva Srinivasan, January 28–31, 2008.

116. Ibid.

117. Ibid.

118. Interview with Dr. P. K. Iyengar, June 7, 2007.

119. Perkovich, *India's Nuclear Bomb*, p. 243.

120. Pugwash Society Meeting, Habitat Center, New Delhi, December 21, 2003.

121. Email correspondence with Dr. Mahadeva Srinivasan, January 28–31, 2008.

122. See "Evolving Indian Nuclear Programme: Rationale and Perspectives," the Lecture by Dr. Anil Kakodkar, chairman of the atomic energy commission at the Indian Academy of Sciences, Bangalore, July 4, 2008, p. 1. The text is available online at http://www.dae.gov.in/lecture.htm.

123. Interview with Dr. P. K. Iyengar, June 7, 2007.

124. Extended conversations in 1998–2001 with the late Dr. Raja Ramanna and in 1998–2007 with Dr P. K. Iyengar.

125. Mark Hibbs, *Nuclear Watch*, June 17, 1998, at http://www.bu.edu/globalbeat/nucwatch/nucwatch061798.html.

126. Karnad, *Nuclear Weapons and Indian Security*, pp. 332–338.

127. T. S. Gopi Rethniraj, "Breakthrough Brings India Closer to an H-Bomb Arsenal," *Jane's Intelligence Review*, January 1998.

128. Interview, P. K. Iyengar, June 7, 2007.

129. Dr. Iyengar hinted of a "neutron" weapon design, among 11 other designs on the shelf, not all of which have been tested. Ibid.

130. This, according to Dr. V. S. Arunachalam, Science Adviser to the Defense Minister in the 1990s. See Stephen Peter Rosen, "Nuclear Proliferation and Alliance Relations," in *The Coming Crisis: Nuclear Proliferation, US Interests, and World Order*, Victor A. Utgoff, ed. (Cambridge, MA: MIT Press, 2000), p. 128.

131. K. Subrahmanyam, "Narasimha Rao and the Bomb," *Strategic Analysis*, 28, No. 4 (2004):595.

132. Karnad, *Nuclear Weapons and Indian Security*, pp. 340–343.

133. Subrahmanyam, "Narasimha Rao and the Bomb," p. 593.

134. Email correspondence with K. Subrahmanyam, September 28, 2007. Subrahmanyam, a former civil servant, is a leading civilian strategist.

135. Perkovich, *India's Nuclear Bomb*, pp. 3, 317.

136. Avner Cohen and Benjamin Frankel, "Opaque Nuclear Proliferation," *Journal of Strategic Studies*, 13, No. 3 (1990).

137. See McGeorge Bundy, "Bishops and the Bomb," *New York Review of Books*, 30, No. 10 (June 16, 1983).

138. Michael Howard, "Nuclear Danger and Nuclear History" (Review essay), *International Security*, 14, No.1 (Summer 1989):181.

139. Jasjit Singh, "A Nuclear Strategy for India" in *Nuclear India* Jasjit Singh, ed. (New Delhi: Knowledge World, 1998).

140. For a critique of "recessed deterrence," see Bharat Karnad, "The Quality of 'Expert' Advice," *Seminar*, No. 444 (August 1996).

141. General Sundarji's personal letter, dated October 18, 1996, to Dr. V. Siddhartha, Officer on Special Duty, Secretariat of Scientific Adviser to Defense Minister. I am grateful to Dr. Siddhartha for providing me with a copy of this letter.

142. M. Granger Morgan, K. Subrahmanyam, K. Sundarji, and Robert M. White, "India and the United States," *The Washington Quarterly*, 18, No. 2 (Spring 1995):164.

143. Perkovich, *India's Nuclear Bomb*, pp. 384–385.

144. Ibid, p. 371.

145. Bharat Karnad, "South Asia: The Irrelevance of Classical Nuclear Deterrence Theory," *India Review*, 4, No. 2 (April 2005):191–193.

146. Sumit Ganguly and Devin T. Hagerty, *Fearful Symmetry: India-Pakistan Crises in the Shadow of Nuclear Weapons* (New Delhi: Oxford University Press, 2005); Gregory S. Jones, *From Testing to Deploying NuclearForces: The Hard Choices Facing India and Pakistan* (Santa Monica: RAND, 2000); Mario E. Carranza, "An Impossible Game: Stable Deterrence After the Indian and Pakistani Tests," *Nonproliferation Review* (Spring-Summer 1999); and Hilary Synott, *The Causes and Consequences of South Asia's Nuclear Tests*, Adelphi Paper 332 (London: International Institute of Strategic Studies, 1999).

147. Karnad, "The Irrelevance of Classical Nuclear Deterrence Theory"; also Karnad, *Nuclear Weapons and Indian Security*, pp. 565–577.

148. Brad Roberts, for instance, attributes the stable deterrence system in the Cold War, among other things, to "unique cultural and geostrategic circumstances not found in the Middle East, South Asia and East Asia" while ignoring the cultural reasons for India-Pakistan wars being comparatively tame affairs. See his "From Nonproliferation to Anti-proliferation," *International Security*, 18, No. 1 (Summer 1993):159.

149. John J. Weltman, "Nuclear Devolution and World Order," *World Politics*, 32, No. 2 (January 1980):170, 174–174.

150. For a historical analysis of the Indian SSBN project, see Karnad, *Nuclear Weapons and Indian Security*, pp. 648–661. For a news report on the Indian SSBN, see Sandeep Unnithan, "The Secret Undersea Weapon," *India Today*, January 25, 2008.

151. Mistry, "The Geostrategic Implications of India's Space Program."

152. 'Prithvi', *FAS WMD Around the World*, online at http://www.fas.org/nuke/guide/india/missile/prithvi.htm.

153. Richard Speier, "India's ICBM—On a 'Glide Path' to Trouble?" February 7, 2006 at http://www.npec-web.org/Essays/060207SpeierICBM.pdf.

154. "Agni," *FAS WMD Around the World*, online at http://www.fas.org/nuke/guide/india/missile/agni.htm.

155. The U.S. Secretary of State Madeleine Albright, for example, condemned the tests as "rash" and "dangerous." See "Albright Breaks Her Silence, Calls Tests 'Grave Historical Error'," May 21, 1998 online at http://www.rediff.com/news/1998/may/21bomb.htm.

156. See Michael A. Levi and Charles D. Ferguson, *US-India Nuclear Cooperation*, Council Special Report No. 16 (New York: Council on Foreign Relations, June 2006), p. 3.

157. See Krishna Menon's speech in the 9th session of the UN General Assembly, October 26, 1954, reproduced in *Krishna Menon on Disarmament: Speeches at the United Nations*, E. S. Reddy and A. K. Damodaran, eds. (New Delhi: Sanchar Publishing House, 1994), pp. 1–26.

158. For a detailed discussion of India's disarmament policy, strategy, and diplomacy, see Karnad, *Nuclear Weapons and Indian Security*, pp. 216–219, 369–390.

CHAPTER 3

1. Atal Bihari Vajpayee was a member of the three-man group that drafted the Party's manifesto in 1961 calling for the augmentation of military power of the state and the

strengthening of national unity on the basis of national defense. As Prime Minister 37 years later, he ordered the nuclear tests. See Craig Baxter, *Jan Sangh: The Biography of an Indian Political Party* (Bombay: Oxford University Press, 1971), pp. 256, 211.

2. Pierre Gallois, *The Balance of Terror: Strategy in the Nuclear Age,* translated by Richard Howard (Boston: Houghton Mifflin & Co., 1961).

3. This letter by General Pierre Gallois to M. L. Sondhi is part of the M. L. Sondhi Papers. My thanks to Mrs. M. L. Sondhi for providing me with a photocopy of this letter.

4. Interview with Brajesh Mishra, April 25, 2007.

5. Ibid.

6. See "PM Vajpayee's Response in Parliament, August 4, 1998," in *Texts & Transcripts of Statements & Debates and Answers to Questions in Parliament on India's Nuclear Tests in May 1998 and Matters Relating Thereto* (New Delhi: Ministry of External Affairs, International Security Division, September 1998).

7. Interview with former Deputy National Security Advisor Satish Chandra, July 3, 2007.

8. Interview with Yashwant Sinha, May 25, 2007.

9. Ibid.

10. See Ambassador Masood Khan, "Results of the NPT Review Conference and Nuclear Policies—Nuclear Options and Policies of Other States," Geneva Center for Security Policy, June 8, 2005, online at http://missions.itu.int/~pakistan/.

11. Interview with A. N. Prasad, July 7, 2007.

12. Ibid.

13. On the controversy about the Indian claim on the yields of the various designs tested in 1998, see Bharat Karnad, *Nuclear Weapons and Indian Security,* 2nd ed. (New Delhi: Macmillan India Ltd., 2002, 2005), pp. 399–419.

14. Dr. Chidambaram , former chairman of the AEC, in a talk at the Indian Institute of Science, Bangalore, December 12, 2002; the text of Chidambaram's talk in the strategic archive of http://www.bharat-rakshak.com; and Ibid, p. 416. On India's not needing to test again owing to its computer simulation prowess, see his interview in *Frontline,* January 2–15, 1999.

15. Regarding the emphasis on testing by American weapons designers at the Lawrence Livermore National Laboratory in the United States, see Hugh Gusterson, *Nuclear Rites: A Weapons Laboratory at the End of the Cold War* (Berkeley, Los Angeles, London: University of California Press, 1996), ch. 6, p. 131.

16. A non-attributable interview; January 12, 2006.

17. National Resources Defense Council, Nuclear Notebook, "French nuclear forces, 2005," *Bulletin of Atomic Scientists* (July/August 2005), p. 75.

18. The U.S. Department of Energy budget request for nuclear weapons-related activities in 2007 was $6.4 billion—$38 million more than in 2006. In 2006, $599.8 million was spent on the thermonuclear explosions simulation program, $543.6 million on ICF, and $238.7 million on manufacturing weapon pits or cores. See Dr. Robert Civak, "Still at It: An Analysis of the Department of Energy's Fiscal Year 2007 Budget Request for Nuclear Weapons Activities" online at http://www.trivalleycares.org.

19. The U.S. Department of Energy's Accelerated Strategic Computing Initiative resulted in a computer capable of 100 teraops (trillion operations per second). For more information on the ASCI and the sheer complexity involved in simulating thermonuclear explosions that India is nowhere in a position to emulate, see Peter D. Zimmerman and David W. Dorn, "Computer Simulation and the Comprehensive Test Ban Treaty,"

Defense Horizons (August 2002) online at http://www.ndu.edu/inss/DefHor/DH17/DH17. htm. The speediest computer BARC has developed for its own use—the ANUPAM-AJEYA—is capable of only 3.70 teraops. See AEC Chairman Anil Kakodkar's speech at the 51st General Conference of IAEA, September 19, 2007, reproduced in *The Indian Express,* September 21, 2007.

20. "Nuclear weapons: Reliable evidence?" *The Economist,* November 17, 2007, p. 84.

21. K. Subrahmanyam, "Narasimha Rao and the Bomb," *Strategic Analysis,* 28, No. 4, 2004, p. 593.

22. Interviews with Jaswant Singh on April 21, 2007, Prime Minister Vajpayee's representative in the strategic dialog with the United States and successively Minister for External Affairs and, for a while, concurrently, Defense Minister, and Finance minister in the BJP government, and with Yashwant Singh on May 25, 2007, Finance Minister and later Minister for External Affairs in the BJP government.

23. Interview with Dr. A. N. Prasad, July 1, 2007.

24. Karnad, *Nuclear Weapons and Indian Security,* pp. 380–381.

25. Interview with Dr. A. N. Prasad, July 1, 2007.

26. "Indian Scientist Opposes Signing CTBT," *Deccan Herald,* February 19, 2000.

27. Dr. Rodriguez's Q&A session at the seminar on "Nuclear India at 60," Center for Policy Research, New Delhi, August 7, 2007.

28. Ashok Parthasarathy's intervention, 2nd session, seminar on "India-US Nuclear Deal: Concerns and Challenges," Center for Air Power Studies, India International Center, New Delhi, February 8, 2008.

29. Email correspondence with Dr. Mahadeva Srinivasan, January 28–31, 2008.

30. Interview with Dr. A. N. Prasad, July 1, 2007.

31. Personal communication from a member of a high level task-force set up by the Ministry of External Affairs to advise it on the posture India should adopt on CTBT and FMCT.

32. See Herman Kahn, *On Thermonuclear War* (Princeton, NJ: Princeton University Press, 1960), fn, p. 244. Also see Lorna Arnold, *Britain and the H-Bomb* (Basingstoke and London: Macmillan, 2001), pp xi–xii.

33. Bruce D. Larkin, *Nuclear Designs: Great Britain, France and China in the Global Governance of Nuclear Weapons* (New Brunswick, NJ: Transaction Publishers, 1996), pp. 51–53.

34. See Kathleen Bailey, *Comprehensive Test Ban: The Worst Arms Control Treaty Ever* (Fairfax, VA: National Institute for Public Policy, 1999).

35. Interview with Admiral Arun Prakash, May 16, 2007.

36. Interview with General Ved Malik, February 21, 2007.

37. Interview with Brajesh Mishra, April 25, 2007.

38. Interview with Satish Chandra, July 3, 2007.

39. Interview with Jaswant Singh, April 21, 2007.

40. Interview with Brajesh Mishra, April 25, 2007.

41. Unattributable interview of a former director, BARC, July 16, 2007 .

42. Interview on an unattributable basis (with request not to reveal date) with a former Chief of an Armed Service.

43. Bharat Karnad, "A Sucker's Payoff," *Seminar,* 485 (January 2000).

44. Minister for External Affairs, Pranab Mukherji, responding to the opposition's charge in the debate in Parliament on the nuclear cooperation deal with the United States

that the Congress Party regime "wanted no more Pokhrans" (Pokhran being the nuclear testing site in the desert state of Rajasthan), stated "How can you say that there will be no ... Pokhran-III or Pokhran-IV?" See "Final Step Still to Be Negotiated: Pranab," *The Asian Age,* December 19, 2006.

45. Admiral David Jeremiah, heading a task force examining the reasons for the intelligence failure on the 1998 Indian nuclear tests, stated: "The identification of the Indian nuclear test preparations posed a difficult [information] collection problem and a difficult analytical problem. Their program was an indigenous program ... not derived from the US, Chinese, Russian or French programs. It was totally within India. And, therefore, there were some characteristics difficult to observe." See "Jeremiah News Conference," June 2, 1998 online at http://www.gwu.edu/~nsarchiv/NSAEBB/NSAEBB187/IN39.pdf.

46. See Raja Ramanna, "Security, Deterrence, and the Future," *USI Journal,* 122 (July-Sept. 1992):509.

47. Interviews with Raja Ramanna in February 2000 and with P.K. Iyengar on June 7, 2007 and December 23, 2007.

48. Ibid.

49. For a succinct explanation of the "Teller-Ulam" design, see Carey Sublette, " 'Teller-Ulam' Summary," *Nuclear Weapons Frequently Asked Questions,* Section 2, online at http://nuclearweaponarchive.org/Library/Teller.html.

50. Interviews with P. K. Iyengar (December 23, 2007) and Mahadeva Srinivasan (by email, January 28–31, 2008).

51. Herbert York, *The Advisors: Oppenheimer, Teller and the Super Bomb* (Stanford, CA: Stanford University Press, 1976), p. 83.

52. Email correspondence, January 28–31, 2008. Mahadeva Srinivasan sought premature retirement in the early 1990s from his post as associate director of the physics group at BARC. Renowned for his mathematical capabilities, he was involved in making all the most complex calculations for the fission, boosted fission, and, perhaps, even the thermonuclear designs produced in BARC.

53. Interview with P. K. Iyengar, December 23, 2007.

54. Ibid.

55. Email interview with Dr. Mahadeva Srinivasan, January 28–31, 2008.

56. R Chidambaram, former chairman of the AEC, in a talk at the Indian Institute of Science, Bangalore, on December 12, 2002.

57. See his "Reactor-Grade Plutonium Can Be Used to Make Powerful and Reliable Nuclear Weapons: Separated Plutonium in the Fuel Cycle Must Be Protected As If It Were Nuclear Weapons," online at http://www.fas.org/rlg/980826-pu.htm.

58. Email correspondence with Mahadeva Srinivasan, January 28–31, 2008. Igniting tritium with deuterium in a boosted weapon, according to *Global Fissile Material Report 2007,* "produces a burst of neutrons that 'boost' the fraction of fissile materials fissioned and thereby the power of the explosion." See *Global Fissile Material Report 2007,* Program on Science and Global Security, Princeton University, p. 112, online at http://www.ipfmlibrary.org/gfmr07.pdf.

59. Zia Mian, A. H. Nayyar, R. Rajaraman, M. V. Ramana, "Plutonium Production in India and the US-India Nuclear Deal," in *Gauging US-India Strategic Cooperation,* Henry Sokolski, ed. (Carlisle Barracks, PA: Strategic Studies Institute, Army War College, March 2007), p. 118.

60. Interview with Air Marshal (Ret.) Vinod Patney, former Vice Chief of the Air Staff and Commander-in-Chief, Western Air Command, Indian Air Force, April 11, 2007. He is presently member of the National Security Advisory Board.

61. Ibid.

62. Alexander Glaser, *Weapon-Grade Plutonium Production Potential in the Indian Prototype Fast Breeder Reactor,* (Revision 10), December 13, 2006, online at http://www.princeton.edu/~aglaser/talk2006_princeton.pdf, p. 39.

63. *Global Fissile Material Report 2007*, p. 15.

64. Interview with Dr. P. K. Iyengar, December 23, 2007.

65. Placid Rodriguez, "Nuclear India at 60."

66. See AEC Chairman Anil Kakodkar's interview in *Businessline,* August 13, 2004.

67. *Global Fissile Material Report 2007,* p. 15.

68. Interview with Dr. Iyengar, December 23, 2007.

69. David Albright, *India's Military Plutonium Inventory, End 2004* (Washington, DC: Institute of Science and International Security), p. 5.

70. Communication from a former Chief of Naval Staff, January 15, 2007.

71. Senior official in government, March 2, 2008.

72. Communication from a senior Indian Navy officer.

73. Interview with Dr. Iyengar, December 23, 2007.

74. David Albright and Susan Basu, "India's Gas Centrifuge Enrichment Program: Growing Capacity for Military Purposes," Institute of Science and International Security, January 18, 2007 at http://www.isis-online.org/publications/southasia/indiagrowingcapacity.pdf. The authors, controversially, mention that India plans to use the Ratnehalli enriched uranium, among other things, in its thermonuclear weapons program. This makes no sense given the fact that the far larger amounts of enriched uranium needed in the weapons would skew the designs and divert this fissile material from its intended primary use in submarine power plants. Indian scientists, in any case, deny any such use of enriched uranium.

75. "Scientists Urged to Pursue Goal of Self-Reliance," *The Hindu,* July 17, 1995.

76. According to P. V. Indiresan, former Director, Indian Institute of Technology, Madras, and Member of the Naval Research Board, but for the sanctions carbon-carbon composites for aircraft and missile cones, mission control computers for missiles and semiconductor/integrated chips of military specifications, for example, would not have been developed indigenously. Personal communication, October 4, 2004. For various assessments on how well or otherwise technology denial regimes have fared, see Brad Roberts, ed., *Weapons Proliferation in the 1990s* (Cambridge, MA: MIT Press, 1995). On the futility of economic sanctions, see Richard N. Haass, *Economic Sanctions and American Diplomacy* (New York: Council on Foreign Relations Press, 1998).

77. Interview, December 23, 2007.

78. See Ashley Tellis, *India's Emerging Nuclear Posture: Between Recessed Deterrent and Ready Arsenal* (Santa Monica: RAND, 2001), fn 353, p. 395. Tellis was reacting to the case this author has made for a China-oriented 300–400 weapons-strong Indian deterrent. See Bharat Karnad, "A Thermonuclear Deterrent," in *India's Nuclear Deterrent: Pokhran II and Beyond* Amitabh Mattoo, ed. (New Delhi: Har-Anand Publications Pvt. Ltd., 1999), pp. 108–149; Bharat Karnad, "India's Force Planning Imperative: The Thermonuclear Option," in *Nuclear India in the Twenty-first Century* D. R. Sardesai and Raju G. C. Thomas, eds. (New York: Palgrave, 2002), pp. 63–84; and Karnad, *Nuclear Weapons and Indian Security,* pp. 614–647. The Indian military, by and large, supports

such nuclear force structure. See, for example, Lt. General (Ret.) Vinay Shankar, "Nuclear Deal versus Nuclear Capability," *Indian Defense Review,* 22, No. 1 (August 2007).

79. Ashley J. Tellis, *Atoms for War? US-Indian civilian nuclear cooperation and India's nuclear arsenal* (Washington, DC: Carnegie Endowment for International Peace, 2006), p. 12.

80. Stephen M. Younger, *Nuclear Weapons in the Twenty-first Century,* June 27, 2000, online at http://www.fas.org/nuke/guide/usa/doctrine/doe/younger.htm.

81. Email correspondence with Mahadeva Srinivasan, January 28–31, 2008.

82. Interview with A. N. Prasad, July 1, 2007.

83. Interview with Dr. P. K. Iyengar, December 23, 2007.

84. See "Suo Moto Statement by Prime Minister Shri Atal Bihari Vajpayee in Parliament on 27th May, 1998," in *Texts and Transcripts of Statements & Debates* (New Delhi: Ministry of External Affairs, International Security division, Sept 1998), p. 3.

85. See Mukherji's response in Ibid.

86. A not-for-attribution communication, February 2007.

87. See Bharat Karnad, "Dangerously Misunderstanding Nehru," *The Asian Age,* November 13, 2004.

88. Email interview with Dr Mahadeva Srinivasan, January 28–31, 2008.

89. See Kalam's autobiography (written with Arun Tiwari) covering the period up to his leadership of DRDO, *Wings of Fire: An Autobiography* (Hyderabad: Universities Press Ltd., 1999).

90. The hard information in this section on Indian missiles and the Agni long range missile program generally, other than the bits that are footnoted, has come from an authoritative source—a retired rocket scientist directly involved in the design and development of the various Agni missiles, communicated to the author in the period 2005–2008 but not on an attributable basis.

91. In late April 2008, the Indian Polar Satellite Launch vehicle injected into precise orbits 10 satellites—one major satellite and a bunch of nano-satellites. See T. S. Subramaniam, "PSLV Puts 10 Satellites in Orbit," *The Hindu,* April 29, 2008.

92. Dinshaw Mistry, "The Geostrategic Implications of India's Strategic Program," *Asian Survey,* 41, No. 6 (Nov/Dec 2001).

93. A senior official in the National Security Adviser's Office, July 24, 2007.

94. Michael D. Swaine and Loren H. Runyon, "Ballistic Missiles and Missile Defense in Asia," *NBR Analysis,* 13, No. 3 (June 2002):22–23.

95. This, according to General Jehangir Karamat, the former Pakistan Army Chief, is a distinct possibility. See his "Missile Acquisition by Pakistan: Military Strategic Imperatives," *South Asia Survey,* 11, No. 2 (2004):175.

96. For a detailed argument along these lines, see Karnad, *Nuclear Weapons and Indian Security,* pp. 571–575.

97. Swaine and Runyon, "Ballistic Missiles and Missile Defense in Asia," p. 23.

98. For Talbott's account of his emphasis on "strategic restraint" in his dialog with Jaswant Singh, see his *Engaging India: Diplomacy, Democracy and the Bomb* (Washington, DC: Brookings, 2004), pp. 146–147.

99. Interview with Jaswant Singh, April 21, 2007.

100. For a newspaper commentary about the IGMP's record of failures, see G. Bharath and Harsh V. Pant, "DRDO's missile mess," *The Asian Age,* February 12, 2008.

101. Interview with A. N. Prasad, July 1, 2007.

102. The BJP government's not developing an ICBM is considered by some Western analysts as a "political choice" made by Delhi. See Gaurav Kampani, "Stakeholders in the Indian Strategic Missile Program," *Nonproliferation Review* (Fall/Winter 2003):67.

103. See Pratap Chakravarty, "India Eyes ICBMs After Testing China-Specific Missile," *Agence France-Presse,* April 15, 2007, online at http://www.spacewar.com/reports/India_Eyes_ICBMs_After_Testing_China_Specific_Missile_999.html.

104. Personal communication, unattributable, by a former senior naval officer, June 27, 2007.

105. T. S. Subramaniam, "Sagarika missile test-fired successfully," *The Hindu,* February 27, 2008.

106. Personal communication, unattributable, former senior naval office, June 27, 2007.

107. Gaurav Kampani said this about the Indian missile program in 2003. See his "Stakeholders in the Indian Missile Program," p. 67.

108. For details of the Indian SSBN project, see Karnad, *Nuclear Weapons and Indian Security,* pp. 648–661.

109. Off the record personal communication by a senior naval officer, June 27, 2007.

110. Omer Farooq, "Hatf, Shaheen no threat, says Saraswat," *The Pioneer,* December 4, 2006.

111. Senior official in the Brahmos program, January 22, 2007.

112. "India to get Scorpene by 2012," *The Times of India,* February 18, 2008.

113. See his "Missile Acquisition by Pakistan: Military Strategic Imperatives," *South Asian Survey,* 11, No. 2 (2004):174.

114. Prahlada Rao, Chief Comptroller, DRDO, is quoted as saying: "For a strategic missile, one needs to test it successfully at least three times." See Rajat Pandit, "With Sub-Launch, India Looks to Complete N-Weapon Triad," *The Times of India,* February 19, 2008.

115. Donald C. Whitmore, "Revisiting Nuclear Deterrence Theory," March 1, 1998, online at http://www.abolishnukes.com.

116. See "L. K. Advani, May 28, 1998," in *Texts and Transcripts of Statements & Debates.*

117. "Opening Remarks by National Security Adviser Mr Brajesh Mishra at the Release of Draft Indian Nuclear Doctrine," August 17, 1999, online at http://meaindia.nic.in/disarmament/dm17aug99.htm.

118. See his "Strategy as a Science," *World Politics,* 1, No. 4 (July 1949):471.

119. See Rodney W. Jones and Thomas Blau, eds., *Small Nuclear Forces and US Security Policy* (New Britian, CT: Lexington Books, 1984).

120. Rodney W. Jones, *Minimum Nuclear Deterrence Postures in South Asia: An Overview* (Washington, DC: US Threat Reduction Agency, 2002).

121. Interview with Satish Chandra, July 3, 2007; Ashley J. Tellis analyzed this supposed Indian posture in some detail. See his *India's Emerging Nuclear Posture,* chs. 4, 5.

122. Tellis, *India's Emerging Nuclear Posture,* fn 49, p, 494.

123. Interview with Dr. Iyengar, December 23, 2007.

124. V. Raghuvanshi, "India to Stay the Course on Nuke Doctrine," *Defense News,* November 1, 2004.

125. Satish Chandra, "The National Security Set Up," *Agni: Studies in International Strategic Issues,* X, No. IV (October–December 2007).

126. Interview, Satish Chandra, July 3, 2007.

127. Interview with Admiral (Ret.) Arun Prakash, May 16, 2007.

128. Interview, April 21, 2007.

129. See Draft Report of National Security Advisory Board on Indian Nuclear Doctrine, August 17, 1999 at http://meaindia.nic.in/disarmament/dm17aug99.htm.

130. See Bharat Karnad, "Deconstructing the Indian Nuclear Doctrine," in *Arms Race and Nuclear Developments in South Asia,* Pervaiz Iqbal Cheema and Imtiaz H. Bokhari, eds. (Islamabad: Islamabad Policy Research Institute, 2004).

131. Interview with Air Chief Marshal S. Krishnaswamy, July 3, 2007.

132. See Henry Kissinger, *Nuclear Weapons and Foreign Policy* (New York: Harper & Brothers, 1957), p. 42.

133. Interview with Air Chief Marshal Krishnaswamy, July 3, 2007.

134. In the "strategic dialog," U.S. Deputy Secretary of State Strobe Talbott's approach was to push India into answering "How much's enough?" "That had, unfortunately," said Jaswant Singh, "become central to the determination of both credibility of deterrence and the definition of minimum." Interview. April 21, 2007.

135. Interview with Satish Chandra, July 3, 2007.

136. Senior DRDO official, August 5, 2007. In fact, General Malik recalls that when he proposed that the military draft a nuclear doctrine in 1997, the then Prime Minister Inder Gujral approved it but not before Dr. Kalam tried but failed to scuttle this exercise by suggesting there was no need for it as DRDO had already written a doctrine. Interview, February 21, 2007.

137. Interview with Satish Chandra, July 3, 2007.

138. George Perkovich, *India's Nuclear Bomb: The Impact on Global Proliferation* (New Delhi: Oxford University Press, 1999), pp. 384–385.

139. See K. Subrahmanyam, "Nuclear Force Design and Minimum Deterrence Strategy for India," in *Future Imperiled: India's Security in the 1990s and Beyond,* Bharat Karnad, ed. (New Delhi: Viking, 1994)

140. See Bernard Brodie, *Strategy in the Missile Age* (Princeton, NJ: Princeton University Press, 1959), pp. 277, 272–273.

141. Interview, unattributable, July 16, 2007.

142. Jasjit Singh, "Nuclear Stability in South Asia: Issues and Challenges," in *India and Pakistan: Pathways Ahead,* Amitabh Mattoo, Kapil Kak, Happymon Jacob, eds. (New Delhi: Knowledge World, 2007), p. 35–36.

143. Interview, May 17, 2007.

144. Interviews with Jaswant Singh on April 21, 2007 and Satish Chandra on July 3, 2007.

145. Interview April 21, 2007.

146. Interview April 25, 2007.

147. Interview on non-attributable basis, September 14, 2007.

148. Interview, April 12, 2007.

149. Max Schmidt, "Military Parity, Political and Military Détente," in *The Arms Race in the 1980s,* David Carlton and Carlo Schaerf, eds. (London and Basingstoke, Macmillan, 1982), p. 63–64.

150. Interview, July 3, 2007.

151. Interview, May 16, 2007.

152. Interview, July 3, 2007.

153. Interview, April 11, 2007.

154. Emailed note from Admiral Arun Prakash; emphases in the original, August 29, 2007.

155. Interview on an non-attributable basis, July 16, 2007.

156. Interview, April 12, 2007.

157. Interview, April 25, 2007.

158. For an assessment of the NSSP, the Defense framework agreement, and the civilian nuclear cooperation deal, see K. Alan Kronstadt, *India-US Relations,* Updated February 13, 2007, CRS Report for Congress, online at http://fpc.state.gov/documemnts/organization/80669.pdf.

159. Interview, May 17, 2007.

160. The former Deputy NSA Satish Chandra opines that several of the new organizations set up in the wake of the 1998 tests, like the National Information Board to formulate national policies on information warfare and information security, "are virtually defunct"; the National Technical Research Organization—"the apex Techint organization"–"remains a shadow" of what was originally envisaged, and the National Security Council Secretariat "has been gutted." See his "The National Security Set Up," pp. 21–22.

161. It was disclosed that India had no more than 35 nuclear weapons and that Pakistan had some more nuclear weapons. See Robert S. Norris, "India's Nuclear Forces, 2002," NRDC Notebook, *The Bulletin of Atomic Scientists,* March 2002.

162. Personal communication, unattributable, from a senior nuclear policy adviser to the government, January 8, 2008.

163. Email correspondence, February 11, 2008.

164. Interview, unattributable, July 16, 2007.

165. Presentation by Major General Ausaf Ali on "Aspects of Pakistan's Nuclear Capability" at the *International Conference on the Nuclearization of South Asia: Consequences, Challenges, Peace Prospects,* The Islamia University of Bahawalpur, Pakistan, March 13–14, 2007. For an American take on Pakistan's nuclear posture and capability, see Peter Lavoy, "Pakistan's Nuclear Posture: Security and Survivability," paper for the Nuclear Proliferation Education Center, Washington, DC, July 26, 2006, p. 14, online at http://www.npec-web.org.

166. All the information about the SPD in this paragraph is from the presentation by Major General Ausaf Ali on "Aspects of Pakistan's Nuclear Capability."

167. Senior official in the prime minister's office, July 24, 2007.

168. Former CINC, SFC, interview, October 8, 2007.

169. Ibid.

170. Interview with Air Marshal Vinod Patney, April 11, 2007.

171. Interview with General Ved Malik, February 21, 2007.

172. Pierre Gallois, *The Balance of Terror: Strategy in the Nuclear Age,* Translated by Richard Howard (Boston: Houghton Mifflin & Co., 1961), p. 135.

173. Interview, April 11, 2007.

174. See his "Massive Retaliation and Graduated Deterrence," *World Politics,* 8, No. 2 (January 1956):230, 234.

175. Kissinger, *Nuclear Weapons and Foreign Policy,* p. 398.

176. Non-attributable interview with a former CINC, SFC, October 8, 2007.

177. A former Naval Chief, non-attributable interview, August 29, 2007.

178. Senior official in the prime minister's office, July 24, 2007.

179. Interview with Satish Chandra, July 3, 2007.

180. Interview, unattributable, with a senior military officer, November 13, 2006.

181. Personal communication from a senior military officer, unattributable, February 25, 2008.

182. Interview with Admiral Arun Prakash, May 16, 2007.

183. Interview with Air Chief Marshal S. Krishnaswamy, July 3, 2007.

184. Interview with Air Marshal Ajit Bhavnani, April 12, 2007.

185. See Ashley Tellis, *India's Emerging Nuclear Posture: Between Recessed Deterrent and Ready Arsenal* (Santa Monica, CA: RAND, 2001).

186. Interviews of Air Marshal Bhavnani and Satish Chandra on April 12, 2007, and July 3, 2007, respectively.

187. Humphrey Hawksley, "India's nuclear muscle," *BBC News,* World edition, January 11, 2003, online at http://news.bbc.co.uk/.

188. Swaine and Runyon, "Ballistic Missiles and Missile Defense in Asia," pp. 22–23.

189. See George Perkovich, "Could Anything Be Done to Stop Them? Lessons From Pakistan," a paper for the Nonproliferation Policy Education Center, Washington, DC, July 26, 2006, p. 9, online at http://www.npec-web.org.

190. For a succinct analysis of the IAF's historic aversion to long range aircraft and why the Soviet offer in 1971 of the Tu-22 was turned down, see Karnad, *Nuclear Weapons and Indian Security,* pp. 661–668.

191. Interview with a former Naval Chief, unattributable, October 12, 2007.

192. Personal communication from a former chief of staff of a Service, unattributable, January 15, 2008.

193. "Nuke sub for the Indian Navy goes on trial in Russian seas," The Press Trust of India (news agency), *The Hindustan Times,* July 1, 2006.

194. Interview with Air Marshal (Ret.) Ajit Bhavnani, April 12, 2007.

195. Interview with Admiral Arun Prakash, May 16, 2007. The admiral is a former naval aviator.

196. The 700-km Agni-I missile was fired for the first time by a unit of the army missile group in late March 2008. See "Army Unit Launches Agni-I for First Time," *The Indian Express,* March 24, 2008.

197. Interview with Satish Chandra, July 3, 2007.

198. Interview with Air Marshal (Ret.) Ajit Bhavnani, April 12, 2007.

199. Sandeep Dikshit, "Armed forces prefer Agni missiles to Prithvi," *The Hindu,* July 10, 2006.

200. The then Defense Minister Pranab Mukherji said there was no external pressure against test-firing the Agni-III missile. "It is just that we have decided," he said, "to have self-imposed restraint." See Seema Mustafa, "US Pressure Halts Agni," *The Asian Age,* May 16, 2006. This "self-restraint" would apply even more strongly to the deployment of this missile.

201. Swaine and Runyon, "Ballistic Missiles and Missile Defense in Asia," pp. 23–24.

202. Prasun K. Sengupta, "New Spatial Frontiers," *Force,* 5, No. 6 (February 2008).

203. Rajat Pandit, "Army Ready for Satellite Spying," *The Times of India,* October 18, 2006.

204. Amitabh Sinha, "With a string of seven satellites, ISRO plans a GPS for South Asia," *The Indian Express,* September 16, 2007.

205. The case for making nuclear missiles invulnerable by basing them in mountain tunnels made in Karnad, *Nuclear Weapons and Indian Security,* pp. 631–635.

206. Interview with Admiral Arun Prakash, May 16, 2007.

207. Senior DRDO and military officers, cross-checked, unattributable information, disclosed in April–June 2007.

208. Senior official in government, December 3, 2007.

209. Israel is increasingly involved in sensitive Indian security projects and has created a lot of trust in the Indian military because of its proven record of keeping secret defense deals secret, the quality of its technology, and its reliability as supplier. In this regard, see the Israeli ambassador Mark Sofer's interview in *Outlook,* February 18, 2008. The growing security cooperation and defense industrial collaboration between the two countries is illustrated by the fact of India's space launch vehicle putting Israel's most advanced reconnaissance satellite into orbit. See Yaacov Katz, "Spy Satellite Launched from India," *The Jerusalem Post,* January 21, 2008, online at http://www.jpost.com/.

210. Personal communication by a former C-in-C, Strategic Forces Command, October 8, 2007.

211. Personal communication from a retired three star rank military officer.

212. Interview with Admiral Arun Prakash, May 16, 2007.

213. Personal communication from a senior officer who served in SFC, 2007.

214. Personal communication from senior DRDO official, October 25, 2007.

215. Interview with Air Marshal (Ret.) Ajit Bhavnani, April 12, 2007.

216. Interview with Admiral Arun Prakash, May 16, 2007.

217. Interview with Satish Chandra, July 3, 2007.

218. Rajat Pandit, "India Gears Up for Wars of Future," *The Times of India,* February 21, 2008.

219. Interview with Admiral (Ret.) Arun Prakash, May 16, 2007.

220. Christopher Eldridge, ed., *Protection, Control and Accounting of Nuclear Materials: International Challenges and National Programs* (Washington, DC: National Academies Press, 2005), pp. 39–40.

221. Charles D. Ferguson, "Assessing the Vulnerability of the Indian Civilian Nuclear Program to Military and Terrorist Attack," in *Gauging US-India Strategic Cooperation,* pp. 141–142.

222. Iftikhar Gilani, "India Plans to Ward Off Radioactive Disaster," *The Daily Times* (Islamabad), December 30, 2006.

223. On the shortfalls of disaster management in South Asia, see R. Rajaraman, Zian Mian, A. H. Nayyar, "Nuclear Civil Defense in South Asia: Is It Feasible?" *Economic and Political Weekly,* November 20, 2004. Also see Dr. Mahnaz Fatima, "Disaster Management Capabilities in the Third World," *The News on Sunday* (Islamabad), January 23, 2006.

224. S. Parasuraman and P. V. Unnikrishnan, eds., *India Disasters Report: Towards a Policy Initiative* (New Delhi: Oxford University Press, 2000).

225. Albert Wohlstetter, "Strength, Interest and New Technologies," *The Writings of Albert Wohlstetter,* January 24, 1968, online at http://www.rand.org.

226. See *Texts and Transcripts of Statements & Debates.*

227. Jacques E. C. Hymans, *The Psychology of Nuclear Proliferation: Identity, Emotions and Foreign Policy* (Cambridge, Cambridge University Press, 2006), p. 180.

228. See Xenia Dormandy "Is India, or Will it Be, a Responsible International Stakeholder?" *The Washington Quarterly,* 30, No. 3 (Summer 2007).

229. For an expostulation of "offensive realism" and historical analysis based on this concept, see John J. Mearsheimer, *The Tragedy of Great Power Politics* (New York & London: W.W. Norton & Company, 2001).

230. Interviews with General (Ret.) Ved Malik and Admiral (Ret.) Arun Prakash on February 21, 2007, and May 16, 2007, respectively.

231. John J. Mearsheimer, "Better to be Godzilla than Bambi," *Foreign Policy,* January/February 2005, online at http://www.foreignpolicy.com/story/cms.php ?story_id=2740.

232. Interview on a non-attributable basis, September 26, 2007.

CHAPTER 4

1. In 1998–2002, China's conventional arms transfers to Pakistan accounted for roughly 64 percent by value of all its military hardware exports. See Bjorn Hagelin, Pieter D. Wezeman, Siemon T. Wezeman, and Nicholas Chipperfield, "International Arms Transfers," in *SIPRI Yearbook 2003: Armaments, Disarmament and International Security* (Oxford: Oxford University Press, 2003), Table 13.1, p. 442.

2. In 2006, Pakistan was the largest importer of U.S. military hardware, signing deals worth $3.5 billion—$1.4 billion for the new version of F-16 aircraft, $890 million for mid-life upgradation kits for an older version of the F-16 already with the Pakistani Air Force, $640 million for missiles and bombs to equip Pakistan's F-16 fleet, and $52 million for 115 self-propelled howitzers. See Richard F. Grimmett, *US Arms Sales to Pakistan,* CRS Report to Congress, November 8, 2007, online at http://www.fas.org/asmp/resources/110th/CRS22757.pdf.

3. The Bharatiya Janata Party–led coalition government headed by Atal Bihari Vajpayee revealed in the May 1998 debate in parliament on the nuclear tests that an American firm, Holmes and Narver, was helping Pakistan build a "Contained Firing Facility" based on a Lawrence Livermore U.S. weapons laboratory "blueprint" for the purposes of refining nuclear weapons and missile warheads. See "Answer by Minister of State for External Affairs Vasundhara Raje," May 27, 1998, in *Texts and Transcripts of Statements & Debates and Answers to Questions in Parliament on India's Nuclear Tests in May 1998 and Matters Relating Thereto* (New Delhi: Ministry of External Affairs, International Security division, September1998).

4. See "Address by the Defense Minister Pranab Mukherji at the Carnegie Endowment for International Peace, Washington DC, on India's strategic perspectives, June 27, 2005," online at http://www.indianembassy.org/.

5. For the case that the U.S. policy of "offshore balancing" of India by beefing up Pakistan may be ending, see Lloyd J. Rudolph and Susan Hoeber Rudolph, "The Making of US Foreign Policy: Offshore Balancing in Historical Perspective," *Economic and Political Weekly,* February 25, 2006.

6. For the concept of "pivotal deterrence" and case study of how the United States applied it to the India-Pakistan dispute over Kashmir in 1962–1965, see Timothy W. Crawford, *Pivotal Deterrence: Third-Party Statecraft and the Pursuit of Peace* (Ithaca, NY, and London: Cornell University Press, 2003), pp. 135–168. For the U.S. role in more recent India-Pakistan conflicts, see P. R. Chari, Pervaiz Iqbal Cheema, and Stephen P. Cohen, *Four Crises and a Peace Process: American Engagement in South Asia* (Washington, DC: Brookings Institution Press, 2007).

7. The Indian Minister for External Affairs Pranab Mukherji visiting Pakistan said: "We share a common heritage and culture, and this commonality" will help resolve

disputes and install peace. See "Shared Past to Act as a Binder: Pranab," *The Times of India,* January 15, 2007.

8. Most Pakistani generals concede these characteristic traits of India-Pakistan wars, most recently Lt. General (Ret.) Asad Durrani, former head of the Pakistan Army's Inter-Services Intelligence, in the 2nd Session, *International Conference on the Nuclearization of South Asia: Consequences, Challenges and Peace Prospects..*

9. For an analysis of India-Pakistan wars along these lines, see Bharat Karnad, "Key to Peace in South Asia: Fostering 'Social Links' between the Armies of India and Pakistan," *Round Table: The Commonwealth Journal of International Affairs,* No. 338 (April 1996); Bharat Karnad, "Key to Confidence-Building in South Asia: Fostering Military to Military Links," *USI Journal,* XCCVI, No. 524 (April–June 1996); and Bharat Karnad, *Nuclear Weapons and Indian Security: The Realist Foundations of Strategy,* 2nd ed. (New Delhi: Macmillan India Ltd., 2002, 2005), pp. 565–572.

10. Hugh Faringdon, *Confrontation: The Strategic Geography of NATO and the Warsaw Pact* (London & New York: Routledge & Kegan Paul, 1986), pp. 249–263.

11. "Nuclear Safety, Nuclear Stability and Nuclear Strategy in Pakistan: A Concise Report of a Visit by Landau Network-Centro Volta," online at http://www.mi.infn .it/~landnet/Doc/pakistan.pdf.

12. Email correspondence with Air Chief Marshal (Ret.) Anil Tipnis, February 19, 2008.

13. In the 1971 War, when India scored a decisive victory and "liberated" Bangladesh, in terms of fighting capabilities vis-à-vis Pakistan, the "combat force ratio"—a composite index used by the Military Operations Directorate, Indian Army Headquarters, was 1.7:1, which ratio had steadily declined to 1.3:1 by 1998. More specifically, the gap in armored forces had declined from 1.91:1 in 1993 to 1.20:1 in 1998, and in mechanized infantry in the same period from 2.89:1 to 2.53:1 See Bharat Karnad, "South Asia: The Irrelevance of Classical Nuclear Deterrence Theory," *India Review,* 4, No. 2 (April 2005):191–192.

14. "Kashmir Militant Extremists," Backgrounder, *Council on Foreign Relations,* updated July 12, 2006, online at http://www.cfr.org/publication/9135/.

15. For an analysis that nuclear weapons make little difference to the subdued nature of India-Pakistan wars, see Karnad, "South Asia: The Irrelevance of Classical Nuclear Deterrence Theory."

16. Hans Delbruck, *History of the Art of War Within the Framework of Political History: The Modern Era* (Westport, CT: Greenwood Publishing Group, 1985).

17. Interview with Air Marshal (Ret.) Vinod Patney, who during the 1999 Operation headed the Indian Air Force's Western Air Command, April 11, 2007.

18. Retired Pakistan Army Brigadier Sher Khan writes about the 1999 Kargil War thus: "The Indians threatened to expand the conflict by crossing the line of control at places of their choosing, perhaps, even violating the international boundary with Pakistan, or even threatening nuclear strike with their newly demonstrated capability. This created panic in our command structure, causing the prime minister to fly post-haste to Washington to seek immediate intervention." See his "Kargil—Nine Years On," *The News* (Islamabad), May 6, 2008.

19. Bruce Riedel, *American Diplomacy and the 1999 Kargil Summit at Blair House,* Policy Paper Series (Philadelphia: Center for the Advanced Study of India, University of Pennsylvania, May 2002).

20. In February 2002, Prime Minister Atal Bihari Vajpayee, referring to the possible Indian preemptive strike, said that if Pakistan thinks India "will wait for them to drop a

bomb and face destruction, they are mistaken." Quote in John E. Peters, James Dickens, Nina Hachigan, Theodore W. Karasik, Rollie Lal, Rachel M. Swanger, Gregory F. Treverton, and Charles Wolf, Jr., *War and Escalation in South Asia* (Santa Monica, CA: RAND, 2006), p. 44.

21. Interview with Brajesh Mishra, Prime Minister Atal Bihari Vajpayee's national security adviser, April 25, 2007. In fact, starting in January 2002 Pakistan Army's 10 Corps began actively to curb infiltration by jihadi terrorists into Indian Kashmir. See Sukumar Muralidharan, "The Lurking Danger," *Frontline,* 19 No. 12 (June 8–21, 2002).

22. Retired Brigadier Feroze Hassan Khan, formerly of the Strategic Plans Division, Pakistan Army, writes that Pakistanis "are always eager to compete with neighbors and accept challenges much greater than might be handled objectively." See his "Comparative Strategic Culture: The Case of Pakistan," *Strategic Insights,* IV,No. 10, Center for Contemporary Conflict, Oct 2005, p. 2.

23. Polly Nayak, " Reducing Collateral Damage to India-Pakistan Relations from the War on Terrorism," The Brookings Institution Policy Brief No. 107, online at http://www.brookings.edu/papers/2002/09southasia_nayak.aspx.

24. See Feroze Hassan Khan, "The Independence-Dependence Paradox: Stability Dilemmas in South Asia," *Arms Control Today,* October 2003.

25. Interview, unattributable, July 16, 2007.

26. Naeem Ahmad Salik, "Missile Issues in South Asia," *The Nonproliferation Review,* Summer 2002, p. 52.

27. Quote in Naeem Salik, "Minimum Deterrence and India and Pakistan Nuclear Dialog: Case Study of Pakistan," Working Paper, Landau Network, Centro Volta, March 2006, p. 10.

28. See Jehangir Karamat, "Missile Acquisition by Pakistan: Military Strategic Imperatives," *South Asian Survey,* 11, No. 2 (2004):169.

29. For example, in his televised address on Pakistan National Day in 2005, President Pervez Musharraf declared that his country faced "no external threat" but only dangers from religious extremism and terrorism inside the country. See Khalida Mazhar, "Bush Tells India: US Will Sell F-16 Jets to Pakistan," *The Pakistan Times,* March 26, 2005, online at http://www.pakistantimes.net/2005/03/26/top.htm.

30. The cochairman of the Pakistan Peoples Party, Asif Ali Zardari, has talked ambitiously of an economic corridor stretching from Gwadar in Baluchistan to the Indian border in the Gujarat province to service the vast Indian market. see "Pakistan, India to Build Economic Empire; Zardari," *The News* (Islamabad), April 26, 2008.

31. Brigadier Agha M. U. Farooq, "Nuclear Deterrence in South Asia: A Strategic Failure or Beginning of Strategic Stability," US Army War College Strategic Research Project, March 19, 2004, online at http://www.strategicstudiesinstitute.army.mil/ksil/files/000168.doc.

32. The Joint Statement issued on June 20, 2004 at the end of the India-Pakistan Experts Level talks on nuclear Confidence Building Measures, in part said that the two countries recognized that the nuclear capabilities of each other, which are based on their national security imperatives, "constitute a factor of stability" in their relations and in the region. See Salik, "Minimum Deterrence and India," p. 34.

33. See Rahul Mukherji, "Wary Neighbors: The Danger of Conflict and the Prospect of Cooperation in South Asia," *Harvard Asia Pacific Review,* Winter 2001, p. 61.

34. The GDP figures in "India," *World Factbook,* last updated February 28, 2008, online at https://www.cia.gov/library/publications/the-world-factbook/print/in.html and in

"Pakistan," *World Factbook,* last updated February 28, 2008, online at https://www.cia.gov/library/publications/the-world-factbook/print/pk.html. And information on market capitalization in "Bombay Stock Exchange," March 4, 2008 at http://www.advfn.com/StockExchanges/about/BSE/BombayStockExchange.html.

35. The Indian and Pakistani defense budget figures for 2007–2008 are some Rs 960 billion and Rs 200 billion respectively. See http://www.ipcs.org/Mar_07_military Defence.pdf and http://www.buzzvines.com/budget-2007-2008-revealed-wao.

36. See John Hawksworth and Gordon Cookson, *The World in 2050: Beyond the BRICs—a Broader Look at Emerging Market Growth Prospects* (London: PricewaterhouseCoopers LLP, 2008).

37. According to Pradeep Kumar, secretary for Defense Production in the Defense Ministry, even if the current 2 percent of GDP rate for military spending is maintained in the future, the economy growing at 8 percent annually will result in $50 billion being allocated for the acquisition of modern military hardware in the next five years. See Mathew Saltmarsh, "Defense Budgets Hold the Line as Civil Aviation Retrenches," *International Herald Tribune,* July 14, 2008.

38. By intellectual reflex or habit, academics in the United States and elsewhere routinely ignore the organic links and cultural factors that make for severely limited India-Pakistan wars and disregard the gross economic inequalities that will make violent confrontation with India growingly infeasible for Pakistan in the future. To cite only a couple of recent studies reflecting this deficient approach, see S. Paul Kapur, *Dangerous Deterrent: Nuclear Weapons Proliferation and Conflict in South Asia* (Stanford, CA: Stanford University Press, 2007) and Sumit Ganguly and Devin T. Hagerty, *Fearful Symmetry: India-Pakistan Crises in the Shadow of Nuclear Weapons* (New Delhi: Oxford University Press, 2005).

39. The cochairman of the ruling Pakistan People's Party and putative prime minister, Asif Ali Zardari, has said that good bilateral relations with India should not be hostage to the Kashmir dispute. See "Zardari's Look-beyond-Kashmir Stance May Bolster Trade Ties," *The Times of India,* March 8, 2008. It is a sentiment increasingly expressed by the Pakistani press. For example, the strong lead editorial "Kashmir and Pakistan's Security" in *The Daily Times* (Islamabad), February 6, 2008 argued that "Pakistan's revisionism of the weaker state" inclined it to use low-intensity warfare against India, which has now rebounded against the country with the well-trained and highly motivated terrorists and Islamic militants turning their guns on the Pakistani society and state.

40. Lead editorial—"How is Pakistan 'equal' to India?" *The Daily Times,* October 25, 2006.

41. Stephen Philip Cohen, "Asian After-Shocks: Strategic Asia, 2002–2003," online at http://www.Brookings.edu/, p. 19.

42. For the difference in Indian and U.S. attitudes in the 1999 and 2002 crises, see Chari, Cheema, Cohen, *Four Crises and a Peace Process,* pp.128–143,151–171.

43. See Pierre Gallois, *The Balance of Terror: Strategy in the Nuclear Age,* Translated by Richard Howard (Boston: Houghton Mifflin & Co., 1961), p. 22.

44. Bernard Brodie, *Strategy in the Missile Age* (Princeton: Princeton University Press, 1959), p. 311.

45. Henry A. Kissinger, "Limited War: Nuclear or Conventional?—A Reappraisal," in *Arms Control, Disarmament and National Security,* Donald G. Brennan, ed. (New York: George Braziller, Inc., 1961), p. 146. Italics in the original.

46. See Thornton Read, "Limited War and Tactical Nuclear War," in *Limited Strategic War,* Klaus Knorr and Thornton Read, eds., (New York: Frederick A. Praeger, 1962), pp. 102–103.

47. Thomas C. Schelling, "Comment" in *Limited Strategic War*, p. 251.

48. Morton H. Halperin, *Limited War in the Nuclear Age* (New York, London: John Wiley & Sons, inc., 1966), p. 9.

49. For the case that the large and politically active Indian Muslim electorate with kith and kin in Pakistan will tolerate the occasional bloodying of Pakistan's nose but not its annihilation, and that this sentiment is a major domestic political constraint on the Indian government against waging a total war with Pakistan or even taking hard actions against terrorists, see Bharat Karnad, "Minorities, Terrorism and Domestic Politics," in *Current Domestic Policy Challenges and Prospects in South Asia* (Islamabad: Institute of Regional Studies, 2003).

50. Karnad, "South Asia: The Irrelevance of Classical Nuclear Deterrence Theory."

51. Pakistani Minister of State for Information and Broadcasting Tariq Azim said: "Our defense posture is guided by the doctrine of minimum credible deterrence. We do not wish to enter into a conventional or strategic arms race with any country." See "Hegemony Not Acceptable, India Told," *Dawn,* February 13, 2007.

52. Karamat, "Missile Acquisition by Pakistan," p. 176.

53. Ibid, p. 174.

54. General Mirza Aslam Beg, "Nuclear Grandeur and Jubilation," in *Nuclearization of South Asia: Problems and Solutions,* P. Cotta-Ramusino and M. Martellini, eds., UNESCO International School of Science and Peace, Como (Italy), May 20–22, 1999, on-line at http://www.mi.infn.it/~landnet/NSA/vol.pdf.

55. Alva Myrdal, *The Game of Disarmament: How the United States and Russia Run the Arms Race,* revised and updated edition (New York: Pantheon Books, 1982), p. xix.

56. Karamat, "Missile Acquisition by Pakistan," p. 175.

57. Julian Critchley, *Warning and Response: A Study of Surprise Attack in the 20th Century and an Analysis of Its Lessons for the Future* (London: Leo Cooper, 1978), p. 87.

58. Albert Wohlstetter, "NATO and Nth+1 Country" in *The Dispersion of Nuclear Weapons* R. N. Rosecrance, ed. (New York: Columbia University Press, 1964), p. 215.

59. Interview with Major General (Ret.) D. N. Khurana, former additional director gneral, Operational Logistics, and commander, 22 Infantry Division, forming part of the II (Strike) Corps in Operation Brasstacks, September 19, 2007.

60. These attributes of the Cold Start capabilities were highlighted in the latest of such corps-level exercises—"Brazen Chariots"—held in March 2008. See Sandeep Unnithan, "Fast and Furious," *India Today,* April 7, 2008.

61. Karamat, "Missile Acquisition by Pakistan," p. 175.

62. General Khalid Mahmud Arif, "Retaining the Nuclear Option," in *Pakistan's Security and the Nuclear Option,* Tariq Jan, ed. (Islamabad: Institute of Policy Studies, 1995), pp. 124–125.

63. Even in 1971, the original military aim was just to capture a small sliver of East Pakistan territory, install there an Awami League government in exile in Calcutta, and have it negotiate a deal with the martial law government headed by General Yahya Khan in Pakistan. But bad domestic politics and even worse military strategy of stretching the defense thin around the East Pakistan borders permitted the Indian land forces to break-through and race to Dhaka without facing much opposition. See Lieutenant General

(Ret.) T. F. R. Jacob, *Surrender at Dhaka: Birth of a Nation* (ew Delhi: Manohar, 1997) Jacob was the chief of general staff of the Eastern Army during the 1971 war.

64. Interviews with Major General (Ret.) D. N. Khurana, September 19, 2007, and Lieutenant General (Ret.) Vijay Oberoi, February 10, 2007.

65. Interview with Major General (Ret.) D. N. Khurana, Septebmer 19, 2007.

66. Karamat, "Missile Acquisition by Pakistan,,p. 175. This scenario is the basis of S. Paul Kapur's case about an India-Pakistan nuclear clash. See his *Dangerous Deterrent.*

67. Karamat, "Missile Acquisition by Pakistan," p. 175.

68. The practicability and benefits of these options discussed in Karnad, *Nuclear Weapons and Indian Security,* pp. 513–517.

69. Paul D. Taylor, "India and Pakistan: Thinking About the Unthinkable—Wargame Scenario Involving Nuclear Weapons," *Naval War College Review,* LIV, No. 3 (Summer 2001).

70. For an account of events in 1990 leading up to the mission by Robert Gates, see J. N. Dixit, *India-Pakistan in War and Peace* (New Delhi: Books Today, 2002), pp. 275–276. Dixit was the Indian foreign secretary at the time.

71. Shireen Mazari, then director general of the government-funded Institute of Strategic Studies, Islamabad, wrote: "It needs to be stated that a nuclear Pakistan located in its critical geostrategic position will by definition be a relevant strategic player—both to states within the region as well as extra regional powers—regardless of the status of its relations with them. In fact it is the relevancy that is seen as an issue by extra regional powers like the US and what we need to ensure against is their effort to reduce this relevancy by getting us bogged down in our internal crises and external absurdities." See her "The State and National Relevancy," *The News* (Islamabad), January 30, 2008.

72. Karamat, "Missile Acquisition by Pakistan," p. 172.

73. Interview with Pervez Musharraf, *The Washington Post,* May 26, 2002.

74. Interviews with Minister for External Affairs Jaswant Singh (April 21, 2007) and Brajesh Mishra, National Security Adviser to Prime Minister Atal Bihari Vajpayee (April 25, 2007).

75. A relieved senior retired Pakistan Air Force officer, Air Marshal Mohammad Ayaz Khan, noting the invariable shortfalls in military supplies owing to Pakistan's military planning only for short wars, wrote: "Fortunately, Indian military planners [also plan for short wars] . . . basically for fear of high attrition and for political reasons." Quoted in Karnad, *Nuclear Weapons and Indian Security,* pp. 566–567.

76. See "Defense Expenditure" in Jaswant Singh, *National Security* (New Delhi: Lancer Publishers and USI, 1996), pp. 76–77.

77. For the classical study from the 1980s on the quality-quantity tradeoff, see Franklin Spinney, *Defense Facts of Life: The Plans/Reality Mismatch* (Boulder, CO: Westview Press, 1985).

78. For the pattern of inflexible Indian military expenditures, see Jaswant Singh, *National Security: An Outline of Our Concerns* (New Delhi: Lancer Publishers, 1996), pp. 76–77. For conventional capability deficits that need to be met, see Bharat Karnad, "Firming Up the Critical Capability Triad: Strategic Muscle, Sub-Conventional Punch and IT-Enabled Network-Centricity and Electro-Magnetic Warfare Clout" in *Army 2020: Shape, Size, Structure and General Doctrine for Emerging Challenges* Lt. Gen. (Ret.) Vijay Oberoi, ed. (New Delhi: Center for Land Warfare Studies and Knowledge World, 2005) and Bharat Karnad, "India's Future Plans and Defense Requirements" in *Emerging India: Security and Foreign Policy Perspectives* N. S. Sisodia and C. Uday

Bhaskar, eds. (New Delhi: Institute for Defense Studies and Analyses and Promilla & Co., Publishers, 2005).

79. Interview with K. Subrahmanyam of the Indian Administrative Service, who was a middle-level official in the Defence Ministry in the early to mid-Sixties and retired as secretary, Defense Production.

80. Personal communication in Spring 1993 from Lieutenant General (Ret.) K. P. Candeth, the Western Army Commander during the 1971 India-Pakistan War.

81. Personal communication (Summer 2003) by General Khalid Mahmud Arif, who as Vice Chief of the Army Staff, ran the Pakistan Army during General Zia ul-Haq's martial law regime.

82. Brigadier (Ret.) Shaukat Qadir, "A Cold Start," *The Daily Times,* September 3, 2005.

83. Interviews with Lieutenant General (Ret.) Vijay Oberoi, February 10, 2007, and Lieutenant General (Ret.) P. S. Joshi, July 7, 2005—both former commanders-in-chief, Western Army.

84. Ali Abbas Rizvi, "The PAF and the SAAB 2000," *The News* (Islamabad), April 18, 2008.

85. Interview with Lieutenant General (Ret.) Vijay Oberoi, February 10, 2007.

86. Walter C. Ladwig III, "A Cold Start for Hot Wars? The Indian Army's New Limited War Doctrine," *International Security,* 32, No.3 (Winter 2007/08).

87. Daniel S. Geller and J. David Singer, *Nations at War: A Scientific Study of International Conflict,* (Cambridge: Cambridge University Press. 1998).

88. Hans J. Morgenthau, "The Four Paradoxes of Nuclear Strategy," *American Political Science Review,* 58, No. 1 (March 1964), p. 24.

89. See his "Opening Address" in *Asia's New Dawn: The Challenges to Peace and Security,* Air Commodore (Ret.) Jasjit Singh, ed. (New Delhi: Institute of Defense Studies and Analyses, 2000), pp. xvi–xvii.

90. Interview with General (Ret.) Malik, February 21, 2007.

91. Quotes of General Pamanabhan and Lieutenant Genreral Oberoi in Karnad, *Nuclear Weapons and Indian Security,* p. 672.

92. See Eugene E. Habiger , "Strategic Deterrence in the 21st Century," Air Force Association, February 27, 1998, online at http://www.globalsecurity.org/.

93. Quotes of Padmanabhan, Oberoi, and Fernandes in Karnad, *Nuclear Weapons and Indian Security,* (New Delhi: Macmillan India Ltd., 2002, 2005), pp. 672–674.

94. Henry A. Kissinger, *Nuclear Weapons and Foreign Policy* (New York: Harper & Brothers, 1957), pp. 133–134.

95. Interview with Air Marshal (Ret.) Ajit Bhavnani, April 12, 2007.

96. Interview with Air Marshal (Ret.) Vinod Patney, April 11, 2007.

97. Interview, unattributable, July 16, 2007.

98. Interview with Air Chief Marshal (Ret.) Krisnaswamy, July 3, 2007.

99. Herman Kahn, *On Escalation: Metaphors and Scenarios* (New York: Frederick A. Praeger, Publishers, 1965), p. 89.

100. Steven Kull, *Minds at War: Nuclear Reality and the Inner Conflicts of Defense Policymakers* (New York: Basic Books 1986), p. 120.

101. Kahn, *On Escalation.*

102. Kull, *Minds at War,* pp. 83–84.

103. Peter Lavoy, "Pakistan's Nuclear Posture: Security and Survivability," The Nuclear Policy Education Center, January 21, 2007, online at http://www.npec-web.org/, pp. 2–3.

104. The former Pakistan foreign minister, Agha Shahi, wrote that the nuclear inequality with India will grow because "Over the years, the existing asymmetry of fissile [material] stockpiles will be further accentuated." Quote in Karnad, "South Asia: The Irrelevance of Classical Nuclear Deterrence Theory," fn 103, p. 212.

105. M. Asghar Khan, "The Nuclear Option" *Dawn* (Karachi), November 3, 2003.

106. Abdul Sattar, "One Year After the Nuclear Tests," in *Nuclearization of South Asia,* p. 99.

107. Kissinger, *Nuclear Weapons and Foreign Policy,* p. 16.

108. The fear of the consequences is what the Clinton Administration officials used to persuade the Pakistan Prime Minister Nawaz Sharif into de-escalating the conflict in the 1999 Kargil War. See Bruce Riedel, *American Diplomacy and the 1999 Kargil Summit at Blair House* (Philadelphia: Center for the Advanced Study of India, University of Pennsylvania, 2002).

109. These attributes of the M-9 missile in Paul Bracken, "Sidewise Technologies: National Security and Global Power Implications," *Military Review,* September-October 2005.

110. Scott Baldauf and Howard LeFranchi, "Why Pakistan Might Turn to Nukes," *Christian Science Monitor,* June 4, 2002.

111. Regarding Cold Start, Brigadier Shaukat Qadir writes: The "synergized" joint services plan for war is to be undertaken with a view "to compel Pakistan to cross the nuclear threshold." See his "A Cold Start."

112. Interview with Lieutenant General Vijay Oberoi, February 10, 2007.

113. Karnad, *Nuclear Weapons and Indian Security,* 2nd ed., pp. 670–672.

114. According to General Oberoi, outfitting 1.1 million troops with eight NBC-relevant items, like anti-radiation suits, dosimeters, etc. would be patently unaffordable. Interview, Feburary 10, 2007.

115. Ibid.

116. Ibid.

117. Halperin, *Limited War in the Nuclear Age,* p. 118.

118. Walter C. Slocombe, "Pre-planned Operations" in *Managing Nuclear Operations,* Ashton B. Carter, John D. Steinbruner, Charles A. Zracket, eds. (Washington, DC: The Brookings Institution, 1987), pp. 122–123.

119. Stephen Peter Rosen, "Nuclear Proliferation and Alliance Relations" in *The Coming Crisis: Nuclear Proliferation, US Interests and World Order,* Victor A. Utgoff, ed. (Cambridge, MA: MIT Press, 2000), p. 129.

120. Lawrence Freedman is of the view that nuclear weapons will discourage "Western involvement in local conflicts." See his "Great Powers, Vital Interests and Nuclear Weapons," *Survival,* 36, No. 4 (Winter 1994–95):47.

121. Patrick M. Morgan, *Deterrence Now* (Cambridge: Cambridge University Press, 2003), p. 51.

122. General Karamat's presentation on "Pakistan's Force Posture" at the International Conference on "A New Nuclear World Order: Asian Perspectives," jointly hosted by the Brookings Institution and the Lee Kuan Yew School of Public Policy, National University of Singapore, Singapore, March 6–7, 2008.

123. Karamat, "Missile Acquisition by Pakistan," p. 175.

124. Michael Krepon, Ziad Haider and Charles Thornton, "Are Tactical Weapons Needed in South Asia?" in *The Nuclear Option in South Asia,* Michael Krepon, Rodney W. Jones and Ziad Haider, eds. (Washington, DC: Henry L. Stimson Center, November 2004), p. 133.

125. The best such study is Chari, Cheema, and Cohen, *Four Crises and a Peace Process.*

126. Morgan, *Deterrence Now,* pp. 23–24.

127. Interview with Air Marshal (Ret.) Patney, April 11, 2007.

128. Kull, *Minds at War,* p. 75.

129. Bernard Brodie, "More about Limited War," *World Politics,* 10, No. 1 (October 1957), p. 117.

130. Karnad, *Nuclear Weapons and Indian Security,* p. 569.

131. Interview with Air Chief Marshal (Ret.) Krishnaswamy, July 3, 2007.

132. Brodie, *Strategy in the Missile Age,* p. 156.

133. Hagerty, "Nuclear Deterrence in South Asia."

134. Interview, unattributable, July 16, 2007.

135. Peters, Dickens, et al., *War and Escalation in South Asia,* p. 77.

136. Cohen, "Asian After-Shocks," p. 19.

137. Bharat Karnad, "Nuclear Commando and Control," *The Asian Age,* January 18, 2008.

138. Rajat Pandit, "Nukes in Jihadi Hands a Worry: Army Chief," *The Times of India,* November 14, 2007.

139. Thomas Donnelly talks of the fear of the India-Pakistan nuclear flashpoint in the U.S. policy circles being supplanted by the fear of terrorists accessing Pakistani nuclear weapons, and the need for Special Forces and rapidly deployable airborne divisions to occupy the uranium centrifuges site at Kahuta, cut off escape routes, etc. See his "Choosing Among Bad Options: The Pakistani 'Loose Nukes' Conundrum," *National Security Outlook,* AEI for Public Policy Research, May 17, 2006.

140. Mirza Aslam Beg's interview, January 1, 2003, online at http://thestar.com.my /news/ (accessed April 2004).

141. See Karnad, "South Asia: The Irrelevance of Classical Nuclear Deterrence Theory," pp. 204–205. Also in this regard, see Shirin Mazari, "A Multilevel Threat: The US, Europe, Terrorism," *The News,* April 9, 2008. It is significant that President Musharraf has held out the threat, if he is removed from his post, of danger to Pakistani nuclear weapons and the possibility of the United States taking Dr. A. Q. Khan into custody for questioning about his proliferation network. See Ashraf Mumtaz, "Musharraf Fears US Will Attack, Take Away AQ Khan if He Quits," *The Indian Express,* April 8, 2008.

142. "Menon Offers Pak Dialog on N-Doctrines," *The Tribune,* April 12, 2007.

143. Karamat, "Missile Acquisition by Pakistan," p. 176.

144. Bharat Karnad, "Immature Technologies," *Force,* April 2004.

145. "India's Missile Defense Cover in 3 Yrs," *The Indian Express,* December 13, 2007.

146. Bolkom, et al., *US Conventional Forces and Nuclear Deterrence,* p. 18.

147. Ayesha Siddiqa, "Is Missile Non-Proliferation a Possibility in South Asia?" *South Asia Survey,* 11, No. 2 (2004):233–234.

148. Devin T. Hagerty, "Nuclear Deterrence in South Asia: The 1990 Indo-Pakistani Crisis," *International Security,* 30, No. 3 (Winter 1995), online at http://www.mtholyoke.edu.

149. The important distinction between the "seriousness" and "credibility" of a threat made by Daryl G. Press. See his *Calculating Credibility: How Leaders Assess Military Threats* (Ithaca, NY, and London: Cornell University Press, 2005), p. 11.

150. International Conference on "The Nuclearization of South Asia: Consequences, Challenges and Peace Prospects," The Islamia University of Bahawalpur, Pakistan, March 13–15, 2007.

151. Andre Beaufre, *Deterrence and Strategy* (London: Faber & Faber, 1965), p. 25.

152. Robert Jervis, *The Illogic of American Nuclear Strategy* (Ithaca, NY: Cornell University Press, 1984).

153. See his *Reckoning with Risk: Learning to Live with Uncertainty* (London: Allen Lane, The Penguin Press, 2002), pp. 26–28.

154. Shauqat Qadir, "India's Cold Start Strategy," *The Daily Times,* May 8, 2004.

155. Tables No. 7.2 and 9.13 in Ayesha Siddiqa, *Military Inc.: Inside Pakistan's Military Economy* (Karachi: Oxford University Press, 2007), pp. 183, 236.

156. See Ayesha Siddiqa, "What's Minimum Deterrence?" *Dawn,* April 4, 2008.

157. Avery Goldstein uses these phrases to describe the Cold War relationship between the second tier nuclear weapon states and the super powers. See his *Deterrence and Security in the 21st Century: China, Britain and France, and the Enduring Legacy of the Nuclear Revolution* (Stanford, CA: Stanford University Press, 2000), pp. 54–55

158. The information in this paragraph is owing to an off-the-record, personal communication by a retired military officer working in the National Security Council secretariat, January 12, 2008.

159. Sujan Dutta, "US disarms Indian ship," *The Telegraph* (Kolkatta), March 1,5 2008.

160. Personal communication from a recently retired Flag-rank officer, unattributable, October 15, 2007.

161. The phrase actually refers to the troubled relationship between Vietnam and Cambodia. See Nayan Chanda, *Brother Enemy: The War After the War* (New York: Harcourt, 1986).

162. Caroline F. Ziemke, Philippe Loustaunau, and Amy Alrich, "Strategic Personality and the Effectiveness of Nuclear Deterrence," IDA Document D-2537, Institute of Defense Analysis, November 2000, p. 116, online at http://www.globalsecurity.org/wmd/library/report/2000/d2537dtra.doc.

163. M. K. Narayanan, National Security Adviser to Prime Minister Manmohan Singh, reaffirmed the "peace begets security" approach by the Indian government at the *1st IISS-Citi India Global Forum,* New Delhi, April 20, 2008.

164. Uyghur Muslims, like the Tibetans, were intent on using the Beijing Olympics to bring their independence movement before the international public. See Howard W. French, "As Uighurs Get Restive, China Takes a Tough Line," *International Herald Tribune,* April 5–6, 2008. For an analysis of the Uyghur natioanlism, see Van Wie Davis, "Uyghur Muslim Ethnic Separatism in Xinjiang, China," January 2008, Asia-Pacific Center for Strategic Studies, Honolulu.

165. Mehmet Ogutcu, "China's Energy Security: Geopolitical Implications for Asia and Beyond," in *Asian Security and China 2000–2010,* K. Santhanam and Srikanth Kondapalli, eds. (New Delhi: Institute of Defense Studies and Analyses and Shipra Publications, 2004).

166. Interview with Yashwant Sinha, May 25, 2007.

167. Regarding the "string of pearls" strategy, former Chief of the Indian Navy Admiral Arun Prakash writes that China has created "right around us what are best described as 'weapon client states': Bangladesh, Myanmar, Sri Lanka, Saudi Arabia, Iran and Pakistan." See his "China's Naval Gazers," *The Indian Express,* September 5, 2007.

168. Christopher J. Pehrson, *String of Pearls: Meeting the Challenge of China's Rising Power Across the Asian Littoral* (Carlisle Barracks, PA: Strategic Studies Institute, US Army War College, July 2006), Table 1, p. 6, online at http://www.strategicstudiesinstitute.army.mil/pubs/display.cfm?pubID=721.

169. Samdhong Rimpoche, Prime Minister of the Tibetan Government-in-Exile in India, says "the Chinese have been razing our culture . . . for the past 50 years." See his interview, *The Times of India,* March 21, 2008.

170. Brian McCartan, "Myanmar Deal Right Neighborly of India," *Asia Times Online,* January 11, 2008, online at http://www.atimes.com.

171. Nitin Sethi, "India, China Team Up to Tackle West Bullying," *The Times of India,* December 8, 2007.

172. In 2002, India and China agreed to identify the differing perceptions of the border on the map, identify the areas of "overlapping claims" and then hammer out a solution. But when the negotiating process moved from the central sector, where there are few disagreements, to the western sector where China has occupied some 37,000 square kms of the Indian Aksai-chin region in Ladakh, the process ground to a halt. See Kanwal Sibal, "Good fences, good neighbors," *The Indian Express,* March 15, 2008.

173. Over 140 armed Chinese incursions were recorded in 2007 alone. See Rajat Pandit, "No Let-up in Chinese Patrolling along LAC," *The Times of India,* March 31, 2008.

174. Nirmalaya Banerjee and Amalendu Kundu, "Chinese Troops Destroy Indian Posts, Bunker," *The Times of India,* December 1, 2007.

175. Pranab Dhal Samanta, "After PM Visit, China Protests Troop Movement in Sikkim," *The Sunday Express,* January 27, 2008.

176. "China 'Concerned' over PM's Arunachal Visit," *The Indian Express,* February 15, 2008.

177. See Saibal Dasgupta, "Beijing Hints at More Wargames with India" and Amalendu Kundu, "China Tries to Sabotage Border Roads," *The Times of India,* December 27, 2007.

178. "China and India: A Rage for Oil," *Businessweek,* September 5, 2005.

179. Somini Sengupta, "India Maneuvers with China in Mind," *International Herald Tribune,* April 5–6, 2008.

180. Rajat Pandit, "Defense Ministry Goes 'Soft' on China," *The Times of India,* March 24, 2008.

181. Pranab Dhal Samanta, "The Engagement Map," *The Indian Express,* January 15, 2008.

182. Jagdish N. Sheth, "Why the Rise of Chindia Will Be Beneficial to the World," *The Times of India,* January 8, 2008. Sheth, professor in the Business School at Emory University, argues that Chindia will become the engine of international economic growth in the new century, as the United States was in the last century.

183. Thierry Apoteker, "India and China: Collision ahead or the Emergence of Chindia?" October 2007, online at http://www.tac-financial.com/publ/Presentation-Chindia_Japan-Oct07.pdf.

184. Mure Dickie, " The Chill beneath a Warming Pacific Friendship," *Financial Times,* February 21, 2008.

185. In Congressional hearings in 2006, answering a question whether conflict with China "was a foregone conclusion," Admiral Willam Fallon, CINC, U.S. Pacific Command, replied in the negative and said the United States and China had many "common interests." Quote in Christopher Bolkom, Shirley A. Kan, and Amy Woolf, *US Conventional Forces and Nuclear Deterrence: A China Case Study,* CRS Report to the Congress, August 11, 2006, p. 13, online at http://www.fas.org/sgp/crs/natsec/RL33607.pdf.

186. Pranab Dhal Samanta, "Economic Ties to Propel Relations with China: PM," *The Indian Express,* January 15, 2008.

187. "China Pips US as India's No.1 Trade Partner," *The Times of India,* February 29, 2008.

188. Wang Jinzhen, Secretary General of the China Council for the Promotion of International Trade said: "Only when the hare (China) naps does the tortoise (India) overtake the hare. China will never 'nap' in the process of economic development." See "China Will Never Let India Overtake Us," Press Trust of India news agency, *The Asian Age,* November 16, 2006.

189. Interview with Admiral Arun Prakash, May 16, 2007.

190. Lars S. Skalnes, *Politics, Markets and Grand Strategy* (Ann Arbor; The University of Michigan Press, 2000), pp. 22–25.

191. Lieutenant General (Ret.) Vinay Shankar, "An Unequal Equation," *The Indian Express,* April 9, 2008.

192. See Kanwal Sibal, "Good Fences, Good Neighbors."

193. "BJP: India Must Voice Concerns of Tibetans," *The Hindu,* March 27, 2008.

194. " 'Army Chief's Remark on LAC unnecessary'," *The Times of India,* March 7, 2008.

195. Ashok K. Mehta, "India Needs a Tibet Policy," *The Pioneer,* March 19, 2008.

196. Retired Indian Navy Chief Admiral Arun Prakash recalls that MEA showed too much concern for China's "sensitivities" in opposing the annual Malabar naval exercises with the United States and other navies. See his "China's Naval Gazers."

197. Personal communication, unattributable, January 7, 2008.

198. Personal communication, unattributable, from a retired additional director general of Military Intelligence, Army Headquarters, June 27, 2007.

199. Email interview with Vikram Sood, April 7, 2008.

200. A former Indian diplomat excoriated the Manmohan Singh government's China policy and, particularly, its response to Chinese claims on the border province of Arunachal Pradesh. See G. Parthasarathy, "Groveling before China," *The Pioneer,* June 14, 2007.

201. Senior official in government, unattributable infomration, February 19, 2008.

202. See his "Chinese Strategic Power: Myths, Intent, and Projections," *Journal of Military and Strategic Studies,* 9, No. 2 (Winter 2006/07).

203. Andrew Scobell, *China's Use of Force: Beyond the Great Wall and the Long March* (Cambridge: Cambridge University Press, 2003).

204. M. Taylor Fravel, "Power Shifts and Escalation: Explaining China's Use of Force in Territorial Disputes," *International Security,* 32, No. 3 (Winter 2007/08):56–57, 68–73.

205. Harold C. Hutchison, "Who Has the Second Best Air Force?" August 10, 2005, online at http://www.strategypage.com/militaryforums/478-2187.aspx; and Harold C. Hutchison, "China and the illusion of Power," April 17, 2006, online at http://www

.strategypage.com/htmw/htmurph/articles/20060417.aspx. A 1995 RAND study assessed that the Chinese Air Force, with "incremental and demonstrably insufficient" modern acquisitions would by 2005 still "not constitute a credible offensive threat" to any major power. Kenneth W. Allen, Glenn Krumel, and Jonathan D. Pollack, *China's Air Force Enters the 21st Century* (Santa Monica: RAND, 1995), p. xiii.

206. Personal communication from Lieutenant General (Ret.) Devraj Singh, former Director General, Infantry, Army Headquarters, March 9, 2007.

207. Ibid.

208. Ibid.

209. Ibid.

210. Interview with Lieutenant General (Ret.) Vijay Oberoi, February 10, 2007.

211. Interview with General Ved Malik, Feruary 21, 2007.

212. Ibid.

213. R. Sukumaran, "The 1962 India-China War and Kargil 1999: Restrictions on the Use of Air Power," *Strategic Analysis,* XXVII, No. 3 (July–September 2003).

214. Interview with General (Ret.) Viajy Oberoi, February 10, 2007.

215. Bharat Karnad, "Getting Tough with China: Negotiating Equitable, Not 'Equal' Security," *Strategic Analysis,* XXI, No. 10 (January 1998), p. 1432

216. The phrase is taken from Richard Ned Lebow's discussion of the U.S.-USSR Cold War system; see his "Deterrence Deadlock: Is There a Way Out?" in *Psychology and Deterrence,* 2nd printing, Robert Jervis, Richard Ned Lebow, and Janice Gross Stein, eds. (Baltimore and London: The Johns Hopkins University Press, 1991).

217. *Indian Maritime Doctrine,* INBR 8, Integrated Headquarters, Ministry of Defense (Navy), June 2004, pp. 54, 64, 69, 70. For an analysis of the Chinese naval buildup in the Indian Ocean, see James R. Holmes and Toshi Yoshihara "China's Naval Ambitions in the Indian Ocean," *The Journal of Strategic Studies,* 31, No. 3 (June 2008).

218. Off-the-record personal communication from a senior official in the prime minister's office, July 24, 2007.

219. *Indian Maritime Doctrine,* p. 110.

220. James Dunnigan, "The Five Nuclear Navies," July 18, 2004, online at http://www.strategypage.com/dls/articles2004/200471823.asp.

221. Personal communication, unattributable, from a retired senior naval person.

222. A former Service Chief of Staff, July 16, 2007.

223. Andrew S. Erickson and Andrew R. Wilson, "China's Aircraft Carrier Dilemma," *Naval War College Review,* 59, No. 4 (Autumn 2006).

224. Senior naval officer, June 27, 2007.

225. See "Secret Sanya—China's New Nuclear Naval Base," *Jane's Intelligence Review,* April 21, 2008. The Indian Navy expects Chinese nuclear submarines from this base to foray into the bay of Bengal and the Indian Ocean. See Rajat Pandit, "China's deep sea plans alarm India," *Times of India,* May 3, 2008.

226. An important leader in the opposition Bharatiya Janata Party coalition and former Defense Minister George Fernandes reiterated that China is the main threat to India. See "Now George Says China Is 'Potential threat No. 1'," *The Times of India,* March 31, 2008.

227. Statement of Admiral Richard W. Mies, C-in-C, U.S. Strategic Command, before the Senate Armed Services Committee, April 14, 1999, online at http://armed-services.senate.gov/.

228. Personal communication from a former Service Chief, December 20, 2007. The Tu-160 aircraft have exercised with the Indian Navy. See Alexei Chernyshev and Ivan

Safronov, "Pacific Fleet Moving South," *Kommersant,* Russian Daily online, September 21, 2005, at http://www.kommersant.com.

229. Jeffrey Lewis, "The Ambiguous Arsenal," *Bulletin of Atomic Scientists,* May/June 2005.

230. Hans M. Kristensen, Robert S. Norris, and Matthew G. Makinzie, *Chinese Nuclear Forces and US Nuclear War Planning,* Federation of American Scientists/National Resources Defense Council, November 2006, p. 36, online at http://www.fas.org/nuke/guide/china/Book2006.pdf.

231. Jeffrey Lewis' presentation "China's Nuclear Posture" at the international conference on "A New Nuclear World Order: Asian Perspectives."

232. Former Chief of Staff of a Service, September 2, 2007.

233. Brahma Chellaney, "China-India Clash Over Chinese Claims to Tibetan Water," Japan Focus, Asia Pacific e-journal, July 3, 2007, online at http://www.japanfocus.org/products/details/2458.

234. Saibal Dasgupta and Diwakar, "Chinese Assurance on Trans-Border Rivers," *Times of India,* January 18, 2008.

235. Among the earliest such reference was Shirley Kan and Zachary Davis, "China," in *Nuclear Proliferation after the Cold War* ed. Mitchell Reiss and Robert Litwak (Washington, DC: Woodrow Wilson Center Press, 1994), p. 148.

236. Somini Sengupta, "Younger Tibetans See No 'Middle Way'," *International Herald Tribune,* March 22–23, 2008.

237. Geoff Dyer and Richard McGregor, "Tibet Untamed," *Financial Times,* April 1, 2008.

238. Kenneth Conboy and James Morrison, *The CIA's Secret War in Tibet* (Lawrence, KS: University of Kansas Press, 2002) and John Kenneth Knaus, *Orphans of the Cold War: America and the Tibetan Struggle for Survival,* new edition (New York: Public Affairs, 2000).

239. Personal communication from a senior Indian Army officer, May 28, 2007.

240. "Red Storm Rising: India's Intractable Maoist Insurgency," *Jane's Intelligence Review,* May 15, 2008.

241. Interview with Brajesh Mishra, April 25, 2007.

242. China's "quest for resources" highlighted in Edward McBride, "A Ravenous Dragon," Special report, *The Economist,* March 15, 2008; and Raphael Minder and Demetri Sevastopulo, "Scramble for Asian Resources Raises Fears," *Financial Times,* June 2, 2008.

243. "India, China Will Flirt, Not Wed, in Foreign Oil," Reuters, December 21, 2005, available online from the China Institute, University of Alberta at http://www.uofaweb.ualberta.ca/chinainstitute/nav03.cfm?nav03=44239&nav=43874&nav=43092.

244. Reeba Zachariah, "ONGC to Acquire Stake in UK's Imperial Energy: Strengthening Presence Abroad With Access To Oil, Gas Fields," *The Times of India,* July 14, 2008.

245. Archana Chaudhury, "India Plans to Spend $300 Billion in Oil Exploration," *Bloomberg News,* April 5, 2008, online at http://www.bloomberg.com/.

246. Sandeep Dikshit, "India Doubles Credit to Africa," *The Hindu,* April 9, 2008.

247. "10 Per cent Hike in Indian Defense Budget," March 2, 2008, online at http://www.india-defence.com/reports-3759.

248. Tracy Quek, "China Unveils Biggest Defence Budget Ever," *The Straits Times* (Singapore), March 5, 2008.

249. David Lague, "Beijing Increases Defense Spending," *International Herald Tribune,* March 4, 2007.

250. "Current and Projected National Security Threats to the United States," Statement by Lieutenant General Michael D. Maples, director, Defense Intelligence Agency, before the Senate Armed Services Committee, February 27, 2007, pp. 14–26.

251. Desmond Ball, "China and Information Warfare," in *Asian Security and China 2000–2010.*

252. Derwin Pereira, "China a Serious Threat to US in Cyberspace, Outer Space," *Straits Times,* March 5, 2008.

253. Personal communication from retired Brigadier Arun Sahgal, formerly Director, Net Assessment, Headquarters, Integrated Defense Staff, April 4, 2008.

254. Communication from an official working on strategic plans, February 29, 2008.

255. Rajat Pandit, "Sukhoi Base in East to Counter China," *The Times of India,* September 28, 2007.

256. Rajat Pandit, "IAF Plans War Doctrine to Expand 'Strategic Reach'," *The Times of India,* August 2, 2007.

257. Interview with Chinese Air Force Lieutenant General Liu Yazhou in *Heartland: Eurasian Review of Geopolitics,* No. 1 (2005), p. 16, online at http://www.eheartland.com/_lib/_docs/2005_01c_China_America_The_Great_Game.pdf.

258. The Tibetan plateau-based missile threat discussed in Ashley J. Tellis, *Emerging Nuclear Posture: Between Recessed Deterrent and Ready Arsenal* (Santa Monica: RAND, 2001), pp. 58–68.

259. Discussions with a senior official in the National Security Council secretariat, July 24, 2007.

260. "India's Missile Defense Cover in 3 Yrs," *The Indian Express,* December 13, 2007.

261. Interview with a former service chief of staff, October 7, 2007.

262. "Cruise Missile Shield to Be in Place within 3 Yrs," *The Indian Express,* December 13, 2007.

263. Rajat Pandit, "India on Way to Joining Exclusive BMD Club," *The Times of India,* November 26, 2007.

264. See A. K. Singh, "Enhance Strategic Calculation," *Strategic Affairs,* 2, No. 6 (February 15, 2007), p. 48.

265. Regarding the missile defense system the George W. Bush Administration has enthusiastically pushed, one of the leading U.S. scientists, Wolfgang K. H. Panofsky, said that because of "the technical difficulties, the large costs and the fiscal constraints, the probability that there ever will be a national missile defense is low." For the quote see Christian Heuss, "Decision to Defy Missile Treaty Sends Dangerous Message," *Stanford Report,* January 30, 2002, online at http://news-service.stanford.edu/.

266. Manu Pubby, "US Offers Help with Missile Shield, Sending Team in Feb," *Indian Express,* January 18, 2008.

267. U.S. Defense Secretary Robert Gates hinted at transfer of missile defense technology to India during his February 2008 visit to India. See Todd Fine, "Missile Defense: A Wrong Turn for US-India Cooperation," Center for Defense Information, March 5, 2008, online at http://www.cdi.org/.

268. See Larry M. Wortzel, "China's Nuclear Forces: Operations, Training, Doctrine, Command, Control and Campaign Planning," Strategic Studies Institute, U.S. Army War

College, May 2007, online at http://www.strategicstudiesinstitute.army.mil/pdffiles/ PUB776.pdf, pp. 8–9.

269. Alastair Iain Johnston, "China's New 'Old Thinking'," *International Security,* 20, No. 3 (Winter 1995/96).

270. This concept is developed in Karnad, *Nuclear Weapons and Indian Security,* pp. 614–647.

271. Email communication with Air Chief Marshal (Ret.) Anil Tipnis, February 11, 2008, and interview with Admiral (Ret.) Arun Prakash, May 16, 2007.

272. Interview with Admiral (Ret.) Arun Prakash, May 16, 2007.

273. Communication from Brigadier (Ret.) Arun Sahgal, April 4, 2008.

274. Interview with Air Chief Marshal (Ret.) S. Krishnaswamy, July 3, 2007.

275. M. Taylor Fravel and Richard J. Samuels, "The US as an Asian Power: Realism or Conceit?" *Audit of Conventional Wisdom,* MIT Center for International Studies, May 2005 pp. 2–3.

276. Quote in Dr. Mark Schneider, "The Nuclear Doctrine and Forces of the People's Republic of China" (Fairfax, VA: National Institute Press, November 2007), p. 30.

277. Kishore Mahbubani, *The New Asian Hemisphere: The Irresistible Shift of Power to the East* (New York: Public Affairs, 2008). Mahbubani is former foreign secretary of Singapore.

278. Zalmay Khalilzad, "Sweet and Sour: Recipe for a New China Policy," Winter 2000, online at http://www.rand.org/publications/randreview/issues/rr.winter.00/ sweet.html.

279. For a discussion about potential areas of U.S.-Japanese discord related to security and Japan's looking to countries like India as counterweight to China, see Robert Sutter, *The United States and East Asia: Dynamics and Implications* (Lanham, MD: Rowman & Littlefield, 2003), pp. 200–215.

280. Ramesh Thakur, "Asian Strategic Triangle: China-India-Japan," *The Hindu,* September 14, 2007.

281. For an overview of growing economic and security links between India and Japan, see "Ambassador Ronen Sen's Remarks at a Luncheon Meeting of the Japan Society in New York," February 15, 2008, online at http://www.indianembassy.org/.

282. Henry Kissinger writes that "In Asia, ... two kinds of adjustments will define 21st-century diplomacy: the relationship between the great Asian powers, China, India, Japan, and possibly Indonesia, and how America and China deal with each other." See his "The Debate We Need," *International Herald Tribune,* April 8, 2008.

283. For the view that the United States is an Asian power but, increasingly, a less influential one, see Fravel and Samuels, "The US an as Asian Power."

284. Dennis Kux, *The United States and Pakistan 1947–2000: Disenchanted Allies* (Karachi: Oxford University Press, 2001).

285. U.S. Deputy Assistant Secretary of Defense James Clad, U.S. Department of Defense Bloggers Round Table, October 30, 2007, at http://www.defenselink.mil/.

286. Allah, Army, and America are supposed to dominate Pakistan; see Hassan Abbas, *Pakistan's Drift into Extremism: Allah, the Army and America's War on Terror* (New York: M.E. Sharpe, Inc., 2004).

287. See his "Nuclear Insecurity," *Foreign Affairs,* 86, No. 5 (September/October 2007), pp. 115–117.

288. Interview with Brajesh Mishra, April 25, 2007.

289. Interview with Yashwant Sinha, May 25, 2007.

290. Amitabh Sinha, "Low on Fuel and No Sign of the Deal, Nuclear Power Plants Take a Hit," *The Indian Express,* March 27, 2008.

291. For a succinct analysis of the kilowatt/hour cost comparisons of various forms of energy, see Brahma Chellaney, "Too Much Hot Air in Nuke Deal," *The Economic Times,* July 4, 2008; and R. Ramachandran, "Power & the Truth," *Frontline,* July 18, 2008.

292. For the plan to use imported reactors to augment speedily electricity production from civilian power plants, see "Evolving Indian Nuclear Programme: Rationale and Perspectives," lecture by chairman of the atomic energy commission, Dr Anil Kakodkar, at the Indian Academy of Sciences, Bangalore, July 4, 2008; the text is available at http://www.dae.gov.in/lecture.htm.

293. "Indo-US Joint Statement," July 18, 2005, online at http://www.hindu.com/thehindu/nic/indousjoint.htm.

294. The opposition to the nuclear deal in the Indian media—mostly in the Indian daily, *The Asian Age,* edited by M. J. Akbar (until he was removed from its editorship) involved in the main, other than the author, P. K. Iyengar, A. G. Gopalkrishnan, A. N. Prasad, and Brahma Chellaney. The "con" view on the deal in this section is distilled from their writings, mostly in the form of newspaper op/ed articles and statements issued to the press by the above-named nuclear scientists. The individual writings can be Googled. On the basis of such writings, BJP leaders like Arun Shourie and Yashwant Sinha mounted a scathing campaign in parliament to reject the deal. The 'pro' sentiment is likewise taken from writings in the Press by those championing this deal, especially K. Subrahmanyam.

295. See his "Remarks before the Foreign Policy Association, New York, February 16, 2000" online at http://www.state.gov/www/global/arms/remarks/holum/holum_fp.html.

296. Televised Press Conference by National Security Adviser M. K. Narayanan, Chairman of the Atomic Energy Commission Dr. Anil Kakodkar, Director of the Strategic Policy Group at the Bhabha Atomic Research Center and member of the safeguards negotiation team Dr. V. B. Grover, and foreign secretary Shiv Shankar Menon, July 12, 2008, Doordarshan TV channel.

297. *Henry J. Hyde United States-India Peaceful Atomic Energy Cooperation Act of 2006,* HR 5682, 109th Cong., 2nd sess. The percentage breakdown of the vote and the text of this Act at http://www.GovTrack.us/.

298. The quote in "Evolving Indian Nuclear Programme:Rationale and Perspectives," the lecture by Dr Anil Kakodkar, chairman of the Indian Atomic Energy Commission, at the Indian Academy of Sciences, Bangalore, July 4, 2008, p. 5. The text of the lecture is available online at http://www.dae.gov.in/lecture.htm.

299. Personal communication from a senior Indian deal negotiator, March 12, 2008.

300. Regarding Indian doubts about this agreement along these lines, see Bharat Karnad, "Safeguards that Erode Security," *Mint* (New Delhi), July 14, 2008; and Prabir Purkayastha, "Does the IAEA Agreement Hide Us from the Hyde Act?" *Hindu,* July 14, 2008. American arms-control experts are equally apprehensive, fearing that the ambiguity relating to the concept of "corrective measures" in the safeguards text there are ready loopholes in the accord that will enable India to test again. See, for example, Henry Sokolski, "Negotiating India's Next Nuclear Explosion," *Wall Street Journal,* July 10, 2008. For the text of the so-called "India-specific" safeguards agreement, see "Full Text of the India-IAEA Safeguards Agreement," July 9, 2008, online at http://im.rediff.com/news/2008/jul/iaea.pdf. At the televised press conference on July 12, 2008, featuring NSA M. K. Narayanan, chairman of the Atomic Energy Commission Anil Kakodkar,

and Foreign Secretary Shiv Shankar Menon, when asked directly if India had the right to withdraw its facilities from the IAEA safeguards, these officials avoided an answer.

301. "If NDA Wins, We Will Renegotiate, Even Scrap Deal: Advani," *The Indian Express,* November 29, 2007.

302. See the Joint Statement by P. K. Iyengar, A. N. Prasad, and A. Gopalakrishnan released to the press on June 24, 2008. The text of the statement may be secured from Dr. Prasad at an_prasad@sify.com.

303. Former U.S. Ambassador to India, Robert Blackwill, at the *1st IISS-Citi India Global Forum,* New Delhi, April 20, 2008.

304. The presentation by former U.S. Ambassador Robert Blackwill at the 1st International Institute of Strategic Studies-Citi India Global Forum, New Delhi, April 20, 2008.

305. Sandy Gordon, "India Is Hungry for Our Uranium," *Canberra Times,* July 14, 2008, online at http://www.canberratimes.com.au/. In the last months of the George W. Bush Administration, Secretary of State Condoleeza Rice in articulating "American Realism for a New World," wrote that it was in the U.S. interest to invest "in strong and rising powers as stakeholders in the international order." See her "Rethinking the National Interest: American Realism for a New World," *Foreign Affairs,* 87, No. 4 (July/August 2008), p. 23.

306. The case for the United States to consider "minimum deterrence" and an inventory of no more than 250 nuclear weapons, an arsenal size espoused by President Jimmy Carter, is made in Jeffrey Lewis, "Minimum Deterrence," *The Bulletin of Atomic Scientists,* July/August 2008.

307. As examples of the arguments of these two camps, see "Perkovich: US-India Draft Nuclear Agreement Ill-considered but Goal of Accommodation with India a Good One," February 24, 2006, interview, Council on Foreign Relations at http://www.cfr.org/; and Bharat Karnad, "The India-United States Rapprochement, the Nuclear Deal, and Indian National Interests," in *Rising India: Friends and Foes,* ed. Prakash Nanda (New Delhi and Olympia Fields, IL: Lancer, 2007)

308. For a news report of the bribes paid opposition members of parliament to vote for the government or to abstain from voting, see Kumar Uttam, "UPA Wins Vote, Loses Trust," *The Pioneer,* July 23, 2008.

309. "Riedel: Delay on US-Indian Nuclear Accord Only a 'Hiccup' on Road to Stronger Ties," interview, October 17, 2007, Council on Foreign Relations, online at http://www.cfr.org/.

Index

About the Author

BHARAT KARNAD is Research Professor in National Security Studies at the Center for Policy Research, New Delhi. He was a member of the (First) National Security Advisory Board, National Security Council, Government of India, member of the Nuclear Doctrine Drafting Group, and Adviser on Defense Expenditure to the Finance Commission, India. He secured a B.A. from the University of California, Santa Barbara, and M.A. from the University of California, Los Angeles, and is the author of *Nuclear Weapons and Indian Security: The Realist Foundations of Strategy,* now in its second edition (2002, 2005).

```
                                  HD
                                  9698
Karnad, Bharat.                   I52
     India's nuclear policy.      K37
                                  2008
```

CARLOW UNIVERSITY
GRACE LIBRARY
PITTSBURGH PA 15213